# Divine Marriage from Eden
# to the End of Days

# Divine Marriage from Eden to the End of Days

## Communion with God as Nuptial Mystery
## in the Story of Salvation

### André Villeneuve

WIPF & STOCK · Eugene, Oregon

DIVINE MARRIAGE FROM EDEN TO THE END OF DAYS
Communion with God as Nuptial Mystery in the Story of Salvation

Wipf & Stock
An Imprint of Wipf and Stock Publishers
199 W. 8th Ave., Suite 3
Eugene, OR 97401

www.wipfandstock.com

PAPERBACK ISBN: 978-1-6667-1834-8
HARDCOVER ISBN: 978-1-6667-1835-5
EBOOK ISBN: 978-1-6667-1836-2

SEPTEMBER 15, 2021

To mom and dad—the first who taught me about spousal love.

"Go forth and look, O daughters of Zion, on King Solomon, with the crown wherewith his mother crowned him on the day of his espousals, on the day of the joy of his heart." "The day of the espousals" refers to the day on which the Law was given, and "the day of the joy of his heart" was that when the building of the Temple was completed. May it soon be rebuilt in our days!

(MISHNAH *TA'ANIT* 4:8)

And I will betroth you to me forever. I will betroth you to me in righteousness and in justice, in steadfast love and in mercy. I will betroth you to me in faithfulness. And you shall know the Lord.

(HOSEA 2:19–20)

Husbands, love your wives, as Christ loved the Church and gave himself up for her, that he might sanctify her, having cleansed her by the washing of water with the word, that he might present the Church to himself in splendor, without spot or wrinkle or any such thing, that she might be holy and without blemish.

(EPHESIANS 5:25–27)

# Contents

*Preface* | ix

*Introduction*
    THE MARRIAGE BETWEEN GOD AND HIS PEOPLE | 1

I.              GOD AND ISRAEL:
        DIVINE MARRIAGE IN THE HEBREW BIBLE

1    IN THE BEGINNING:
      *Marriage with Creation in the Garden of Eden* | 19

2    REDEMPTION AND COVENANT:
      *Betrothal at Mount Sinai* | 30

3    IN THE BRIDAL CHAMBER:
      *Union in the Tabernacle and Temple* | 49

4    BETROTHED FOREVER:
      *Mystical Marriage in the Messianic Age* | 75

II.          COMMUNION WITH GOD THROUGH LOVE
                  AND WISDOM

5    THE MYSTERY OF LOVE:
      *The Song of Songs as Journey to God* | 107

6    THE MYSTERY OF WISDOM:
      *Lady Wisdom's Banquet as Path to Love* | 126

III.  CHRIST AND THE CHURCH:
DIVINE MARRIAGE IN THE NEW TESTAMENT

7 THE BRIDEGROOM AND THE KINGDOM:
*The Gospel of Matthew* | 159

8 THE ONE WHOM MY SOUL LOVES:
*The Gospel of John* | 169

9 TEMPLE OF THE HOLY SPIRIT:
*First Corinthians* | 227

10 LIVING BETWEEN THE TIMES:
*Second Corinthians* | 240

11 ONE FLESH:
*Ephesians* | 250

12 THE WEDDING FEAST OF THE LAMB:
*The Apocalypse* | 277


*Conclusion*
FROM SALVATION HISTORY TO FOUR SENSES OF SCRIPTURE | 295

*Epilogue*
FROM DIVINE TO HUMAN MARRIAGE | 302


*Bibliography* | 315

# Preface

THIS BOOK HAS BEEN a long time in the making. Its genesis goes back to my days as a PhD student at the Hebrew University in Jerusalem. The project began as a thesis entitled "Mystical Marriage and Temple Imagery in the New Testament: A Case of Mystagogy in Scripture," which I wrote in 2007–8. This work became the nucleus of my dissertation, written over the next several years and submitted to the Hebrew University in 2012 under the title "Nuptial Symbolism at Key Moments of Salvation History."

As I worked on the manuscript, huddling day after day in the libraries of the Hebrew University and the *École Biblique*, I used to say in jest to my friends: "writing a dissertation is not quite the same level of commitment as being married; but it's a close second." Nearly fifteen years later, the saying has proven true. With that kind of commitment, I knew I had to pick my topic wisely—and it was fitting that I chose to write about the mystery of marriage as the sign *par excellence* of God's love for man.

In many ways, this project reflects my own intellectual and spiritual journey. First, it expresses my love for the great story of Scripture. While most dissertations focus on narrow, ultra-specialized topics, I was determined to write about the *whole Bible*, drawing out the big picture of salvation history in a way that would capture the interest not only of specialists but of all students of Scripture.

Second, the work reflects my love for both Judaism and Christianity—a love that largely grew out of my years living in Jerusalem. Of course, the rediscovery of the Jewish roots of Jesus and Christianity is not new but has now been under way for quite some time. It is now standard practice for any scholarly work on the New Testament to integrate not only the Hebrew Scriptures (the Old Testament), but also Second Temple Jewish literature and sometimes the later Rabbinic exegesis of the Bible.

My topic, even if primarily focused on Christian theology, digs deep into its Jewish roots.

Third, my study of marriage symbolism brings together the ancient and modern worlds. While my professors and mentors at the Hebrew University were specialists in ancient Judaism and Christianity, this book draws from the past but does not remain there. It also speaks to modern readers, informing our contemporary understanding of love and marriage in light of the wisdom of the ancients.

Fourth, though dissertations are typically highly academic and technical, I wanted mine to be also of pastoral or catechetical relevance to its readers, informing and edifying their faith. Although the book draws primarily from the Old Testament, the New Testament, and ancient Jewish sources, it also points to a Catholic and sacramental view of marriage as a faithful covenantal bond that fulfills every person's deepest aspirations for both divine and human love.

Finally, the book's exploration of love and marriage touches upon a topic that concerns every human person, for as the *Catechism of the Catholic Church* states, "God who created man out of love also calls him to love—the fundamental and innate vocation of every human being. For man is created in the image and likeness of God who is himself love."[1] Love is the deepest calling of every person. Yet it is no secret that marriage today is in a profound crisis. Perhaps this crisis stems from the fact that modern man has lost sight of the mystery of marriage as deeply rooted in God's loving designs and revealed in the story of salvation. This book intends to rekindle interest in this wondrous mystery.

These were my goals as I set out on this journey of exploring the mystery of divine love as reflected in human marriage. Four years after the completion and submission of the dissertation, it was published in lightly edited form as *Nuptial Symbolism in Second Temple Writings, the New Testament, and Rabbinic Literature: Divine Marriage at Key Moments of Salvation History.*[2] *Nuptial Symbolism* surveys the development of the theology of marriage in a wide range of sources including the Hebrew prophets, wisdom literature, deuterocanonical and apocryphal texts, Philo, the New Testament, Jewish and Christian pseudepigraphical texts, and rabbinic literature.

---

1. *Catechism of the Catholic Church*, 1604.

2. André Villeneuve, *Nuptial Symbolism in Second Temple Writings, the New Testament and Rabbinic Literature* (Leiden: Brill, 2016).

Now the moment has come to publish a book for a wider audience. Although still a scholarly work, *Divine Marriage from Eden to the End of Days* introduces the mystery of God's marriage with his people throughout salvation history in streamlined form. While specialists seeking a fuller treatment of the topic will find it in *Nuptial Symbolism*, *Divine Marriage* is more suitable for readers who are looking for a simpler introduction to the topic.

This book would not have been possible without many dear friends and colleagues who have played vital roles in my intellectual and spiritual growth at various homes along my personal journey. I would like to thank especially Scott Hahn, John Bergsma, Curtis Mitch, and Bob Rice at Franciscan University of Steubenville; Serge Ruzer, Israel Yuval, and Justin Taylor at the Hebrew University in Jerusalem; Sean Innerst and Mark Giszczak at Saint John Vianney Seminary and the Augustine Institute in Denver, and Barbara Nicolosi at Azusa Pacific University in Los Angeles. Your scholarship, work, and especially the testimony of your lives have had a deep impact on my life that transcends the pages of this book.

*Introduction*

# The Marriage between God and His People

GOD IS LOVE (1 John 4:16). Perhaps no truth about God captures his essence as well as those three words from the First Epistle of John. The story of the Bible is the story of God's love for his people. From Genesis to Revelation, Scripture communicates the same timeless message: God has redeemed his people out of love for them, and he calls them to love him in return. And so, at the heart of the biblical faith stands the great exhortation of the *Shema*: "you shall love the Lord your God with all your heart and with all your soul and with all your might" (Deut 6:5). This is not a matter of mere sentimentality but a question of life and death: faithfulness results in blessings and prosperity; unfaithfulness leads to curse and calamity (Deut 30:15–20). This exclusive covenantal union of love between God and his people is vividly portrayed in the Scriptures through the metaphor of a tender, loving, and permanent marriage bond between husband and wife.

This marital image grew out of the fertile soil of many myths in the ancient world involving either sexual unions between deities or divine-human marriages. And yet despite the proliferation of these myths, the biblical tradition is unique in its portrayal of a deity entering into an exclusive and faithful marriage with an entire *people*.[1] For the Old Testament prophets, God is Israel's husband and Israel is God's bride. This marriage is a rocky one: Israel's love is fickle, and she is often guilty of unfaithfulness that leads to her own debased humiliation. Yet the divine husband, in his steadfast and persevering love, patiently awaits her

1. Cohen, "The Song of Songs and the Jewish Religious Mentality," 6.

1

repentance so that he may restore her to himself, the source of all joy and blessings. No less unique is the fact that the marriage between God and Israel always remains strictly *monogamous*: despite the bride's infidelities, the bridegroom is never tempted to find himself another wife—quite in contrast to the norm in surrounding cultures where polygamy was a common occurrence. The prophets also frequently personify Israel as the *daughter of Zion*, a female allegorical figure portrayed as either a virgin or a mother with child. In Wisdom literature, the nuptial metaphor takes on another form through the mediating figure of *Lady Wisdom* who seductively courts men and invites them to follow her and be united with her.

In the New Testament, God's love for his people is reaffirmed through the life, teachings, death, and resurrection of Jesus Christ. Christ takes on the role of the divine bridegroom, the Church assumes Israel's role as bride, and the attendant commandment to love him in return is upheld and even intensified. Though at times the Church struggles to remain faithful to her bridegroom, she is nevertheless promised a glorious eschatological wedding feast with him at the end of times.

The nuptial imagery of the Bible raises an important question: What does the marriage between God and his people intend to portray in its deepest essence? Is it a mere metaphor, an allegorical way of illustrating God's love for humanity? Or does it attempt to describe a mystical, metaphysical union between the human and the divine? Evidence points to the fact that in some cultures of the ancient world the nuptial imagery was understood as an act of "*spiritual fusion*" between God and man, a "transfusion of divine energy into the world" whereby the Bridegroom, by uniting himself to humanity, raised it to the heaven from which he came.[2] One sees a recurring pattern in ancient Jewish and Christian texts whereby the Redeemer unites himself to the unholy in order to make it holy. The nuptial texts portray this union as occurring at four distinct stages of history: First, God formed a primeval, idyllic marriage with humanity at the dawn of creation; but the bond was broken through sin. Second, the marriage was restored by a new divine initiative and great redemptive event. Third, this nuptial redemptive event was extended into time through liturgical worship, recalling and reenacting the redemptive marriage for later generations. Fourth, the same liturgical worship anticipated a final, eschatological fulfillment of the divine-human marriage at the end of history.

---

2. Chavasse, *The Bride of Christ*, 17; Seaich, *A Great Mystery*, 1–2.

The present book explores the ancient Jewish and Christian theology of the marriage between God and his people as a nuptial covenant dynamically moving through salvation history. In the first part, we introduce these four stages of nuptial imagery in the ancient Jewish exegesis of the Old Testament. In the second part, we demonstrate how the same four stages of nuptial symbolism are developed in the ancient interpretation of the Song of Songs and in wisdom literature. In the third part, we discover how these four stages are taken up in the New Testament and applied to the marriage between Christ and the Church.

## Part I: God and Israel: Divine Marriage in the Hebrew Bible

Reading the Old Testament in light of ancient Jewish commentaries reveals that the story of the Bible is the story of God's romance with humanity. In Part I, our first four chapters investigate how this nuptial mystery is unveiled at four key moments of Israel's biblical history:

1. Covenant with Creation in the Garden of Eden

2. Betrothal at the Time of the Exodus and at Mount Sinai

3. Nuptial Union in the Tabernacle and Temple

4. Divine Marriage at the End of Days

These four moments reveal an overarching thread in God's plan of salvation, whereby his initial marital covenant with humanity, wounded by sin, is restored at the great redemptive event of the Sinai revelation, then extended into time by means of sacrificial liturgy and worship in Israel's sanctuary. This worship, in turn, anticipates and foreshadows the final restoration of God's marriage with Israel and humanity in the messianic age.

## 1. Covenant with Creation in the Garden of Eden

The Old Testament and its ancient Jewish commentaries depict God's work of creation and covenant with man in Eden as a divinely instituted *marriage* covenant serving as the ideal prototype of God's future marriage with Israel. According to rabbinic commentaries on Genesis, God's work of creation anticipated and foreshadowed Israel's central religious institutions such as the Torah and the Temple. Moreover, when God created Adam and Eve, he not only *wedded* them to one another but also *wedded* the world and the Sabbath, anticipating Israel's future "marriage" with the Sabbath at Mount Sinai. The Garden of Eden is thus a primeval sanctuary in which dwells the divine presence and glory that would be revealed later to Israel on Mount Sinai, in the Temple, and on the Sabbath. The rabbis develop this nuptial imagery by portraying Adam and Eve's sin and expulsion from Eden as a divorce, resulting in the loss of divine glory that would be mirrored in the future destruction of the Temple. *Chapter 1* sets us off on our journey through salvation history as we examine the communion between God and man at the dawn of creation in the primeval abode of humanity.

## 2. Betrothal at the Time of the Exodus and at Mount Sinai

Ancient Jews believed that the rupture between God and man that occurred at the fall was repaired by a single great redemptive event—the Exodus from Egypt and especially the covenant at Mount Sinai. They viewed this redemptive event as a *nuptial* event—a *marriage* covenant between God and Israel. This is the focus of *chapter 2*. In contrast to the ten plagues—portrayed as the "de-creation" of Egypt—the Exodus is a "new creation" through which God fashions his newly-formed covenant people and fulfills the original commandment given to Adam to "be fruitful and multiply." The rabbis depict the great redemptive moments of the Exodus—the Passover, the crossing of the Red Sea, and especially the Sinai Theophany— as nuptial moments that enact God's betrothal of Israel. The Lord reveals his glory and holiness to his people through the giving of the Torah and commandments, which the rabbis equate to divine "kisses." The divine-human marriage sealed at the Sinai covenant is the completion of God's new creation, acting as a corrective to the fall and restoring in Israel the divine presence that was lost in Eden—especially through the commemoration and observance of the Sabbath. But the sin of the golden calf quickly undoes the newly formed marriage. Israel's betrayal of the nuptial covenant—the nation's own "original sin"—is a new act of human de-creation and alienation that calls for a new divine initiative and means of restoring God's presence among his people.

### 3. Nuptial Union in the Tabernacle and Temple

Following the golden calf crisis, the marriage between God and Israel is restored, reenacted, and sustained over time in Israel's history through liturgical worship in the nation's sanctuary: the desert Tabernacle and its successor, the Jerusalem Temple. In *chapter 3*, we investigate the role of the sanctuary as locus of God's marriage with Israel. The Tabernacle actualizes and perpetuates the Sinai theophany for future generations of Israelites. As counterpart to the Sabbath—God's *sacred time* commemorating his covenant with creation and with Israel—the sanctuary is God's *sacred space* where he dwells among his people. Thematic connections between holiness, Sabbath, Eden, and sanctuary indicate that the Tabernacle is a type of new creation. The sages, moreover, believed that the Tabernacle and Temple were a nuptial chamber in which God and Israel consummated their union. This view of the sanctuary as nuptial chamber is vividly illustrated in an ancient tradition holding that the two cherubim in the Holy of Holies embraced one another to symbolize the "face of God," his male-female image, his nuptial love for Israel, and the male-female union in human marriage. Moreover, the Jerusalem Temple was imbued with cosmic symbolism: the rabbis considered it to be a microcosm or "world in miniature." In other words, God's marriage with Israel in the sanctuary recalled and reflected his marriage with creation in Eden. From this identification of the Temple with Eden, it follows that the Temple service was viewed as a source of divine, Edenic blessing because it was the place of the indwelling *Shekhinah*—God's presence on earth.

### 4. Divine Marriage at the End of Days

Finally, the love between God and Israel tends towards a definitive consummation and fulfillment in the Messianic Age at the end of human history. *Chapter 4* explores the eschatological fulfillment of biblical nuptial symbolism in the prophetic and rabbinic texts. While the prophets Hosea, Jeremiah, Ezekiel, and Isaiah employ a mostly negative metaphor—portraying Israel's idolatry as spiritual adultery—they also anticipate a marvelous restoration of God's marriage with his people at the end of time, revealing his divine glory and holiness through all creation. The rabbis express a similar hope for the eschatological restoration of Zion, expressing through rich midrashic commentaries how God will heal his marriage with Israel. This eschatological hope emerged out of Ezekiel's famous vision of the divine chariot or *Merkavah* during the Babylonian exile. As moveable seat of the divine presence, the *Merkavah* provided hope that God's glory was not bound to a physical sanctuary but could reveal itself anywhere—even in exile. The *Merkavah* was not only a mystical actualization of the Holy of Holies, but also a visible manifestation of the Sinai theophany and echo of God's work of creation. The idea that Israel could mystically access the Temple, the Sinai covenant, and even the Garden of Eden through the *Merkavah* developed into the belief that faithful Jews could encounter God's holiness and glory—that is, experience anew nuptial communion with him—even without a physical sanctuary. Indeed, the idea of a spiritual temple in exile led to the concept of an *anthropological temple* whereby God could be found in the community and even in the soul of individual believers.

## Part II: Communion with God through Love and Wisdom

The concept of the believer as spiritual sanctuary and dwelling place of the divine presence was further developed in ancient interpretations of the Song of Songs and in the Wisdom books. This is the focus of Part II, which explores the story of God's marriage with his people through the nuptial drama of the Song of Songs and the mysterious figure of Lady Wisdom.

## The Song of Songs: Allegory of God's Love for Israel and "Holy of Holies" of Scripture

From the second century onwards, the book that stands out as the outstanding symbol of the marriage between God and his people is the *Song of Songs*. Traditionally attributed to King Solomon, most scholars now believe that the Canticle was originally an erotic love song portraying the nuptials between Solomon and the daughter of Pharaoh, or between a young shepherd and a country maiden. Yet for most of the Song's history of interpretation, the Canticle was primarily interpreted as the allegorical description of the courtship and union between God and his mystical bride. Ancient Jewish exegetes interpreted Israel's history in light of the romantic verses of the Song, or—even more remarkably—reinterpreted the entire Song as the romance between God and Israel through the nation's history. Christian writers followed suit, reading the Song as a portrait of the marriage between Christ and the Church. This spiritual reading of the Canticle eventually became the foundation of Christian mysticism.[3]

Yet some early rabbis, concerned about the Canticle's nature as erotic love song, opposed its very inclusion into the canon of Scripture. At the beginning of the second century CE, Rabbi Akiva (d. 135) vigorously defended the sanctity of the Canticle in response to its detractors, exclaiming: "God forbid!—no man in Israel ever disputed about the Song of Songs . . . for all the ages are not worth the day on which the Song of Songs was given to Israel; for all the Writings are holy, but the Song of Songs is the Holy of Holies."[4] The same Rabbi Akiva even denied the world to come to those who read the Canticle as a secular song in a profane context.[5] The rhetorical force of these sayings indicates that Akiva and others believed the Canticle to be much more than a common love poem: as the "Holy of Holies" of sacred Scripture, it was considered to be a gateway into the mystery of God's love for his people.

We discern two main threads of nuptial traditions in the rabbinic commentaries on the Song: in the first, the sages associate verses from the Canticle with historical texts, thereby transforming the history of Israel—and especially the Exodus—into a nuptial drama. As Gershon Cohen has noted, when the rabbis located the consecration of the marriage between God and his bride at the time of the Exodus and at Sinai, they were "merely amplifying what they had already found in Scripture," namely, the vow of fidelity that God demanded of his people as expressed in the prophets.[6] The use of the Canticle to describe the redemptive events of the Exodus shows that the sages read it as a sacred love poem between God and Israel that allegorically depicted his salvific deeds as a divine romance. This is, no doubt, one good reason that would have strengthened Akiva's conviction that the Song was the "Holy of Holies" of Scripture.

---

3. For a survey of the history of exegesis of the Song, see Pope, *Song of Songs*, 89–229.

4. *M. Yadaim* 3:6; cf. also *t. Yadaim* 2:14; *b. Megillah* 7a; *CantR* 1:1 §11.

5. *T. Sanhedrin* 12.10: "Rabbi Akiva says, 'Whoever sings the Song of Songs with tremulous voice in a banquet hall and (so) treats it as a sort of ditty has no share in the world to come.'" Cf. also *b. Sanhedrin* 101a.

6. Cohen, "The Song of Songs and the Jewish Religious Mentality," 11.

And yet a second, more mystical rabbinic tradition further explains the Song's identification with the Holy of Holies. While discussing the Song's canonicity, Rabbi Akiva speaks of the day when the Canticle was *"given"* to Israel—an expression generally used to denote the giving of the Torah.[7] Some rabbis believed that the Song of Songs was indeed *divinely* given to Israel—long before Solomon—either at the Red Sea, at Mount Sinai, in the Tabernacle, or in the Temple, as a secret mystical level of Torah.[8] Another remarkable statement is attributed to Akiva: "Had the Torah not been given to Israel, the world could have been conducted by the Song of Songs."[9] This indicates that Akiva saw not only Sinai as the original setting of the Song but also the Canticle as "the heart of revelation, the secret love-gift that God gave to Israel along with the more public Torah of history, law, and covenant."[10] *Chapter 5* focuses on the rabbinic interpretation of the Song of Songs and especially its Targum, which rewrites the entire Song as a romanticized allegory of the history of Israel.

## Wisdom as Path to Love

In wisdom literature, the nuptial union with God takes a different form through the presence of Lady Wisdom. In contrast to the prophetic books—where the divine protagonist is male and the human one is a collective female (personified Israel)—in the wisdom books the quasi-divine Lady Wisdom is female and the human protagonists are individual males who are invited to "marry" her.

Scholars have noticed a definite affinity between wisdom and *eros* in the Bible.[11] The quest for Wisdom is a quest for the beloved, and the pursuit of Lady Wisdom is described with the language and imagery of

---

7. *M. Yadaim* 3:5.

8. *CantR* 1:2 §1. In Green's words ("Shekhinah, the Virgin Mary and the Song of Songs," 3), Rabbi Akiva held that "the Song of Songs was first spoken—a living dialogic event that took place among God, the angels, and the community of Israel—at Sinai." Green, "The Song of Songs in Early Jewish Mysticism," 52; "The Children in Egypt and the Theophany at the Sea," 452–53.

9. *Agadat Shir Hashirim* 5, quoted in Green, "Shekhinah, the Virgin Mary and the Song of Songs," 8.

10. Green, "Shekhinah, the Virgin Mary and the Song of Songs," 3; "The Song of Songs," 52.

11. Murphy, *The Tree of Life*, 78–79, 106–107.

love: Wisdom is "found" (Prov 3:13; 8:17, 35) just as one "finds" a good wife (Prov 18:22; 31:10). The author of Proverbs uses the same language to indicate that both are the way to obtain favor from the Lord:

> For he who finds me [wisdom] finds life and obtains favor from the Lord. (Prov 8:35)

> He who finds a wife finds a good thing and obtains favor from the Lord. (Prov 18:22)

Moreover, the language of love applied to Lady Wisdom sometimes echoes the passionate language of the Song of Songs. Men are advised to love and embrace Lady Wisdom as the Canticle's lover embraces his beloved (Prov 4:6–8; Cant 2:6), while she declares in response: "I love those who love me" (Prov 8:17; Cant 4:9). Wisdom is called "my sister" (Prov 7:4), as is the bride of the Canticle (Cant 4:9–5:1). Sirach exhorts his readers to take hold of Wisdom and not to let her go (Sir 6:27), just as the Song's bride will not let go of her lover (Cant 3:4). Also, using the exact same expression, both the pursuer of Wisdom and the Song's beloved are said to "peer through her windows" (Sir 14:23; Cant 2:9). To seek Wisdom is thus a romantic pursuit framed in the language of the Song of Songs.

The wisdom texts reveal that Lady Wisdom is present throughout salvation history, at the same four key moments introduced above: She participates in the work of creation and is identified with the Tree of Life. She is identified with the Torah—implying that she came down and "embraced" Israel for the first time at Mount Sinai. She dwells in the sanctuary of the Tabernacle and Temple, and it is in the liturgical service that men may find her. Finally, Wisdom is eternal; she will endure until the end of time. Lady Wisdom's presence on earth, her association with the bride of the Song of Songs, and her suggestive invitations to "eat," "drink," and "live" with her imply that all who seek her, find her, and are joined to her undergo a mystical, life-giving, transformative union. *Chapter 6* examines nuptial symbolism in wisdom literature, focusing especially on Lady Wisdom's song of praise in Sirach 24.

## Part III: Christ and the Church:
## Divine Marriage in the New Testament

In Part III, we turn to nuptial symbolism in the New Testament, where the marriage between God and Israel evolves into the nuptials of Christ and the Church. We will examine six books of the New Testament that employ nuptial symbolism, beginning with two Gospels that focus primarily on the person of Jesus as bridegroom. In the Gospel of Matthew (*chapter 7*), Jesus refers to himself as "the bridegroom" and teaches about the kingdom of heaven via two nuptial parables—the parable of the wedding feast and the parable of the ten virgins. In the Gospel of John (*chapter 8*), we discover a plethora of nuptial allusions such as the Wedding at Cana's echo of the Sinai covenant, John the Baptist's designation of Jesus as "the bridegroom," the betrothal-type scene in Jesus' conversation with the Samaritan woman, and echoes of the Song of Songs at the anointing in Bethany and the resurrection appearance to Mary Magdalene. We then turn to three Pauline Epistles, which primarily develop the idea of the Church as Christ's bride. In 1 Corinthians (*chapter 9*), Paul develops a rich ecclesiology in his description of the Church as Temple of the Holy Spirit and Body of Christ. A strong nuptial theme emerges from this ecclesiology, combined with warnings against sexual immorality, typological references to Adam and Eve, and teachings on baptism and the Eucharist as the sacramental means to be joined to Christ. In 2 Corinthians (*chapter 10*), Paul further develops the analogy of the body as Temple of the Holy Spirit, explaining how Christ imparts the superior glory of the New Covenant to believers in the frail "tabernacle" of their bodies and in the Church, which is "a pure virgin betrothed to Christ." Paul's Epistle to the Ephesians (*chapter 11*) develops a high Christology and rich theology of the Church as Christ's temple, body, and bride. It provides us with the most extensive nuptial passage of the New Testament, presenting the union of Christ and the Church as the model for the sacrificial one-flesh union of a man with his wife. Finally, the Book of Revelation (*chapter 12*) depicts the final consummation of the mystical marriage between Christ and the Church—the "New Jerusalem coming down out of heaven from God, prepared as a bride adorned for her husband."

Our study of these books will reveal a close correlation between New Testament and Old Testament nuptial symbolism through the reinterpretation of the four key moments of salvation history:

## 1. Christ as New Adam; Church as New Eve

In the New Testament, the marriage between Christ and the Church evokes the union of Adam and Eve in Eden. The New Testament authors presuppose the tradition of an ideal, first marriage formed at the dawn of creation but followed by rupture and disorder. Nuptial passages reflect Adam/Eve typology, recalling the original order of creation and damage caused by Adam's sin, and explaining how it was repaired by Christ. Christ is portrayed as new Adam and the Church as new Eve, and their marriage signifies a restoration of humanity to the original state of Eden.

## 2. New Covenant Wedding through Christ's Paschal Sacrifice

As the marriage between God and Israel is formed at the great redemptive event of the Sinai theophany, so the marriage between Christ and the Church is established through the great redemptive event of Christ's paschal mystery. Christ's nuptial covenant with the Church, sealed by his self-sacrifice as "Lamb of God who takes away the sin of the world," echoes God's betrothal of Israel at the Passover, the Exodus, and the Sinai covenant.

## 3. Marriage in the Temple of the Holy Spirit through Baptism and the Eucharist

Jesus is the Word made flesh who "tabernacled" among us—the new Temple in whom dwells the fullness of the deity. Christ's Incarnation enables the Christian community (and the individual believer) to also become a Temple of the Holy Spirit in which the nuptial union between God and man takes place. The marriage between Christ and the Church (or Christ and the soul), evoking Old Testament Temple and sacrificial typology, occurs especially in the sacraments of Baptism and the Eucharist. Just as Israel's sanctuary perpetuated the Sinai covenant through the history of Israel, so the spiritual temple—the Church and the believer—is the liturgical extension, commemoration, and actualization over time of the nuptial covenant that Jesus sealed with his beloved bride-people at the cross.

## 4. The Eternal Wedding Feast of the Lamb

The ecclesial, spiritual temple of the Church and believer anticipates the eschatological fulfillment of the sacred marriage at the end of time. The marriage between Christ and the Church, still veiled sacramentally as it journeys through history, moves towards its ultimate consummation in the wedding feast of the Lamb that will take place in the eternal, heavenly Temple, as depicted in the Book of Revelation.

# Meet the Rabbis:
# Ancient Jewish Commentaries on Scripture

Throughout our study (especially in Part I), we will consult the ancient rabbis. Ancient rabbinic writings and commentaries on Scripture provide a treasure trove of insights into how ancient Jews understood and interpreted the biblical texts, often by means of *midrash*, or creative expansions and embellishments of the biblical narratives.[12] Since these rabbinic texts are often unfamiliar to Christian readers, we present here a brief introduction to our main sources.

The *Mishnah* (*m.*) is the earliest and most foundational compilation of Jewish oral law, edited and redacted in the early third century CE. It is composed of six major sections (called "orders") containing 63 tractates, which are further divided into chapters and paragraphs. Its tractates cover in systematic fashion all aspects of Jewish law (known as the *halakhah*) as taught by the rabbis until its redaction around 200 CE. It is decidedly a *legal* text, terse and difficult to read, that contains little narrative material. The *Mishnah* is cited by the letter *m.* followed by the name of the tractate, chapter, and paragraph (e.g. *m. Yoma* 2:3).[13]

The *Tosefta* (*t.*) is a compilation of Jewish oral laws roughly contemporary to the Mishnah (third century CE). Its content supplements the Mishnah with additional materials, though considered less authoritative. It is organized in the same way as the Mishnah with the same division of

---

12. A *midrash* (pl. *midrashim*) is an ancient Jewish commentary on Scripture that seeks to explain and shed light on the content of the Hebrew Bible. The term *midrash* can refer either to an entire collection of texts compiled in a book (such as the *Mekhilta* or *Genesis Rabbah*), or to a short section of text embellishing or commenting on a specific passage of Scripture.

13. Danby, *The Mishnah*; Strack and Stemberger, *Introduction to the Talmud and Midrash*, 108–48.

orders and tractates. The *Tosefta* is cited by the letter *t.* followed by the name of the tractate, chapter, and paragraph (e.g. *t. Berachot* 1:6).[14]

The *Mekhilta de-Rabbi Ishmael* (*Mekh*) is one of the oldest halakhic midrashim, dated to the second half of the third century CE.[15] The *Mekhilta* is a commentary on Exodus 12:1–23:19, 31:12–17, and 35:1–3, covering the story of Israel's escape from Egypt beginning with the Passover and crossing of the Red Sea, the first wanderings through the desert and feeding of the manna, the Sinai theophany and giving of the Ten Commandments, and most of the covenant code, with two additional exhortations on the observance of the Sabbath. The *Mekhilta* is relevant to our purposes because it associates verses of the Song of Songs with the events of the Exodus, thereby giving them a nuptial meaning. It is organized in nine treatises, known by their Aramaic names, each devoted to a section of Exodus. The main treatises we refer to are *Pisḥa* (on the Passover, Exod 12:1–13:6), *Beshallaḥ* (on the Exodus and crossing of the Red Sea, 13:17–14:71), *Shirata* (on the Song at the Sea, 15:1–21), and *Baḥodesh* (on the revelation at Mount Sinai, 19:1–20:23).[16]

*Sifre Devarim* or *Sifre Deuteronomy* (*Sifre Deut*) is a halakhic midrash edited and compiled sometime in the third century in the Land of Israel on sections of the book of Deuteronomy, including the historical prologue (1:1–30), the prayer of Moses (3:23–4:1), the *Shema* (6:4–9), the book's legal core (11:10–26:15), the transfer of office to Joshua (31:14), the Song of Moses, his final blessing, and his death (32:1–34:12). The narrative context is thus set some forty years after the initial events of the Exodus. *Sifre* develops the nuptial meaning of the Torah as Wisdom, the motif of the Temple as place of marital encounter between God and Israel, the realization of this union in the nation's history, and its eschatological consummation in the Messianic age.[17]

The *Babylonian Talmud* (*b.*) is an extensive commentary on the Mishnah. Written in Mishnaic Hebrew and Jewish Babylonian Aramaic, it is the longer and more authoritative of the two Talmuds (the other being the Palestinian or Jerusalem Talmud). Like the *Tosefta*, it is organized

14. Strack and Stemberger, *Introduction to the Talmud and Midrash*, 149–63.

15. A *halakhic* midrash is a *legal* midrash that focuses on identifying the sources of Jewish law in the Bible and determining its practical applications in Jewish life.

16. Lauterbach, *Mekhilta De-Rabbi Ishmael*; Strack and Stemberger, *Introduction to the Talmud and Midrash*, 251–57.

17. Hammer, *Sifre Deuteronomy*; Strack and Stemberger, *Introduction to the Talmud and Midrash*, 294–99.

(with some discrepancies) according to the orders and tractates of the Mishnah. The Babylonian Talmud is a massive, encyclopedic work that has come to be known as the most important text of rabbinic Judaism and the primary source of Jewish law and theology. It is cited by the letter *b.* followed by the name of the tractate, folio (page) number and side (a or b) according to the standard Vilna edition (e.g. *b. Yoma* 39b).[18]

*Genesis Rabbah* (*GenR*) is one of the oldest haggadic exegetical midrashim (dated around 400 CE), commenting verse-by-verse on the book of Genesis.[19] As a midrash on the first book of the Bible, it contains many motifs touching upon cosmology, how the universe came to be, the origins of mankind, and how the later religious institutions of Israel were foreshadowed at creation and at the dawn of human history. *Genesis Rabbah* is divided into 100 *parashiyot* (chapters or midrashic units); somewhat confusingly, the *parashiyot* numbers do not correspond to the chapters and verses of Genesis.[20]

*Leviticus Rabbah* (*LevR*) is a haggadic midrash that was probably redacted sometime during the fifth century CE, consisting of 37 homilies on Leviticus. Accordingly, its primary context is the time of the Exodus immediately after Israel received the Torah at Mount Sinai; its chief interests are the laws concerning sacrifices and offerings, the priesthood, legal purity, and laws of holiness. *Leviticus Rabbah* makes considerable use of the nuptial motif on this legal material. Like *Genesis Rabbah*, it is interested in connecting Israel's religious institutions with the origins of mankind and with salvation history. Like *Genesis Rabbah*, the 37 *parashiyot* of *LevR* do not correspond to the chapter numbers of Leviticus.[21]

*Pesikta de-Rab Kahana* (*PRK*) is a haggadic homiletic midrash on the readings that were read in the synagogue on Jewish feasts (such as

---

18. Strack and Stemberger, *Introduction to the Talmud and Midrash*, 190–224.

19. In contrast to *halakhic* midrashim, a *haggadic* midrash is a narrative (non-legal) commentary on Scripture that focuses on interpreting the Bible in terms of ethics and devotion, often through narrative expansions of the biblical text. An *exegetical* midrash offers a running commentary (sometimes verse-by-verse) on a given book of the Bible.

20. For example, *Genesis Rabbah* 8:1 comments on Genesis 1:26. Freedman and Simon, *Midrash Rabbah*, Vol. 1; Neusner, *Genesis Rabbah: The Judaic Commentary to the Book of Genesis*; Strack and Stemberger, *Introduction to the Talmud and Midrash*, 300–308.

21. Freedman and Simon, *Midrash Rabbah*, Vol. 4; Strack and Stemberger, *Introduction to the Talmud and Midrash*, 313–17.

Hanukkah, Passover, or Shavuot) and special Sabbaths.[22] It is dated to the fifth century CE and approximately contemporaneous with *Leviticus Rabbah*. PRK is organized into 28 homilies or chapters (called *piskas* or *piskaʾot*). It makes extensive use of nuptial symbolism in several of those homilies—especially those given at Hanukkah, Shavuot, and the Sabbaths of consolation following Tisha b'Av (the national day of mourning in the Jewish calendar).[23]

*Canticles Rabbah* or *Song of Songs Rabbah* (*CantR*) is an exegetical Midrash from the Land of Israel, written in mishnaic Hebrew and some Galilean Aramaic, and redacted around the mid-sixth century. The Midrash expounds the Song of Songs verse-by-verse, combining materials from previous works with many original interpretations. *CantR* is tremendously significant for our study of biblical nuptial symbolism: Whereas the previously mentioned rabbinic works make occasional references to the Song while commenting on other books of Scripture and events in Israel's history, *Canticles Rabbah* is entirely dedicated to interpreting the Song as an allegory of the love between God and Israel. The fact that it presents many layers of interpretation of each verse of the Song—often spanning many periods of the nation's history in a single verse—makes it a complex and rich text. It is organized into eight *parashiyot* that correspond to the chapter numbers of the Song of Songs.[24]

*Targum Canticles* (*TgCant*) is an Aramaic "translation" of the Song of Songs—and there is a good reason why the word "translation" is placed in quotation marks: Generally, Targums are Aramaic translations of books of the Hebrew Bible. Such translations became necessary when spoken Hebrew fell into disuse among the Jews and Aramaic became their common spoken language. While some Targums translate the Hebrew text quite literally, others take considerable liberties with it, expanding the text with paraphrases and explanations. The Targum on the Song of Songs is an extreme example of the latter. Much more than a translation, it is really a paraphrase of the Song, which it creatively reinterprets as an allegory of the history of Israel. Although the Targum closely follows the

---

22. In contrast to *exegetical* midrashim, a *homiletic* midrash organizes its materials thematically, commenting on lectionary readings from the synagogue's liturgy.

23. Braude and Kapstein, *Pesikta de-Rab Kahana*; Strack and Stemberger, *Introduction to the Talmud and Midrash*, 317–22.

24. Freedman and Simon, *Midrash Rabbah*, Vol. 9. Herr, "Song of Songs Rabbah" in *Encyclopaedia Judaica*, 152–54; Strack and Stemberger, *Introduction to the Talmud and Midrash*, 342–44.

chapter/verse structure of the Song, it reinterprets it so freely that one must often look carefully to see the connection between the Canticle and its corresponding verse in the Targum. The origins of the Targum are uncertain. Scholars have proposed a date of redaction oscillating between the fifth and eighth centuries CE while recognizing that its traditions go back much earlier.[25]

---

25. Menn, "Targum of the Song of Songs and the Dynamics of Historical Allegory," 423; Alexander, "Tradition and Originality in the Targum of the Song of Songs," 318–39; Alexander, *The Targum of Canticles*, 55–58; Loewe, "Apologetic Motifs in the Targum to the Song of Songs," 636–38.

# I

# God and Israel:
# Divine Marriage in the Hebrew Bible

*1*

# In the Beginning

*Marriage with Creation in the Garden of Eden*

THE BIBLE TELLS A LOVE STORY—the story of God's love for humankind. Indeed, the Scriptures begin and end with a wedding—from the "one flesh" union of Adam and Eve (Gen 2:23–24) to the "marriage supper of the Lamb" (Rev 19:9).[1] Yet the first chapters of Genesis say nothing about divine love or a marriage between God and humanity. The creation and Garden of Eden narratives are concise, providing few details and leaving much to the reader's imagination. Ancient Jewish interpreters, aware that these stories left much unsaid, filled in the gaps and expanded the biblical narrative by means of rich midrashic commentaries. These commentaries reveal that for the rabbis, God's act of creation and his covenant with humankind was the first act of his wedding with the world.

## The World as Wedding

### Creation as Cosmic Temple

The first chapter of Genesis describes the cosmological narrative of the days of creation. The story is well-known: God created the world in six "days." In the first three days he created the realms of creation by a process of separation and distinction—separating the day from the night (first day), the waters below the firmament from the waters above it (second

1. Hahn, "The World as Wedding," 4.

19

day), and the dry land from the seas (third day). In the next three days he filled these realms with life—creating the sun, moon and stars to rule over day and night (fourth day), the fish and birds to rule over the sky and seas (fifth day), and the animals and man to rule over the earth (sixth day). On the seventh day, God finished his work, "rested" from his creative activity, then "blessed the seventh day and sanctified it" (Gen 1:1–2:3).[2]

For the ancient rabbis, the creation of the world and origins of mankind foreshadowed the later religious institutions of Israel. The Midrash *Genesis Rabbah* tells us that six things preceded the creation of the world. Two were actually *created* before the beginnings of the world: the Torah, identified with divine Wisdom (cf. Prov 8:22), and the throne of glory (cf. Ps 93:2). Four other things were "contemplated," that is, they existed conceptually in the divine mind: the patriarchs, Israel, the Temple, and the name of the Messiah.[3] These concepts anticipate the unfolding of salvation history. For the rabbis, the Torah—the Word of God—preceded creation; it waited, as it were, for the moment of its future public revelation on Mount Sinai while Israel was being conceived, formed, and prepared through the life of the patriarchs. The idea of the Temple was also pre-existent, waiting for the moment of its construction when it would become the seat of God's presence in Israel. God even planned from the beginning the final messianic age by knowing the name of the Messiah who would usher in the final redemption and grant Israel eternal access to the divine throne of glory. Thus, for the sages, God already anticipates in his work of creation the entire history of his relationship with Israel, including the revelation of his Word—the Torah—at Sinai, the building of his dwelling place, the Temple, and the manifestation of his throne of glory in the messianic age.

Elsewhere, the rabbis associate God's creation of the world with Israel's future sanctuary in greater detail: The Midrash tells us that at the beginning of creation God foresaw that the Temple would be built, destroyed and rebuilt: "*In the beginning God created*" refers to the building of the Temple (cf. Isa 51:16); "*and the earth was without form*" refers to its destruction (cf. Jer 4:23); and "*let there be light*" refers to its reconstruction in the world to come (cf. Isa 60:1).[4] Another sage holds that the primeval light called into existence by God's word at creation (Gen 1:3) was in fact

---

2. Cf. Thomas Aquinas, *Summa Theologiae*, I. Q.70, A.1; Hahn, *A Father Who Keeps His Promises*, 43–45.

3. *GenR* 1:4.

4. *GenR* 2:5.

"created from the place of the Temple" and was identical with the glory of God that entered Ezekiel's Temple when *the earth shone with his glory* (Ezek 43:2).[5] The creation of the world is also identified with the future raising of the Tabernacle in the wilderness: According to the Midrash, when the Tabernacle was completed, God declared: "It is as if on that day, I actually created the world."[6] These correlations between God's work of creation and the sanctuary imply that the world is a macro-temple—God's home in which he is pleased to dwell among his people. Conversely, because it reflects the creation of the universe, Israel's sanctuary is a microcosm, a miniature representation of the world that is to constantly remind Israel of God's creation and covenant with the cosmos.

## God's Image: Male and Female

It is within this cosmic temple of the world that God creates humanity and the institution of marriage. On the sixth day, God creates man "in his own image, in the image of God he created him; male and female he created them" (Gen 1:27). Commenting on this verse, the Midrash claims that the first human was actually androgynous—*both* male and female—before God separated it into man and woman: God "created him with two faces, then sawed him into two and made a back on one side, and a back on the other." [7] This original male-female unity, followed by separation of the two sexes, would explain their perennial mutual attraction and desire to be reunited with their "other half." The sages also associate Adam's "side" with the "side" of the Tabernacle (Exod 26:20), hinting at the idea that he is in fact a human temple, created to receive the divine presence within himself. As we shall see, the metaphor of man as temple is a key motif in the development of both Jewish and Christian nuptial symbolism.

### God Weds Adam and Eve

The Midrash develops the nuptial dimension of the creation narrative by depicting God as an active player in the union of Adam and Eve. According to the sages, "the Holy One, blessed be He, took a cup of blessing

5. *GenR* 3:4.
6. *GenR* 3:9.
7. *GenR* 8:1.

and blessed them"—as is traditionally done at Jewish weddings—for God "blesses bridegrooms and adorns brides."[8] By blessing the newlyweds, God becomes Adam and Eve's matchmaker and mediator who plans and arranges their marriage—a role known in Judaism as the *shoshbin*. God's blessing upon Adam and Eve's wedding further establishes their marriage—together with all future human marriages—as a divinely instituted covenant.

### God Weds the World

The rabbis also attribute a nuptial meaning to God's entire work of creation, which he declares to be *very good* (Gen 1:31). The Midrash compares the Creator of the world to a king who married off his daughter and prepared a marriage canopy (*chuppah*) and home for her:

> He saw it and it pleased him. He said, 'O my daughter, my daughter, may this marriage canopy always charm me as it charms me at this hour.' So said the Holy One, blessed be he, to his world, 'O my world, my world! May you always charm me as you charm me at this hour.'[9]

In this parable, the king is a figure of God; his daughter who charms him is the world—presumably mankind. The *chuppah* and house made for the daughter also represent the world—the physical and material creation that serves as home for mankind. Thus, the creation of the world is portrayed as the marriage of God's daughter (mankind) under the *chuppah* of creation. Going far beyond celebrating the marriage between Adam and Eve, the Midrash celebrates the completion of God's creative activity as a cosmic wedding that is a source of great joy and delight to him.

### Kedushah and the Sabbath

#### The Concept of Kedushah

At the conclusion of the work of creation, "God blessed the seventh day and sanctified it" (Gen 2:3)—that is, he made it holy—*kadosh*—or consecrated for his purpose. The concept of *kedushah* (holiness) is

8. *GenR* 8:13.

9. *GenR* 9:4.

foundational to the Bible's nuptial theology. *Kedushah* most profoundly describes God's own essence: He is *kadosh* in the sense of being set apart and transcendent from this world.[10] When applied to things or people, the word *kedushah* does not primarily refer to moral perfection but rather to consecration for a special purpose: to encounter the divine. Thus, the all-holy God sanctifies certain realms of creation in which he will encounter his people in a particularly intimate way: a realm of *sacred time*—the Sabbath, and a realm of *sacred place*—the Temple. These two central institutions of ancient Israel were deeply rooted in *kedushah*; they were the realms in which the mystical union of God and Israel occurred.

In this light, it is significant that the Hebrew root *k.d.sh* is also used in a sexual or nuptial context: *kedeshah* is one of the words used in the Bible to describe a prostitute ("dedicated" to the act of harlotry).[11] In the Mishnah, *kiddushin* describes the act of the bridegroom sanctifying his bride to himself in the act of marriage.[12] The derivative verb *kiddesh* thus means both "to sanctify" and "to betroth," for both actions signify the act of setting apart and consecrating a person by a solemn oath for the purpose of establishing an enduring covenantal bond between the two parties.

## God Marries the Sabbath

As the pinnacle of creation, the Sabbath is a *sanctuary in time*. This is the only place in Genesis that speaks of *kedushah*: when "God blessed the seventh day and sanctified it," he set it apart for the special purpose of forming his covenant with creation and uniting himself with humanity. The inherent holiness of the seventh day of creation is beautifully illustrated in a second nuptial parable that imbues the Sabbath with nuptial meaning. The Midrash compares the completion of God's work of creation on the seventh day to a king who made a *chuppah* for himself. The only thing lacking was a bride to come into it. "So too what did the world lack? It was the Sabbath."[13] Thus, the Sabbath became God's (or the world's) bride who completed the marriage of creation. Just as mankind marries the Sabbath, so also does a heavenly-earthly marriage between God and the Sabbath take place under the *chuppah* of creation.

10. Exod 15:11; Amos 4:2. Berman, *The Temple*, 1–19.

11. Gen 38:21–22; Deut 23:17; Hos 4:14. Berman, *The Temple*, 5–6.

12. Through the act of betrothal, the husband "prohibits her to the whole world as a sacred object" (*b. Kiddushin* 2b).

13. *GenR* 10:9.

## The Sabbath Marries Israel

In a third parable, the Midrash presents a marriage joining heaven and earth. Here, *the Sabbath* complains to the Holy One that it has no mate—in contrast to the first six days of creation who are paired up with one another: "the first day of the week has the second, the third has the fourth, the fifth has the sixth, but the Sabbath has no partner." God replies that the community of Israel is to be her mate. And so, much later:

> When Israel stood before Mount Sinai, the Holy One blessed be He, said to them, 'Remember what I said to the Sabbath: 'The community of Israel is your mate." Now therefore: *remember the Sabbath day to keep it holy.* (Exod 20:8)[14]

The meaning of the passage is elucidated in the double meaning of "keep it holy" (*lekadsho*). Since the verb *kiddesh* means both "to sanctify" and "to betroth," the Midrash reads the commandment in Exodus 20:8 to "remember the Sabbath day, to keep it holy" as "remember the Sabbath day, to *consecrate it in marriage.*" Thus, God's establishment of the Sabbath at creation anticipates and announces the marriage between the Sabbath and Israel that will take place much later at the time of the Sinai revelation. This implies that the nuptial covenant between God and Israel was not *instituted* at Mount Sinai (with the giving of the Ten Commandments, including the one prescribing the sanctification of the Sabbath), but merely *recalled*, for it had been already sealed at creation. The obligation to keep the Sabbath, given to Israel at Sinai, rests upon the original betrothal made at the dawn of history.

The etymological connection between sanctity and betrothal is the foundation for nuptial symbolism in other rabbinic interpretations of the Old Testament. The rabbis not only equate God's sanctification of the Sabbath at the conclusion of creation with him *betrothing* the Sabbath. As we will see, they reinterpret the Sinai covenant—when God chose and sanctified Israel as his people—as the moment when God *betrothed* the community of Israel to himself. They also see the Temple as the place where the sacred nuptial union between God and Israel was consummated, anticipating the day when God's *kedushah* will be manifest to all creation at the end of history.

---

14. *GenR* 11:8.

## Garden of Eden as Sanctuary and Bridal Chamber

The second chapter of Genesis focuses on the creation of man. In this narrative, God "formed the man of dust from the ground and breathed into his nostrils the breath of life, and the man became a living creature" (Gen 2:7). He then "planted a garden in Eden," and "there he put the man whom he had formed" (2:8). In the garden are two notable trees: the tree of life, and the tree of the knowledge of good and evil. A riverhead flows out of Eden, which divides into four rivers—the Pishon, the Gihon, the Tigris, and the Euphrates (2:10–14). God places the man in the garden "to till it and keep it," then commands him not to eat of the fruit of the tree of knowledge under pain of death (2:15–17). After Adam names the animals, God makes the woman—"a helper fit for him"—out of his "rib" (or "side") and brings her to him, leading to his great exclamation of wonder: "This at last is bone of my bones and flesh of my flesh; she shall be called Woman, because she was taken out of Man" (2:21–23).

## Shekhinah and Glory in Eden

As the first home of humanity, the Garden of Eden exemplifies the primeval abode of God with man. The anthropomorphic description of God "walking in the garden" (Gen 3:8) emphasizes the unhindered communion between him and the first couple before it was broken and they were expelled from Eden. According to some apocryphal texts, the divine glory radiated from Eden and was especially granted to Adam. Jubilees 2:32 reveals that at the completion of creation the Creator blessed the Sabbath "which he had created for blessing and holiness and glory above all days." Thus, as Wenham notes:

> The Garden of Eden is not viewed by the author of Genesis simply as a piece of Mesopotamian farmland, but as an archetypal sanctuary, that is a place where God dwells and where man should worship him. Many of the features of the garden may also be found in later sanctuaries particularly the tabernacle or Jerusalem temple. These parallels suggest that the garden itself is understood as a sort of sanctuary.[15]

The Midrash connects the Eden story with the future temple and the age to come. God's planting of the Garden (Gen 2:8) is associated with

15. Wenham, "Sanctuary Symbolism in the Garden of Eden Story," 399.

"the trees of the Lord" and "the cedars of Lebanon which he planted" (Ps 104:16). According to the Midrash, the cedars of Eden were created for the sake of the Temple. Another sage recalls that cedars will be planted in the wilderness in the age to come (cf. Isa 41:19).[16] In other words, the cedars of Eden anticipate the future Temple and Messianic age. The rabbis also connect Eden and the future sanctuary by noting that the gold of Eden's neighboring land of Havilah (Gen 2:11–12) existed for the sake of the Temple.[17]

## God's Bridal Chamber

For the sages, the Garden of Eden was not only God's first sanctuary; it was also his original home and nuptial chamber in which he dwelt with mankind. *Canticles Rabbah* reinterprets the lover's exclamation in Cant 5:1 ("I have come into my garden, my sister, my bride . . . ") as follows:

> *I am come into my garden.* R. Menahem . . . said . . . It does not say here, 'I am come into *the* garden,' but *I am come into my garden* (*ganni*): as if to say, to my bridal-chamber (*ginnuni*): to the place which was my real home originally; for was not the original home of the Shechinah in the lower realm, as it says, *And they heard the voice of the Lord God walking in the garden* (Gen. 3:8)?

By means of a pun, *Canticles Rabbah* reads "my garden" (*ganni*)—a euphemism for the bride in the Song of Songs—as "my bridal-chamber" (*ginnuni*), i.e. the Garden of Eden where God's presence—the *Shechinah*— "walked" and communed with Adam and Eve.

*Genesis Rabbah* links Eden with the future Sinai theophany via the observance of the Sabbath and Adam's charge to "work" and "keep" the garden. R. Berekiah says that God placed Adam in the Garden of Eden to give him repose, protect and delight him with all the trees of the garden; in other words, he gave him the precept of the Sabbath—anticipating God's future gift of the Sabbath to Israel. Adam's task to "till" or "work" (Heb. *avad*) and "keep" the garden (Heb. *shamar*) (Gen 2:15) anticipates Israel's obligation to "work" for six days and to "keep" the Sabbath (Exod 20:9 Deut 5:12). In another interpretation, Adam's task to work and keep the garden is associated with Israel's obligation to serve (*avad*) God

16. *GenR* 15:1.
17. *GenR* 16:2.

on Sinai (Exod 3:21) by keeping (*shamar*) the commandment to offer him sacrifices.[18] The nuptial theme returns when, commenting on the moment when God made the woman out of the man's rib and brought her to him (Gen 2:22), R. Shimon bar Yochai portrays him as the divine matchmaker who "adorned her like a bride and brought her to him."[19] The Talmud adds: "and brought her to Adam . . . This teaches that the Holy One, blessed be he, served as the groomsman (*shoshbin*) for the first man."[20]

In short, the Midrash displays several motifs attributing a nuptial meaning to the dawn of creation and humanity—from the portrait of God as a king marrying off his daughter in the *chuppah* of the world, to the mystical marriage between the Creator-king and Sabbath-bride, to the mating between Israel and the Sabbath anticipated at creation, to Eden as the *Shekhinah*'s original bridal chamber. By means of creative literary devices, the nuptial meaning of creation is related to the Torah, the Tabernacle and Temple, the throne of glory, and the Messianic age.

## Broken Marriage and Paradise Lost

### The Fall of Man

Adam and Eve's idyllic communion with God in the Garden was short-lived. Tempted by the serpent, they disobeyed God's commandment and ate of the forbidden fruit from the tree of the knowledge of good and evil (Gen 3:1–6). Immediately, their eyes are opened. They recognize their nakedness yet evade responsibility for their action (Gen 3:7–13). As a result, God declares that the woman will bear children in pain and be subject to desire for her husband, who will rule over her (Gen 3:16). To Adam, God curses the ground, imposing toil and hard labor on human existence until he returns to the ground, "for out of it you were taken; for you are dust, and to dust you shall return" (Gen 3:17–19). Suffering and death make their entrance into human history. The Lord drives Adam and Eve out of the Garden, placing "the cherubim and a flaming sword that turned every way to guard the way to the tree of life" (Gen 3:22–24).

---

18. *GenR* 16:5.
19. *GenR* 18:1.
20. *B. Berakhot* 61a.

The sages depict the drama of Adam and Eve's sin and their banishment from Eden as a marital drama. They view God's casting of Adam and Eve out of the garden as a divorce: "like the daughter of a priest who has been divorced and cannot return [to her husband]," or more leniently, "like the daughter of an Israelite [i.e. a non-priest] who has been divorced and is able to return."[21] The expulsion is also compared to the future ruin of the Temple: "So he drove out the man . . . which intimates that he showed him the destruction of the Temple."[22] The exile from Eden is thus understood as a break in the original marriage between God and humanity (represented by Adam and Eve), just as the Temple's destruction later signifies a rupture in the spousal relationship between God and Israel. Yet something else was lost: God originally established the Sabbath as a source of light for all creation, but this light was extinguished because of Adam's sin. Some rabbis opine that Adam sinned on the eve of the Sabbath. Yet because of the sanctity of the Sabbath, God extended a grace period, so to speak, before inflicting punishment upon him. Even though the lights were spoiled on the eve of the Sabbath, God allowed the light to tarry on throughout the Sabbath: "The glory stayed the night, but at the end of the Sabbath, [God] took the splendor from him and drove him out of the Garden of Eden."[23]

By sinning, Adam also lost the divine glory that the Lord had bestowed upon him. The apocryphal *Apocalypse of Moses* records that Adam exclaimed to the serpent after he ate from the tree: "Why have you done this to me in that you have deprived me of the glory with which I was clothed?" (20:2); and to Eve who led him astray: "O wicked woman! What have I done to you? You have alienated me from the glory of God!" (21:6).[24] The same book also depicts the Garden of Eden as seat of the divine Presence: After Adam dies, he is brought back to Paradise for judgment; God appears there "mounted on the chariot of his cherubim" with his throne being "fixed where the Tree of Life was" (22:3–4).[25]

---

21. *GenR* 21:8.

22. The Hebrew word for "drove out" (*giresh*, Gen 3:24) is the same word used to describe a man "sending away" his wife when he divorces her. *GenR* 21:8.

23. *GenR* 11:2.

24. The Dead Sea Scrolls also attest to the "glory of Adam" (1QS 4:23; CD 3:20; 1QH 17:15). Hayward, *The Jewish Temple*, 45.

25. On Adam's loss of the glory of God, cf. 3 *Bar* 4:16; 4 *Ezra* 7:118–124; 8:50–52; *Test Abr* 11:8–9. The idea was adopted and expanded in rabbinic literature, which depicts the presence of the *Shekhinah* dwelling in Eden before the fall of Adam and Eve.

## The Cherubim in Eden

After the expulsion of Adam and Eve, God placed winged cherubim at the east of paradise to guard the way to the Tree of Life by means of "a flaming sword that turned every way" (Gen 3:24). As we have seen, Eden was not only the home of the first couple and primeval abode of humanity; it was also the dwelling place of God where he "walked" (Gen 3:8) and conversed with them. By preventing the return of mankind to Eden and to the Tree of Life, the guarding cherubim symbolize the rupture of communion between God and humanity. While Genesis tells us virtually nothing about the cherubim, the prophet Ezekiel attests to their presence in paradise: in his oracle against the proud king of Tyre, Ezekiel seems to identify the king with Adam, created "full of wisdom and perfect in beauty," beautifully bedecked with precious jewels, and placed in "Eden, God's garden" and "God's sacred mountain," in the presence of an anointed guardian cherub (Ezek 28:12–14). After the king rebelled, sinned, and "profaned his sanctuaries," the cherub banished him from the divine mountain (28:16) and cast him down to the ground to suffer a dreadful end (28:18–19). As we continue our survey of salvation history, we will encounter the cherubim anew and see how they continue to guard the renewed access to God's presence.

## Out of Eden

There is a tragic irony in the story of the Garden of Eden: from its original purpose as place of blessing and communion with God, it became instead the locus of alienation and curse. Once Eden is lost, the world becomes the arena of two opposing forces that remain continuously at war: On the one hand, God-centered *creation* is characterized by harmony, order, and blessing; on the other hand, man-centered *decreation* results in alienation, chaos, and curse.[26] The estrangement from God brought about by sin calls for restoration and reconciliation. Redemption, in this sense, is but a re-implementation of creation and restoration of humanity to its rightly intended created order.

---

Cf. *PRK* 1; *CantR* 5:1 §1.

26. Och, "Creation and Redemption," 229.

# 2

# Redemption and Covenant
## *Betrothal at Mount Sinai*

## From Eden to Egypt

AFTER THE FALL, sin proliferates in the world. The flood is a type of decreation and new creation by which God refashions the world anew through his covenant with Noah (Gen 6–9). With the call of Abraham, God begins to form a family that will become his instrument of salvation for the world. God promises to Abraham, Isaac, and Jacob that their descendants will become a great nation, a great name, and a blessing to all the families of the earth (Gen 12–22). The second half of Genesis narrates the story of the patriarchs and the growth of their family into the twelve tribes of Israel, concluding with their deliverance from famine, migration to Egypt, and settlement in the land of Goshen. The stage is set for the next act in humanity's nuptial drama, told in the book of Exodus: It will take a great redemptive event to repair man's break from Eden and alienation from God—indeed, a new creation.

## The Exodus as Renewal of Creation

The theme of creation is paramount in the Exodus narrative. Scholars have noted that the language used to describe the multiplication of the Israelites in Egypt, who "were fruitful and increased greatly" and "multiplied and grew exceedingly strong" (Exod 1:7), evokes the original commandment given to Adam to be fruitful and multiply (Gen 1:28).[1] The forming of Israel is the creation of a people *ex nihilo*—out of the "nothingness" of Egyptian slavery. It is a *new creation*, modeled on the first, cosmic creation, and its historical counterpart and completion. Bernard Och calls the birth of Israel in Egypt a "microcosmic fulfillment of God's macrocosmic plan for the world."[2] As new creation, Israel is called to be fruitful and multiply to mediate God's life-giving presence and redemption to the world. But this calling is thwarted by Pharaoh's oppressive measures, which are "fundamentally antilife and anticreation." These measures are the embodiment of the primeval forces of chaos that threaten "a return of the entire cosmos to its precreation state."[3] The consequence of Pharaoh's corrupt moral order is God's judgment in the form of devastating plagues unleashed upon Egypt, which correspond to the suffering that Pharaoh previously inflicted upon the Israelites. These are epitomized by the penultimate plague of darkness—signifying a reversion to the chaos of the pre-creation state, and the death of the first-born as the final and irreversible snuffing out of life.[4] In stark contrast to the "de-creation" of Egypt stand the events of the Exodus and deliverance of Israel, portrayed as reversals of the plagues and as a re-creation ultimately carried out for the sake of the entire world.[5]

---

1. Cf. also Gen 9:1, 7.

2. Och, "Creation and Redemption," 234–35.

3. Fretheim, "The Plagues as Ecological Signs of Historical Disaster," 385; "The Reclamation of Creation: Redemption and Law in Exodus," 357.

4. So Fretheim ("The Plagues," 395): "Pharaoh has been subverting God's creational work, so the consequences are oppressive, pervasive, public, prolonged, depersonalizing, heart-rending, and cosmic because such has been the effect on Egypt's sins upon Israel—indeed, upon the earth."

5. Fretheim, "The Plagues," 392. Fretheim (395) demonstrates how the events of the Exodus reverse the plagues: a) the Song at the Sea uses creational language; b) after the first plague the Egyptians "could not drink the water" (Exod 7:24), but when the Israelites "could not drink the (bitter) water" Moses made it sweet (Exod 15:23); c) God destroyed the food by "raining" hail upon Egypt (9:18, 23), but he "rained" bread from heaven for the Israelites (Exod 16:4); d) locusts "came up" and "covered" the land of Egypt, destroying the food (10:14–15), while quails "came up" and "covered" the Israelite camp (16:13). See also Carmichael, *The Story of Creation*, 17.

## The Exodus as Nuptial Event

### The Passover

In several midrashic texts, the sages attribute a nuptial meaning to the events of the Exodus by associating them with the Song of Songs and other Old Testament nuptial passages. They view Israel enslaved in Egypt as a *rose of Sharon* and *lily among thorns* (Cant 2:1–2) in dire need of redemption.[6] In the *Mekhilta*, one sage recalls the moment of Israel's redemption when the Passover lamb was slaughtered and eaten (Exod 12:6) as the *"time of love"* of Ezekiel 16:8. In this nuptial parable, Ezekiel personifies Jerusalem (or Israel) as a naked and destitute maiden. When God passed by her, he spread his garment over her, covered her nakedness, swore an oath, and entered into a covenant with her. The girl's former state—*naked and bare* (Ezek 16:7)—points to Israel's lack of religious deeds before the Lord delivered her from Egypt. This lack was remedied by the Passover sacrifice and circumcision of Israelite males. As Ezekiel's maiden was *weltering in her blood*, God saw her and said to her: "*I said to you in your blood, 'Live!'*" (Ezek 16:6). The *Mekhilta* associates this blood with the *blood of the covenant*, that is, the blood of the Passover sacrifice and blood of circumcision.[7] Another rabbi illustrates Israel's chastity in Egypt with Cant 4:12: the chaste behavior of Israel's men and women in Egypt is depicted as the Song's Shulamite, called a *garden locked* and *fountain sealed*.[8] The *Mekhilta* thus presents the Passover as a nuptial event—the first stage of the betrothal between God and Israel—where Israel is identified as Ezekiel's maiden and the Song's bride.[9]

On the night of the Passover, the Lord commanded Israel to eat the Passover in haste (Exod 12:11). The *Mekhilta* associates this commandment with the haste of the divine presence—the *Shekhinah*—in delivering Israel from the Egyptians. The *Shekhinah*, in turn, is identified with the lover of Cant 2:8–9, *leaping upon the mountains, skipping upon the hills*, and *standing behind our wall*.[10] The same *"leaping"* is equated with God skipping over the houses of his children as he goes to smite the Egyptian

---

6. *CantR* 2:1–2; *LevR* 23:1.

7. The identification of the blood of circumcision with the maiden's blood in Ezek 16:6 is also seen in *Pisḥa* 16; *PRK* 5:6, 7:4; *CantR* 1:5 §1.

8. Cf. also *LevR* 32:5, *PRK* 11:6.

9. *Mekh Pisḥa* 5.

10. *Mekh Pisḥa* 7.

first-born and sees the blood of the Passover smeared on the doors of the Israelites (Exod 12:13). The *Mekhilta* thus portrays the Passover in terms of the romantic drama of the Canticle, with God's *Shekhinah* portrayed as the Song's lover coming to take his beloved away with him.

Other events of the Exodus are allegorized and given a nuptial meaning: *Mekhilta* identifies the articles of gold and silver that the Israelites plundered from the Egyptians (Exod 12:35–36) with the ornaments that God gave to Ezekiel's maiden prior to her betrothal, and with the Shulamite's *circlets of gold* and *studs of silver* (Cant 1:11). Hence the plunder taken from the Egyptians is seen as a nuptial gift from the divine Bridegroom to his bride.[11] Moreover, the 600,000 Israelite men leaving Egypt (Exod 12:37) are associated with the Song's *litter of Solomon*, accompanied with *sixty mighty men coming up from the wilderness, perfumed with myrrh and frankincense* on the way to his wedding (Cant 3:7–11).[12] These connections with nuptial texts indicate that the sages saw the Passover as God's betrothal with Israel and the Exodus as Israel's wedding procession.

## The Red Sea

Following their flight from Egypt, the Israelites are caught in a panic between the pursuing Egyptians and the Red Sea (Exod 14:9–10). The sages describe the frightened people as a dove fleeing from a hawk (the Egyptians behind them) about to enter a cleft in the rock where there is a hissing serpent (the sea before them). This desperate situation causes them to set their mind on prayer. God's reply comes in the form of the lover praising his bride in the Song: "*O my dove, in the clefts of the rock . . . let me see your face, let me hear your voice; for your voice is sweet, and your face is lovely*" (Cant 2:14). According to the rabbis, the "voice" of the bride (the "dove") in the Canticle refers here to Israel's prayer, and her "face" is her study of Torah or good deeds.[13]

The divine lover guides his people on dry ground through the sea while the Egyptians drown in the returning waters (Exod 14:26–31). As the crossing concludes, a window into the future is opened, revealing that the deliverance from Egypt is a sign of the eschatological ingathering

11. *Mekh Pisḥa* 13.

12. *Mekh Pisḥa* 14.

13. *Mekh Beshallaḥ* 3; Cf. *CantR* 2:14 §2–4.

of the exiles, expressed by the beloved inviting his bride to come out of Lebanon with him (Cant 4:8). The *Mekhilta* further emphasizes the nuptial meaning of the future redemption by identifying it with the eschatological betrothal spoken of in Hosea 2:21–22: "*I will betroth you to Me forever . . . and I will betroth you unto Me because of faithfulness.*"[14]

The Israelites then begin to sing the Song at the Sea (Exod 15:1). The *Mekhilta* identifies God as the beloved of Cant 5:10–15 ("*My beloved is radiant and ruddy . . .* ").[15] The nuptial symbolism is developed in an exegesis of the first words of the Song at the Sea ("*This is my God, and I will praise him,*" Exod 15:2) that is particularly rich in nuptial allusions. R. Eliezer relates that what a common maidservant saw at the sea was more exalted than the visions of God seen by Isaiah and Ezekiel (Isa 6; Ezek 1). The *Mekhilta* then develops a sustained dialogue between Israel and the nations that begins and ends with the beloved and bride—God and Israel—communing together in the (future) Temple. Rabbi Akiva recalls how the nations of the world asked Israel:

> What is your beloved more than another beloved, that you thus adjure us? (Cant 5:9), that you are so ready to die for him, and so ready to let yourselves be killed for him? For it is said: "*Therefore do the maidens love Thee*" (Cant 1:3), meaning, they love thee unto death. And it is also written: "*nay but for Your sake we are killed all day long*" (Ps 44:23). "You are handsome, you are mighty, come and intermingle with us."[16]

The inquiry of the daughters of Jerusalem, asking the bride why she loves her beloved so much (Cant 5:9), becomes a metaphor of the nations asking Israel why she loves her divine Bridegroom to the point of dying for him. To the Gentiles' ensuing invitation to come and intermingle with them, Israel replies with the praise of God in the words of Cant 5:10 ("*My beloved is radiant and ruddy . . .* "). The beauty of the divine Lover is such that the nations wish to join themselves to Israel, asking: "*Where has your beloved gone, O fairest among women? Where has your beloved turned aside, that we may seek him with you?*" (Cant 6:1). But Israel jealously guards the Bridegroom for herself: "You can have no share in him,

---

14. *Mekh Beshallaḥ* 7.

15. *Mekh Shirata* 1.

16. *Mekh Shirata* 3. The argument rests upon a pun between "*maidens*" (*alamot*) and "unto death" (*ad mot*). The willingness to be martyred for the sake of divine love is related to the commandment of the *Shema* to love God with all of one's heart, soul and strength. Cf. *m. Berakhot* 9:5; Fishbane, *The Kiss of God*, 3–12.

but *My beloved is mine and I am his* (Cant 2:16), *I am my beloved's and my beloved is mine* (Cant 6:3)." For other sages, the text refers to Israel accompanying God into his Temple. This is illustrated with the parable of a king who followed his son on numerous trips to faraway countries. The king represents the *Shekhinah* following Israel from Canaan to Egypt, then out of Egypt, through the sea, and into the wilderness, "until they brought him with them to his holy Temple. And so it also says: *Scarcely had I passed by them, when I found the one I love*" (Cant 3:4). The rest of the Canticle's verse is revealing: "*I held him and would not let him go, until I had brought him to the house of my mother, and into the chamber of her who conceived me.*" Hence the deliverance from the Egyptians at the Red Sea offers occasion for a dialogue in which Israel proclaims to the nations her willingness to be martyred for the sake of her divine Lover. Her ultimate desire is to be united with him in his holy Temple, which is equated with the house and (nuptial) chamber of the Shulamite's mother in the Song of Songs.[17]

Following other references to the Canticle in the midrashic exposition of the Song of the Sea,[18] the *Mekhilta* identifies the moment when Israel goes into the wilderness (Exod 15:22) as the time of the betrothal between God and Israel spoken of by Jeremiah (2:2) when he wrote of "*the kindness of your youth, the love of your betrothal, when you went after Me in the wilderness.*"[19] Yet most rabbinic traditions situate the marriage between God and Israel at the moment of the Sinai theophany and covenant.

## Covenant and Betrothal at Mount Sinai

### Divine Kavod and Kedushah

The new creation is completed at Mount Sinai with the establishment of God's covenant with Israel, grounded in mutual love, revealing God's *kavod* (glory), and endowing Israel with his own *kedushah* (holiness). God's glory appears in the Old Testament as a visible and powerful manifestation to men, often in the form of a cloud.[20] While the glory

17. *Mekh Shirata* 3.

18. For example, in *Shirata* 6 (on Exod 15:7–8), the Egyptians are identified with the foxes of Cant 2:15.

19. *Mekh Vayassa* 1.

20. On the identification of the divine glory with the cloud, Patai (*The Hebrew*

of the Lord had already appeared in the cloud to the Israelites in the Wilderness of Sin (Exod 16:10), it becomes especially manifest at Mount Sinai, when Moses mediates the covenant and "the glory of the LORD rested on Mount Sinai, and the cloud covered it six days," resulting in a sight that was "like a consuming fire on the top of the mountain" (Exod 24:16–17).[21]

At Sinai, God calls Israel to be "a kingdom of priests and a holy nation" (*goy kadosh*).[22] The *kedushah* of Israel stems from the fact that it has entered into a national covenant with God. This means that they are to be dedicated to the Lord, segregated and set apart for his service through formal, legal restrictions: "And you shall be holy to Me, for I the Lord am holy, and have separated you from the peoples, that you should be Mine."[23] The covenant is based on mutual love, and the commandments set the people apart from the nations of the world (Deut 7:6–9).[24] God thus imparts *kedushah* on his people, first, by revealing his glory to them, and second, by setting them apart for the special purpose of serving him and being witnesses of his glory and love to the world.

## The Day of God's Espousals

The sages expand upon the idea of Sinai as the revelation of divine glory, turning it into the place where the Lord receives Israel as a bride. Indeed, the idea of the Sinai theophany as betrothal between God and Israel pervades the rabbinic exegesis of the Song. In a commentary on Cant 3:11, the Mishnah comments:

---

*Goddess*, 97) writes: "A careful perusal of the passages referring to the manifestation of God in the sanctuary shows that the nouns 'cloud' and 'glory' are used interchangeably, and that the 'cloud' was undoubtedly regarded as the visible form taken by the 'glory' of Yahweh when He wished to indicate His presence in His earthly abode, the sanctuary."

21. Later, when God instructs Moses to construct the Tabernacle, the Lord reveals that He will be the source of its sanctity, since it "shall be sanctified by My glory" (Exod 29:43). But when Moses asks to see the Lord's glory, he is told that this is impossible in his present mortal state (Exod 33:18–23). The manifestation of divine glory at Sinai is also described in Deut 5:24.

22. Exod 19:6. Cf. 22:30; 30:32, 37; Lev 11:43–45; 19:2; 20:26; 21:7–8; Num 15:39–40; Deut 7:3–6; 14:1–2, 21; 23:15.

23. Lev 20:26. Cf. Berman, *The Temple*, 6.

24. See also Deut 28:9 and Berman's discussion on *kedushah* and covenant (*The Temple*, 7–10).

"Go forth and look, O daughters of Zion, on King Solomon, with the crown wherewith his mother crowned him on the day of his espousals, on the day of the joy of his heart" [Cant 3:11]. "The day of the espousals" refers to the day on which the Law was given, and "the day of the joy of his heart" was that when the building of the Temple was completed. May it soon be rebuilt in our days![25]

According to this saying, the "day of King Solomon's espousals" designates the day of the giving of the Torah on Mount Sinai, when lover and beloved—God and Israel—are wedded. The sages richly develop this nuptial theme. The *Mekhilta* identifies Israel arriving at Sinai and setting camp before the mountain (Exod 19:1) as the Song's "*fairest among women*" (Cant 1:8),[26] then as "*my dove, my perfect one*" (Cant 6:9) as God declares his intention to make of Israel "a kingdom of priests and a holy nation" (Exod 19:6).[27]

## Divine Kisses

*Canticles Rabbah* comments on the Shulamite's passionate exclamation of desire that opens the Song of Songs: "*Let him kiss me with the kisses of his mouth! For your love is better than wine*" (Cant 1:2). The sages turn this exclamation into Israel's longing to receive God's "kisses" at Mount Sinai. And what are those kisses? None other than the commandments that God gave to Israel! Rabbi Yohanan illustrates this by means of a parable: a king wanted to marry a wife of a noble family and sent an envoy to speak with her. The lady said to the envoy: "I am not worthy to be his handmaid, but all the same I desire to hear from his own mouth." The king here represents God, the woman is Israel, and the envoy is Moses. The parable conveys the idea that Israel was not content to hear only the words of Moses but wanted to "hear from God's own mouth," that is, to "receive his kisses"—to hear his voice and receive his commandments (Exod 19:8–9). Hence God's "kisses"—the affectionate expression of his love for Israel—are embodied in the Torah and commandments.[28]

---

25. *M. Taʿanit* 4:8; cf. *CantR* 3:11 §2.
26. *Mekh Baḥodesh* 1.
27. *Mekh Baḥodesh* 2.
28. *CantR* 1:2 §3.

R. Judan presents an eschatological variation of this theme: Israel's longing for the *"kisses of his lips"* represents the people's longing for a direct and unmediated knowledge of Torah in their hearts. Yet God replies that this desire will only be fulfilled in the future days foretold by the prophets when he will put his law within them (Jer 31:33) and remove their heart of stone (Ezek 36:26). In this way, a nuptial link is made between Sinai and the end of history: Israel's desire for "kisses" is partially fulfilled by receiving the Torah and commandments at Sinai, yet only in a transitory way since they are still liable to forget what they have learnt. Only when God will "kiss them with the kisses of his mouth" by definitively writing his Torah on their hearts in the Messianic age will their longing be completely fulfilled.[29]

## Holy Inebriation

In another parable, God is compared to a king who had a cellar of wine. He mixed a cup for a first guest, then another for a second guest, but when his son came, he gave him the whole cellar. The wine stands for the Torah and commandments: While God gave just a few commandments (one cup of wine) to each of the patriarchs (Adam, Noah, Abraham, Isaac, Jacob, Judah), he gave the whole Torah (the entire cellar) to Israel.[30] The Midrash further develops the association of Torah with wine elsewhere in a commentary on Cant 2:4: *"He brought me to the banqueting house* (literally: *"house of wine"*), *and his banner over me was love."* The lover bringing his beloved to the *"house of wine"* is interpreted as God bringing Israel to Sinai, called a "great cellar of wine" to symbolize the abundant outpouring of love and joy that flows from the study of Torah. The Torah is thus the *"banner of love"* that the lover raised over his beloved.[31]

## The King at His Table

We now come to the theophany itself. God's appearance on Sinai *on the third day*, with thundering and lightnings, a thick cloud, and the loud sound of trumpet (Exod 19:16), is said to be "confirmed" by Cant 1:12: *"While the king was on his couch, my nard gave forth its fragrance."* One

29. *CantR* 1:2 §4.
30. *CantR* 1:2 §5.
31. *CantR* 2:4 §1.

may assume that the "king on his couch" is God about to form the covenant with Israel, and the "fragrance" presumably refers to the sights and sounds of the theophany. The *Mekhilta* then presents the moment when Moses *brought the people out of the camp to meet God, and they stood at the foot of the mountain* (Exod 19:17) as *the* great nuptial moment between God and Israel:

> Judah used to expound: *The Lord came from Sinai* (Deut 33:2). Do not read it thus, but read: "The Lord came to Sinai" to give the Torah to Israel. I, however, do not interpret it thus, but: *The Lord came from Sinai* to receive Israel as a bridegroom comes forth to meet the bride.[32]

This interpretation places Moses, who brings the bride Israel to her divine bridegroom, in the position of the *shoshbin*, the mediator responsible for arranging the wedding. The Torah, moreover, is Israel's *ketubah* or marriage contract.[33] The *Mekhilta* reinforces the view of Sinai as nuptial moment by a renewed mention of the *dove in the clefts of the rock* (Cant 2:14). Whereas this expression elsewhere depicts Israel at the Red Sea, here it refers to Israel coming near and standing *below the mountain*. The bride's lovely "*face*" represents the twelve pillars erected for the twelve tribes of Israel, and her sweet "*voice*" the people's response to the Ten Commandments.[34] Elsewhere, God is portrayed as the lover who is "*like an apple tree*" (Cant 2:3), shunned by all people on the day of the giving of the Torah; only Israel, like the Shulamite, longed to "*sit in his shadow*." The woman's longing is an image of Israel longing for the Torah, and his fruit "*sweet to my taste*" refers to the people at Mount Sinai feasting on the words of Torah.[35] In another identification of God as divine bridegroom, the Holy One assisting Israel at Sinai is described as the Canticle's lover whose "*left hand is under my head and his right hand embraces me* (Cant 2:6)."[36]

---

32. *Mekh Baḥodesh* 3.

33. On the Torah as *ketubah*, cf. *Sifre Deut* 305; *PRK* 19:4; *Exodus Rabbah* 46:1.

34. *Mekh Baḥodesh* 3. Cf. *CantR* 2:14 §2–4.

35. *CantR* 2:3 §1–3; *TgCant* 2:3.

36. *Mekh Baḥodesh* 9.

## Decalogue, Kedushah and Sabbath: A New Creation

At Sinai, God gives the Ten Commandments to Israel—the heart of the Torah (Exod 20). The first three commandments directly pertain to Israel's covenant faithfulness to God. Significantly, the *Mekhilta* associates the second commandment ("Thou shalt have no other gods before me," Exod 20:3) with the seventh ("Thou shalt not commit adultery," Exod 20:14). With this association, the *Mekhilta* follows the classic view of the prophets (cf. Ezek 16:32; Hos 3:1), holding that "if one worships idols it is accounted to him as though he committed adultery, breaking his covenant with God."[37]

The fourth commandment instructs Israel to remember (or "observe," Deut 5:12) the Sabbath day. Yet the Sabbath is much more than an obligatory day of rest. It is also a "temporal shrine" and eternal sign bearing witness to God's covenant with Israel.[38] The Sabbath links the Sinai covenant with the creation of the world via God's *kedushah* (Gen 2:2–3; Exod 31:12–17).[39] As the Sabbath commemorates God's creation of the world and his covenant with humanity, so the Sabbath commemorates God's "creation" of Israel and his covenant with his newly formed people.

Second Temple Jewish Literature emphasizes the connection between creation and Sinai. According to the Book of Jubilees, God pre-ordained the birth of Israel at creation and established the Sabbath as sign of his future covenant with them.[40] For the rabbis, although the Sabbath was "married" in the first place to God, she was also espoused to Israel. She thus plays a mediating role between her two partners. Drawing from the double meaning of the word *kiddesh,* the Sages interpret the commandment that Israel sanctify the Sabbath (Exod 20:8) as a

---

37. *Mekh Baḥodesh* 8.

38. Exod 31:13–17; Isa 56:4–6; Lev 23:2–3. Cf. Berman, *The Temple,* 11.

39. In Exod 24:16, the cloud covering Sinai for six days followed by the Lord calling Moses on the seventh day hints at the six days of creation followed by the Sabbath.

40. [Upon creating the seventh day, God said:] "Behold, I will separate unto Myself a people from among all the peoples, and these shall keep the Sabbath day, and I will sanctify them unto Myself as My people, and will bless them; as I have sanctified the Sabbath day and do sanctify (it) unto Myself, even so will I bless them, and they shall be My people and I will be their God. And I have chosen the seed of Jacob from amongst all that I have seen, and have written him down as My first-born son, and have sanctified him unto Myself for ever and ever; and I will teach them the Sabbath day, that they may keep Sabbath thereon from all work." (Jub 2:19–21; cf. also 2:31–32)

commandment to *betroth* her.[41] To them, the meaning of the word "sanctify" (*kiddesh*) was to impress upon Israel its destiny to be "the groom of the sacred day;" it was a commandment for Israel to "espouse the seventh day."[42] As sign of the covenant between God and Israel, the Sabbath not only commemorates the seventh day of creation and the giving of the Torah on Mount Sinai; she is also a bride endowed with *kedushah* calling for the companionship of man to be celebrated like a wedding ceremony.

## The Bride's Response

Canticles Rabbah expands on the allegorical reading of Cant 1:12, "*While the king was on his couch, my nard gave forth its fragrance,*" by interpreting the Shulamite's fragrance as Israel's response to the covenant. The rabbis dispute whether the nard refers to Israel's fragrant obedience to God at Sinai, or whether it was rather the stench rising to heaven when they adored the golden calf (Exod 32). R. Meir takes the negative approach, but he is rebuked by R. Judah who tells him that the Song should not be expounded in a bad sense, for it was "revealed only for the praise of Israel." Thus, *while the king was on his couch* refers to the moment when "the supreme King of Kings, the Holy One, blessed be He, was at his table in the firmament, Israel sent forth a fragrance before Mount Sinai and said '*All that the Lord has spoken we will do, and we will be obedient*'" (Exod 24:7), and *the glory of the Lord dwelt on Mount Sinai* (Exod 24:16).[43] According to the Midrash, "it is with reference to that occasion that Scripture said: *You are all fair, my love; and there is no flaw in you*" (Cant 4:7).[44]

## Precious Commandments

In *Sifre Deuteronomy*, Israel's observance of the Torah and commandments is also given a nuptial meaning. Commenting on the *Shema*

---

41. Cf. *b. Shabbat* 119a; *b. Baba Qama* 32b; *GenR* 10:9. *Shabbat* is the bride of Israel in *GenR* 11:8 and God's Queen in *LevR* 27:10. On the Sabbath's role as bride, cf. Heschel, *The Sabbath*, 45–55; Green, "Shekhinah, the Virgin Mary, and the Song of Songs," 19; Patai, *The Hebrew Goddess*, 255–76; Pope, *Song of Songs*, 171–79.

42. Heschel, *The Sabbath*, 54.

43. *CantR* 1:12 §1.

44. *CantR* 4:7 §1; *LevR* 18:4.

(Deut 6:9), *Sifre* compares the commandments adorning Israel to jewelry adorning the wife of a king and to the beauty of the Shulamite (Cant 6:4).[45] The Midrash equates keeping the commandments (Deut 11:22) with *seeking wisdom as silver* (Prov 2:4). Through several biblical verses, *Sifre* establishes connections between Torah, wisdom, divine love, water, wine, and honey. The Torah is the source of *cold waters to a faint soul* (Prov 25:25), forever free to anyone who wishes to restore his soul. Just as water is priceless, "so are words of Torah priceless, as it is said, *she* (wisdom) *is more precious than rubies*" (Prov 3:15). The words of Torah, identified with divine Wisdom, are equated with the love of God that makes the heart rejoice, just as wine makes the heart of lovers rejoice: *For thy love is better than wine* (Cant 1:2, cf. Ps 19:9). Moreover, *Sifre* states that the Torah is good for both the head and the body, as the ointment of the Song's lover is good for head and body (Cant 1:3); the Torah is also *sweeter than the honey and the honeycomb* (Ps 19:11). Yet the ultimate reason for studying Torah should be "*to love the Lord your God*" (Deut 11:22). The Torah should be studied for its own sake because *she is a tree of life to those who lay hold of her* (Prov 3:18). *Sifre* underlines the nuptial metaphor by identifying the rewards of Torah study with Lady Wisdom's love for those who seek her—both in this world and in the world to come: *She will place on your head a garland of grace* (in this world), and *a crown of glory she will bestow on you* (in the world to come) (Prov 4:9).[46] Given that garlands and crowns were worn by bridegrooms and brides in the ancient world, this implies that studying Torah and seeking Wisdom is a romantic pursuit leading to the marriage of Lady Wisdom with those who seek her.

## Divine Love in Pesikta de-Rab Kahana

### Arise, My Love, and Come Away!

*Pesikta de-Rab Kahana* adroitly brings together much of the imagery seen above. Piska 5 reinterprets the Lord's redemptive action from Egypt to Sinai as the drama of the lovers in the Song of Songs. *PRK* reads the Exodus in light of Cant 5:2, which describes the lover knocking at his beloved's door:

45. *Sifre Deut* 36.
46. *Sifre Deut* 48.

*Hark! My beloved knocks* (Cant 5:2)—that is, Moses knocks, declaring, "Thus says the Lord: About midnight will I go out into the midst of Egypt" (Exod 11:4). By *Open to Me* (Cant 5:2) . . . the Holy One was saying: Make an opening for Me in you . . . By *My sister* (*ibid.*), God was saying: Israel, My own, My kin—you who bound yourselves irrevocably to Me in Egypt by two covenants of blood, the blood of Passover and the blood of circumcision. By *My love*, He was referring to Israel at the Red Sea—at the Red Sea where Israel showed their love of him, saying "The Lord shall reign for ever and ever" (Exod 15:18). By *My dove* (*ibid.*), He was referring to Israel at Marah where Israel . . . came to have the iridescence of a docile dove. By *My perfect one*, He was referring to Israel at Sinai—at Sinai, where they became pure in My sight when they said to Me, "We will do, and then hear" (Exod 24:7).[47]

Thus, the lover knocking on the door of his beloved represents God's deliverance of Israel on the night of the Passover, the crossing of the Red Sea, the water incident at Marah, and Israel's acceptance of the covenant at Sinai. *PRK* also re-reads the story of the redemption from Egypt from the perspective of the beloved woman (Israel), who sees and hears her lover (God) invite her to come away with him—to Sinai (Cant 2:9–10):

*My Beloved is like a gazelle or a young hart* (Song 2:9) . . . as a gazelle leaps and skips from tree to tree, from thicket to thicket, from grove to grove, so the Holy One leaped from Egypt to the Red Sea and from the Red Sea to Sinai. The children of Israel saw him in Egypt, as is said *I will go through the land of Egypt in that night* (Exod. 12:12). They saw him at the Red Sea: *And Israel saw the great work* (Exod. 14:31). They saw him at Sinai: *Moses . . . said, The Lord came to Sinai . . .* (Deut. 33:2) . . . *Behold, He stands behind our wall* (Song 2:9), [waiting to enter into our encampment], as is said "For the third day the Lord will come down in the sight of all the people upon Mount Sinai" (Exod. 19:11). *He looks out through the windows* (Song 2:9) [of heaven, waiting to come down]: "And the Lord came down upon Mount Sinai, to the top of the Mount" (Exod. 19:20). *He sings out through the lattice* (Song 2:9), as when He said, "I am the Lord thy God" (Exod. 20:2), and goes on, as we are told, *My Beloved spoke, and said unto me: "Rise up, My love, My fair one, and come away"* (Song 2:10). And before saying, "*Come away* . . . " what words did He speak to me? The words "I am the Lord thy God" (Exod. 20:2).[48]

47. *PRK* 5:6.
48. *PRK* 5:8.

In short, as the Canticle's beloved man leaps like a gazelle, the Lord leaps from Egypt to the Red Sea to Sinai, where he patiently waits for Israel to recognize him so he can enter into a marriage covenant with her.

## Torah as Wedding Gift

Piska 12 is a homily for Pentecost discussing Exodus 19:1, the giving of Torah, and its many levels of eternal meaning. Its nuptial symbolism revolves around the Sinai event, portrayed as the climax of the entire history that preceded it. The homily begins with an account of the original commandments given to Adam in the Garden, then to Noah, Abraham, and the other patriarchs. All these were surpassed at Sinai when God gave 613 commandments to Israel.[49] The Shulamite's longing that her lover "*sustain me with raisin cakes, refresh me with apples; for I am sick with love*" (Cant 2:5) refers to Israel's longing for words of Torah, and her lovesickness is every man's yearning to hear a word of Scripture.[50] The words of Torah are compared to spiced wine, containing wine, honey and pepper, as Torah has the goodness of wine (Cant 1:2), the sweetness of honey and the sharpness of pepper.[51] *PRK* 12:10 quotes the Canticle again: "*as an apple tree among the trees of the woods, so is my beloved among the sons*" (Cant 2:3). As the apple tree is shunned because it gives no shade, so the nations shunned the Holy One on the day of the giving of the Torah, while Israel delighted to sit in his shadow. The nuptial dimension of the Sinai revelation follows, where the giving of the Torah to Israel is equated with the bride entering the *chuppah*:

> Consider an analogy with a king who betrothed a noble woman and set a time [for the wedding]. When the time came, he was told, "The hour has come for the bride to enter the nuptial chamber." So, too, when the time came for the Torah to be given, the announcement was made, "The time has come for the Torah to be given to Israel."[52]

Other nuptial parables follow: just as a king decided to count the years of this era beginning with the month of the wedding of his daughter, so God decreed that the years of this era should be counted

49. *PRK* 12:1.
50. *PRK* 12:3.
51. *PRK* 12:5.
52. *PRK* 12:11.

beginning with the month of the giving of Torah. Thus, the giving of the Torah is equated with the daughter's wedding. In another parable, Israel is compared to a noble woman whom a king wanted to marry; but he first wished to do something generous on her behalf before asking her hand. So he *"clothed [her] in embroidered cloth"* (Ezek 16:10), brought her safely across the Red Sea, and delivered her from the Amalekites. R. Eleazar tells of a similar story: the king gave the woman loaves of bread, spiced wine, force-fed birds and figs—respectively figures of the manna (Exod 16:4), water from the well (Num 21:17), quails (Num 11:31), and honey from the rock (Deut 32:13). Both parables portray the Exodus as God's courtship of Israel. A final parable presents the Sinai covenant and giving of the Torah as the reuniting of heaven and earth: R. Abba bar Yudan tells of a king who had previously forbidden marriages with people from across the sea. But when he gave his own daughter in marriage [to one beyond the sea], he withdrew the decree. So too, before the Torah was given, God had decreed the separation of heaven and earth (cf. Ps 115:16); but after the Torah was given from heaven, God withdrew this decree and enabled the union between heaven and earth (i.e. between himself and Israel) at Sinai, when Moses went up to God and he came down on the mountain (Exod 19:3, 20).[53]

*PRK* further considers the giving of the Ten Commandments (Exod 20) in light of God's chariot and myriads of ministering angels present at Sinai (cf. Ps 68:18). The Lord outshines even the beautiful radiance of the angels, being identified with the beloved of Cant 5:10 who is *white and ruddy, chief among ten thousand*.[54] The Midrash describes the various "forms" under which God appeared to Israel: as a mighty man waging war at the Sea, a scribe who teaches Torah at Sinai, an elder teaching Torah in the days of Daniel, and a young man in the days of Solomon who is *"like Lebanon, young as the cedars"* (Cant 5:15).[55] These metaphors imply that the great nuptial encounter with the divine Lover at Sinai is also a vision of his divine glory as it appeared at the greatest moments of revelation in the history of Israel.

---

53. *PRK* 12:11.
54. *PRK* 12:22.
55. *PRK* 12:24.

## Completion of the New Creation

The return of God's sanctified Presence on earth in the midst of his newly created people, reestablishing the relationship that had been broken in Eden, means that redemption is nothing less than the restoration and renewal of creation. Sinai is a corrective to the fall and the completion of what had begun in Eden.[56] This explains the Torah's emphasis on abundant life and growth as the natural fruit of faithfulness to the covenant and the logical outcome of the commandment to "be fruitful and multiply." Obedience to the law means conformity to the creational order that God has restored by his sovereign redemptive activity; it is the very source of life.[57]

The Sages developed the idea of the Sinai revelation and gift of the Torah as a corrective and remedy to the Fall, and the way for Israel to regain the divine image lost when Adam sinned.[58] Israel's cosmic role is seen in a midrash stating that the extension of God's cosmic plan to all creation was dependent upon Israel's acceptance of the (pre-existent) Torah at Sinai.[59] Similarly, the Ten Commandments establishing God's divine law are elevated to a position of cosmic importance by

56. In Och's words ("Creation and Redemption," 238): "The journey of man which began at the Garden of Eden moves on to its ultimate destination: Mount Sinai. The theophany at Sinai marks the culmination and fulfillment of God's creational plan. The encounter between God and Israel at Sinai can be seen as a return to beginnings, an iterative event which is a reenactment of the original encounter between God and man at Eden. For this purpose, God has created a new people to stand before him at Sinai as Adam stood in His presence at Eden. What began at Eden is now completed at Sinai. At Sinai, the people of Israel are called on to become participants in the renewal and maintenance of the created order."

57. Deut 4:40; 11:8–9; 16:20; 22:7. Cf. Fretheim, "The Reclamation of Creation," 360, 362. Philo (*On the Creation of the World* 3) writes that the law corresponds to the world and the world to the law.

58. "When the serpent came upon Eve he injected lust into her: [as for] the Israelites who stood at Mount Sinai, their lustfulness departed" (*b. Yebamot* 103b). Cf. GenR 19:7; CantR 5:1 §1; *b. Shabbat* 145b–146a; *b. Avodah Zara* 22b. On Sinai as remedy to the fall, see Scroggs, *The Last Adam*, 52–54.

59. "God said to the objects of creation, 'If Israel accepts the Torah, you shall continue and endure, otherwise, I shall turn everything back into chaos again.' The whole of creation was thus kept in dread and suspense until the revelation at Sinai, when Israel received and accepted the Torah, and so fulfilled the condition made by God when He created the universe" (*b. Shabbat* 88a). Cf. Och, "Creation and Redemption," 238. The eternal nature of the Torah is the basic premise of the Book of Jubilees; cf. Jub 1:29; 2:22, 29; 3:10, 14, 31.

corresponding to the ten words by which the world was created. The words of the Commandments and the tablets on which they are engraved are divine, created by God's own hand at twilight on the eve of the first Sabbath of creation, and thus they form the foundation to the entire created order.[60] Israel's cosmic role in completing the created order is also seen in the correlation between Adam's responsibility to work (*avad*) and keep (*shamar*) the Garden (Gen 2:15) and Israel's calling to serve (*avad*) the Lord and keep (*shamar*) the commandments.[61] This implies that Israel's observance of the law is the continuation of Adam's care of the Garden of Eden.

The redemptive event of Sinai is thus the completion and renewal of creation and the initiation of its repair back to its original state before the fall.[62] The connection is well attested in the Old Testament. We have mentioned how the *kedushah* of the Sabbath forms a common thread between creation and Sinai. Deut 4:32 calls the Exodus and Sinai revelation the greatest event since the creation of the world.[63] Jer 31:31–37, which describes in nuptial terms God's covenant with Israel, compares this event with the fixed order of creation, using the language of Genesis 1 (day and night; sun and moon; heaven, earth and sea). Jeremiah also praises the Lord both for having made the heavens and the earth by his great power and outstretched arm, and for having brought Israel out of Egypt with signs and wonders, with a strong hand and outstretched arm (Jer 32:17–21; cf. Amos 9:5–7). Psalm 136 first praises God for his work of creation (vv. 5–9) and then for the events of the Exodus (vv. 10–21). Isaiah's depiction of redemption as "new Exodus" is typically linked with the elements of nature (earth, sea, rivers, animals, vegetation) associated with creation.[64] Finally, the author of the Wisdom of Solomon clearly illustrates the creation-Exodus relationship as he concludes a long description of the events of the Exodus by stating that in it "the whole creation in

---

60. *M. Avot* 5:1; *GenR* 17:1; *b. Rosh HaShanah* 32a. Cf. Och, *"Creation and Redemption,"* 239; Carmichael, *The Story of Creation,* 28–29.

61. *Sifre Deut* 41; *GenR* 16:5; *CantR* 1:2.

62. As Och states: "At Sinai, the destructive forces of decreation unleashed by man in Eden are neutralized and brought under control by a Divine/human act of restoration and recreation. Eden and Sinai are parametric events which set up a historical continuum on which the drama of creation and decreation is played out" (Och, "Creation and Redemption," 230–31).

63. Cf. also Exod 34:10. Carmichael, *The Story of Creation,* 4–5.

64. Isa 41:17–20; 42:5–17; 43:15–21; 51:10.

its nature was fashioned anew" (Wis 19:6). These passages indicate that the biblical authors saw an intrinsic connection between creation and the Exodus as God's two greatest deeds.

## The Golden Calf: Israel's "Original Sin"

Yet like Eden, which began as a paradise of communion but ended in alienation, Sinai ends in tragedy. Israel's worship of the golden calf (Exod 32) amounts to such a shockingly quick betrayal of the newly formed (nuptial) covenant that the rabbis considered it the equivalent of a bride committing harlotry while still under the *chuppah*: "shameless is the bride who fornicates in her own bridal canopy."[65] Here again Moses acts as the *shoshbin*, pleading with God that he would extend mercy upon his wayward bride and be reconciled with her.[66] Other sources compare the building of the calf to Adam's eating of the forbidden fruit in Eden and his subsequent loss of the divine nature.[67] The golden calf is thus a reenactment of man's turning away from God—an act of divine creation followed by an act of human de-creation and renewed alienation. Israel's journey from Sinai resumes mankind's journey that began with the expulsion from Eden. As the flaming sword barred Adam and Eve from reentering the Garden, the flaming pillar of fire accompanying the Israelites in the wilderness—while indicating God's presence and protection for his people—also stands between them as the sign of his inapproachability.

Just as the Shulamite is *"dark but lovely"* (Cant 1:5), as the Midrash point out, so is Israel dark (sinful and rebellious) yet lovely (repentant and obedient) at the major stations of the Exodus: in Egypt, at the Passover, by the Red Sea, at Horeb, at the setting up of the Tabernacle, and at later moments of Israel's history until its final redemption. Thus, God's bride can say: *"I am black in this world and lovely in the world to come."*[68] This failure of Israel to fulfill her calling as agent of God's work of (re-) creation and redemption calls for a more sustained means of actualizing the divine Presence among his people.

---

65. *B. Shabbat* 88b; cf. *b. Gittin* 36b; *Deuteronomy Rabbah* 3:10; Pope, *Song of Songs*, 349.

66. *Exodus Rabbah* 46:1; *Deuteronomy Rabbah* 3:17.

67. *Exodus Rabbah* 32:1; *Numbers Rabbah* 16:24; *LevR* 11:1, 3; *CantR* 3:6–7. Cf. Scroggs, *The Last Adam*, 53.

68. *CantR* 1:5 §1.

*3*

# In the Bridal Chamber

## Union in the Tabernacle and Temple

### The Tabernacle: God Dwells with Israel

#### Liturgical Actualization of Sinai

THE BETROTHAL BETWEEN GOD AND ISRAEL at Mount Sinai was a one-time event that lasted only as long as the Israelites remained at the foot of the mount. Moreover, it had been seriously breached by the worship of the golden calf. This breach called for a more permanent mode of God's presence among his people. The Tabernacle is the continued locus of the covenant and nuptial union between the Lord and Israel for the next generations as they wander through the desert towards the Promised Land. The holy sanctuary, coming into existence by divine decree at Sinai, constitutes the liturgical extension, actualization in the present, and perpetuation into the future of God's union with Israel formed at Sinai. Like Sinai, the Tabernacle is the meeting point between God and Israel—between heaven and earth. Jewish scholar Umberto Cassuto expresses this well:

> In order to understand the significance and purpose of the Tab-
> ernacle, we must realize that the children of Israel, after they had
> been privileged to witness the Revelation of God on Mount Si-
> nai, were about to journey from there and thus draw away from
> the site of the theophany. So long as they were encamped in the

49

place, they were conscious of God's nearness; but once they set out on their journey, it would seem to them as though the link had been broken, unless there were in their midst a tangible symbol of God's presence among them. It was the function of the Tabernacle [literally, "dwelling"] to serve as such a symbol . . . The nexus between Israel and the Tabernacle is a perpetual extension of the bond that was forged at Sinai between the people and their God.[1]

The connection between the Sinai covenant and Tabernacle service is underlined by several literary devices in the Pentateuch. Parallels between the finale of the Sinai theophany and the last stages of the Tabernacle's construction indicate that both are viewed as the locus of God meeting with his people: The cloud covered both Mount Sinai (Exod 24:15) and the Tent of Meeting (Exod 40:34); the glory of the Lord settled on the mount (Exod 24:16) and filled the Tabernacle (Exod 40:34); it appeared in both places as a consuming fire (Exod 24:17; Lev 9:23–24); the Lord called Moses out of the cloud (Exod 24:16) and from the tent (Lev 1:1); all the people saw both theophanies (Exod 24:17; Lev 9:24); and Moses went up the mountain and into the tent (Exod 24:18; Lev 9:23).[2]

Berman has noted other connections between Sinai and the Tabernacle: At Sinai, the divine voice (*kol*) spoken to the people (Exod 19:5; Deut 4:12, 33, 36; 5:22–26) was the audible manifestation of God's will, communicating to Israel his commandments and directives. After Sinai, the *kol* continues to be heard from above the mercy seat upon the Ark of the Covenant, between the cherubim (Num 7:89). It is from above the Ark that God promises to Moses: "I will meet with you" and "I will speak with you of all that I will give you in commandment for the people of Israel" (Exod 25:22). The Tabernacle is the locus of divine instruction, as Mount Sinai had been at the moment of Revelation. God's appearance to Israel at Sinai in the thick cloud (Exod 19:9, 16; 24:15–18) signified his proximity through a shield of protection from his immediate Presence which, if seen "face to face" would cause death (Exod 33:20). The same cloud of glory continued to accompany the Israelites in the Tabernacle (Exod 40:34–38). In addition, the cloud of incense rising up in the sanctuary from the altar of incense, positioned in front of the curtain of the innermost sanctuary (Exod 30:1–10, 34–38; Lev 16:12–13), acted as a

1. Cassuto, *A Commentary on the Book of Exodus*, 319. Cited in Berman, *The Temple*, 41.

2. Berman, *The Temple*, 41–42.

protective veil and "symbolic buffer" between the outer chamber and the divine Presence in the Holy of Holies, as the cloud had done at Sinai. The altar of burnt offerings at the entrance of the Tabernacle also "simulates" the great consuming fire of God's unapproachable Presence that had previously engulfed Mount Sinai (Exod 24:17; Deut 5:20–22). Finally, another key link between Sinai and Sanctuary is the sacrificial system, divinely instituted at Horeb and perpetually reenacted in the courts of the sanctuary as the means to atone for sins and enable the communion with God that was first experienced on the mountain.[3]

## Kedushah, Sabbath and Sanctuary

What the Sabbath is to time, the Tabernacle is to space. If the Sabbath constituted the *sacred time* for the covenantal union between God and Israel, the sanctuary is its *sacred place* (Exod 25:8; 29:43–45). The Tabernacle is called "tent of meeting" (*ohel moed*), "dwelling place" (*mishkan*), "sanctuary" (*mikdash*), or "holy place" (*kodesh*). These names reveal it as a "house of holiness," a consecrated, sacred space for divine service, where the divine presence dwells and meets with God's covenantal people. As realms of sacred time and sacred space, the Sabbath and Tabernacle are closely linked: The commandment to keep the Sabbath and abstain from performing any work on it (Exod 31:12–17) is reiterated immediately after instructions are given to build the Tabernacle (Exod 31:1–11), just before God gives Moses the two tablets of the testimony (Exod 31:18). As signs of the covenant and privileged realms of *kedushah*, both Sabbath and Sanctuary are to be guarded with the same diligence: "You shall keep My Sabbaths and reverence My Sanctuary: I am the Lord" (Lev 19:30; 26:2). The connections between the Tabernacle and the Sabbath imply that the Tabernacle is also a type of new creation. Parallels between the accounts of the completion of creation and of the Tabernacle—both of which use the language of completion, blessing, and sanctification—indeed present the sanctuary as the spiritual completion of the universe.[4]

3. Berman, *The Temple*, 45.

4. The Genesis account states that "the heavens and the earth were finished . . . and on the seventh day God finished his work which he had done, and he rested on the seventh day from all his work which he had done. So God blessed the seventh day and hallowed it" (Gen 2:1–2). The account of the completion of the Tabernacle echoes this language: "Thus all the work of the tabernacle of the tent of meeting was finished" (Exod 39:32); "and Moses saw all the work, and behold, they had done it . . . And

## The Cherubim in the Tabernacle

At the heart of the Tabernacle, in the Holy of Holies, were two cherubim of solid gold overshadowing the Ark of the Covenant. The biblical text says nothing about their appearance or form.[5] Exodus 25:18–22 (and 37:7–9) tells us that they faced each other with their wings stretched upwards, covering the mercy seat—the throne upon which the glory of God rested. From there, God communed with Israel and spoke to Moses: "And there I will meet with you, and I will speak with you from above the mercy seat, from between the two cherubim which are on the ark of the Testimony" (Exod 25:22). Cherubim figures were also woven into the ten curtains of the Tabernacle and on the veil that separated the holy place from the Holy of Holies (Exod 26:1, 31; 36:8, 35). The predominance of cherubim motifs throughout the Tabernacle precinct points to the former cherubim at the entrance of the Garden of Eden. As the cherubim guarded the access to the Garden after the fall, so they now guarded God's presence in the sanctuary—indicating that Tabernacle worship now provided the way back to God's presence which had been lost in Eden.

## Tabernacle as Nuptial Chamber

From the belief that the Tabernacle was the sacred place of God's covenant with Israel, the rabbis developed the idea that the sanctuary was the *nuptial chamber* where their union was enacted. *Pesikta de-Rab Kahana* provides a masterful treatment of the Tabernacle as nuptial chamber. Its first homily is a lesson for the Sabbath during Hanukkah—when Jews commemorate in their liturgy the rededication of the Temple by the Maccabees. As background to the Temple's dedication, the homily discusses the original dedication of the Tabernacle as described in Num 7:1: "*On the day when Moses had finished setting up the tabernacle, and had anointed and consecrated it . . .*" Surprisingly, the midrash reads this verse loosely as "*It was on [Israel's] bridal day that Moses brought to a conclusion [the coming back to earth that God had begun in the days of Abraham]*."

---

Moses blessed them" (Exod 39:43); "So Moses finished the work" (Exod 40:33). Cf. Berman, *The Temple*, 13–14.

5. They possibly resembled the figures with a human face and two outstretched wings attached to the arms known from Egyptian art, or Assyrian winged human figures. Josephus claims that no one knew what shape they had (*Antiquities* 3.6.5). Carol Meyers, "Cherubim" in *Anchor Bible Dictionary*, 899–900.

The midrash immediately frames the dedication of the Tabernacle as a nuptial event by quoting Cant 5:1 (*"I have come to my garden, my sister, my bride . . . "*)—where the words of the lover to his bride represent the words of God speaking to Israel as he enters his "garden"—the sanctuary.

R. Azariah explains this by telling the parable of a king who became angry at his wife, deposed her, and cast her out of his palace; but he later wished to restore her back to her place. The queen asked him to first restore his former practice of receiving gifts from her. The parable is elucidated as follows: God (the king) who formerly withdrew from men (the wife), now desires to draw close to them again, but this is on the condition that he first receives Israel's gifts—the sacrifices offered in the Tabernacle. Thus, when Israel offers God their sacrifices, he becomes willing to return to his bride in their nuptial chamber—the sanctuary.

Another sage quotes Cant 4:16–5:1 to illustrate that *"a groom [God] is not to enter the bridal canopy [the Tabernacle] until his bride [Israel] gives him permission"*: first, she extends to him the invitation (*"let my beloved come his garden"*), and only afterwards does he respond (*"I have come to my garden"*). As in *Canticles Rabbah*, by means of a pun, the Song's garden (*ganni*) is identified with the divine bridal chamber (*ginuni*)—the Tabernacle—while the lover in his "garden" is the divine root of the *Shekhinah* on earth and in the Garden of Eden at the beginning of time. This is related to God's interaction with Adam and Eve, who heard the "voice" of the Lord "walking" in the Garden (Gen 3:8). *PRK* takes this as God walking *away* from Adam and Eve, from earth towards heaven. The midrash explains that the root of the *Shekhinah*, originally located on earth, progressively withdrew from earth back to heaven with every successive sinful generation: Following the sin of Adam, the wicked generations of Enosh, the flood, Babel, the Egyptians of Abraham's time, the Sodomites, and the Egyptians of Moses' day caused the *Shekhinah* to gradually withdraw from the first to the seventh level of heaven. Abraham initiated the reversal of this process, and the merits of later patriarchs and priests (Isaac, Jacob, Levi, Kohath, and Amram) each drew the *Shekhinah* down by one level of heaven until it returned to earth when Moses completed the Tabernacle. This leads back to the opening verse (Num 7:1), now charged with a nuptial meaning through a pun on the "day of completion" (*kalot*) of the Tabernacle, rendered as Israel's "bridal day" (*kalat*). Hence *PRK* considers the day of the completion of the Tabernacle, when the divine presence returned to earth and entered the sanctuary, as the day when God espoused Israel and joined her in their nuptial chamber.[6]

*PRK* further establishes the nuptial meaning of the Tabernacle by identifying it with King Solomon's palanquin (Cant 3:9). Solomon's making of the palanquin in the Canticle becomes a metaphor for God constructing the Tabernacle so that he can privately communicate with Israel. This is explained in another parable: A king who had a young daughter felt free to talk to her in the marketplace and streets while she was still small. But after she reached puberty, the king said: "It does not suit the deference owed to my daughter that I speak to her in public. Make a pavilion for her, and I will speak to her in privacy within the pavilion." The care-free relationship between king and young daughter reflects the relationship between God and Israel in Egypt, at the Red Sea, and at Sinai. But once Israel accepted the Torah (i.e. the daughter reached puberty), it was no longer fitting for God to speak to her in public, so he commanded the construction of the Tabernacle as the place of private encounter between them: "Make the Tabernacle for Me, and then I shall speak to them [in privacy] from within the Tabernacle." To reinforce the nuptial symbolism, the midrash goes on to identify the parts of Solomon's palanquin (Cant 3:9–10) with those of the Tabernacle (Exodus 26–27).[7]

The nuptial metaphor continues with a commentary on Cant 3:11—in which the daughters of Zion are exhorted to behold King Solomon *"with the crown with which his mother crowned him on the day of his wedding, the day of the gladness of his heart."* Solomon (whose name means "peace") is a figure of God ("the King of the universe who has the power to make peace"), and the daughters of Zion represent the children of Israel who are bidden to behold him. Solomon's crown is thus God's "crown" that he wore on the day of his wedding—"the Tent of Meeting because, like a crown, it is topped with blue, purple and scarlet." Within this nuptial context, the cosmic symbolism of the earthly Tabernacle is

---

6. *PRK* 1:1. *CantR* 5:1 §1 follows the same line of interpretation: the Song's "garden" is the *Shekhinah*'s bridal chamber and her original home in the Garden of Eden; the lover's declaration *"I have come into my garden"* refers to the *Shekhinah* entering the Tabernacle when Moses completed it.

7. The palanquin's boards of wood are identified with the Tabernacle's boards of wood (Exod 26:15); its pillars of silver with the Tabernacle's silver hooks (Exod 27:10); its support of gold with the Tabernacle's boards overlaid with gold (Exod 26:29); its seat of purple with the blue and purple veil of the Holy of Holies (Exod 26:31); and its inside *"paved with love,"* with the study of Torah, merits of the righteous, and presence of the *Shekhinah*. *PRK* 1:2; cf. *CantR* 3:9 §1; 3:10 §1.

highlighted. Made after the pattern of the heavenly tabernacle revealed to Moses on the mountain (Exod 25:40), its standing boards of shittim (Exod 26:15) reflect the standing seraphim (Isa 6:2), and its golden clasps represent the stars of the firmament. The conformity of the earthly and heavenly sanctuaries enables God to leave his heavenly counselors above and condense his *Shekhinah* to dwell among his people below. As for the "*day of [Solomon's] wedding*" and "*day of gladness of his heart*," these symbolize the day of God's betrothal of Israel at Sinai and the day he entered the Tent of Meeting (or, alternatively, the day he entered the Tent of Meeting and the day of the construction of the Temple).[8]

The cosmic role of the Tabernacle continues to be expounded in the next section, which opens with a commentary on God's cosmic omnipresence and omnipotence as described in Prov 30:4: "*Who has ascended into heaven, or descended? Who has gathered the wind in his fists? Who has bound the waters in a garment? Who has established all the ends of the earth?*" These actions are primarily attributed to God, yet they are also those of righteous men such as Moses who ascended and descended the mountain (heaven) and established the ends of the earth by building the Tabernacle. Num 7:1 is again cited to assert that through the Tabernacle the stability of the earth was achieved: "until the Tabernacle was set up, the earth was unstable. After the Tabernacle was set up, the earth became stable." The section concludes by reiterating that the day when Moses completed the Tabernacle was in fact "the day that [Israel] entered the bridal chamber as God's bride.[9] The benefits of this union carried over to all creation: "Until the Tabernacle was set up, there was enmity, jealousy, rivalry, wrangling, and dissension in the world. But after the Tabernacle was set up, love, affection, friendship, mercy, and peace were bestowed upon the world."[10]

*Pesikta de-Rab Kahana* masterfully crafts the story of the *Shekhinah*: From her original dwelling in the Garden of Eden, she withdrew back to heaven after the sin of Adam and his descendants. Her gradual return to earth culminated in Moses' building of the Tabernacle. This act is portrayed as a cosmic event that sustains the world, charged with nuptial meaning through numerous references to the Song of Songs.

8. *PRK* 1:3.

9. *PRK* 1:4.

10. *PRK* 1:5.

## The Davidic Kingdom and Solomonic Temple

The Tabernacle was the heart of Israel's liturgical life during the wanderings in the wilderness. After the death of Moses and the conquest of the Promised Land under the leadership of Joshua, its role remained unchanged—though it is mentioned far less frequently in the centuries of political instability that followed under the leadership of the judges until the rise of the Israelite kingdom. After the failed reign of Saul, God chooses David, the son of Jesse, to establish the kingdom. With the Davidic Kingdom, God's promise to make a "great name" of Abraham's seed (Gen 12:2; 17:4–6) comes to pass: The Lord establishes an everlasting covenant with David (2 Sam 7), which comes to fruition under the reign of David's son, Solomon. King Solomon builds the successor of the Tabernacle, the Jerusalem Temple—a new center of Israelite worship that will henceforth take on the former role of the Tabernacle (1 Kgs 6). The continuity between both places of worship is seen in the parallels between the inauguration of Solomon's Temple and the former inauguration of the Tabernacle: just as the cloud of glory manifest at Sinai had filled the Tabernacle at the time of its dedication so thickly that it was not possible to enter, so the same manifestation of God's glory was visible at the dedication of Solomon's Temple (1 Kgs 8:10–11).[11]

## Temple as Nuptial Chamber

The Temple as place of union between the divine and human is the dwelling place of God's *kedushah*—a term whose root *k.d.sh.*, as we have seen, carries both cultic and nuptial/sexual connotations. Temples in the ancient world were regarded as nuptial chambers where the divine powers of fertility celebrated their wedding feast for the purpose of ensuring the fruitfulness of the earth.[12] Likewise, the Jewish Temple was imbued with a nuptial meaning that gradually developed into the full-blown metaphor of the Temple as nuptial chamber for God and his bride, the community of Israel—represented by the High Priest.[13] The Temple plays a prominent

---

11. Cf. Exod 40:34–35; Lev 9:6, 23; 2 Chr 5:14; 2 Chr 7:1–3.

12. Cf. Patai, *Man and Temple*, 88–90.

13. Rachel Elior notes the affinity in the ancient world between "the sanctity of the Temple, ceremonially expressed through interlocking septuples of time, place, and ritual in the Holy of Holies (*kodesh kodashim*) . . . and *kidushin*, 'sanctification,' the Hebrew term for betrothal and conjugal union—a personal covenant whose purpose is to

role as the place of nuptial union between God and Israel in the rabbinic exegesis of the Song of Songs—beginning with the Mishnah's comment on the *"day of [Solomon's] espousals"* (Cant 3:11), which identifies the *"day of the joy of his heart"* with the day of completion of the building of the Temple.[14]

The Midrash presents Cant 1:15–16 as the classic dialogue of love between God and Israel. God declares to Israel: *"Behold, you are beautiful, my love; behold, you are beautiful; your eyes are doves;"* and Israel responds: *"Behold, you are beautiful, my beloved, truly lovely."*[15] The Midrash reveals that the *"green couch"* where they are joined is the Temple, the home of the *Shekhinah*. R. Azariah illustrates the transition from Tabernacle to Temple with a parable: He compares God's dwelling with the story of a king who went out into the desert and slept in a short bed that was uncomfortable and cramping for his limbs. When he came to the city he was brought a longer bed upon which he could stretch himself and loosen his limbs: "So until the Temple was built the *Shechinah* was confined between the two staves of the ark, but when the Temple was built, then . . . the staves were prolonged."[16] In other words, God was content with temporary "uncomfortable" accommodations in the Tabernacle as long as Israel wandered without a home; but once they settled in Jerusalem, God found a more permanent and comfortable home in the Temple. As nuptial chamber, the Temple is a source of stability and fruitfulness causing the people of Israel to multiply:

> *Also our couch is leafy.* Until the Temple was built the *Shekhinah* was tossed about from place to place, as it says, *But I have walked in a tent and in a tabernacle"* (2 Sam 7:6), but after the Temple was built, [God said], *this is my resting-place for ever* (Ps 132:14) . . . *Also our couch is leafy.* Just as a couch is only for propagation, so before the Temple was built [David could say], *Go, number Israel* (1 Chr 21:2), but after it was built *Judah and Israel were many, as the sand* (1 Kgs 4:20).[17]

---

perpetuate life, also associated with ceremony and number, with cycle and counting, with sanctity and purity. Both the sanctity of the Temple and betrothal connect with the number seven, with oaths, with 'a covenant for all time,' with blessing and fertility and the cycle of life." Elior, *The Three Temples*, 54–55.

14. M. Ta'anit 4:8.

15. CantR 1:15 §1; 1:16 §1.

16. CantR 1:16 §2.

17. CantR 1:16 §3.

What does the connection between nuptial symbolism, Sinai, the Tabernacle, and the Temple signify? One might argue that at its heart lies the two related notions of covenantal love and sacrifice. The sacrificial themes of sanctification/setting apart, renunciation, drawing close, atonement, purification, restitution, and restoring communion through a covenantal meal are all related to nuptial love. Early Jewish texts constantly suggest that the necessary condition for a nuptial encounter with the divine is precisely sacrifice, instituted as the central component of the Sinai covenant and perpetually offered in the sanctuary courts. We will return to the relationship between love and sacrifice in our study of the Epistle to the Ephesians below.

## The Embracing Cherubim in the Holy of Holies

The cherubim continued to guard the access to the Holy of Holies in the Temple of Solomon. The biblical tradition recalls the two cherubim of the Solomonic Temple as massive, ten cubits high (15 feet) and the same length from one wing tip to the other (1 Kgs 6:23–28). Made of olive wood and overlaid with gold, they overshadowed the Ark of the Covenant as in the former Tabernacle.[18] According to the chronicler, however, the figures no longer faced each other as they did in the Tabernacle but stood side by side, together facing "the house" (presumably the Holy Place) with their wing tips spanning the entire width of the Holy of Holies, the outer wings touching the sanctuary's walls and the inner wings touching each other in the center (2 Chr 3:10–13). The entire Temple structure was decorated with figures of cherubim, including the walls of the inner and outer sanctuaries, the inner and outer doors (1 Kgs 6:29–35; 2 Chr 3:7), the veil leading into the Holy of Holies (2 Chr 3:14), and the bases of the ten lavers (1 Kgs 7:29, 36). The predominance of cherubim figures all over the Temple and their role as sign of the divine presence was such that the Lord eventually became known as "the One who dwells between the cherubim."[19]

The cherubim are of great significance to help us understand the nuptial symbolism between God and Israel in ancient Judaism. This topic is well developed in the writings of first-century Jewish philosopher Philo.

---

18. 1 Kgs 8:6–7; 1 Chr 28:18; 2 Chr 5:7–8.

19. 1 Sam 4:4; 6:2; 2 Kgs 19:15; Isa 37:16; Ps 80:1; 99:1; LXX Dan 3:55.

Eugene Seaich has identified a four-fold symbolism of the cherubim that we will follow here:

1. The cherubim represented the "face of God."

2. They were a symbol of God's male-female image.

3. They were a symbol of God's redemptive marriage to Israel.

4. They were a paradigm for human marriage, patterned after God's male-female image.[20]

## The Cherubim as Representation of the "Face of God"

Some scholars have argued that the commandment that every male Israelite should *"appear* ('be seen') three times a year before the face of the Lord" (Exod 23:17; Deut 16:16) originally meant to actively "see" the face of God.[21] This opportunity to "see the face of God" during the three pilgrim festivals possibly consisted in getting a glimpse of the Ark and cherubim after the veil of the Holy of Holies was temporarily removed. The cherubim, therefore, were believed to be the visual representation of the face of God. Philo—perhaps referring to the cherubim—claimed that it was possible to "see" God in the Holy of Holies, a divine vision which he considered to be "the beginning and end of happiness." He identifies the Holy Place with the visible world perceptible to the senses, the Holy of Holies with the incorporeal world of the divine, and the veil that separated the two chambers as the *Logos* mediating between the two realms.[22]

## The Cherubim as Symbol of God's Male-Female Image

If the two cherubim were a visual representation of the "face of God," for Philo they were also a symbol of God's male-female image and "an allegorical figure of the whole heaven."[23] The cherubim in Eden—anticipating those of the sanctuary—represented the two supreme powers of the divinity: the creative power of goodness by which he created

20. Seaich, *A Great Mystery*, 9–22.

21. Seaich, *A Great Mystery*, 9–10; Anderson, "To See Where God Dwells," 23–24.

22. *Questions on Exodus* 2:51–52, 94; Cf. Seaich, *A Great Mystery*, 10; Anderson, "To See Where God Dwells," 35–36.

23. *On the Cherubim* 21–25.

everything (called 'God'), and his royal power of authority by which he governs creation (called 'Lord').[24] God's two powers, symbolized by the cherubim, are joined in a perfect union, begetting virtues for the benefit of humanity.[25] This fusion is not an impersonal one; it is inspired and motivated by mutual love. The cherubim were placed before paradise so that "in consequence of a continued sight and contemplation of one another, the two powers might conceive an affection for one another, the all-bounteous God inspiring them with a winged and heavenly love."[26]

The coupling of the cherubim symbolizing the union of the two powers of God is correlated with the idea of the sacred marriage between God and Wisdom, borrowed from Wisdom literature (Wis 8:3). For Philo, God is the "husband of wisdom," joined to her for the sake of sowing virtue in the souls of men: "God is both a house, the incorporeal abode of incorporeal ideas, and the Father of all things, inasmuch as it is he who has created them; and the husband of wisdom, sowing for the race of mankind the seed of happiness in good and virgin soil."[27]

Elsewhere, the nuptial union between the male and female powers of the divinity is even more explicit: God is the Father of creation who is joined with his own knowledge (or wisdom), personified as "mother and nurse of the universe." Wisdom receives the Creator's "seed" and gives birth to their "son"—the visible world.[28] For Philo, the cherubim thus represent the marriage between the divine attributes of goodness and power (God and Lord), or between God and Wisdom (the Father-Creator and his wife, the mother of the world). As Patai says, this means that Philo sees the process of *creation* as *procreation*.[29]

---

24. *Questions on Genesis* I:57; *On the Life of Moses*, II:98–99. Philo attributes these powers to both the cherubim of Eden and those of the sanctuary, which he views interchangeably.

25. *On the Cherubim* 27–29.

26. *On the Cherubim* 20.

27. *On the Cherubim* 49.

28. *On Drunkenness* 30–31.

29. Patai, *The Hebrew Goddess*, 77.

## The Cherubim as Symbol of
## God's Redemptive Marriage to Israel

If for Philo the cherubim were a symbol of the union between the male and female aspects of the divinity, for the Talmud they concealed another stunning secret: they represented the nuptial love between God and Israel. A revealing Talmudic passage associates the staves that held the Ark and protruded through the veil of the Holy of Holies (1 Kgs 8:8) with the breasts of the bride in the Song of Songs: "Scripture says: '[The staves] could not be seen from outside.' How so? They bulged out and protruded like a woman's two breasts, as it is said: *My beloved is unto me as a bag of myrrh that lies between my breasts* (Cant 1:13)."[30] This stunning metaphor implies that not only the divine Bridegroom but also *the bride* (Israel) is mystically present in the Holy of Holies, consorting with her Husband. This is confirmed by the explanation that follows: According to this mysterious tradition, the cherubim interacted lovingly with each other as long as Israel remained in good favor with God, and their love would be displayed to the Jewish public during the festivals as a way of reminding them of God's love for them: "Whenever Israel came up for the pilgrim festival, the curtain would be removed for them and the cherubim were shown to them, whose bodies were intertwined with one another, and they would say to them: See how you are beloved before God, as the love between man and woman."[31] The cherubim in embrace in the Temple, the innermost and holiest symbol of the sanctuary, were thus viewed as a symbolic expression of the nuptial union between God and Israel.

When the objection is raised that such gazing upon the holiest objects should lead to certain death according to the Torah (Num 4:20), a curious reply is given: "That may be compared to a bride: As long as she is in her father's house, she is reserved in regard to her husband, but when she comes to her father-in-law's house, she is no more so reserved in regard to him."[32] The short parable implies that while the children of Israel were in the desert during the Exodus, they were bashful and could not yet directly look at the *Shekhinah*—the awesome visible presence of God. Once settled in their land, however, Israel reached sufficient maturity and familiarity with her divine Husband so that she could feast her

30. *b. Yoma* 54a.
31. *b. Yoma* 54a.
32. *b. Yoma* 54a.

eyes upon him.[33] The argument underlines a historical consciousness of the marriage between God and his bride; the growth in maturity of Israel over time gained her the privilege of contemplating the cherubim in the Temple: a feat that would have been impossible (and indeed deadly) at the time of the betrothal of her youth in the desert.

It is easy to see why the Jews would have wished to conceal such a display of religious eroticism from their pagan neighbors. Indeed, the Talmud testifies to the embarrassment that this scene caused when it was discovered by the conquering gentiles:

> When the heathens entered the Temple and saw the cherubim whose bodies were intertwisted with one another, they carried them out and said: These Israelites, whose blessing is a blessing, and whose curse is a curse, occupy themselves with such things! And immediately they despised them, as it is said: All that honored her, despised her, because they have seen her nakedness.[34]

Another Talmudic passage adds to the mystery of the embracing cherubim by ingeniously harmonizing the difference in their orientation: did the cherubim face each other (Exod 25:20), or did they stand side-by-side with their faces turned toward the veil (2 Chronicles 3:13)? The Talmud explains this discrepancy by positing that the cherubim were miraculously endowed with the ability to move and change position in accordance with Israel's righteous obedience to God, or lack thereof:

> How did [the cherubim] stand? . . . One Says: They faced each other; and the other says: Their faces were inward. But according to him who says that they faced each other, [it may be asked]: Is it not written, and their faces were inward? — [This is] no difficulty: The former [was] at a time when Israel obeyed the will of the Omnipresent; the latter [was] at a time when Israel did not obey the will of the Omnipresent.[35]

The dynamic positioning of the cherubim is thus perceived as reflecting the state of the relationship between Bridegroom and bride.

Philo attests that the nuptial view of the cherubim was known in the first century. He considers the cherubim to be "mirrors" of Wisdom, reflecting her role as "divine surrogate" between God and the human

---

33. Cf. Patai, *The Hebrew Goddess*, 307 n. 57; Seaich, *A Great Mystery*, 16.

34. *b. Yoma* 54b.

35. *b. Baba Bathra* 99a.

soul.[36] Philo develops the theme of Wisdom's nuptial relationship with men flowing out of her mystical union with God.[37] As mediatrix of the divine essence, she must first be "impregnated by God" before she can impregnate those who 'marry' her.[38] For Philo, God effects a spiritual procreation in the souls of the righteous, "impregnating" the patriarchs and Moses with the seeds of Wisdom by divine inspiration.[39] By conversing with the human soul and introducing into it "unpolluted virtues," God restores man's virginity, so to speak, so that the soul of man may "live the virgin life in the house of God and cling to knowledge."[40] Philo thus considers the wise man to be taken into God's presence through a nuptial union with Wisdom, a union that is symbolically represented by the cherubim.

## The Cherubim as Paradigm for Human Marriage and the Original Androgynous Man

Given that the cherubim symbolized the union of God's male and female aspects, and that God created man in his "image and likeness" as "male and female" to "be fruitful and multiply" by becoming "one flesh" (Gen 1:26–28; 2:24), it follows that the embracing cherubim also represented a paradigm for the male-female union in human marriage, patterned after God's male-female image.[41] Philo indeed holds that the union of man and woman reflects the divine nature. Borrowing from Plato,[42] he asserts that in the beginning, before Eve was taken out of Adam, the original man was androgynous, with its two halves (male and female) perfectly

---

36. *Questions on Genesis* 1:57; cf. Seaich, *A Great Mystery,* 41. As we will see below, the idea of Lady Wisdom as "divine surrogate" or intermediate between God and man is borrowed from wisdom literature.

37. *On the Posterity of Cain* 78. Cf. Horsley, "Spiritual Marriage with Sophia," 34–36.

38. Seaich, *A Great Mystery,* 33–35.

39. *On the Preliminary Studies* 130–35; *On the Cherubim* 44–47.

40. *On the Cherubim* 49–52. Cf. Horsley, "Spiritual Marriage with Sophia," 37; Seaich, *A Great Mystery,* 47–48.

41. Seaich, *A Great Mystery,* 19–22.

42. In the *Symposium* (189–93), Plato describes the primal separation of the sexes which resulted in each half constantly seeking his partner to be grafted again into a single person. Cf. Batey, "The μία σάρξ Union of Christ and the Church," 274; Batey, *New Testament Nuptial Imagery,* 32–33.

united into one. It is the subsequent separation out of this original unity that is at the root of the sexual attraction of each side for the missing half. The first human (created in Gen 1:26–27) was thus a complete, harmonious person at a pre-sexual stage, made according to the image of God, "perceptible only by the intellect, incorporeal, neither male nor female, imperishable by nature." By contrast, the person created in Gen 2:7 is "perceptible to the external senses, partaking of qualities, consisting of body and soul, man or woman, by nature mortal."[43] In other words, "having first modelled the generic man, in whom they say that the male and female sexes are contained, he afterwards created the specific man Adam."[44]

In summary, Philo considered the two cherubim in the Temple to be not only a representation of the "face of God," but also a symbol of the male-female aspects of the divinity which united God and Lord, Father and Mother, Husband and Wife, Begetter and Bearer, Creator and Nurturer, Reason and Wisdom. This dualism constitutes the earliest indication that the two cherubim consisted in a male and a female figure. At the same time, for Philo the male-female dynamism within the divinity corresponded to God's relationship with Israel—anticipating the Talmud's cherubim representing the love between God and Israel. Finally, the cherubim also pointed to the original unity of the first male-female human person.

## Temple as Microcosm

While the Temple is the ongoing actualization of the Sinai covenant for Israel's future generations, its role extends far beyond the celebration of a national alliance limited to the elect people. In line with many ancient near eastern traditions, the Jerusalem Temple was also imbued with cosmic symbolism. It was viewed as a microcosm that represented, renewed,

---

43. *On the Creation of the World* 134.

44. *Allegorical Interpretation* 2:13. Cf. *On the Creation of the World* 76, 151–52; *Who is the Heir?* 164; *Questions on Genesis* 1:25–26. Scroggs, *The Last Adam*, 115–122; Seaich, *A Great Mystery*, 48–49. The tradition that the marital embrace of husband and wife was a human reenactment of the divine male-female union and fecundity is also preserved in a rabbinic tradition that underlines the reason for the divine imperative for marriage, based on the belief that the *Shekhinah* abides between the worthy husband and wife: "He who does not marry thereby diminishes the image of God." (*t. Yebamot* 8:4).

and sustained the entire universe.[45] The basis for this symbolism is found in the idea that the Temple's predecessor, the Tabernacle, was a copy of the heavenly Temple. Moses was to build the Tabernacle and its furnishings in conformity with a divinely revealed blueprint, "according to the pattern for them, which is being shown you on the mountain" (Exod 25:40).

As the earthly Temple manifests a measure of the ineffable glory of the heavenly Temple, so does all creation: When Isaiah in his great mystical vision sees the Lord seated on his throne and hears the seraphim proclaim that "the whole earth is full of his glory" (Isa 6:3), he is implying that the world is the visible manifestation of God sitting enthroned in his Temple.[46] The universe is a cosmic Temple, full of the divine presence, holiness, and *kavod* that was made manifest at Sinai and continues to be present in "concentrated" form in the Temple (1 Kgs 8:27; Isa 66:1–2; Sir 24:3–11). Literary correspondences illustrate how both the Temple and creation are visible manifestations of the invisible divine realm.[47] When the psalmist declares that God built his sanctuary on Mount Zion "like the heights" (i.e. the heavens) and "like the earth that he established forever" (Ps 78:69), he is implying that the Temple represents heaven and earth. The idea is manifest in the parallels between the creation narrative and building of the Tabernacle, linked together by the *kedushah* of the Sabbath.[48] In short, the origins of the cosmos are portrayed as a Temple, and the Temple is depicted as a microcosm—both linked by the Sabbath.

45. For studies on the Temple as microcosm and world as macrotemple, see Barker, *The Gate of Heaven*, 65–67, 108–14; Patai, *Man and Temple*, 84–87, 105–32; Levenson, "The Temple and the World"; *Sinai and Zion*, 137–42; *Creation and the Persistence of Evil*, 90–99; Elior, *The Three Temples*, 37.

46. Levenson, "The Temple and the World," 290.

47. John Walton summarizes this Temple/cosmos correspondence in five points: (1) In the Bible and in the ANE the Temple is viewed as a microcosm; (2) the Temple is designed with the imagery of the cosmos; (3) the Temple is related to the functions of the cosmos; (4) the creation of the Temple is parallel to the creation of the cosmos; (5) In the Bible the cosmos can be viewed as a Temple. Walton, *The Lost World of Genesis One*, 84.

48. Berman notes other similarities between creation, Sabbath, and Sanctuary: (1) creation was completed in seven days; the Temple took seven years to complete (1 Kgs 6:35) and was dedicated on the seven-day long Sukkot festival on the seventh month of the year (1 Kgs 8:2); (2) both the creation of the world and of the Tabernacle were done by wisdom, understanding, and knowledge (Exod 31:3; Prov 3:19–20); (3) like the Sabbath, the Temple is a place of divine rest (Ps 132:7–8, 13–14; 2 Chr 6:41); (4) both are connected with the opposite concept of *melakhah* (creative work). "The covenant at Sinai established God and the Jewish people as partners in the process of creation. The Sabbath—covenantally commemorative time—recalls the creation of the

The correspondence between earthly and heavenly sanctuaries is evident in the Wisdom of Solomon, which asserts that the Jerusalem Temple is but a temporal manifestation of the eternal Temple: "You have given command to build a temple on your holy mountain, and an altar in the city of your habitation, a copy of the holy tent which you prepared from the beginning" (Wis 9:8).[49] The cosmic symbolism of the Temple is even more vivid in the writings of Philo. In continuity with the Wisdom of Solomon, he views creation as a copy of the heavenly world and the whole universe as "the highest and truest temple of God."[50] He adds a level of cosmic anthropology, proposing that both the cosmos and the human soul reflect the divine image.[51] Elsewhere, Philo describes the cosmic symbolism of the Temple in detail: The menorah represents the sun and stars in heaven; the altar of incense is an emblem of the things of earth; and the table of showbread symbolizes the nourishment proceeding from heaven and earth.[52] Following Wisdom tradition,[53] he narrows down his cosmic anthropology to the figure of the high priest.[54] Thus, for Philo the high priest represents all of humanity: "Whenever [the high priest] enters the temple to offer up the prayers and sacrifices in use

---

universe through the *melakhah* of God. The Sanctuary—covenantally commemorative space—represents a completion of the process of creation through the *melakhah* of the Jewish people." Berman, *The Temple,* 18. Cf. also Levenson, "The Temple and the World," 288–89.

49. This theme is extensively developed in the Epistle to the Hebrews, which speaks of the Temple sacrifices and priesthood as "a copy and shadow of the heavenly sanctuary" which is "the true tent which is set up not by man but by the Lord"— namely heaven itself, which Christ entered by merit of his own self-sacrifice (Heb 8:2, 5; 9:23–24).

50. *On the Special Laws* I:66–67. For studies of Philo's view of the Temple and its cosmic symbolism, see Hayward, *The Jewish Temple,* 108–41; Briggs, *Jewish Temple Imagery in the Book of Revelation,* 204–8.

51. "For there are, as it seems, two temples belonging to God; one being this world, in which the high priest is the divine word, his own firstborn son. The other is the rational soul, the priest of which is the real true man . . . " (*On Dreams* 1:215).

52. *On the Life of Moses* II:102–105.

53. Sir 50 and Wis 18:24: "For upon [Aaron's] long robe the whole world was depicted, and the glories of the fathers were engraved on the four rows of stones, and thy majesty on the diadem upon his head."

54. The sacred vestments of the high priest are a "copy and representation of the world; and the parts are a representation of the separate parts of the world." *On the Life of Moses* II:117–124.

among his nation, all the world may likewise enter in with him."[55] For Philo, therefore, the heavenly world and divine image is revealed through a process of increasing concentration:

Divine/heavenly realm > visible world > temple > high priest

When one considers Philo's cosmic view of the temple in light of his nuptial symbolism—illustrated by the cherubim in the Holy of Holies representing the marriage between God and Wisdom (or between Wisdom and man)—one arrives at a vision of the world as a cosmic wedding, where the marriage between Wisdom and creation is typified and reenacted in the Temple through the ministry of the high priest.

The correspondence between Temple and creation is also common in rabbinic literature, often appearing side-by-side with cosmic nuptial symbolism. On a first level, legends depict the creation of the world as a sort of cosmic mating between the "upper male waters" and "lower female waters."[56] According to some rabbis, this cosmic (re-)union is reenacted every time it rains, when the lower female waters rise to receive the upper male waters.[57] In other traditions, the rain comes down to mate with the earth to fructify it.[58] On a second level, the abundant rains and ensuing fruitfulness of the earth originate from the Temple, or more specifically from the nuptial union between God and Israel taking place within it,

55. *On the Life of Moses* II.133. Josephus (*Ant.* 3.7.7) also describes the Tabernacle and high priestly garments as "made in way of imitation and representation of the universe." He describes the Temple in similar terms (*Wars* 5.5.4–5). For Josephus, therefore, the Temple is "an *eikon*, an image, an epitome of the world . . . It is the world *in nuce*, and the world is the Temple *in extenso*" (Levenson, "The Temple and the World," 285).

56. According to those legends, the waters were originally united (*GenR* 5:2) until God separated them, relegating half to the firmament above and half to the ocean below (*GenR* 4:5). The waters were so distressed by this separation that they wept (*GenR* 5:4) and, since then, unceasingly long to be reunited: "the only desire of the rains is for the earth" (*GenR* 20:7; *CantR* 7:10 as interpretation of "I am my beloved's, and his desire is for me").

57. In a saying attributed to R. Levi: "The upper waters are male while the lower waters are female. And they say one to the other: Receive us, you are the creation of the Holy One and we are His envoys. Immediately they receive them . . . like a female who receives the male" (*GenR* 13:13). Cf. Patai, *Man and Temple*, 67.

58. Referring to Isaiah's words about the rain coming down to water the earth to make it bring forth and bud (Isa 55:10), R. Judah says that "rain is the husband of the soil" (*b. Ta'anit* 6b).

enacted through the sacrificial service.[59] The rabbis identify the Temple with Solomon's *leafy couch* or with the lovers' *house* to portray it as source of the world's fertility and fruitfulness.[60] They also identify the Temple with Solomon's palanquin (Cant 3:9): In an impressive cosmic recapitulation, *Canticles Rabbah* identifies the palanquin with the Tabernacle, the Ark of the Covenant, the Temple, the world, and the heavenly Throne of Glory. The cosmic symbolism is especially visible in the connection between the palanquin and the stone upon which the Ark rested in the Holy of Holies, known in Jewish tradition as the *even shetiyah*. This was considered to be the foundation stone upon which the world was established.[61] The identification of the palanquin with these realms—the Tabernacle, Ark, Temple, world, and throne of glory—and the interconnections between them indicates that they are multiple facets of the same reality: the most sacred dwelling of God. The sanctuary is not only a sacred place of nuptial encounter between God and his people; it is also a microcosm representing the entire world. Conversely, the world's identification with the palanquin means that the universe is itself a macro- or cosmic Temple in which the divinity lovingly dwells.

Other traditions recall that the first ray of light that illuminated the world emanated from this same foundation stone upon which the Temple was built as symbol of health, life, joy and success.[62] The Temple on God's cosmic mountain of Zion, rising upon the *even shetiyah*, was known to be the center or "navel of the world," the *axis mundi* or meeting point of heaven and earth out of which flowed the primeval waters of the deep. The world was nourished by these life-giving waters just as an embryo receives its nourishment from the navel.[63] While discussing the *even shetiyah* upon which the Ark of the Covenant had laid, the Talmud states that "from it the world was founded" and "the world was created

---

59. For example, the water libation ritual during the feast of Sukkot was intended to re-enact the creation of the world and induce rainfall. Cf. Patai, *Man and Temple*, 24–47.

60. *Mekh Pisḥa* 14; *PRK* 1:4; *CantR* 1:16; *TgCant* 1:16–17; 3:7. The nuptial role of the Temple as source of fertility and life is well illustrated in a midrashic comment on the "couch" of Cant 3:7: "And why was the Temple compared to a couch? Because just as this couch serves fruitfulness and multiplication, even so everything that was in the Temple was fruitful and multiplied" (*Midrash Tanḥuma*). Cf. Patai, *Man and Temple*, 87, 90.

61. *PRK* 1:2; *CantR* 3:9–10; *TgCant* 3:9–10.

62. *GenR* 3:4.

63. On the Temple as navel of the world, cf. Patai, *Man and Temple*, 85–87; Levenson, *Sinai and Zion*, 115–122; 134–37.

beginning from Zion."[64] Having conceptually existed since the beginning of creation, the Temple is thus a microcosm, made to correspond to the creation of the world and to be responsible for the stability of the universe.

Significantly, these Talmudic remarks on the foundation of the world originating from Zion follow the discussions about the staves of the Ark protruding through the curtain as the breasts of a woman, and the intertwined cherubim in the Holy of Holies representing the love of God for Israel. This points again to the idea that the creation of the world originating from the Temple is seen as a nuptial act. In the same vein, the Temple's frequent identification with the Shulamite's *"chamber of her who conceived me"* (Cant 3:4),[65] or *"garden"* (Cant 4:16, 5:1) indicates that it is the divine bridal chamber and place of God's return to earth.[66] As the home of the indwelling *Shekhinah,* providing a dwelling place for God who is the source of all blessings, the Temple—mystically representing the origins of the cosmos—is a source of divine, Edenic blessing, fruitfulness and welfare on nature, multiplying crops and warding off catastrophes not only to Israel but also to the whole world.[67]

64. The passage continues by stating that "both [the generations of the heavens and the earth (Gen 2:4)] were created from Zion, as Scripture says: 'Out of Zion, the perfection of beauty, God hath shined forth', that means from it the beauty of the world was perfected" (*b. Yoma* 54b). Cf. Levenson, *Sinai and Zion*, 118.

65. *Mekh Shirata* 3; *LevR* 1:10; *CantR* 3:4 §1; *TgCant* 3:4.

66. *LevR* 9:6; *PRK* 1:1; *CantR* 1:2; 1:4a §1; 5:1 §1; *TgCant* 4:16, 5:1, 6:2, 11.

67. The idea of the Temple's influence on the forces of nature is attested as early as the prophet Haggai, who lamented that the heavens withheld the dew and the earth its produce because the Lord's House laid waste (Hag 1:9–11). M. *Avot* 1:2 tells us that one of the three things upon which the world rests is the Temple service; *PRK* 1:5 claims that the earth became stable after the Tabernacle was built; *b. Rosh Hashanah* 16a describes how the bringing of offerings at each feast brings a corresponding blessing on the crops or rain; *b. Ketubot* 111b–112a depicts how the offering of sacrifices brought an extraordinary fertility to Israel which disappeared when the Temple was destroyed; *b. Baba Bathra* 25a–25b states that the rain stopped with the end of the Temple. Cf. Patai, *Man and Temple*, 121–124. In Levenson's words, chaos is neutralized by cult: as creation emerged from chaos in Gen 1:1–2:3, "it is through the cult that we are enabled to cope with evil, for it is the cult that builds and maintains order, transforms chaos into creation, ennobles humanity, and realizes the kingship of the God who has ordained the cult and commanded that it be guarded and practiced" (*Creation and the Persistence of Evil*, 127).

## Temple as Garden of Eden

As dwelling-place of the sacred, the Temple erects through its laws of worship a barrier of holiness between the common and the sanctified. It is the ideal place where time stands still, or a pure and pristine "enclave of ideal reality within the world of profanity."[68] From this it is but a small step to arrive at the Temple's identification with the Garden of Eden. As Walton says, the Temple represents both the cosmos at large and Eden as the "innermost" sacred space of the universe and archetypal sanctuary.[69] The Temple is intentionally designed to recall ancient traditions of the Garden of Eden, understood to be a "prototype of the conditions and environment in which man can intimately encounter God."[70]

Before examining the connection between *the Temple and Eden*, it is fitting to consider the relationship between *Israel and Eden*. Berman has shown how the land of Israel could be seen as a "conceptual expansion of the garden of Eden."[71] For example, the covenantal language of Lev 26:3–12, promising to Israel abundant rains, a fertile land, plentiful fruit, vintage and bread, peace and security, and the absence of evil beasts if they keep God's Sabbaths, reverence his sanctuary, and observe his commandments, seems to be a "simulation of the garden of Eden." As was the case for Adam in the Garden, Israel's covenant with God requires the observance of commandments (Lev 26:3). As God planted the Garden and made the rivers of Eden, he will grant rain, fertility, and peace in the land if Israel remains faithful. As Adam and Eve were told to be fruitful and multiply, God will make Israel fruitful and multiply them (Lev 26:9). Finally, just as God "walked" in the Garden, he will "walk" among his people as long as they remain faithful to the covenant (Lev 26:12). And just as Adam and Eve's disobedience led to their expulsion from Eden, sin and disobedience will lead to Israel's banishment and exile from the land (Lev 26:33). This view of Israel as Eden is also reflected in texts such

---

68. Levenson, *Sinai and Zion*, 127–128.

69. "The Garden of Eden was sacred space and the temple/tabernacle contained imagery of the garden and the cosmos . . . The temple is a microcosm, and Eden is represented in the antechamber that serves as sacred space adjoining the Presence of God as an archetypal sanctuary" (Walton, *The Lost World of Genesis One*, 83).

70. Berman, *The Temple*, 22. On the Temple as Eden, see Barker, *The Gate of Heaven*, 57–103; Elior, "The Jerusalem Temple," 134–36; Levenson, *Sinai and Zion*, 128–37; Wenham, "Sanctuary Symbolism in the Garden of Eden Story."

71. Berman, *The Temple*, 23–26.

as Isa 51:3, where restored Zion is compared to Eden and the "Garden of the Lord."

If the Land of Israel is a "simulation of Eden" where the Israelites encounter God, the Temple, as spiritual center of the nation, is the apex of this communion—and it too follows the paradigm of Eden. At the center of the Garden stood the Tree of Life. At the heart of the sanctuary is the Ark of the Covenant containing the tablets of the testimony which symbolize the Torah, source of life (Deut 30:15-16), later identified with Wisdom—known as a "Tree of Life" (Prov 3:18; Sir 24:23).[72] As the cherubim guarded the presence of God and access to the Tree in the Garden (Gen 3:24), cherubim "guard" the divine Presence in the Holy of Holies (Exod 25:20-21). As God "walked" in the Garden (Gen 3:8), so he "walks" in the sanctuary (Deut 23:14; 2 Sam 7:6-7). As Adam was commanded to "work" (avad) and "keep" or "guard" (shamar) the Garden (Gen 2:15), so the priests and Levites "work" (avad) and "guard" (shamar) the sanctuary.[73] Both Eden and the sanctuary were entered from the East. There was gold in both Eden and the Temple. Several texts record a tradition of waters flowing from the Temple, which evoke the rivers of Eden.[74] Both sanctified domains were highly regulated, and infraction was punishable by death (Gen 2:17; Exod 28:43; Lev 10:9). The Midrash takes these biblical parallels to their logical conclusion: when God banished Adam from Eden, he revealed to him the future destruction of the Temple because both events represent the same thing: the end of communion with God brought about by human sin.[75]

In summary, we may illustrate the concentric levels of Temple symbolism in the following way. The Temple represents in its broadest sense the world, then Israel, then Eden:

$$Temple = Cosmos > Israel > Eden$$

This multi-layered symbolism corresponds to the concentric structure of the courts of the Jerusalem Temple and their increasing

---

72. Scholars have proposed that the menorah was a stylized tree of life. Wenham, "Sanctuary Symbolism," 401.

73. Num 3:7-8, 38; 4:23, 47; 8:26; 18:5-7. Cf. *GenR* 16:5.

74. This tradition is preserved in the psalms (36:9; 46:4), prophets (Ezek 47:1-12; Joel 4:17-18; Zech 14:8-9), wisdom literature (Sir 24:25-27), and rabbinic texts (*LevR* 34:15; *TgCant* 4:12, 15).

75. *GenR* 21:8.

sanctity. As one approached the sanctuary, one first had to cross the court of Gentiles—representing the world and open to everyone. Then one had to walk through the court of women and the court of Israel (off limits to Gentiles). Then, only priests could enter the court of priests and sanctuary. Finally, only the high priest could enter the Holy of Holies (on the Day of Atonement) which, guarded by the cherubim, most strongly evoked the lost Garden of Eden.

Second Temple literature amply attests to the Temple's identification with Eden. As we will see, Sirach 24 portrays an Edenic setting of the sanctuary on God's holy mountain (chapter 6 below). According to the Book of Jubilees, the Garden of Eden is "holier than all the earth besides" (Jub 3:12). There, Adam made an offering of frankincense, galbanum and stacte (Jub 3:27)—the ingredients later used to make incense for the Tabernacle service. Hence for the author of Jubilees the Edenic sanctuary was an integral part of creation from the very beginning, and Adam was the first priest, representative of the human race, who offered the first sacrifice.[76] Enoch later returned there as well:

> And [Enoch] offered the incense which is acceptable before the Lord in the evening at the holy place on Mount Qater. For the Lord has four (sacred) places upon the earth: the *Garden of Eden* and the mountain of the East and this mountain which you are upon today, *Mount Sinai*, and *Mount Zion*, which will be sanctified in the new creation for a sanctification of the earth. (Jub 4:25–26, emphasis added)

In this stunning passage, Jubilees closely associates the Garden of Eden, Mount Sinai, and Mount Zion, identifying these holy places with God's mythical holy mountain which constituted the foundation of all creation. According to Jubilees, Noah also recognized the Garden as the "Holy of Holies" and "dwelling of the Lord":

> And [Noah] knew that the *Garden of Eden* was the *holy of holies* and the dwelling of the Lord. And *Mount Sinai* (was) in the midst of the desert and *Mount Zion* (was) in the midst of the

---

76. In discussing the image of Eden as primeval sanctuary in Jubilees, Hayward notes that if the expulsion of Adam and Eve from Eden was seen as their removal from the place of God's most immediate presence, the high priest's entrance into the Holy of Holies on Yom Kippur might "typologically correspond to the first man's return to Eden, for a season, to be reconciled with his Maker face to face" (*The Jewish Temple*, 89).

navel of the earth. These three were created as holy places, one facing the other. (Jub 8:19)

Similar traditions are preserved in the *Apocalypse of Moses* and *Life of Adam and Eve*, where Adam takes sweet spices and fragrant herbs from Eden as an offering to God after he leaves paradise (*Apoc. Mos.* 29:3–6; *Vita* 43:3). Other texts confirm that Eden is God's sanctuary: In *Apoc. Mos.* 22:3–4, "God went up into paradise, mounted on the chariot of his cherubim . . . and the throne of God was fixed where the Tree of Life was." In 1 Enoch 25, Enoch sees the Tree of Life "transplanted to the holy place, to the temple of the Lord" situated on a high mountain which is the throne of God. Finally, according to 2 Baruch 4:3–6, God revealed the heavenly Temple to Adam in Eden, to Abraham when he established his covenant with him, and to Moses on Mount Sinai.

We find many Eden-Temple associations in rabbinic literature as well: the Temple's cedar and gold originate in the Garden of Eden (*GenR* 15:1; 16:2); Israel's sacrificial worship is associated with Adam's work in the Garden (*GenR* 16:5; cf. *LevR* 2:7–8); and the water libations brought into the Temple at the Feast of Tabernacles are identified with the waters of creation (*t. Suk* 3:3–11). When one adds the nuptial element to these Eden-Temple connections, one easily arrives at the view held by *PRK* that the *Shekhinah* originally dwelt in Eden, was lost because of human sin, and was restored anew by her solemn entrance into the Tabernacle, expressed in the suggestive words of the Canticle: "*I come into my garden, my sister, my bride*" (Cant 5:1). These associations also lead to the understanding of the destruction of the Temple as a re-enactment of the expulsion from Eden and type of spiritual "divorce" (*GenR* 20:7).

## Memory, Liturgy, Eschatology:
## Cosmic, Mystical, and Ultimate Marriage

Israel's sanctuary fulfilled several roles: First, it commemorated and perpetuated the Sinai covenant, reenacting it and extending it through time in Israel's sacrificial liturgy. Second, the Temple acted as the symbolic nuptial chamber where the covenantal union between God and Israel was consummated. Third, the Temple was a microcosm or "world in miniature" that recalled the cosmic covenant between God and mankind and acted as a source of blessing and fruitfulness for the entire earth. Fourth, the Temple liturgy provided Israel with a symbolic access back to the primeval sanctuary of humanity in the Garden of Eden and to the unhindered communion with God that it signified.

Yet the Temple's role did not only recall the past. It also pointed towards the future, anticipating its own fulfillment in the eschatological wedding of the messianic age. This eschatological symbolism became particularly acute after the catastrophic destruction of the Jerusalem Temple and exile of the nation to Babylonia in 586 B.C. It is to this last aspect of nuptial symbolism that we now turn.

# 4

# Betrothed Forever

## *Mystical Marriage in the Messianic Age*

THE MODERN READER CAN HARDLY GRASP the impact of the destruction of the Temple and exile of the Jews to Babylonia. These events were a tragedy of incalculable proportions. In the nation's national and religious consciousness, they would have appeared to be the definitive end of the covenant between God and his people. It is no wonder that the rabbis associated Israel's exile with the expulsion of Adam and Eve from paradise and viewed it as a kind of divine divorce.[1] Yet the breakup was not final. For it is precisely during the exile that the memory of Eden, of the Sinai covenant, and of the lost Sanctuary helped foster hope for an eschatological restoration of God's marriage with his people.

We now turn to the eschatological dimension of the marriage between God and Israel, or how it was expected to be consummated during the Messianic Age at the end of history, thereby recapitulating its previous layers of symbolism. We will first consider nuptial passages in the Hebrew prophets, paying close attention to their eschatological dimension. Second, we will examine the eschatological treatment of nuptial symbolism selections in select Rabbinic writings. Third, we will consider the development of realized eschatology, that is, how the tragic events in Israel's history led to the conceptual transformation of the Temple and theological relocalization of the seat of the divine presence. We will look at one particular form of realized eschatology in Ezekiel's chariot or

1. *GenR* 21:8.

75

*Merkavah,* and how it conceptually enabled ancient Jews to experience the mystical marriage that formerly took place in the Holy of Holies, at Mount Sinai, and in the Garden of Eden. Fourth, we will consider an alternate form of realized eschatology—an "anthropological eschatology" identifying the community or human person with the Temple.

## The Prophets: Spiritual Adultery and Hope of Restored Marriage

The portrayal of Israel as God's spouse is a prominent feature in the writings of four prophets: Hosea, Jeremiah, Ezekiel, and Isaiah. This symbolism involves a pronounced cultic element, indicating that Israel's marital covenant with God was inseparable from her worship. The metaphor is rarely flattering towards Israel: drawing on other texts that lament the nation's "whoring" after other gods, often in the context of cultic sacrifice, it portrays her frequent infidelities as fornication, adultery, and prostitution.[2] Nevertheless, the prophets express hope that God will one day restore the marriage to a condition of pristine perfection. This wondrous future restoration evokes a return to the origins of mankind and to a place of perfect harmony between man and woman flowing from an unhindered communion with God.

### Hosea

#### *Betrayed Marriage*

In the mid-eighth century BCE, shortly before the fall of the northern kingdom of Israel, Hosea is divinely summoned to take a "wife of harlotry" and "children of harlotry" as a symbol of the people who have "committed great harlotry by forsaking the LORD" (Hos 1:2).[3] Hosea's unhappy love for Gomer, who is "loved by a lover and an adulteress" (Hos 3:1), reflects the frustrated love of the Lord for the children of Israel on account of their idolatrous love for other gods. While the nuptial elements in chapters 1 and 3 focus on Hosea's own troubled marriage, chapter 2 develops the

2. Cf. Exod 34:14–16; Lev 17:7; 20:5–6; Deut 31:16; Ps 73:27; 106:38–39; 1 Chr 5:25; 2 Chr 21:11,13.

3. On Hosea's nuptial symbolism, cf. Fensham, "The Marriage Metaphor in Hosea"; Abma, *Bonds of Love,* 110–213; Moughtin-Mumby, *Sexual and Marital Metaphors,* 206–68; Levenson, *Sinai and Zion,* 75–80..

nuptial metaphor as applied to God and Israel, whom Hosea describes as "husband" and "wife" (2:2). The first part (2:2–13) is a description of Israel's misdeeds and a severe castigation of her unfaithfulness and betrayal, while the second part (2:14–23) describes her future restoration and rehabilitation. God initially appears to repudiate his adulterous wife: "she is not my wife, nor am I her Husband" (2:2). Israel's punishment is a humiliating public display of her nudity, turning her into an arid wilderness that recalls "the day she was born" (2:3). The association of Israel's "birth" with the wilderness wanderings is reinforced with an allusion to the blessings of the Sinai covenant: Israel hopes to find material abundance in the pursuit of her lovers (2:5), oblivious that she received all her grain, wine, and oil from God as sign of his covenant faithfulness.[4] In response, God impedes her paths so that she will no longer be able to find her lovers (2:6–7) and will be constrained to return to him, realizing that her former condition with her "first husband" was better than her current state. God causes all mirth to cease, bringing an end to her Sabbaths and festivals (2:11) and destroying her vines and fig trees (2:12) because she has forgotten him (2:13). Israel's marital betrayal represents a Baal fertility cult which includes wine and oil libations, grain, silver and gold offerings and the burning of incense to foreign divinities (2:5, 8, 13). This illicit cult competes with the Temple worship due to God, especially on Israel's "feast days, her New Moons, her Sabbaths—all her appointed feasts" (2:11).[5]

### Future Reconciliation

The purpose of this divine castigation is not divorce, however, but rather correction and restoration. The second part of the chapter (2:14–23) is a message of mercy and hope that foresees a future restoration of the broken marriage. This restoration will begin in the wilderness, the place of the first love, again recalling the time of the Exodus and Sinai covenant (2:14–15). The sustained use of the future tense and repetition of the expression "on that day" (2:16, 18, 21) points to an eschatological fulfillment: "On that day," not God but the Baals will be forgotten. Hosea

4. "Grain, wine, and oil" (2:8, 22) symbolize the full range of God's agricultural blessings to Israel. Deut 7:13; 11:14; 12:17; 14:23; 18:4; 28:51.

5. The cultic and sacrificial aspects of Israel's idolatry are particularly evident in Hos 4:10–19, where she plays out her "harlotry" and "adultery" by offering sacrifices on the mountaintops and burning incense on the hills.

expresses this future reality with a pun: "you will call me 'My Husband' (my *ish*) and no longer call me 'my Master' (my *baal*)" (2:16). Israel's rehabilitation is depicted with covenantal language: "And I will make for you a covenant on that day with the beasts of the field, the birds of the air, and the creeping things of the ground" (2:18). This terminology recalls the language of creation and Eden (Gen 1:28; 2:19–20). Thus, the nuptial covenant has a double point of reference: proximately, the Sinai covenant, and remotely, the primeval relationship between God and man in Eden.

God's covenant faithfulness to Israel is then expressed in a triple promise of a future betrothal which unequivocally overrides the previous threat of divorce. The verb "betroth" is used here in an unusual way: whereas it normally describes a man's espousals with a virgin, here it denotes the betrothal of an adulteress wife, rehabilitated by the mercy and faithfulness of her husband: "And I will espouse you for ever; I will espouse you in righteousness and in justice, in steadfast love, and in mercy. I will espouse you in faithfulness; and you shall know the LORD" (2:19–20).

In short, Hosea's nuptial metaphor is clearly situated within the context of salvation history. The setting of Israel's birth (or youth) and God's "first love" for her is the time of the Exodus (2:3, 15). Israel's marital infidelity is expressed as illegitimate cultic sacrifices, set in contrast to her lawful Temple worship. Moreover, Hosea's covenantal language recalls the creation and Eden narratives (2:18). Finally, the vision of the future marriage restored to an idyllic state, the disappearance of instruments of war (2:18), and the renewed fecundity of the earth (2:22) all point to a marvelous eschatological restoration of the marriage between God and Israel.[6]

## Jeremiah

### *Broken Love of Former Betrothal (Jer 2:1–4:4)*

About a century after Hosea, shortly before the destruction of Jerusalem, Jeremiah also makes abundant use of the nuptial metaphor, personifying

---

6. As Levenson (*Sinai and Zion*, 79) has noted, for Hosea, the covenant moves beyond its original juridical function and becomes "the stuff and substance of a vision of cosmic renewal. The entire universe takes part in the sacred remarriage of YHWH and Israel." Covenant is thus "the teleological end of creation and of history."

Jerusalem as God's bride.[7] Jeremiah tries in vain to remind the city of her former love for the Lord during the wilderness wanderings. As in Hosea, the wilderness is referred to as a period of betrothal: "I remember the devotion of your youth, your love as a bride, how you followed me in the wilderness, in a land not sown" (Jer 2:2). Now, however, Israel has forsaken her God. In an allusion to cultic prostitution and Baal fertility rites, she has gone up "on every high hill and under every green tree" and "bowed down as a harlot" (2:20). In contrast to a faithful virgin and bride, Israel's pursuit of the Baals reveals the extent to which she has forgotten her divine Husband (2:32–33).

The unflattering nuptial metaphor continues in chapter 3. Jeremiah designates again the Lord as husband and Judah as his wife (Jer 3:1) who has greatly polluted the land by "play[ing] the harlot with many lovers" (3:1). The severity of her offense is underlined by an allusion to the Torah's prohibition that a husband take back his divorced wife (Deut 24:1–4). Yet the exhortation for her to return indicates that not all hope is lost. The prophet then turns to the bad example of the former northern kingdom, now in ruins and exiled to Assyria (Jer 3:6). God's warnings went unheeded. Because of her adulteries, he "sent her away with a decree of divorce" (3:8). Despite this terrifying end, Israel's "treacherous sister" Judah did not fear, but "she too went and played the harlot." "She polluted the land, committing adultery with stone and tree" (3:9), dealing treacherously with God "as a treacherous wife leaves her husband" (3:20). Still, despite this dismal record, God's marriage with Judah still stands, and he pleads to her children to return to him so he can take them back to Zion at a future time: "'Return, O faithless children,' says the Lord; 'for I am married to you. I will take you . . . and I will bring you to Zion'" (3:14).

The Temple as meeting place between the Lord and his bride is alluded to in Jeremiah's mention of the Ark of the Covenant (Jer 3:16). The seat of the divine presence, now desecrated by the bride's adultery and on the brink of disaster at the hands of the Babylonians, will be forgotten when the marriage between God and Israel is restored. In its place, the whole city of Jerusalem will be "the throne of the Lord," gathering not only Israel but also all the nations, when they no longer follow the dictates of their hearts and recognize the sovereignty of the Lord (3:16–17). Jeremiah further develops his nuptial metaphor with the "daughter of

7. On nuptial symbolism in Jeremiah, cf. Abma, *Bonds of Love*, 214–252; Moughtin-Mumby, *Sexual and Marital Metaphors*, 80–116.

Zion" motif—a personification of Jerusalem as either virgin or mother with child. Her vain attempts to beautify herself for her lovers are grotesquely caricatured as useless, for they will not prevent the anguish and misery that the same lovers will soon inflict upon her (Jer 4:30–31).[8]

## The Voice of the Bridegroom and Voice of the Bride

Nuptial language also occurs in Jeremiah's reference to "the voice of the bridegroom and the voice of the bride"—an indication of peace, joy, and prosperity in Israel. Conversely, their absence signifies a time of desolation and destruction. The expression appears four times, three times in a context of condemnation and once in a context of consolation and hope. The first occurrence is associated with Israel's corrupt Temple worship. Jeremiah is summoned to stand "in the gate of the Lord's house" to castigate those who think they are safe in the Temple despite their grave sins (Jer 7:2–4). The Temple has become a den of thieves (7:11), defiled by illicit offerings to other gods (7:18). God rejects their sacrifices because they are not offered in a spirit of obedience or justice (7:21–26). They have polluted the Temple by setting abominations in it, even burning their children on high places (7:30–31). As a result, the Lord declares: "I will cause to cease from the cities of Judah and from the streets of Jerusalem the voice of mirth and the voice of gladness, the voice of the bridegroom and the voice of the bride" (Jer 7:34). Here too, the point of reference is the Exodus: The prophet recalls that obedience was more important than sacrifice already at the origin of the nation's history when the Lord delivered his people from Egypt (Jer 7:22–25). Just as they disobeyed then, so they are still disobeying at the present critical hour of the nation's history.

The voice of the bridegroom and bride returns in chapter 16. Like Hosea, Jeremiah's personal experience mirrors God's feelings towards his people. Yet in contrast to Hosea, Jeremiah is commanded *not* to take a wife and thus not to have children (16:2) as a sign of the mourning that will soon overtake the land. The absence of marital and family love reflects Israel's grim situation at the time of impending destruction when one will soon no longer hear the voice of the bridegroom and voice of the bride (16:9). The covenantal point of reference is again the Exodus

---

8. Cf. Jer 6:2; 23–26; 8:19; 18:13; 2 Kgs 19:21; Ps 9:14; Lam 1:6, 15; 2:1–18; 4:22; Amos 5:2; Mic 1:13; 4:8–13; Zeph 3:14; Zech 2:10; 9:9.

(16:14), and it points to a future new Exodus when the Lord will take Israel out of many nations and bring them back into their own land (16:15). The castigation of Israel's sins and threat of exile also appears in chapter 25, where the prophet declares again that the destruction of Jerusalem will result in the disappearance of "the voice of mirth and the voice of gladness, the voice of the bridegroom and the voice of the bride" (Jer 25:10).

## Everlasting Love (Jer 31)

In Jeremiah's book of consolation, God declares that he has loved the "virgin Israel" with an "everlasting love" (Jer 31:3–4). Commentators have noticed common themes between this chapter and Jer 2:1–4:4. One is the announcement of Israel's future salvation and the promise of a new exodus as a pilgrimage to Zion (Jer 31:6–9, 12–14) that will follow the time of desolation that Israel experienced because of her infidelity. Again, we are told that Israel will encounter grace in the wilderness (31:2). The eschatological pilgrimage to Zion displays ties with the Sinai covenant in its promise of abundant produce of the land, including the covenantal signs of "wheat, new wine and oil" (31:12) as material benefits of the restored relationship between God and Israel.[9] In a possible Edenic allusion, the souls of those who will come up to Zion will be "like a well-watered garden," forever freed of sorrows and joyfully satiated by the Lord's goodness (31:12–14). This redemptive action will be a radically new thing, expressed in the language of creation with an expression of odd sexual connotation: "For the LORD has created a new thing in the earth—a woman shall encompass a man" (31:22). It is within this context that the well-known promise of a new covenant is given to Israel and Judah, set in contrast to the (nuptial) covenant given when they were led out of Egypt: the covenant "that they broke, though I was their husband" (31:31–32). Unlike the broken Sinai covenant, the new covenant will be permanent, likened to the covenant with creation and its ordinances of the sun, moon and stars, and heaven and earth (31:35–37; 33:20–22). The obvious reference to Genesis 1 is another indication that the nuptial metaphor is related not only to Sinai but also to the order of creation and original covenant between God and humanity.

9. Cf. Hosea 2:22.

The voice of the bridegroom and bride returns in Jer 33:10–11. The prophet tells us that in the place that was once desolate there shall be heard again "the voice of mirth and the voice of gladness, the voice of the bridegroom and the voice of the bride, the voices of those who sing, as they bring thank offerings to the house of the LORD: 'Give thanks to the LORD of hosts, for the LORD is good, for his mercy endures forever!'" (Jer 33:11). The wider context of this last nuptial passage summarizes Jeremiah's interrelated motifs: The permanent nature of God's covenant with Judah and Israel is again illustrated with the covenant of creation (33:20–22, 25), together with the promise of an eschatological new exodus (33:7, 26) that will bring healing and forgiveness (33:6–8). The voice of the bridegroom and bride will join the voice of praise of those sacrificing in the Temple (33:11), and Temple sacrifices will thrive (33:18) when the messianic king will rule in the land (33:15–16).

In summary, Jeremiah, like Hosea, presents the marriage covenant between God and Israel/Judah as firmly placed within the context of salvation history. Having originated in the wilderness at the time of the Exodus, its drama is played out in the cultic history of the two nations, whether faithfully centered around the Ark of the Covenant and Temple, or (more frequently) violated through cultic harlotry and adultery with the Baals. The marriage finds a remote, ideal point of reference in the Genesis creation account. The memory of the idyllic state of creation provides hope that the marriage will not remain in its current wounded state forever, but is moving towards an eschatological restoration in the new Exodus that will lead Israel from its barren state to the marvelously fruitful heights of Mount Zion.

## Ezekiel

Ezekiel also makes rich use of nuptial symbolism.[10] Speaking from the perspective of the Babylonian exile, he provides two dramatic descriptions of the stormy relationship between God and his bride: in chapter 16, Jerusalem is a destitute maiden who was tenderly adopted by God, only to grievously betray him; in chapter 23, Samaria and Jerusalem are portrayed as the two harlot sisters Oholah and Oholibah.

---

10. On Ezekiel's nuptial imagery, cf. Moughtin-Mumby, *Sexual and Marital Metaphors*, 156–205.

## *Jerusalem, Faithless Maiden*

Chapter 16 can be divided into five scenes. The first (16:3–6a) describes the miserable origins and condition of Jerusalem. She was an infant girl from Canaan, born of an Amorite father and Hittite mother. She was unwashed, loathed, and mercilessly abandoned in an open field, left to wallow in her own blood. The second scene (6b–14) describes God adopting and betrothing the maiden. In a prophetic, creative act, the Lord speaks life into her and makes her "flourish like a plant in the field" so that she "grew up, became tall, and arrived at full maidenhood" though still remaining "naked and bare" (16:7). This intermediate state lasts until a moving covenant-making ceremony takes place:

> When I passed by you again and looked upon you, behold, you were at the age for love; and I spread my garment over you and covered your nakedness. Yes, I swore an oath to you and entered into a covenant with you, says the Lord God, and you became mine." (Ezek 16:8)

The covenant whereby the Lord "spreads his garment" over the abandoned maiden and takes her as his own is undoubtedly a nuptial moment. Following the ceremony, the divine Bridegroom lavishes upon his bride all the best things. Beginning with a washing and purification in water (a bridal bath?), he effects a splendid metamorphosis of the maiden's formerly miserable state by anointing her with oil, clothing her with fine linen and silk, adorning her with a crown and precious jewels of gold and silver, and providing her with the finest foods (16:9–13a). At the end of this process, Jerusalem "grew exceedingly beautiful and advanced to royalty;" her renown went forth among the nations because of her beauty, made perfect through the splendor that God he bestowed on her (16:13–14).

As Renée Bloch has shown, Ezekiel 16 appears to be a *historical allegory* or anthology of biblical allusions to Israel's history, beginning with the time of the patriarchs and leading up to the eve of the Temple's destruction at the hand of the Babylonians.[11] The humble origin and "birth" of the maiden in the "land of the Canaanites" likely refers to the sojourn of the patriarchs in Canaan. The miserable time when she "wallowed in her blood" is the period of Egyptian slavery, and the language used to describe her fruitful growth (16:7) recalls the description of the nation's

---

11. Bloch, "Ezéchiel XVI," 212–17.

rapid multiplication in Egypt (Exod 1:7, 12). The nuptial and covenantal "time of love" corresponds to the Exodus and Sinai covenant (Ezek 16:8; 19:4–6) when the Lord showered his bride with gifts (Ezek 16:9–13). The climax of the narrative and the maiden's most glorious hour when her "renown went forth among the nations" (Ezek 16:14) refers to the reigns of David and especially Solomon, when Jerusalem became the capital of Israel, greatly admired by neighboring nations (1 Kgs 10).

But everything goes downhill from there. The third scene (Ezek 16:15–34) describes the shameful betrayal and degradation of the bride. Rather than responding gratefully to the generosity of her protector and husband, she trusts in her own beauty and turns to idolatry. Borrowing from Hosea and Jeremiah, Ezekiel underlines the cultic and sacrificial aspects of Israel's harlotry: using priestly language, she offers as a "pleasing odor" to her lovers—the foreign divinities—the bread, cakes, oil, and honey that the Lord had given her. To this grave offense is added the abomination of child sacrifice (16:19–21). Ezekiel's account of Israel's betrayal is even worse than Hosea's—for whom Israel's betrayal was at least partly motivated by material gain. For Ezekiel, she is worse than a harlot because she does not even ask her lovers for payment (16:31–34). This scene has an evident historical connection, as the Assyrians and Chaldeans (16:28–29)—the two peoples who would exile the two kingdoms—are identified as Israel's lovers.

The fourth scene (Ezek 16:35–59) describes God's wrath and punishment towards his unfaithful bride, which would be carried out by the foreign nations she courted. Jerusalem became even more corrupt than her "elder and younger sisters," respectively Samaria and Sodom. God's "jealousy" appears within the context of the nuptial metaphor as an expression of his passionate love for his bride (16:38, 42). Though exile awaits Jerusalem because of her waywardness, the fifth scene (16:60–63) is a testimony to the triumph of mercy over judgment, in which the Lord promises to remember his former covenant with Israel from "the days of [her] youth" and to (re)establish this everlasting covenant with her.

### Oholah and Oholibah

In chapter 23 the nuptial metaphor is extended to the two adulterous sisters Oholah/Samaria and Oholibah/Jerusalem, who are whoring with Assyria and Babylon, respectively. Unlike in Hosea and Jeremiah, the time of the Exodus is not idealized here as a period of pristine romance but remembered as a time when Israel already committed harlotry (23:2, 8, 19–21, 27). Oholah and Oholibah's adultery is identified with the defilement of the Lord's sanctuary and profanation of his Sabbaths (23:38–39). Allusions to the misuse of the Temple furnishings, incense, and oil are visible in the reproach that Israel "sat on a stately couch, with a table prepared before it, on which you had set My incense and My oil" (Ezek 23:41). This chapter does not conclude with a reversal of the situation and 'happy end,' but with a harsh judgment meted out to the two wayward sisters.

In summary, the historical component of the nuptial metaphor is evident in Ezekiel 16 and 23. Egypt and the Exodus are the point of reference for the marriage, but far from depicting this period as an idyllic time of romantic betrothal, Ezekiel asserts that Israel was already promiscuous back then. In both chapters 16 and 23, the cultic element of Israel's adultery and its defiling effect on the Temple is predominant. Ezekiel also expects an eschatological restoration of the God-Israel marriage in his promise that a future "everlasting covenant" will atone for Israel's sins (16:60–63).

## Isaiah

### Wayward Daughter of Zion

Of all the prophets, Isaiah contains the most nuptial passages. While the first chapters of the book focus on the present broken state of the marriage between God and Israel, its last chapters focus on God's future restoration of the marriage. In the first chapter, the prophet laments that Jerusalem, the "daughter of Zion" and "faithful city" has "become a harlot" (1:8, 21). There is a heavy emphasis on Israel's cult. The problem is not illegitimate worship offered to foreign divinities (as in Hosea and Jeremiah) but rather that legitimate cultic practices—such as the offering of sacrifices and incense, or the celebration of Sabbaths and feasts—are tainted by social injustice. Despite this dire situation, the prophet expresses hope that after a time of purgation Zion will again be called "the city of righteousness, the faithful city" (1:26).[12]

---

12. The female personification of Jerusalem as the "daughter of Zion" recurs several times throughout the entire book; cf. Isa 10:32; 16:1; 37:22; 52:2; 62:11.

Another nuptial allusion is seen in the messianic passage on the "branch of the Lord" (4:2–6). At the revelation of the Lord's beautiful and glorious branch, all the inhabitants of Jerusalem will be called "holy." This will occur "when the Lord has washed away the filth of the daughters of Zion and cleansed the bloodstains of Jerusalem from its midst" (Isa 4:4). This washing recalls God washing off the blood of his bride in Ezekiel 16:9. This purification will lead to a restored communion between God and Israel, recalling former times when God dwelt with his people in the wilderness. Worthy of note is the presence of a *chuppah*—a "bridal canopy" over the divine glory: "Then the Lord will create above every dwelling place of Mount Zion, and above her assemblies, a cloud and smoke by day and the shining of a flaming fire by night. For over all the glory there will be a covering (*chuppah*)" (Isa 4:5).

Isaiah's Song of the Vineyard follows (5:1–7), opening with the words: "Let me sing for my beloved a love song regarding his vineyard" (5:1). The song displays three levels of symbolism: At the literal level, it expresses the disappointment of the vinedresser towards his vine, which has produced sour grapes. On a second level, this symbolizes the disappointment of a man who laments his failed love. This second level points to a third one—the frustrated love of God for his people. The vine is a common biblical symbol of either Israel or a beloved woman.[13] The vineyard is thus symbolic of the song's bride, who is in turn a symbol of Israel, the bride of the Lord. Moreover, the fact that Isaiah calls God "my beloved" could indicate that the prophet is taking on the role of the *shoshbin*—the male friend of the bridegroom who negotiates the Jewish marriage contract.

### As the Bridegroom Rejoices over the Bride . . .

The nuptial motif resumes in Isaiah's songs of consolation to Israel. While some passages continue to castigate Israel as unfaithful bride, others express great hope for a glorious eschatological marriage. Isa 49:14–26 depicts God's enduring fidelity as he assures Zion that she will "clothe herself" with her sons returning from exile "as an ornament" and put them on herself as a bride puts on her attire (49:18). In answer to her

---

13. For the vine as symbol of Israel, cf. Deut 32:32; Hos 10:1; Jer 2:21; 5:10; 6:9; 8:13; 12:10; Ezek 15:1–8; 19:10–14; Ps 80:9–19. For the vine as symbol of a beloved woman, cf. Cant 1:6; 7:9; 8:12.

concerns that she has been forgotten or even divorced, God speaks of his love as the love of a mother, unable to forget the child of her womb (49:15). In chapter 50, the metaphor shifts: a distinction is made between the mother who was given a bill of divorce (a transcendent Israel?) and her children (the individual Israelites?). As if replying to accusations that he unjustly repudiated her, the Lord replies that he put her away not because of a lack of faithfulness on his part but because of her children's transgressions (50:1).

Yet Zion will be restored. This eschatological restoration when Zion will blossom recalls the memory of the lush Garden of Eden: "For the LORD will comfort Zion, he will comfort all her waste places; he will make her wilderness like Eden, and her desert like the garden of the LORD; Joy and gladness will be found in her, thanksgiving and the voice of song" (Isa 51:3).

The personification of the daughter of Zion and promise of her future glorification is developed in chapter 52, where she is exhorted to put on splendid garments and leave behind her former oppressed condition: "Awake, awake! Put on your strength, O Zion; Put on your beautiful garments, O Jerusalem, the holy city! . . . Shake yourself from the dust, arise; O captive Jerusalem! Loose the bonds from your neck, O captive daughter of Zion!" (Isa 52:1–2). What is this glorious event for which the daughter of Zion must prepare? It is an eschatological new exodus (52:4, 8) that will reenact the Exodus from Egypt. The bride must put on her wedding garments in preparation for the wedding described in chapter 54—one of the most beautiful nuptial poems of the Hebrew Bible. Israel's former destitute state—when she was barren and desolate (54:1), ashamed and confounded (54:4), forsaken and grieved in spirit (54:6)—will soon be entirely forgotten, giving way to the exultation and jubilation of a newly found fruitfulness. Israel will "forget the shame of [her] youth, and will not remember the reproach of [her] widowhood anymore" (54:4), thanks to the bountiful mercies of her divine husband:

> For your Maker is your husband, the LORD of hosts is his name; and the Holy One of Israel is your Redeemer, the God of the whole earth he is called. For the LORD has called you like a wife forsaken and grieved in spirit, like a wife of youth when she is cast off, says your God. For a brief moment I forsook you, but with great compassion I will gather you. In overflowing wrath for a moment I hid my face from you, but with everlasting mercy

I will have compassion on you, says the LORD, your Redeemer.
(Isa 54:5–8)

God's role as redeemer, set here in a nuptial context, indicates that he is carrying out a social obligation to provide shelter and protection to an abandoned widow (cf. Ruth 3:8, 12–13). The concrete expression of God's mercy and love for his bride will be the ingathering from exile, which was but a temporary "hiding of his face" for the sake of purifying the nation towards final union.[14]

The last nuptial passage in Isaiah (61:10–62:12) provides more consolation and hope, returning to motifs such as Zion's garments of salvation and robes of righteousness (cf. 52:1), compared with the glorious adorning of bridegroom and bride (cf. 49:18):

> I will greatly rejoice in the LORD, My soul shall be joyful in my God; For he has clothed me with the garments of salvation, he has covered me with the robe of righteousness, as a bridegroom decks himself with ornaments and as a bride adorns herself with her jewels. (Isa 61:10)

This leads to a final song of praise for the glorious bride (Isa 62:1–5). The prophet refuses to remain silent until Zion's righteousness and salvation shine forth and are universally recognized by all nations and kings. She is to be a "crown of glory" and "royal diadem" in the hand of the Lord, who will rejoice and delight in her as a bridegroom rejoices over his bride.

> You shall no longer be termed Forsaken, nor shall your land any more be termed Desolate; But you shall be called Hephzibah, and your land Beulah; For the LORD delights in you, and your land shall be married. For as a young man marries a virgin, so shall your sons marry you; And as the bridegroom rejoices over the bride, so shall your God rejoice over you. (Isa 62:3–5)

The marriage here takes on several dimensions. The bridal figure of Zion represents not only the city of Jerusalem but also the land of Israel.

---

14. The nuptial/sexual motif also appears in Isa 57:3–9, but with a tone of severe castigation akin to that of Hosea, Jeremiah, and Ezekiel. The Israelites are called "offspring of the adulterer and the harlot" (57:3), and the language suggests both sexual and cultic infidelity: they are inflaming themselves with gods under every green tree (57:5), bringing drink offerings and grain offerings to them (57:6). Israel's idolatry is described in terms of "setting her bed" before the foreign divinities, "uncovering herself" to them and making a covenant with them (57:7–9).

This is a remarkable marriage: On the one hand, Zion is the personified city and God's beloved bride. Yet on the other hand, Zion's "sons" will also marry her. Transcendent, personified Zion is a mediating figure, married to God in the heavenly realm, but also married to her "sons"—the children of Israel, here on earth. We will find a similar mediating role attributed to the figure of Lady Wisdom in the wisdom literature.

## From Broken Marriage to Restored Divine Glory

The prophetic books connect their nuptial symbolism with the time of the Exodus, either by idealizing it as a time of pristine, youthful love (Hosea, Jeremiah), depicting it as a time when Israel already engaged in harlotry (Ezekiel), or using it as a pattern for the eschatological new exodus (Isaiah). The prophets also draw a strong connection between nuptial symbolism and Israel's cultic worship. This is often expressed negatively, with the people's idolatry described as adultery that violates and desecrates the legitimate Temple service. And yet the prophets view the wounded marriage between God and Israel as moving forward towards an eschatological restoration. No matter how bad the present conjugal situation appears, all express great hope that it will be gloriously restored at the end of days.

Despite the destruction of the Temple and Israel's exile, Ezekiel foresaw the return of "the glory of the God of Israel" to a future eschatological Temple (Ezek 43:2–5; 44:4). Haggai had similar insights: despite the modest appearance of the Second Temple, he prophesied that "the glory of this latter house shall be greater than that of the former" (2:6–9). The universal manifestation of God's *kavod* was anticipated by prophets and psalmists who echoed Habakkuk's words: "For the earth will be filled with the knowledge of the glory of the Lord."[15] The eschatological restoration of the divine presence and glory also appears in apocryphal writings, where it is often portrayed as a return to Eden: In the *Apocalypse of Moses*, Seth the son of Adam is promised that he will eat from the Tree of Life at the end of the times when the *kedushah* of God is universally restored: "Then will all flesh be raised up from Adam till that great day, as many as will be a holy people. Then will every delight of paradise be given to them and God will be in their midst."[16] Even Adam is promised a future

---

15. Hab 2:14. Cf. Isa 4:5; 11:10; 24:23; 40:5; 43:7; 60:1; Ps 84:11; 85:9.
16. *Apoc. Mos.* 13:2–4.

restoration of the glory he lost: "I will transform you to your former glory and set you on the throne of the one who deceived you."[17] The *Testament of Dan* (5:12) likewise announces that "the saints shall rest in Eden, and in the New Jerusalem shall the righteous rejoice, and it shall be unto the glory of God forever." The *Testament of Levi* (18:6–11) describes the glory of God resting upon the eschatological priest who will open the gates of paradise and give to the saints to eat from the tree of life. And 2 *Baruch* describes the glory of those who have been justified as being changed "from beauty into loveliness, and from light into the splendor of glory."[18]

## Kedushah, Sabbath and World to Come

Hope for the future restoration of creation is also expressed in the Jewish theology of the Sabbath. As we have seen, the Sabbath commemorated God's covenant with creation; it was the sign of God's redemptive covenant with Israel; and as Israel's sacred time during which the covenant was commemorated, it was closely linked with Israel's sacred space—the Sanctuary. In addition, the *kedushah* of the Sabbath anticipates the world to come. An old tradition is preserved to this day in the Shabbat prayer at the end of grace after meals: "May the All-merciful let us inherit the day which will be all Sabbath and rest in the life eternal." The idea that the Shabbat is "something like the world to come" is of ancient origin. In the apocryphal *Life of Adam and Eve* (51:2) we read that "the seventh day is the sign of the resurrection and the rest of the age to come." The *Mekhilta* on Exod 31:13 adds that the world to come is "characterized by the kind of holiness possessed by the Sabbath in this world. We thus learn that the Sabbath possesses a holiness like that of the world to come."[19] A rabbinic tradition attributed to Rabbi Akiva also states that the world to come is "the day which will be all Sabbath in the life eternal."[20] The *kedushah* of the Sabbath thus links creation/Eden, Sinai, the Temple, and the eschaton.

17. *Apoc. Mos.* 39:2.

18. 2 *Baruch* 51:3, 10–11.

19. *Mekh Shabbata* 1.

20. *M. Tamid* 6:7; *b. Rosh Hashanah* 31a.

## Rabbinic Hope: Restored Marriage
## in the Messianic Age

The Sages also expected a restoration of the *Shekhinah* and divine glory in the Messianic age and Temple, in an eschatological marriage that they expected to be *collective, historical,* and *earthly.* With the sanctuary in ruins and the Jews scattered in the diaspora, rabbinic nuptial symbolism naturally emphasizes the hope for the eschatological ingathering of the exiles and its consummation in the messianic age.

*Pesikta de-Rab Kahana* provides several illustrations of eschatological nuptial symbolism. In Piska 5, for example, the Song's beloved, *leaping upon the mountains* and inviting his maiden to come away with him (Cant 2:8–13), represents both Moses leading Israel's first redemption from Egypt, and the Messiah leading Israel's final redemption from exile at the end of days.[21]

## Torah as Ketubah

Piskas 19–22 are dedicated to the prophetic (*haftarah*) readings (all from Isaiah) of the Sabbaths of Consolation following the Ninth of Ab—the day of national calamity in Jewish history. These homilies provide messages of hope and comfort for Israel, who is exhorted not to despair in the face of exile but to look forward to the glorious restoration of Zion to come. Piska 19 comments on Isa 51:12 ("*I, I am he who comforts you*"). While discussing the hardships of exile, the midrash uses a parable to compare the Torah to a marriage settlement (*ketubah*): A king betrothed a noble-woman and wrote out a pledge of a substantial settlement, promising her elegant chambers, ornaments, and treasures before he traveled to a far country for many years. Her companions eventually began to mock her for waiting so long for her absent husband, telling her to find herself another man. She remained faithful by going into her house, reading her *ketubah* and being comforted until the king came back many years later and said to his wife:

> "My little one, I marvel that you could wait around for me all these years." She replied: "My lord the king, but for the substantial marriage settlement which you pledged to me in writing, my companions would long since have got me to give you up."

21. *PRK* 5:7–9; cf. *CantR* 2:8–10.

The parable is an image of the nations of the world who mock Israel for sacrificing herself to God and remaining faithful to the Torah.[22] The story is eschatological: the return of the king to his wife represents the final time of redemption when God returns to Israel and marvels that she waited for him all these years. She responds that her faithfulness is only due to the *ketubah*—the Torah as marriage settlement—that he gave her before leaving.[23]

## Barren One Turned Fruitful

If the nuptial symbolism of Piska 19 is one of *hope*, encouraging patient endurance in the face of adversity, the next piskas elaborate on the *glory* of the eschatological wedding. Piska 20 is a commentary on Isa 54:1 (*"Sing, O barren one, who did not bear . . . "*), which foretells the future restoration of Zion when the once-barren Jerusalem will become miraculously fruitful and rise to the divine throne of glory. Commenting on this passage, the Midrash portrays Zion as the last of seven barren wives (following Sarah, Rebekah, Rachel, Leah, Manoah's wife, and Hannah) whom God finally blesses with children. Hope is expressed that Zion will one day no longer be exiled and barren but restored to her former splendor. Her present barrenness is equated with the Temple's desolation (20:5), but in the age to come *"there will be an abundance of grain in the earth"* (Ps 72:16) when God restores the abundance of the Garden of Eden that Adam and Eve enjoyed before the fall (20:6). In the last section (20:7), the Sages turn their attention to the future Jerusalem: not only will the barren wife become fruitful again; in the messianic age she will also become the throne and resting place of the Lord (cf. Jer 3:17, Ps 132:14).[24]

---

22. The nations say to Israel: "How long will you sacrifice yourselves for your God, giving up your lives for him, letting yourselves be slain for His sake? . . . Get yourselves over to us, and we shall make you captains, prefects, and commanders-in-chief!" Israel's reply to the nations is to go into synagogues and into houses of study, take the Torah Scroll and read in it [God's pledges to her]: *"For I will look on you favorably and make you fruitful, multiply you and confirm My covenant with you"* (Lev 26:9)." Cf. *Mekh Shirata* 3; *Sifre Deut* 343.

23. *PRK* 19:4.

24. *PRK* 20:1–7.

## Final Marriage as Light to the Nations

Piska 21 is a commentary on Isa 60:1 ("*Arise, shine, for your light has come
. . .* "). It develops the theme of God's restoration of Zion as he bestows
the radiance of his glory upon the city. It also speaks of the eternity of the
Temple as part of God's design, envisioned as built, destroyed, and rebuilt
in Zion from the origins of creation. Resh Lakish tells a parable about a
king whose daughter was sought for marriage by several unworthy men.
They were all sent away until a worthy candidate asked for her hand; the
king agreed, echoing to his daughter the words of Isaiah: "*Rise, give light,
for the light of your life has come.*" Oddly enough, the marriage here seems
to be between Israel and Zion, as God entrusts his people to Zion which
proved itself more worthy than all others. Within the context of this
marriage, "there will come a time when the Holy One will bring Sinai,
Tabor and Carmel together and build the Temple on top of them." The
eschatological role of the Temple as beacon for all nations is associated
with Isaiah's mountain of the Lord (Isa 2:2), and its eternal cosmic role
is underlined: according to R. Hiyya, its construction, destruction, and
rebuilding are all implied in the first three verses of Genesis.[25] Finally,
the Temple that will send light out into all the world is identified with
Ezekiel's eschatological Temple (Ezek 43:2) and Jeremiah's eternal throne
of glory (Jer 17:12).[26]

## Utter Joy!

Piska 22 is the lesson on the seventh and last Sabbath of Consolation
following the Ninth of Ab. The reading is from Isaiah 61:10 ("*I will
greatly rejoice in the Lord . . .* ")—a key nuptial verse. Of the joy spoken
of by Isaiah, a parable is told on the commandment to be fruitful and
multiply. When a married woman bore no children for ten years, her
husband wished to divorce her. As compensation, he told her: "take any
precious object I have in my house, take it and go back to your father's
house." The woman proceeded to prepare a great feast, gave her husband
too much to drink so that he fell asleep, and then had him brought to her
father's house. After the husband woke up, she explained that she had
no object more precious than him and therefore took him to her father's

25. Cf. *GenR* 2:5.
26. *PRK* 21:3–5.

house. Following this, R. Shimon bar Yochai prayed for them and they were blessed with children. The moral of the story: as the woman rejoiced over her husband as her most prized possession, so will Israel greatly rejoice over God since she looked forward to his deliverance for so many years—hence the opening verse: "I will greatly rejoice in the Lord." This is followed by another nuptial parable of a noble woman whose husband, sons, and sons-in-law went to a far country. Although the return of the sons and the sons-in-law caused joy to her daughters-in-law and daughters, only when the husband returned did she exclaim: "Joy! Utter joy!" And so when the prophets announce to Jerusalem that her exiled sons and daughters are returning, she is glad, but only when the prophets tell her: "*Behold, your King [God] is coming to you*" (Zech 9:9), she is overjoyed and replies: "*I will greatly rejoice in the Lord.*"[27]

Nuptial symbolism through salvation history takes again the center stage in sections 4 and 5: Isa 61:10 ("*as a bridegroom decks himself with a garland, and as a bride adorns herself with her jewels*") is quoted to portray Israel bedecked like a bride when she stood at Mount Sinai. This is followed by a compilation of ten places in Scripture where Israel is called "bride": six by Solomon (Cant 4:8, 9, 10, 11, 12, 5:1), three by Isaiah (49:18, 61:10, 62:5), and one by Jeremiah (33:11). The piska ends on an eschatological and messianic note, recalling the six things that God will renew in the world to come: heaven and earth, heart and spirit, the name of the Messiah, and the name of Jerusalem.[28]

## Realized Eschatology and the Merkavah

### From Disaster to Eschatological Hope

Both the prophets and the rabbis hoped for the ultimate restoration of the marriage between God and Israel and anticipated its consummation at the end of human history. Yet how was the nuptial relationship to be sustained in the meantime, in the absence of a temple? As we will now see, the exile led to the development of a *realized eschatology* that enabled an unmediated encounter with the divine in a supernatural state transcending normal earthly life. This extraordinary breaking forth of the divine presence into time functioned as an intermediary state between

27. *PRK* 22:2–3. Cf. *CantR* 1:4c §2.
28. *PRK* 22:4–5.

the physical Temple (traditional home of the *Shekhinah*, yet strictly off limits to common people), and the messianic age (when the *Shekhinah* would become openly manifest to the whole world). It behooves us now to briefly examine this conceptual transformation of the Temple in early Jewish manifestations of realized eschatology.

How did the Temple become associated with the world to come? Can we trace a conceptual development in the relocation of the seat of the divine Presence from Temple to eschaton? The destruction of the Temple became the occasion of great theological developments in Judaism. The Jews exiled in Babylon had to face the grave implications of the destruction and exile, and seek to answer the inevitable question: had God forsaken his people?[29] Ezekiel expresses hope in the midst of desolation: despite the departure of the divine glory from the sanctuary (Ezek 9:3; 10:19; 11:23) and the subsequent fall and capture of the city (33:21), the prophet is confident that not only will the land be rebuilt and the cities resettled (Ezek 36–37), but the divine glory will also return to dwell in an eschatological Temple (Ezek 43:1–5) out of which will flow miraculous waters for the healing of the nations (Ezek 47:1–12).

## The Merkavah: Seat of the Divine Presence

What is most remarkable about Ezekiel is his dramatic vision of the divine chariot—the *Merkavah*—by the River Chebar in Babylon (Ezek 1). For the first time in Israel's sacred history since the Exodus, the vision of the divine glory is revealed *outside* of the Temple, of Jerusalem, and even of Israel. In the midst of national tragedy, the divine *kavod* has left the Temple but not entirely abandoned God's people. The glory is no longer bound to a physical Holy of Holies: it now follows Israel even in captivity. Ezekiel's vision of the *Merkavah* provides the conceptual framework for the theological development of realized eschatology—the transformation of the earthly Temple service into mystical rites believed to grant access

---

29. This despair is exemplified in the Book of Lamentations, which comes to grips with the desolate state of the virgin daughter of Zion: the former princess now become slave (Lam 1:1), abandoned by her former lovers (1:2, 19), with her former splendor now gone (1:6), and her sanctuary defiled by the nations (1:10). Most troubling is the fact that the Lord himself has done violence to his Tabernacle, spurning his altar and abandoning his sanctuary (2:6–7). Yet not all hope is lost. In the midst of desolation, the author expresses hope that "the Lord will not cast off forever" and in due time will "show compassion according to the multitude of his mercies" (Lam 3:31–32).

to celestial shrines, anticipating the unmediated encounter with God expected at the end of time.[30]

Ezekiel's *Merkavah* is relevant to our study not only because of its role as transitional locus of realized eschatology between Temple and eschaton, but also because it constitutes yet another biblical motif tying together the great moments of salvation history by connecting the Temple, Mount Sinai, and Garden of Eden.

## The Merkavah as Moveable Sanctuary

As the seat of the divine throne and glory of God (Ezek 1:28; 10:1–4), the *Merkavah* is a type of mobile, mystical Temple. Ezekiel identifies the four living creatures of the terrifying vision (Ezek 1:5–11) as *cherubim* (Ezek 10:1–22)—bearers and movers of the throne of God upon which rested the divine *kavod*, represented as a thick cloud and intense brightness. Although the living creatures of Ezekiel's chariot resemble the winged cherubim of the former Holy of Holies, these moveable four-faced and four-winged cherubim are much more complex than the silent, immobile figures that dwelt in the Tabernacle and Temple.[31] The *Merkavah* thus represents "a visionary, mystical transformation of the Holy of Holies, a composite of details from the Temple which expressed the very essence of the sacred precinct."[32] The *Merkavah* also anticipates Ezekiel's eschatological Temple: the prophet identifies the return of the divine glory into the future Temple—also adorned with numerous cherubim (41:18, 20, 25)—with his vision of the chariot at the River Chebar (Ezek 43:2–3).[33]

---

30. Cf. Elior, "From Earthly Temple to Heavenly Shrines," 242; Elior, *The Three Temples*, 31–34.

31. 1 Kgs 6:23–28; 8:6–8; 2 Chr 3:10–13. The idea that God majestically "rides" on cherubs recalls other biblical references to the deity "riding on the clouds." Cf. 1 Chr 28:18; Ps 18:10; 104:3–4; Isa 19:1; Hab 3:8; Patai, *The Hebrew Goddess*, 72–75.

32. Elior, *The Three Temples*, 63. *LevR* 2:7–8 identifies the glory of the Temple with the glory of Ezekiel's *Merkavah*.

33. Other references to Ezekiel's chariot and its identification with the heavenly Temple are found in Sir 49:8; 1 Enoch 14:8–25; Rev 4:2–11; *Vita Adae Evae* 25–29; *Apoc. Mos.* 33:1–5; *Apoc. Abr.* 18.

## The Merkavah as "Echo" of Mount Sinai

Scholars have also noted numerous parallels between the *Merkavah* and Sinai theophany. These are linked especially by the festival of *Shavuot* (the Feast of Weeks), which was the liturgical commemoration of the giving of the Torah and the nuptial covenant between God and Israel, perceived as a "pact or oath of betrothal, matrimony, and sacred conjugality in the supernal worlds."[34] We have seen an example of this commemoration of Sinai in *Pesikta de-Rab Kahana* 12 (expounding Exod 19:1–20:26), which was read during *Shavuot*. In addition to highlighting the nuptial dimension of the covenant, the midrash claims that "with the Holy One there came down 22,000 chariots, and each and every chariot was like the chariot which Ezekiel saw."[35] Thus, for *PRK*, Ezekiel's *Merkavah* is but a miniature echo of the Sinai revelation.

The correlation between Sinai and Ezekiel's *Merkavah* well pre-dates this rabbinic homily, for it is already evident in the biblical texts. As Elior summarizes:

> Like the Sinai Covenant . . . in which God came down on the mountain 'in a thick cloud' (Exod 19:9) accompanied by 'thunder and lightning and a dense cloud . . . smoke . . . and fire . . . thunder and flaming torches' (Exod 19:16, 18: 20:18)—Ezekiel too saw in his vision 'a huge cloud and flashing fire' (Ezek 1:4), 'burning coals of fire . . . suggestive of torches' as well as 'fire and lightning' (Ezek 1:13–14) and heavenly sounds (1:24–25). Like the vision of 'the God of Israel, under His feet . . . the likeness of a pavement of sapphire' (Exod 24:10) . . . —Ezekiel saw 'the semblance of a throne, in appearance like sapphire' (Ezek 1:26) and 'something like sapphire stone . . . resembling a throne' (Ezek 10:1). Like 'the Presence of the Lord . . . as a consuming fire' (Exod 24:17), Ezekiel saw . . . 'the semblance of the Presence of the Lord' as a 'surrounding radiance' (Ezek 1:28). Like the vision described by Moses as "the Lord our God has just shown us His majestic Presence, and we have heard his voice out of the fire' (Deut 5:21), Ezekiel, having seen 'the radiance of the Presence of the Lord' (Ezek 10:4), describes [it]': 'I saw a gleam as

34. Elior, *The Three Temples*, 157. On the Sinai-Merkavah tradition, cf. Halperin, *The Faces of the Chariot*, 16–19.

35. *PRK* 12:22. The tradition of chariots at Sinai is based on Ps 68:18. Cf. Halperin, *Faces of the Chariot*, 141–49. As Halperin notes (18), until today the Torah portion read at *Shavuot* is the passage describing the Sinai theophany (Exod 19), while the prophetic reading is Ezekiel's vision of the *Merkavah* (*m. Meg.* 3:5; *b. Meg.* 31a–b).

of amber – what looked like a fire . . . ; and from what appeared
as his loins down, I saw what looked like fire, and there was a
radiance all about him' (Ezek 1:27).[36]

The similarities between the two theophanies imply that Ezekiel's
vision is not solely a "mystical and visionary metamorphosis of the
Holy of Holies in Solomon's Temple" or "heavenly memorialization of
the ruined earthly Temple in a heavenly counterpart and an archetypal
cosmic model"; it is also a renewed experience of the Sinai theophany—a
mystical metamorphosis of the covenants concluded between heaven and
earth (on *Shavuot*), binding sacred time (covenant, oath, seven weeks)
and sacred place (Sinai, Merkavah, Temple, earthly and heavenly Holy of
Holies).[37] Thus, the God who formed a nuptial covenant with his people
at Sinai and dwelt with them in the Temple now continues to make his
presence known to them via the *Merkavah* vision, itself a foretaste of the
eternal heavenly sanctuary.[38]

## The Merkavah, Creation, and the Garden of Eden

As Levenson notes, the identification of the Temple with the world to
come was predictable because both realms are representative of a return
of humanity to its idyllic origin.[39] The idea of protology as prefigurement
of eschatology indeed became so established that the term "Garden of
Eden" came to be known as a synonym for the future age. Given the
association between protology and eschatology, it is not surprising that
the *Merkavah* motif also became associated with creation and paradise.
Wacholder has highlighted a number of links between Ezekiel's chariot
and the Genesis creation account. These include the heavens opening
up (Ezek 1:1; Gen 1:1), Ezekiel's repeated used of "and I looked" (cf. the
repeated use of "and God saw" in Gen 1), the wind (*ruach*), cloud, fire,
and brilliant radiance of Ezek 1:4, which may allude to the spirit (*ruach*)
hovering over the waters and the light in Gen 1:2–3, Ezekiel's "living

---

36. Elior, *The Three Temples*, 156. Cf. also Halperin, *The Faces of the Chariot*, 16–18.

37. Elior, *The Three Temples*, 157.

38. As Green suggests: "The merkavah voyager saw himself to be repeating the journey of Moses, who stepped off the mountaintop and entered into the heavenly chambers. The merkavah journey is a way in which the individual repeats the ascent of Moses." Green, *Keter*, 86.

39. Levenson, *Sinai and Zion*, 182–83.

creatures" (cf. the living creatures mentioned 6 times in Gen 1–2), the firmament (5 times in Ezek 1:22–26; 10:1; 9 times in Gen 1), and the divine voice of Ezek 1:24–25, at whose command the world was called into being.[40] These links imply that Ezekiel's vision of the *Merkavah* is an indirect vision of creation—not only an encounter with the One who created *ex nihilo* but also an insight into the very design of creation reflecting the Creator enthroned in glory upon the *Merkavah*.

Ancient Jewish interpreters located the divine chariot in the primeval Garden of Eden. The *Apocalypse of Moses* sees the eschaton as a return to Eden, where God had already "set up his throne" after Adam and Eve ate of the forbidden fruit (*Apoc. Mos.* 8:1).[41] The picture that emerges from this text is a blurring of the boundary between the earthly Garden of Eden and the heavenly paradise—called "third heaven"—with God's chariot and throne seemingly present in both locations. On the one hand, the throne of God and cherubim are situated by the earthly Tree of Life; on the other hand, the same throne and chariot are in heaven, receiving the souls of the deceased. Finally, a general return of humanity to the earthly Tree of Life is expected after the resurrection.[42]

40. Wacholder, "Creation in Ezekiel's Merkabah: Ezekiel 1 and Genesis 1."

41. The story narrates how Adam falls sick after the expulsion from Eden. He sends Eve and Seth back to paradise to bring him fruit from the tree that "flows with oil" that could heal him (*Apoc. Mos.* 9:3). But the archangel Michael announces that access to the tree will only be renewed at the end of times (13:2–4). Eve recalls how Adam became "alienated from the glory of God" (20:6) because of his sin. God then went up into paradise, "mounted on the chariot of his cherubim" to judge him, and "the throne of God was fixed where the Tree of Life was" (22:3–4). After having set the cherubim to guard the entrance to paradise, the Lord promised to Adam and Eve a renewed access to the Tree of Life at the time of the resurrection (28:4). Adam then took crocus, nard, calamus, and cinnamon, in order to offer sacrifice to God (29:3–6). At the moment of Adam's death, Eve sees "a chariot of light, born by four bright eagles, (and) it were impossible for any man born of woman to tell the glory of them or behold their face and angels going before the chariot." As the chariot and its seraphim come to a halt, Eve beholds "golden censers" and "all the angels with censers and frankincense came in haste to the incense-offering and blew upon it and the smoke of the incense veiled the firmaments" (33:2–4). Following this vision of the heavenly liturgy upon the *merkavah*, Adam is taken into "paradise," called "third heaven" (37:5). Yet his body remained "lying upon the earth in paradise" and he was buried there after being told that he would be transformed again to his former glory (39:1–2; 40:6).

42. Cf. the correlation between Eden, eschaton and Temple in 1 Enoch 24:1–25:7, where Enoch is shown the Tree of Life on a magnificent mountain whose summit is "like the throne of God." The fruit of the tree is inaccessible until the final judgment and consummation of time when it will be "given to the righteous and holy. Its fruit shall be for food to the elect: it shall be transplanted to the holy place, to the temple

To sum up, the *Merkavah* was not only a manifestation of realized eschatology. It also provided a conceptual, spiritual access to the heavenly Holy of Holies—even after the earthly sanctuary was no longer in existence. It offered faithful Jews the opportunity to mystically experience anew the Sinai theophany, celebrated at *Shavuot* as the betrothal between God and Israel. It even transported the believer back to the Garden of Eden at the dawn of creation, which was at the same time identified with the heavenly world to come. Thus, the *Merkavah* provided ancient Jews with a theological framework grounded in salvation history in which they could mystically experience the spiritual marriage with God, where protology was joined with eschatology.

## Sanctuary in Exile: Community and Man as Temple

### Community as Temple

The awesome, mystical vision of the *Merkavah* was perhaps a bit much for average pious Jew. Fortunately for common mortals, for whom such lofty visionary metamorphoses were out of reach, the *Merkavah* was not the only means of communion with God. Ezekiel had also spoken of a "sanctuary in exile"—that the Lord would be a "little sanctuary" for Israel in the countries in which they were scattered (Ezek 11:16). The prophet thus announces not only the future building of an eschatological Temple (Ezek 40–48) but also the edification of an *anthropological temple* whereby the Lord would give a "new heart" to Israel and put his own Spirit within them (Ezek 36:26–27). Ezekiel uses strong temple language to describe this eternal covenant by which he would establish his sanctuary among his people:

> I will make a covenant of peace with them; it shall be an ever-
> lasting covenant with them; I will establish them and multiply
> them, and I will set My sanctuary in their midst forevermore.
> My dwelling place shall be with them, and I will be their God,
> and they shall be My people. Then the nations will know that

---

of the Lord, the Eternal King (1 Enoch 25:5). The protology-eschatology correlation is also found in *T. Lev.*, which portrays heaven as a temple (3:4–8; 5:1) and announces that at the time of the messianic priest "the heavens shall be opened, and from the temple of glory shall come upon him sanctification." This priest will "open the gates of paradise and shall remove the threatening sword against Adam. And he shall give to the saints to eat from the tree of life, and the spirit of holiness shall be on them" (18:6, 10–11; cf. Briggs, *Jewish Temple Imagery*, 128–131). Cf. Rev 22:1–3.

I am the LORD who sanctifies Israel, when My sanctuary is in their midst forevermore.[43]

In this sense, also, Ezekiel is revolutionary because he paves the way for the concept of the community of believers as temple that will become characteristic of the Dead Sea sect and of Paul.[44] This is another form of realized eschatology, one that we might designate as "anthropological eschatology." It is a transitional, mystical state between temple and eschaton—the anticipated experience *now* in the life of the community of that glorious communion with the Lord that was previously dependent upon the physical temple and is still to be fully disclosed at the end of time.

## Man as Temple and Microcosm

The idea of the community as temple further developed into the concept of the individual believer as temple. This reflects a process of gradual personalization and "contraction" of the seat of the divine presence, going from the Temple building, to the community of the elect, to the heart of the believer. The identification *man = temple* eventually became combined with the *temple = microcosm* symbolism, resulting in the equation *man = temple = microcosm*. These ideas begin to emerge in Second Temple writings, come to fruition in Philo and Paul, and become quite detailed in later rabbinic writings. One later midrash states, for example, that "the Temple corresponds to the whole world and to the creation of man who is a small world."[45]

We have seen that for Philo, the Temple is a shadow of the visible cosmos, which in turn is a shadow of incorporeal reality, and the *Logos* is high priest of the temple of the cosmos. Yet the Alexandrian does not limit the role of priesthood and sanctuary to Israel's high priest; he also extends it to every person, explaining that man was made to be "an abode

---

43. Ezek 37:26–28. Cf. also Ezek 43:7. Other post-exilic prophets refer to God's promise of dwelling among His people in Zion and sanctifying them in a spiritual Temple (cf. Joel 3:17; Zech 2:10).

44. On the community as Temple, cf. 1QS 8:4–9; 9:3–7; 11:8; 4QFlor 1:6; 1 Cor 3:16–17; 6:19; 2 Cor 6:16; Eph 2:21; 4 Ezra 9:38–10:54. Cf. Gärtner, *The Temple and the Community,* 16–46; McKelvey, *The New Temple,* 46–53; Kerr, *The Temple of Jesus' Body,* 54–57; 296–98; Coloe, *God Dwells With Us,* 167–171; Corriveau, "Temple, Holiness, and the Liturgy of Life," 149; Briggs, *Jewish Temple Imagery,* 147–190.

45. *Midrash Tanhuma,* Pequde 3. See Patai, *Man and Temple,* 113–17; McKelvey, *The New Temple,* 53–55.

or sacred temple for a reasonable soul."[46] Elsewhere, Philo depicts the rational soul as a temple, and man as the priest who ministers within his own human sanctuary and represents the universe.[47] This shows that for Philo, a person and the universe participate in a "micro-macrocosmic" relationship.[48] When one considers this alongside Philo's nuptial symbolism, in which God joins himself to men via his surrogate Wisdom, one arrives at a convincing anthropological and mystical version of the (human) Holy of Holies as nuptial chamber.

We have observed a remarkable transformation of the eschatological motif, from the hope of the prophets for the future reign of God on earth, to the dramatic breaking forth in time of the divine Presence in Ezekiel's *Merkavah*, to the imparting of the same presence to the believing community, to its mystical infusion into the soul of the devout believer. At every stage, it seems, the eschaton "draws nearer" to man. One might say that the eschatological perspective between the time of the prophets and the late Second Temple period becomes progressively less distant and more present—going from a future to a realized, anthropological eschatology. This realized anthropological eschatology, whereby man can enter into nuptial communion with

46. *On the Creation of the World* 137. On Philo's Logos, cf. Barker, *The Gate of Heaven*, 115–118.

47. "For there are, as it seems, two temples belonging to God; one being this world, in which the high priest is the divine Logos, his own firstborn son. The other is the rational soul, the priest of which is the real true man, the copy of whom, perceptible to the senses, is he who performs his paternal vows and sacrifices, to whom it is enjoined to put on the aforesaid tunic, the representation of the universal heaven, in order that the world may join with the man in offering sacrifice, and that the man may likewise co-operate with the universe" (*On Dreams* 1:215). Elsewhere, Philo explains that the Temple of the soul, called the "earthly habitation of the invisible God" is to be prepared for the divinity's indwelling through knowledge and the virtues: "Since, therefore, he invisibly enters into this region of the soul, let us prepare that place in the best way the case admits of, to be an abode worthy of God . . . what sort of habitation ought we to prepare for the King of kings, for God the ruler of the whole universe . . . we call the invisible soul the terrestrial habitation of the invisible God . . . but that the house may be firm and beautiful, let a good disposition and knowledge be laid as its foundations, and on these foundations let the virtues be built up in union with good actions" (*On the Cherubim* 98–101).

48. This motif resurfaces in other texts. In 2 Enoch 30:8–10, 13, a midrash on the creation of man, Adam's identification with the universe is seen in his being formed out of seven elements of nature: his flesh from the earth, his blood from the dew, his eyes from the sun, his bones from stone, his intelligence from the swiftness of the angels and from cloud, his veins and his hair from the grass of the earth, and his soul from God's breath. Scroggs, *The Last Adam*, 113–14.

God here and now in this life, continues to be developed in the rabbinic interpretation of the Song of Songs and in wisdom literature.

# II

# Communion with God
# through Love and Wisdom

## 5

# The Mystery of Love

### *The Song of Songs as Journey to God*

## The Song of Songs and its Allegorical Interpretation

IN PART I, WE HAVE PROVIDED numerous examples demonstrating how the Song of Songs was interpreted allegorically to represent the love between God and Israel. When did this type of allegorical interpretation begin? Though it is difficult to trace back its origins, a few clues indicate that it long preceded Rabbi Akiva's declaration that the Song is the "Holy of Holies" of Scripture. First, the apocryphal book of 4 Ezra (1st century A.D.) uses some of the Song's language to refer to Israel as "lily" (5:24), "dove" (5:26) and (in some manuscripts) "bride" (7:26)—hinting at an allegorical reading of the Song. Second, the influence of the Canticle on passages in the New Testament, where the Canticle's lover is identified with Jesus and the beloved with the Church, also testifies to a first century allegorical interpretation of the Song.[1] Third, the presence of fragments of the Canticle among the Dead Sea Scrolls also points to its religious interpretation among the members of the Qumran sect.[2] Finally, some

1. Cf. Matt 9:14–15; 25:1–13; Mark 2:18–20; Luke 5:33–35; John 3:29 and chapters 7–8 below.

2. Alexander ("The Song of Songs as Historical Allegory," 15 n. 3.) writes that the presence the Song among the DSS "suggests that already by the first century BCE the book was being read allegorically, since it is hardly conceivable, given the religious outlook of the group behind the Scrolls, that they would have read the text literally."

scholars have argued that the very inclusion of the Canticle into the canon of Scripture assumes its allegorical reading. As Paschal Parente remarks:

> It is exactly its spiritual and allegorical interpretation that has vindicated to the Canticle of Canticles a divine origin and a place among the *canonical* books in both Jewish and Christian tradition. Otherwise, how could a book be considered as divinely inspired for our instruction and edification in which the name of God is never mentioned and no religious or supernatural idea ever seems to occur? How could the Canticle of Canticles be numbered among the sacred books of both the Synagogue and the Christian Church if it were to be understood simply in its literal sense as an epithalamium, a melodramatic interpretation of the delights and anxieties of the wedded love of Solomon and Pharaoh's daughter or, perhaps, a country maiden?[3]

This is a fair question: how can one explain the presence of this erotic love song in the canon of Scripture unless the ancients viewed it as a sacred text that mysteriously reflected God's love for his people? Although the origins of the Song's allegorical reading remain obscure, we know that it soon became the "center of gravity" for both rabbinic and patristic nuptial symbolism.

Early commentaries associating the Song's romantic verses with the history of Israel paved the way for the later emergence of complete systematic Jewish allegorical expositions of the Canticle.[4] We have seen that some rabbinic texts attribute a nuptial meaning to events in Israel's history by associating these events with occasional verses from the Canticle. Such is the case with *Genesis Rabbah* (focused on Genesis), the *Mekhilta* (focused on Exodus), and *Sifre Devarim* (focused on Deuteronomy). Other rabbinic compilations achieve a similar result by a reverse process, commenting primarily on the Song of Songs and associating its verses with events from Israel's history. Texts like the Midrash

---

3. Parente, "The Canticle of Canticles in Mystical Theology," 144. Feuillet ("Le Cantique des Cantiques et la tradition biblique," 706–733), also argues that the Song of Songs reflects Israel's biblical and prophetic tradition: the bridegroom (God) is portrayed as king and shepherd; the bride wishes that he were her brother and teacher; she is associated with the bridegroom's flock and compared to the city of Jerusalem, to a land and to a garden. Feuillet also notes that the Canticle's themes of sleep, vigilance, awakening, and finding and seeking all find parallels in the prophetic literature.

4. Cf. Green, "The Children in Egypt and the Theophany at the Sea"; "The Song of Songs in Early Jewish Mysticism"; "Shekhinah, the Virgin Mary, and the Song of Songs."

*Canticles Rabbah* and the *Targum Canticles* thus reread and reinterpret the entire Song of Songs as the story of the romance between God and Israel, played out through the various moments of the nation's history. In the present chapter, we first briefly recapitulate how the Song of Songs and its Midrash evokes the key moments of salvation history. We then look at the text that most systematically reads the Song as the history of Israel: *Targum Canticles.*

## Song of Songs as Journey through Salvation History

### The Song of Songs as Return to Eden

There is a natural connection between the Song of Songs and the Garden of Eden. The Song is set in a mysterious garden (Cant 4:12–5:1; 6:2) that carries many echoes of Eden: The former paradise was lost through disobedience and sin; in the Canticle it is regained through love. Landy has argued that "the Song constitutes an inversion of the Genesis narrative" in which man rediscovers the Paradise lost in Eden.[5] Both gardens are secluded and inaccessible; both relate to a tree and its fruit (Cant 2:3; 8:5). In Genesis, the Tree of Knowledge and the Tree of Life stand in opposition to each other; in the Song they are reunited. In Genesis, knowledge is death; in the Song, knowledge is life. Genesis presents a world where man was naked and unashamed; the Canticle describes a return to this world.[6] The Song's fountain of living waters (4:15) recall the rivers of Eden; a multitude of animals are present in both gardens; death is excluded from both places; and the beloved herself becomes the Garden of Eden in the Song of Songs (4:12, 5:1). In short, Gen 2–3 begins with the unity of Adam and Eve and ends in their division and exile; in the Song, lover and beloved are reunited.[7] These textual connections demonstrate that the

---

5. Landy, *Paradoxes of Paradise*, 172; Landy, "The Song of Songs and the Garden of Eden," 524.

6. Landy, *Paradoxes of Paradise*, 214.

7. Landy writes: "The detailed correspondence of thematic material is so extensive that the Song constitutes an inversion of the Genesis narrative . . . Both texts find their complement in the other, and, moreover, imply the other. The Genesis myth points outside the garden; the Song goes back to it. Their opposition conceals a hidden identity, for the Song is not merely a commentary on the Garden of Eden, but a reenactment, almost a hallucination of it." *Paradoxes of Paradise*, 172.

rabbinic identification of the Song's "garden" with the *Shekhinah's* bridal chamber and original home in Eden is well supported by the Song itself.[8]

## The Song of Songs "Given" at Sinai

As mentioned in the introduction, some rabbis believed that the Song was "said"—that is, *divinely given*—to Israel at Mount Sinai. We have seen how the rabbis spare no effort in pointing to the Exodus and Sinai as the setting *par excellence* of the love between God and his people. For *Canticles Rabbah*, the romance of the Song of Songs mystically reveals God's nuptial covenant with Israel formed at Sinai: The Shulamite's passionate longing, "*let him kiss me with the kisses of his mouth*" is a metaphor for Israel asking to receive God's Torah and commandments—also portrayed as his best *wine* (*CantR* 1:2). Her "*darkness*" points to the sin of the golden calf (1:5); the fragrance of her nard is either the stench of that same sin or Israel's obedience response to the covenant (1:12). The "*rose of Sharon*" is Israel sitting in the shadow of her beloved "*as an apple tree*"—God—who brings her to the "*house of wine*"—Sinai—where she enjoys his *sweet fruit* and *banner of love*—the words of the Torah (2:1–4). The lover standing *behind our wall* and *gazing through the windows* is God at Sinai (2:9), while the *dove in the clefts of the rock* is Israel standing before the mountain (2:14). These metaphors lead to the conclusion that the *day of [Solomon's] espousals* is the day when Israel received the Torah at Sinai (3:11).

## The Song of Songs as Sanctuary and God's Dwelling

Other sages believed that God gave the Song to Israel in either the Tent of Meeting or the Temple—a view that follows from their understanding of the sanctuary as the liturgical actualization of Sinai. It is possible that the author of the Canticle alludes to the Temple as the place of union between lover and beloved: Scholars have proposed that the description of the bridegroom in Cant 5:10–16 is a veiled description of Solomon's Temple.[9] *Canticles Rabbah* clearly depicts the sanctuary

8. Cf. *PRK* 1:1; *CantR* 5:1 §1.

9. E.g. the lover's head of gold points to the gold of the Holy of Holies (1 Kgs 6:20–21; 2 Chr 3:8); his wavy locks (LXX: "like palms") to the palms decorating the sanctuary (1 Kgs 6:18, 29, 32, 35); his eyes "like springs of water" to the water of the

as a bridal chamber in which the *Shekhinah* dwelt and enjoyed Israel's offerings (*CantR* 1:2). The Midrash reinterprets images from the Song—such as the green *couch* (1:16), the *chamber of her who conceived me* (3:4), the *palanquin* (3:9), or *Lebanon* (4:8)—as descriptions of the sanctuary, and the *dove in the clefts of the rock* as Israel in the shelter of the Tent of Meeting and Temple (2:14). Particularly rich is the rabbinic interpretation of Cant 4:16 ("*Awake, O north wind, and come, O south wind! Blow upon my garden, let its spices flow. Let my beloved come to his garden and eat its choicest fruits*"). The sages interpret the "*north wind*" as the burnt offerings killed on the north side of the altar, and the "*south wind*" as the peace offerings slaughtered on the south side. "*My garden*" refers to the Tent or Temple; "*let its spices flow*" alludes to the incense of spices offered in the sanctuary; and "*let my beloved come to his garden and eat his delicious fruits*" is Israel's invitation to the *Shekhinah* to enter the sanctuary and receive the sacrifices. The lover's exclamation "*I have come into my garden*" (5:1) is thus God entering the Tabernacle. Accordingly, the Midrash's ensuing exposition of Cant 5:1 refers to God's response to Israel's sacrificial liturgy: "*I have gathered my myrrh with my spice*" refers to God receiving with delight the incense and frankincense rising from the sanctuary; "*I have eaten my honeycomb with my honey*" speaks of the burnt-offerings; "*I have drunk my wine with my milk*" refers to the drink-offerings. The Midrash then reinterprets the Song's exhortation to *eat* and *drink* as God's invitation to Moses and Aaron, Nadab and Abihu to feast while on the top of Mount Sinai (Exod 24:11).[10]

## The Song of Songs as Israel's Final Redemption

Finally, human love in the Song overcomes all obstacles and endures beyond the grave; it is "strong as death" (Cant 8:6). The Midrash, accordingly, reads it as the story of God's enduring love that will steadfastly accompany Israel until the nation's final redemption. Israel's longing for the *kisses of his mouth* will only be fully satisfied in the world to come when

---

brazen sea (1 Kgs 7:23–26; 2 Chr 4:2–5); his lips like "lilies" to the flowers on the Temple's walls (1 Kgs 6:29) and top of the pillars in the shape of lilies (1 Kgs 7:22); his appearance like the cedars of Lebanon to the boards of the Temple, made of cedar of Lebanon (1 Kgs 6:9–18). Robert, *Le Cantique des Cantiques*, 48–49; Feuillet, "Le Cantique des Cantiques et la tradition biblique," 716–18.

10. Cf. *PRK* 1:1.

God fulfills the promises of the prophets and writes the Torah on their hearts (*CantR* 1:2). Only then will she fully shed the Shulamite's darkness and possess her loveliness (1:5). Only then will she fully blossom as the *rose of Sharon*, more fully than she bloomed at the Passover in Egypt, at the Red Sea, and at Mount Sinai (2:1). For now, she must be patient: The adjuration to the daughters of Jerusalem to "*not stir up nor awaken love until it pleases*" is an exhortation to Israel not to rebel against the yoke of foreign dominations nor attempt to return from exile by force—for this will be the role of the King Messiah (2:7). The lover *leaping upon the mountains like a gazelle* refers to God leaping over the great moments of the Exodus (Egypt, the Red Sea and Sinai) and forward to the future redemption (2:8–9). The messianic age will be the blossoming springtime of love (2:10–13) when it is finally appropriate to stir up and awaken love.

## The Song as Israel's History: The Targum on Canticles

### Introduction

The Targum on the Song of Songs is a *tour de force*. Although not the first work that allegorically associates the events of Israel's history with the verses of the Song, it is the first to draw out Israel's historical narrative as the "overarching structure for understanding the entire book of the Song of Songs from beginning to end,"[11] systematically translating the universal experience of human love into the particular events of Israel's history. In other words, the Targum rewrites the Song of Songs as the history of Israel. Presenting the Garden of Eden, Mount Sinai, the Jerusalem Temple, and the Messianic Age as the privileged moments of communion between God and his people, the Targum represents the crystallization of the nuptial interpretation developed in earlier rabbinic texts.

The Targum is the story of the divine presence, the *Shekhinah*, who accompanies God's people throughout history. The *Shekhinah* is the manifestation of the divinity on earth, united with Israel in a tender nuptial union (1:16) as long as they remain faithful to God's commandments. She guides, nourishes, and protects Israel (1:4; 2:1–2), ensures her fruitfulness and multiplication (1:16), and even banishes demons (4:6). The presence of the *Shekhinah* is likened to a return to the Garden of Eden (2:1). She was present at Mount Sinai (1:13; 2:3; 3:1–2) and accompanied

---

11. Menn, "Targum of the Song of Songs and the Dynamics of Historical Allegory," 424.

Israel during the wilderness wanderings, appearing as the pillar of cloud or fire (1:4, 16) and dwelling in the Tabernacle (1:5; 3:2–4). She dwells in the Temple, between the cherubim (3:10; 4:6; 5:1; 6:3, 11; 8:14), but when Israel sins or is exiled, she withdraws (2:2; 5:3, 6; 6:1; 7:11) to heaven, where she originated (3:1; 5:3, 8:14).

Written from the perspective of the exile of Edom—the Roman exile of the Jews that followed the destruction of the Second Temple in 70 A.D.—the Targum describes God's relationship with Israel as it progresses through the pivotal periods of the nation's history. The text could be outlined as follows:

1. Preamble, including the Midrash of the Ten Songs and an opening benediction (1:1–2)

2. The Exodus, including the Passover, the crossing of the Red Sea, the giving of the law at Sinai, the wilderness wanderings, and the conquest of the land (1:3–3:6)

3. First account (1:3–8); (b) Second account (1:9–2:7); (c) Third account (2:8–3:6)

4. The First Temple Period (3:7–5:1)

5. The Babylonian Exile (5:2–6:1)

6. The Second Temple Period (6:2–7:10)

7. The Exile of Edom (7:11–14)

8. The Messianic Age (8:1–12)

9. Peroration (8:13–14) [12]

## Midrash of the Ten Songs

The historical perspective of the marriage between God and Israel is introduced at the outset with the "Midrash of the Ten Songs," a long

---

12. Alexander (*Targum of Canticles*, 13, 15) outlines the Targum differently to emphasize the thrice-recurring pattern of Israel's estrangement from God, reconciliation, and communion, with three exiles (Egypt, Babylon, and Edom), three exoduses (under Moses, Cyrus, and the Messiah), culminating in three Jewish States (under Solomon, the Hasmoneans, and the Messiah): 1. From the Exile of Egypt to King Solomon (1:3–5:1); 2. From the Babylonian Exile to the Hasmonean period (5:2–7:11); 3. From the Exile of Edom to the Messiah's Coming (7:12–8:12).

exposition of Cant 1:1 and adaptation of an existing midrashic tradition.[13]
This Midrash lists ten songs that were "spoken in this world" by the great
figures of Israel's history, from Adam to the Messiah. Among them, the
Canticle is the ninth song, sung by Solomon and called "the best of them
all." This indicates that the Targum's narrative will be historical, spanning
from creation to consummation, from Adam to the Messianic Age, from
the Garden of Eden to the final redemption from Exile.

## Exodus and Mount Sinai

Following the prologue, the first scene of the Targum (1:2–3:6) is set at
the time of the Exodus, which is described in three accounts. Each "back-
tracks" from the preceding one, opening with an earlier scene: The first
begins at Mount Sinai; the second, at the Red Sea; and the third, in Egypt
at the Passover. In all three accounts, God declares his love for his bride
by means of the Torah and promises that his abiding presence will remain
with her in the Tabernacle as they set out towards the Promised Land.

### First Account of the Exodus

The first account of the Exodus opens with the longing words of the
Shulamite imploring the beloved: "*Let him kiss me with the kisses of his
mouth*" (1:2). For the targumist, the beloved's kisses that Israel longs
for are the words of the Torah, "*better than wine,*" that God lovingly
spoke to Israel.[14] The young maidens who love him in return (1:3) are
the righteous Israelites who follow the path of God's goodness revealed
on the mount. The divine Lover expresses his love by actively guiding,
protecting and providing for his bride: The Song's king who brings the
maiden to his chambers (1:4) is the "*Shekhinah* of the Lord of the World"
appearing as pillar of cloud or fire and guiding his bride Israel to the base
of Mount Sinai. Given that Sinai is the great romantic moment between
God and his people, it is no wonder that Israel is eager for the encounter.
The Targum rewrites the Shulamite's longing for her lover ("*draw me after
you; let us run. The king has brought me into his chambers. We will exult
and rejoice in you; we will extol your love more than wine; rightly do they
love you*") as Israel's longing for God's appearance:

13. *Mekh Shirata* 1. Cf. Alexander, *The Targum of Canticles*, 206–209.

14. Cf. *Sifre Deut* 48; *CantR* 1:2a §2; 1:2b §3.

> Draw us after You, and we will run in the way of Your good-
> ness. Bring us near to the foot of Mount Sinai, and give us Your
> Torah from out of Your heavenly treasury, and we will be glad
> and rejoice in the twenty-two letters in which it is written. We
> will remember them and love Your divinity and shun the idols
> of the nations. And all the righteous who do what is right before
> You will fear You and love Your commandments.[15]

At Sinai, God grants Israel the *kisses of his mouth*, that is, the Torah
from the "heavenly treasury." Sinai is established as the meeting point
between heaven and earth—the moment when the celestial and impen-
etrable Law becomes expressed in human language as a gift of divine
love. But the sublime quickly makes way for betrayal and disgrace: the
Shulamite who is "dark but lovely" (1:5) represents Israel's "darkness"
when they worshiped the golden calf, and her "loveliness" when they
repented and "the splendor of their faces' glory increased like the angels."
They were forgiven on account of the Tabernacle's curtains (the "*curtains
of Solomon*") which caused the presence of the *Shekhinah* to dwell among
them.

## Second Account of the Exodus

The second account of the Exodus begins with Cant 1:9, which the Targum
interprets as the departure of the Israelites from Egypt. The Shulamite,
like *a mare among Pharaoh's chariots*, evokes the Egyptian chariots that
pursued the Israelites at the Red Sea.[16] After they cross the sea and set
out into the wilderness, the Shulamite's cheeks, *lovely with ornaments*
(1:10), are a figure of the Torah's precepts that are to bridle the jaws of
the Israelites so that they do not stray from the right path, and her neck
adorned with *strings of jewels* represents the yoke of God's commands on
Israel's neck. The Shulamite's *ornaments of gold* (1:11) are the tablets of
stone, "hewn from the sapphire of [God's] glorious throne, bright as pure
gold," and her *studs of silver* are the Ten Commandments, "refined more
than silver."[17] The *king at his couch* (or table) (1:12) alludes to Moses, the
mediator between the God and his bride who went up to the firmament
to get the heavenly tablets of the Law. The king's banquet may also refer

---

15. *TgCant* 1:4 (Alexander, 81).
16. Cf. *Mekh Beshallaḥ* 7; *CantR* 1:9 §4–5.
17. Cf. *CantR* 1:11 §1.

to the covenantal meal that Moses, Aaron, Nadab, Abihu and the seventy elders ate when they saw God (Exod 24:9–11) and he solemnly sealed his covenant with Israel. For the targumist, the Shulamite's fragrance of nard symbolizes the idolatrous stench of the golden calf worship that took place in the Israelite camp below while the covenantal ceremony and meal were being celebrated on the mount above.[18]

In this context, the Tabernacle is described again as the remedy for Israel's sins. The building of the Tabernacle and Ark, together with the offering of sacrifices, provides atonement for the sin of the calf. The Shulamite's designation of her beloved as *"a cluster of henna blooms in the vineyards of Ein Gedi"* (1:14) points to the grape clusters that the sons of Aaron picked from the vineyards of Ein Gedi, providing the wine libations that accompanied the atoning sacrifices. The Tabernacle—built, consecrated and set in operation at the foot of Horeb—extends the theophany into time. As Israel's nuptial chamber, it not only provides atonement but also assures the Israelites of the continued presence of the *Shekhinah* after they leave the Holy Mount behind them.

Although the targumist's narrative of Israel's history generally moves linearly from the Exodus to the Messianic age, he also adds flashbacks to the original home of mankind—the Garden of Eden—as the idyllic prototype for the love between God and Israel. This occurs in 1:16–2:5. The Targum identifies the lovers' green (or leafy) couch (1:16) with the sanctuary, home of the *Shekhinah* and source of great fruitfulness deriving from Israel's union with Her.[19] The "green couch" is compared to a fruitful marriage bed out of which springs an abundance of new life as long as the *Shekhinah* dwells upon it:

> You cause love to dwell in the bridal bed so that our children
> are many on the earth, and we increase and multiply like a tree
> planted by a spring of water, whose leaves are beautiful and
> whose fruit is abundant.

The "houses" of the two lovers, made with beams of cedar and rafters of cypress (1:17), refer to two future Temples—of Solomon and of the Messiah—whose beams will be from the cedars of the Garden of Eden and whose pillars will be from fir, juniper, and cypress.[20] The covenantal

---

18. Cf. *Mekh Baḥodesh* 3; *CantR* 1:12 §1–2.

19. Cf. *CantR* 1:16 §2–3.

20. According to *GenR* 15.1 (on Gen 2:8) cedars were among the trees of Eden, created for the sake of the Temple.

language of procreation borrowed from the creation narrative (Gen 1:28), juxtaposed with the mention of Eden, Sinai, the Temple, and the days of the Messiah, points to the targumist's interest in situating the love between God and Israel from the origins of history until its consummation.

At the same time, the fruit of Eden is enjoyed at Sinai, for it is Sinai that enables Israel to return to an Eden-like state. The bride's self-identification as the "*rose of the Sharon*" and "*lily of the valleys*" (Cant 2:1) stands for the Assembly of Israel joyfully proclaiming that the presence of the *Shekhinah* at Sinai makes her "like the narcissus fresh from the Garden of Eden," and her actions "beautiful like the rose in the plain of the Garden of Eden." Israel is the Canticle's *lily among brambles* (2:2), and God is *as an apple tree among the trees of the wood* (2:3), "praised among the angels when he revealed himself on Mount Sinai" and gave the Torah to his people.[21] His "*shadow*" is the shadow of the *Shekhinah*, and his fruit (sweet to his bride's taste) stands for the commandments of Torah (like spice to Israel's palate) whose observance stores up rewards for her in the world to come. The Targum further interprets the king's "*house of wine*" (2:4) as the house of study at Sinai, and "*his banner over me*" is the banner of his commandments that Israel received with love.[22] The Torah and commandments are not only inebriating as wine; they are sweet as the apples of the Garden of Eden (2:5)—a generous gift of divine love that grants the delights of Eden to those who taste them (cf. Prov 9:5). The Torah, moreover, is another means of actualizing Sinai: Since the Law was given at Sinai—the place of the revelation of the *Shekhinah*—studying the Torah ushers in her presence. By associating the words of Torah with the apples of the Garden of Eden, the Targum views Torah study not only as an actualization of Sinai but also as the way back to the lost paradise.[23] The Torah also plays a cosmic role: the world is based on its words, and like the Temple service, it sustains all creation (2:5). Thus, the lush, intimate setting of the garden and its feast of delights for the Shulamite and her lover in Cant 1:16–2:5 represents the marriage between God and Israel situated in Eden, at Sinai, in the Temple, and at the eschaton.

---

21. Cf. *Sifre Deut* 355; *CantR* 2:3 §1–3.

22. Cf. *CantR* 2:4 §1.

23. *Pirkei Avot* 3:7 states that the *Shekhinah* resides with those who study Torah, which is identified with Wisdom and thus called "a Tree of Life to those who take hold of it" (cf. *m. Avot* 6:7; Prov 3:18).

### Third Account of the Exodus

The third account of the Exodus begins in Cant 2:8. The *"voice of the beloved"* is the glory of the Lord revealed to Moses in the burning bush at Mount Horeb, sending him back to Egypt to deliver Israel. God "skipped" to the appointed end of the time of Egyptian slavery because of the merits of the patriarchs and matriarchs. In the next verse (2:9), the Song's lover is the same divine glory revealed on the night of Passover who, when *standing behind the wall* and *looking through the lattice*, saw the blood of the Passover sacrifice and circumcision that protected Israel from the destroying angel and initiated their redemption.[24] The lover's tender invitation, calling out *"arise, my love, my dove, my fair one, and come away; for behold, the winter is past, the rain is over and gone"* (2:10–11) is God calling Israel to depart from the Egyptian slavery, for their time of her servitude has ended. The *flowers appearing on the earth* (2:12) are Moses and Aaron performing miracles in Egypt, the *time of pruning* is the time for the slaying of the firstborn sons, and the *voice of the turtledove* is the voice of the Holy Spirit of redemption. The *fig tree* (2:13) is another metaphor for Israel, now singing the Song at the Sea. As in the *Mekhilta*, the *"dove in the clefts of the rock"* (2:14) symbolizes Israel trapped between a hawk and a snake (the Egyptians and the Red Sea); her "sweet voice" is her prayers, and her "lovely face" her good deeds.[25] In the next verse (2:15), the Targum associates the Song's disturbing *"foxes"* with wicked Amalek waging war against Israel.[26]

Canticle 3:1 reveals an abrupt change of setting: The Shulamite lies in bed, alone at night, seeking the one she loves (3:1). The Targum interprets this scene as Israel left in darkness after the calf incident. Consequently, the clouds of glory departed from them and the "crown of holiness" given to them at Sinai was removed. The woman going into the city to look for her lover (3:2) refers to the Israelites going to the Tent of Meeting built by Moses (Exod 33:7–11) to seek instruction from God. When the Shulamite finally finds her man and brings him into the house of her mother (3:4), this is interpreted as the *Shekhinah* entering and dwelling into the Tabernacle (Exod 40:33–34). The depiction of the Tabernacle as the chamber into which the Shulamite brings her lover means that it is a marriage chamber as much as it is a place of worship, where sacrifices

---

24. Cf. *Mekh Pisḥa* 7; *CantR* 2:9 §1.

25. Cf. *Mekh Beshallaḥ* 3; *CantR* 2:14 §2–4, 6.

26. Cf. *Mekh Shirata* 6; *CantR* 2:15 §1.

are offered to God and the Torah is studied. The Tabernacle is thus not only the extension of Sinai into time but also the wedding chamber of God and Israel where they continue to consummate the marriage that was sealed at Sinai.

## The First Temple

As the successor of the Tent of Meeting, the Temple is the direct link to Sinai and home of the *Shekhinah* for future generations of Israelites. The entire section of the Targum from 3:7 to 5:1 focuses on Solomon's Temple, pictured as Solomon's bed (3:7) and palanquin built from the wood of Lebanon (3:9). Lebanon is a symbolic name for the Temple, built with cedar from Lebanon (1 Kgs 5:6–36) and overlaid with pure gold (1 Kgs 6:21). The Targum turns the parts of the palanquin (3:10) into a description of the most important cultic items of the sanctuary: The palanquin's pillars represent the Ark of the Covenant, "the pillar of the world." The two tablets of the Law are said to be more precious than the palanquin's silver and gold; its purple seat alludes to the blue and purple curtain in the sanctuary; and the "inside" of the palanquin, "*paved with love*," refers to the space between the cherubim on the mercy-seat where the *Shekhinah* dwells. The description of these sacred objects and the divine love dwelling between the cherubim is a preparation for the "*day of [Solomon's] wedding*" (3:11), pointing to the day of the Temple's dedication (1 Kgs 8:63–66), which for the targumist is a sacred marriage associated with the Feast of Tabernacles.

For the Targum, the exclamation "*behold, you are fair, my love*" (4:1) is spoken by God, praising the Assembly of Israel and its leaders who became beautiful after Solomon offered a thousand burnt offerings in the Temple (1 Kgs 8:62–64; 2 Chr 7:7). The Targum's allegorical description of the Temple service as a romance between lovers highlights the work of the priests and Levites. These are represented as the beloved's white teeth (4:2), while the prayer of the high priest on Yom Kippur is portrayed as the Shulamite's "*lips like a strand of scarlet*" (4:3). The *mountain of myrrh* and *hill of frankincense* (4:6) stand for the glorious *Shekhinah* dwelling in the Temple and the smell of incense and spices which causes demons (the Canticle's "shadows") to flee. In Cant 4:8, the beloved's invitation to his spouse to come with him *from* Lebanon (read by the targumist as going "*to* Lebanon") is interpreted as God inviting Israel, his chaste bride, to enter the Temple ("Lebanon") with him.[27]

The Targum's interpretation of Cant 4:12–16 is rich in Edenic allusions. In 4:12, the bride, called a *locked garden*, represents the married women of Israel, while the image of a *fountain sealed* depicts the virgins sealed like the Garden of Eden, from which humanity was excluded. The Canticle's spring is associated with the Edenic spring of living water which according to the Targum "issued from beneath the Tree." The Canticle's locked garden and sealed fountain, alluding to the faithful love between bridegroom and bride and excluding all potential rivals, become an image of the chastity of Israel's women, reminiscent of the Edenic paradise which excluded all evil. Cant 4:13–14 describes the Shulamite as an "*orchard of pomegranates with all choicest fruits, fragrant henna with nard, nard and saffron, calamus and cinnamon, with all trees of frankincense, myrrh and aloes, with all chief spices.*" For the targumist, these are the "sweet spices of the Garden of Eden"[28] and the spices used to make the anointing oil in the Temple (Exod 30:23–25). Then, the "*fountain of gardens, a well of living waters, and streams from Lebanon*" (4:15) are rendered as the waters of Shiloah (cf. Isa 8:6) irrigating the land of Israel for the sake of those immersed with the study of Torah,[29] and by merit of the water libations in the Temple.[30]

In Cant 4:16, the Shulamite invites her lover in no uncertain terms: "*Awake, O north wind, and come, O south wind! Blow upon my garden, let its spices flow. Let my beloved come to his garden and eat its choicest fruits.*" The Targum takes this to be Israel inviting God to take up residence in his Temple. The north and south winds refer to the furnishings of the sanctuary—the table of showbread (on the north side of the sanctuary) and the menorah (on the south side). The "blowing upon the garden" alludes to the offering of sacrifices, the beloved's spices are the spice incense rising from the altar (Exod 40:22–27), and the eating of the fruit is God consuming the Temple offerings. The invitation to the beloved to "*come to his garden and eat its choicest fruits*" is thus Israel inviting God, her

---

27. Cf. *Mekh Pisḥa* 14; *CantR* 4:8 §1.

28. Cf. 1 Enoch 30, 32; Apoc. Mos 29:3–6, where Adam takes the ingredients of the Temple incense from Paradise.

29. For the imagery of Torah as well of living waters, cf. Isa 55:1; Jer 2:13; *GenR* 41:9; 66:1; 69:5; 97:3.

30. Cf. *m. Sukkah* 4:9.

beloved, to enter the Temple and favorably receive the sacrifices of his people.[31]

The divine lover obliges in Cant 5:1 ("*I have come to my garden, my sister, my bride . . .*"). For the targumist, the lover entering his "garden" is God entering the Temple which Israel—his "sister" and "chaste bride"—has built for him (1 Kgs 8:10–13). There he receives the people's incense of spices ("*my myrrh with my spice*"), consumed burnt offerings and holy sacrifices ("*my honeycomb with my honey*") (2 Chr 7:1), and libations of red and white wine ("*my wine with my milk*"). The invitation to his friends to eat and drink is an invitation to the priests to come and eat the offerings (Exod 29:32; Lev 8:31–32). The Song's intimate union between beloved and bride thus becomes a metaphor for God's communion with Israel as a cultic banquet in the Temple.[32] When read in context with 4:12–13, the association of the Garden with the Temple suggests another connection: The beloved's entrance into "*his garden*" (his spouse) not only refers to God entering his bridal chamber (the Temple) to consume the sacrifices and receive the incense; it also implies that the union of lover and beloved is tantamount to a return to Eden.

## The Second Temple

Following a schematic description of the Babylonian Exile based upon Cant 5:2–6:1, the Targum dedicates Cant 6:2–7:10 to the Second Temple, portrayed with the same imagery as the First. It is introduced as the beloved man's "*gardens*" in 6:2, while his "*beds of spices*" are the sacrifices and spice incense that God favorably receives. The Shulamite's total surrender to her lover ("*I am my beloved's, and my beloved is mine*") is an expression of Israel's worship of the Lord who "*feeds his flock among the lilies*" (6:3)—again interpreted as a cultic nuptial feast where God feeds his people with delicacies in the Temple. As in the First Temple, the beloved's "*white teeth*" represent the priests and Levites bringing offerings to the Lord (6:6). The Shulamite, *lovely as Jerusalem* (6:4), is equated with the beauty of the Second Temple, which is also the "*garden of nuts*" inhabited by the *Shekhinah* (6:11)—possibly another allusion to Eden.

---

31. Cf. *GenR* 22:5; 34:9; *LevR* 9:6; *CantR* 1:2a §1; *PRK* 1:1.
32. Cf. *CantR* 5:1 §1; *PRK* 1:1.

## Eschatological Messianic Age

The Second Temple period comes to an end with the exile of Edom (7:11)—the Roman exile of 70 A.D. This new tragedy rekindles the hope of redemption and expectation of the Messiah who will rebuild the Temple in Jerusalem at the end of history. The eschatological hope, mentioned in passing throughout the text, becomes the main focus of attention from 7:11 to the end, when the King Messiah ushers in the final redemption. The eschatological perspective already appeared in the Targum's opening verses: The Torah was given at Mount Sinai so that the righteous may possess "this world and the world to come" (1:3). The coming of the Messiah is anticipated in the narrative on the Exodus (1:8), associated with the Song's "*shepherd's tent.*" Two Messiahs, the son of Ephraim and the son of David are symbolized by the two breasts of the Shulamite, almost identically in both sections on the First and Second Temples (4:5, 7:3).

The entire final section of the Targum is set in the Messianic Age. It is characterized by the permanent indwelling of the *Shekhinah* in Israel, described as the lovers' mutual belonging and passion for each other (7:10) after God has ingathered his people from the Exile of Edom and brought them back to Jerusalem where they offer burnt offerings and holy oblations (7:12). God tells the Messiah about the merits of the righteous (the *fragrance of mandrakes*) and the studies of the scholars (*choice fruits*) which have created the right conditions for redemption (7:13). The bride's longing that her beloved be "*like a brother who nursed at my mother's breasts*" (8:1) is an expression of Israel's love for the Messiah, where the "mother" is the Torah nourishing Israel as a mother nourishes her child.

In Cant 8:2, the Shulamite pledges to bring her lover into "*the house of my mother, she who used to teach me*" and give him "*spiced wine to drink, the juice of my pomegranate.*" For the Targum, this means that Israel will lead the Messiah-King into the Temple at the end of days, where he will teach her to walk in his ways. Together they will partake of the "Feast of Leviathan," which, according to Talmudic tradition, refers to the Messianic feast where the righteous will eat the flesh of the giant leviathan.[33] The spiced wine is the wine of the messianic banquet, preserved since the day the world was created "from pomegranates and fruits prepared for the righteous in the Garden of Eden."[34] Recalling that

33. Cf. *B. Baba Bathra* 74a. Cf. also 1QSa 2:11–12; Matt 26:29; 2 Bar 29:4; *b. Shabbat* 153a; *b. Hagigah* 14b.

34. Cf. *b. Berakhot* 34b; *b. Sanhedrin* 99a on the special Messianic drink.

"*the house of my mother*" previously referred to the desert Tabernacle (3:4), this verse therefore encompasses in a nutshell the history of the world, from the primordial Garden of Eden via the Exodus to the Messianic Temple and eschatological banquet. In Cant 8:3, the two hands of the beloved embracing his bride represent the *tefillin* and *mezuzah*, two important symbols of obedience and love towards the Torah providing the right conditions for redemption and protection from demons, as well as recalling the Passover and the destroyer that slayed the Egyptian firstborns (Exod 12:13, 23).[35]

Cant 8:5 asks: "*Who is that [woman] coming up from the wilderness, leaning upon her beloved?*" She responds: "*Under the apple tree I awakened you. There your mother was in labor with you.*" The Targum interprets this as the return from exile and resurrection of the dead, when the people of the earth will ask:

> What is the merit of this people that comes up from the earth in myriads upon myriads, as on the day when she came up from the wilderness to the land of Israel, and that delights in the love of her Lord as on the day when she appeared beneath Mount Sinai to receive the Torah?

The comparison of the Messianic ingathering and final resurrection with the Exodus is known from the prophets (Jer 23:7–8; Isa 52:12). The beloved's location *under the apple tree* signifies the place "beneath" Mount Sinai where Israel received the Torah. This confirms the double identification of the apple tree with Eden and Sinai seen above (2:3, 5). At the same time, the return from exile is a birthing process whereby "Zion, the mother of Israel, will give birth to her sons and Jerusalem will receive her exiles." The ingathering of the exiles in the Messianic Age and the final resurrection of the dead are therefore related to the Garden of Eden, the Exodus from Egypt, the revelation at Sinai, and Zion travailing and giving birth—a metaphor no doubt inspired by Isaiah's eschatological prophecy of Zion's "birth pangs of redemption" (Isa 54:1).

The language of love of Cant 8:6 ("*set me as a seal upon your heart . . .*") is Israel's plea to God that they may become as the seal of a ring on his heart and arm so that they may never again be exiled, thanks to his love that is "*strong as death.*" God responds favorably to their request, for just as "*many waters cannot quench love,*" so even if all the nations gather against Israel they could not quench God's love for his people (8:7), who

35. Cf. *CantR* 2:6 §1.

will find mercy in the eyes of the Lord through the words of Torah (8:10). A final reference to the bride sitting in *"the gardens"* (8:13) represents the Assembly of Israel sitting in the house of study, learning the words of the Law. Having taken his readers on a long journey across salvation history, the targumist pragmatically reminds them that the study of the Torah is *the* way for Jews to bring the exile to an end and rediscover the delights of Eden, renew and actualize the Sinai covenant, commune with the *Shekhinah* in the Temple, and usher in the great eschatological marriage between God and his people. In the last verse (8:14), spoken from the perspective of the Exile, the elders of the Assembly of Israel call upon God to flee from the polluted world and let his *Shekhinah* dwell in heaven above, looking upon Israel's affliction until the final redemption when he will bring them to the *"mountains of spices"*—the mountains of (heavenly?) Jerusalem—where priests will burn the incense of spices as an eternal offering to him.

## Summary: The Song as Romance between God and Israel

The Targum's masterful historical allegory of the Canticle transforms the lovers' passionate dialogue into the story of the romance between God and Israel through its highest peaks and lowest valleys. The idealized prototype of the divine-human love is the long-lost Garden of Eden, with its arousing odors of rich spices and sweet savors of abundant fruit. What humanity lost when Adam and Eve were expelled from Eden, Israel regained at Mount Sinai when God entered a nuptial covenant with his newly adopted people and bestowed on them the Torah as guarantee of his enduring faithfulness. The valley of tears, however, remains present throughout the nation's vicissitudes. If humanity's exile from Eden is only implicit in the Targum as the faint remembrance of the lost idyllic garden of love, Israel's long exile through history is real, beginning with the years of wandering in the wilderness. During this time, the Tabernacle remains the commemoration and actualization of Sinai and the sign of the *Shekhinah*'s loving presence among God's people. The building of Solomon's Temple on Mount Zion signifies not only the end of their wanderings and establishment of a permanent spiritual home; it also signifies the enduring presence of the Garden of Eden in the midst of Israel via the nuptial chamber in which God continues to lovingly dwell with his people. Even when the Temple is destroyed, all is not lost: the Torah remains Israel's connection with her divine Lover; its study ushers in the presence of the *Shekhinah* as they experienced it at Sinai and in the Temple. When the Jews return to Jerusalem and rebuild the Temple, the nation experiences a renewed romance with the *Shekhinah*, but it comes to an end with the exile of Edom. It is from the perspective of this exile that the Targum is written, longingly recalling the delights of Eden, the betrothal ceremony at Sinai, the intimacy of the Temple's bridal chamber, and forcefully reminding its readers that the Torah remains their only link with the glorious moments of the past. The study of the sacred books is the activity that sustains the enduring love between the divine Bridegroom and his human bride until it becomes again fully manifest in the great nuptial feast in the eschatological Temple of the Messianic Age.

# 6

# The Mystery of Wisdom

*Lady Wisdom's Banquet as Path to Love*

## The Quest for Wisdom as Divine Romance

THE WISDOM LITERATURE of the Bible BEARS a unique character. Whereas earlier wisdom books (such as Proverbs, Ecclesiastes, and Job) are largely detached from the historical tradition of Israel, later books (such as Sirach, Baruch, and the Wisdom of Solomon) tend to "Judaize" Wisdom and reintegrate her into the historical and religious traditions of Israel, so that she is depicted as present throughout the nation's history. This national particularism coexists with a wider universalism whereby Wisdom is seen as the inheritance of all humanity: On some occasions she is identified with Israel's Torah, while in other places she is thought of as the eternal, intelligent principle and source of the entire cosmos. In Proverbs, Wisdom is said to have a divine origin. Later, in the Wisdom of Solomon, she takes on the form of an emanation of God identified with the divine spirit. Moreover, in what some have called "the most striking personification in the entire Bible,"[1] divine Wisdom is personified as the figure of *Lady Wisdom*, a female hypostasis who takes on the traits of a mother or wife. Accordingly, the relationship of Lady Wisdom with men is described in nuptial language: her beauty is praised, she is desired and loved like a bride, she courts her followers, and she seductively invites

---

1. Murphy, *The Tree of Life*, 133.

them to eat at her table, promising them riches, honors, and abundant life.

Nuptial imagery in wisdom literature takes on a radically different shape from that of the prophets. Whereas in Hosea, Jeremiah, Ezekiel and Isaiah the male figure is always God and the female (as bride, virgin, mother, harlot, or adulteress) always Jerusalem or Israel, in the wisdom books these roles are reversed. Now, the female protagonist is the quasi-divine figure, Lady Wisdom, and the humans she courts are implicitly male. Moreover, God in a certain sense fades into the background. Instead of a direct nuptial relationship between the Lord and his people, Wisdom now acts as intermediary between God and humans. She is a "divine surrogate," mediating the role of the divinity who seeks communion with men, and in relationship with two different partners: she is the bride of both God and the wise man, resulting in what Zimmermann has called a "peculiar love triangle."[2] If such "love triangles" generally result in jealousy and discord in human relationships, this is not the case with the God-Wisdom-man triangle. Lady Wisdom' two relationships do not compete with one another. On the contrary, the love between God and Wisdom, becomes "the archetype of human love for Wisdom and of love in general."[3] In addition, the human protagonists are no longer viewed as one personalized, collective figure representing the entire people. The collectivity of Israel in the prophets gives way to the individuality of each person whom Wisdom invites to communion with her.

In this chapter, we study the figure of Lady Wisdom and her role in the history of Israel and of the world. We will begin with a brief survey of her features in the books of Proverbs, Baruch, and the Wisdom of Solomon. Next, we will dive into a deeper study of her complex role in the book of Sirach. Finally, we will sketch out a summative overview of Wisdom's wanderings through the history of Israel and of mankind.

## Meet Lady Wisdom

### Lady Wisdom's Banquet: Proverbs

The female personification of Wisdom appears for the first time in the book of Proverbs. On three occasions, Wisdom calls aloud outside and

2. Zimmermann, "The Love Triangle of Lady Wisdom," 244.
3. Zimmermann, "The Love Triangle of Lady Wisdom," 258.

in the streets, raising her voice in the open squares and exhorting simple ones and fools to give heed to her (Prov 1:20–33; 8:1–36; 9:1–6). The reader is encouraged to "love" and "embrace" her (Prov 4:6, 8). She speaks noble things: from her lips come what is right and her mouth utters truth (8:6–7). In her is found justice, prudence, knowledge and counsel (8:8–9; 12–16; 20) and her instruction is beyond price (8:10–11). In Proverbs, Wisdom is the first of God's creation. She claims that "the Lord acquired me at the beginning of his way" (8:22), and before anything else existed she was "brought forth" or "begotten" (8:25–29). She was thus already present at creation, standing beside God "like a master workman" (8:30); it was by her that the Lord founded the earth and established the heavens (3:19–20). In Prov 9:1–6, Lady Wisdom invites men to a sumptuous banquet. After having built her house, set up her seven pillars, slaughtered her beasts, mixed her wine, and set her table, she sends out her maids to invite all to come to her feast: "Come, eat of her bread and drink of the wine that I have mixed!" This invitation to pursue Wisdom and dine with her competes with that of her arch-rival, Dame Folly, represented as an adulteress who attempts to entice men by her charms (Prov 2:16–22; 5:1–20; 6:20–35; 7:5–27; 9:13–18). Whereas dishonor, destruction and death lie in wait behind Folly's temptations, truth, understanding and life are found at Wisdom's table.

Who—or *what*, ontologically—is the Lady Wisdom of Proverbs? Though she is of divine origin, intelligent, personal, loving, existing before creation and even playing a role in it, she remains nonetheless a created entity—perhaps the form in which the Lord makes himself present in the world, or the thoughts he expressed in creating the world.

## Wisdom as Torah and Mother: Baruch

Baruch is a short book that combines different genres, including historical, prophetic, and wisdom passages. Two major sections of the book are of interest to our study. The first is the hymn of praise of Wisdom (Bar 3:9–4:4); the second is the song of encouragement to Israel (4:5–5:9), where Jerusalem is depicted as an innocent mother and widow who mourns the loss of her children.

Bar 3:9–4:4, speaking to Israel in exile, takes up the motif of personalized Wisdom seen in Proverbs. Wisdom is a feminine "she."[4] Israel

---

4. Wisdom is called *phronesis* (3:9, 14, 18) or *sophia* (3:12, 23) in Baruch.

is in exile because they have "forsaken the fountain of Wisdom" which is the "way of God" (3:12–13). Borrowing a theme from Job (28:12–28), Baruch underlines the elusiveness of Wisdom who was not found by the powerful, the wealthy, and the strong (3:16–21), and was not heard of in foreign nations (3:22–23) or even known among the men of old in ancient Israel (3:24–28). Wisdom is seen as God's plan in creation, and no one knows the way to her except the Creator (3:29–35). At the height of this tension, the identity of wisdom is revealed. Despite her apparently ineffable and unreachable character, God has revealed to Israel the way to her. She has in fact "appeared upon earth and lived among men" as "the book of the commandment of God, and the law that endures forever. All who hold her fast will live, and those who forsake her will die" (3:36–4:1). Wisdom is thus identified with the Torah that was given at Sinai.

The second nuptial element of Baruch is found in the song of encouragement to Israel in the last section of the book (4:5–5:9). Here Lady Wisdom makes way for the return of personified Jerusalem as mourning mother and widow (cf. Isa 50:1; 54:4). Familiar prophetic images return of God as Father who raised Israel, and Jerusalem as mother who reared and nurtured them as her children (4:8, 11) but is now deprived of them. Her sons and daughters were sold to the foreign nations because they sacrificed to demons rather than to God (4:6–7). This passage, however, reveals a noticeable development from the personification of Jerusalem/Zion as seen in the prophets. In contrast to the nuptial passages in Hosea, Jeremiah, Ezekiel and Isaiah, where the mother and spouse is an unfaithful adulteress and the children pay the consequences through deportation and exile (Hos 2:6; Jer 31:15–22; Isa 49:20–23), in Baruch Jerusalem—distinct from her wayward children—remains pure and innocent, yet she is repudiated because of their fault (Bar 4:12).[5]

While the motif of the mother rejected because of the sins of her children appears in Isa 50:1, Isaiah says nothing about the innocence of the mother. For Baruch, however, this is a central theme and a theological novelty.[6] Grieving Jerusalem has no sins to confess. Her identity somehow transcends the individual Israelites and their faults. While in former times she nurtured her children with joy, Jerusalem is now "a widow and bereaved of many" (Bar 4:12). Although the widow analogy is not entirely consistent (her husband—God—has not died), it represents the

5. Infante, *Lo sposo e la sposa*, 63–64.

6. Contrast the guilt of Jerusalem and her responsibility for the exile in Lam 1:8, 9, 14, 18.

lonely woman's desolate state and loss of her sons and daughters (4:16). In the face of this desolation and exile of her children, the faithful mother exhorts them to endure their hardships with patience and trust that God will soon deliver them (4:21–29). At the same time, she intercedes before God on their behalf (4:20, 22). Hope for their salvation is inseparable from the expectation of a return from exile: mother Jerusalem is reassured that her sons will come back to her (4:23, 36–37; 5:5–6) in a glorious eschatological event that recalls the key nuptial texts of Isaiah: Jerusalem will take off the garment of her sorrow and affliction and "put on forever the beauty of the glory from God" along with "the robe of the righteousness of God" and "the diadem of the glory of the Everlasting" (5:1–2; cf. Isa 52:1; 61:3, 10).

## Loving Wisdom: The Wisdom of Solomon

Wisdom's divine origin, her female personification, and the love of the righteous for her are themes that continue to be developed in the Wisdom of Solomon, though with a distinctly Hellenistic flavor. Whereas in Proverbs Wisdom originated in God but was nonetheless created, here she is virtually identified with the deity: She is called "a breath of the power of God, and a pure emanation of the glory of the Almighty . . . a reflection of eternal light, a spotless mirror of the working of God, and an image of his goodness" (7:25–26). The nuptial element comes out strongly: The author, professing to be Solomon, writes that he "loved her more than health and beauty" (Wis 7:10). He is so enraptured by Lady Wisdom's beauty that he wishes to marry her: "I loved her and sought her from my youth, and I desired to take her for my bride, and I became a lover of her beauty" (8:2). Lady Wisdom shares in the very life of God, or "lives with him," and God loves her in return (8:3). This language of marital cohabitation implies that Wisdom is indeed God's wife. In imitation of God, therefore, Solomon determined to take Lady Wisdom to live with him (8:9). We see the crystallization of her role as mediating figure married to God in the heavenly realm while connected with the earthly realm as she invites men to marry her: "Intercourse with Sophia thus imitates God's union with her, and is the sage's personal *experience* of the Divine—revelation, salvation and divinization."[7]

---

7. Horsley, "Spiritual Marriage with Sophia," 34.

## Lady Wisdom's Journey through History in Sirach

Sirach echoes Proverbs in affirming that the Lord created Wisdom before all things (Sir 1:4, 7). The feminine personality of Wisdom (*sophia*) as mother and wife particularly shines through in this book. With tender motherly care she "exalts her sons and gives help to those who seek her" (4:11). Loving her is a source of life and abundance: "Whoever loves her loves life, and those who seek her early will be filled with joy" (4:12). Though at first her discipline seems "harsh to the uninstructed" (4:17; 6:20), in the end she will "gladden him, and will reveal her secrets to him" (4:18). Her wise followers "will wear her like a glorious robe, and put her on like a crown of gladness" (6:31), and so they are encouraged to encamp near her house and pitch their tent near her and thus "lodge in an excellent lodging place" (14:24-25). Lady Wisdom will come to meet the man who fears the Lord "like a mother, and like the wife of his youth she will welcome him" (15:2). As in Proverbs, communion with her is depicted as the sharing of a meal with her: "She will feed him with the bread of understanding and give him the water of wisdom to drink" (15:3). For this reason, men's souls remain thirsty when they refuse to draw near to her (51:24).

Lady Wisdom's song of praise in chapter 24 is the centerpiece of the book; it is also a text of great interest for our study because of its marked nuptial character. The poem, permeated with allusions to the Song of Songs, describes a personified Lady Wisdom who seductively invites men to join her in intimate communion so that they can "eat" and "drink" her. In addition, rich biblical imagery depicts Lady Wisdom as active throughout Israel's history: she is especially present in Eden, at Sinai, in the Temple, and at the end of days. We will proceed with a verse by verse exegesis of Sirach 24, divided into its main sections:

- Lady Wisdom's Origin and Universality (24:1–7)
- Lady Wisdom's Indwelling in Israel (24:8–12)
- Lady Wisdom, Trees and Spices (24:13–17)
- Lady Wisdom's Banquet (24:19–22)
- Lady Wisdom as the Torah Personified (24:23–34)

## Lady Wisdom's Origin and Universality (Sir 24:1–7)

The poem begins by announcing that Wisdom will "praise herself" and "glory in the midst of her people." Verse 2 adds: "In the assembly of the Most High she will open her mouth, and in the presence of his host she will glory." The personal character of Lady Wisdom is established through the anthropomorphic metaphor of her praising herself, opening her mouth to speak (cf. Prov 8:6–8), and glorying among "her people" and the "assembly of the Most High." While the assembly of the Most High and "his host" are no doubt the angelic attendants at God's throne, "her people" likely refers to the people of Israel.

Wisdom then begins her own song of praise, disclosing her origin in God and her universality. She "came forth from the mouth of the Most High and covered the earth like a mist" (24:3). Her origin from God's mouth suggests an identification with God's creative word. The fact that God created Wisdom "from eternity, in the beginning" (24:9) implies that she was present at the time of creation (cf. Prov 8:22–31). The scene with "mist" covering the earth is reminiscent of the dark chaos that reigned at the beginning of creation when "the Spirit of God was hovering over the face of the waters" (Gen 1:2) and God's word, indeed "coming out of his mouth," brought the universe into being (Gen 1:3).[8]

At that time, Wisdom dwelt in "high places" (Sir 24:4). Do these high places refer to heaven or to an earthly elevation? From the immediate context, one might think that Wisdom's dwelling is in heaven. But the "high places" could also be inspired by Prov 8:2, where Wisdom "takes her stand on the top of the high hill." This is no doubt a reference to the mountain of the Lord, the "holy hill of Zion" (Ps 2:6; 24:3) elsewhere identified as Jerusalem (Ps 48:1–2; Isa 2:2–3; Ezek 20:40), where the Temple stood. Given the central place of the sanctuary in Sir 24, perhaps Sirach alludes to *both* heavenly and earthly high places, since the Temple on God's holy hill was understood to be a replication of the sanctuary in heaven.[9] Wisdom's throne is located "in a pillar of cloud," which recalls the pillar of cloud that led the Israelites through the wilderness and rested above the sanctuary as sign of God's presence.[10] This would confirm the

---

8. Cf. Sheppard, *Wisdom as a Hermeneutical Construct*, 22–26.

9. Cf. Wis 9:8; Sheppard, *Wisdom as a Hermeneutical Construct*, 30.

10. Cf. Exod 13:21–22; 14:19, 24; 19:9; 33:9–10; 40:34–38; Num 12:5; 14:14; Deut 31:15; Ps 98:7.

double location of Wisdom's dwelling, both in heaven and on earth, with the cloud acting as bridge between the two realms.[11]

Verses 5–6 underline the cosmic universality of Wisdom, her ancient origins and omnipresence over all creation. She "made the circuit of the vault of heaven" and "walked in the depths of the abyss." The "vault of heaven" is identified in Job 22:14 as the place where God walks, and the "abyss" alludes to the "deep" that prevailed over the formless earth at creation (Gen 1:2; cf. Prov 8:24–28). Not only did Wisdom exist from the beginning: she is also present everywhere, "in the waves of the sea, in the whole earth" (cf. Prov 8:29) and "in every people and nation" (cf. Prov 8:15–16). Her total dominion is expressed by four polar dimensions encompassing the entire universe: vertically, the extremes of the heavens and the abyss; horizontally, the elements of the sea and the earth. Nevertheless, despite her omnipresence and cosmic universality, she sought a place where she could dwell and a "resting place" where she might lodge (24:7). This paradoxical wish serves as a bridge between the *universalism* of verses 3–6 and the *particularism* of verses 8–12. Lady Wisdom, infinite and eternal, boasts of her absolute rule over the whole universe in time and space. Yet this was somehow not satisfying to her, and she desired to make her home among one particular people, limiting herself in a kind of self-contraction bound by the limits of time and space. In a movement of descent and concentration, Wisdom is on a journey from heaven to earth, from the mouth of God to Israel.[12]

## Lady Wisdom's Indwelling in Israel (Sir 24:8–12)

Verses 8–17 depict the "earthly adventure" of Wisdom, or how she forsook her heavenly throne to come and dwell on earth. The first part (24:8–12) describes how Wisdom "contracted" herself from her eternal,

11. The idea of Wisdom sitting by God's throne in heaven and coming down to earth, and her identification with the cloud is also taken up in the Wisdom of Solomon: In Wis 10:17–19 it is Wisdom herself who led the Israelites out of Egypt, having become "a shelter to them by day and a starry flame through the night." She "brought them over the Red Sea and through deep waters," and she even is the one who drowned the Egyptians.

12. Compare a similar but less successful journey in 1 Enoch 42:1–2: "Wisdom found no place where she might dwell; then a dwelling-place was assigned her in the heavens. Wisdom went forth to make her dwelling among the children of men, and found no dwelling-place: Wisdom returned to her place, and took her seat among the angels."

universal reign over all creation to the limited realm of Israel. The second part (24:13–17) illustrates this sojourn among her people on earth.

In verse 8, God assigns a place for Wisdom's "tent" (skene), commanding her to make her dwelling (kataskeno, i.e. to "tabernacle" or "pitch a tent") in Israel. The use of these terms evokes the *mishkan*, the desert Tabernacle in which dwelt God's *Shekhinah*—his divine presence on earth (cf. Exod 25:8–9; 33:7–11). After highlighting Wisdom's eternal existence, spanning from the beginning to the end of creation (24:9), Sirach describes the conclusion of her process of self-contraction as she settles in the Tabernacle: "In the holy tabernacle (skene) I ministered before him, and so I was established in Zion" (24:10). Which tabernacle is this? Although the term *skene* seems to refer to the Tent of Meeting, the location of Wisdom's tent in "Israel" and "Zion" points to the Jerusalem Temple. Yet the mention of Wisdom's eternal existence and her liturgical ministry before the Creator also indicates that the "holy tabernacle" could be the eternal, heavenly sanctuary. The ambiguity is possibly intentional given that the earthly tabernacle was modeled on the heavenly blueprint that God showed to Moses (Exod 25:8–9). Wisdom thus ministered before God in the heavenly Tabernacle and continued the same liturgical function after she came to dwell in Israel's tent.

Following her remarkable self-contraction from heaven's glory to the frail earthly tabernacle, Wisdom begins to geographically expand her domain again, stretching out from the sanctuary to Zion to the whole people and land of Israel. Jerusalem—the "beloved city" (24:11)—is the "resting place" that Wisdom previously sought and which has now become her dominion. Wisdom further spreads out her presence from Jerusalem to all of Israel, taking root in "an honored people (or "glorified" people), in the portion of the Lord, who is their inheritance" (24:12). This glory of God's people could well be a veiled reference to the divine glory that prevailed in the dwelling place of God.[13]

The first twelve verses of Sirach 24 thus situate Lady Wisdom at the beginning of creation, at the time of the Exodus under the form of the pillar of cloud, in the Tabernacle and/or Temple on Mount Zion, and at the end of times. Her omnipresence is further developed in the following verses.

---

13. Exod 24:16–17; 40:34–35; 1 Kgs 8:10–11; 2 Chr 5:14; 2 Chr 7:1–3.

## Lady Wisdom, Trees and Spices (Sir 24:13–17)

Having announced that Wisdom "took root" in an honored people (24:12), Sirach now describes the trees that grew out of this root. He does so with a rich description of lush vegetation and spices evoking not only the flora of the land of Israel but also the language of the Song of Songs and our four nuptial moments of the Garden of Eden, Mount Sinai, the Temple, and the end of days.

> [13] I grew tall like a cedar in Lebanon,
> and like a cypress on the heights of Hermon.
> [14] I grew tall like a palm tree in Ein-Gedi,
> and like rose plants in Jericho;
> like a beautiful olive tree in the field,
> and like a plane tree I grew tall.
> [15] Like cassia [cinnamon] and camel's thorn I gave forth the aroma of spices,
> and like choice myrrh I spread a pleasant odor,
> like galbanum, onycha, and stacte,
> and like the fragrance of frankincense in the tabernacle.
> [16] Like a terebinth I spread out my branches,
> and my branches are glorious and graceful.
> [17] Like a vine I caused loveliness to bud,
> and my blossoms became glorious and abundant fruit. (Sir 24:13–17)

### Trees and Spices in the Song of Songs

Sirach's metaphors of trees and flowers (and their geographical locations) echo the Canticle's passionate language of love.[14] In the Song of Songs, the beams of the lovers' house are made of cedar, their rafters are of cypress (Cant 1:17), Solomon's palanquin is made out of wood of Lebanon (3:9), and the beloved invites his bride to come out with him from Lebanon and from the top of Hermon (4:8).[15] Ein Gedi is another common geographical feature between both texts (Cant 1:14). Also noteworthy is Sirach's mention of the terebinth (24:16), which may allude to the frequent association of this tree with cultic prostitution at idol shrines.[16] Wisdom's appearance like "rose plants" (Sir 24:14) and her "blossoms" (Sir 24:17)

14. On the Canticle's nature imagery, cf. Munro, *Spikenard and Saffron*, 80–87.

15. See Cant 4:11; 5:15 for other references to Lebanon.

16. On cultic role of the terebinth, oak or "green tree," cf. Gen 35:4; Jos 24:26; Isa 1:29–30; 57:5; Jer 2:20; Hos 4:13. Cf. Gilbert, "L'éloge de la Sagesse (Siracide 24)," 333; Skehan and Di Lella, *The Wisdom of Ben Sira*, 335.

also recalls the abundant imagery of flowers in the Song of Songs, where the bride is called "rose of Sharon" and "lily of the valleys" (2:1–2), and her lover pastures his flock "among the lilies" (2:16; 6:2–3).

Lady Wisdom's rich aroma of spices in Sirach 24:15 also echoes the Song's fragrances.[17] The Canticle opens mentioning the fragrance of the beloved's good ointments (1:3), for he is to his bride a "bag" or "mountain" of myrrh and a "hill of frankincense" (1:13; 4:6). His cheeks are "like beds of spices, yielding fragrance," his lips are lilies "distilling liquid myrrh" (5:13), and Solomon's couch is "perfumed with myrrh and frankincense" (3:6). As for the bride, the scent of her perfumes is better than all spices (4:10), and her hands and fingers drip with myrrh (5:5). In the Song's most fragrant passage, the bride's "garden" is said to be spiced with "henna with nard, nard and saffron, calamus and cinnamon, with all trees of frankincense, myrrh and aloes, with all chief spices" (Cant 4:13–14)—revealing three spices common to Sirach 24 (cinnamon, frankincense, and myrrh). The lover also portrays the consummation of their union as gathering his myrrh with his spice (5:1; also 6:2).[18]

Both Sirach 24 and the Canticle also speak of a budding vine and fruit harvest. In the Song, the beloved goes down to the valley of nuts to see the "fruits of the valley" and "whether the vine had budded" (Cant 6:11). Lady Wisdom seems to answer his query as she says: "Like a vine I caused loveliness to bud, and my blossoms became glorious and abundant fruit" (Sir 24:17). These parallels indicate that communion with Lady Wisdom is an encounter of love, evocative of the love expressed in the Song of Songs.

### Trees and Spices in Eden

The imagery of trees, flowers and spices in Sir 24:13–17 also evokes the Edenic paradise: Lady Wisdom, located in Jerusalem, thrives luxuriously like the original garden. Sheppard has noted the implications of this imagery: "The city of Jerusalem has been painted as wonderland of Wisdom, a restoration of the Garden of Eden." To partake of her, therefore, "is to experience paradise."[19] Although Genesis 2–3 tells us virtually

---

17. Cf. Munro, *Spikenard and Saffron*, 48–52.

18. The use of spices in a nuptial or sexual context is also seen in Ps 45:8; Prov 7:17; Esther 2:12.

19. Sheppard, *Wisdom as a Hermeneutical Construct*, 52–53.

nothing about the trees in Eden, Ezekiel 31:8–9 provides more details about its vegetation. Three of the trees described there are the same as those in Sirach 24, namely cedars, cypress (or fir) trees, and plane trees. Ezekiel also describes the mass of branches of the cedar in Eden in a way that recalls Sirach's Wisdom spreading out her "glorious and graceful" branches (Sir 24:16).

Lady Wisdom's aroma of spices also connects Sirach 24 and the Garden of Eden. Though the Bible does not attest to the presence of spices in Eden, this ancient tradition is found elsewhere. The Book of Jubilees relates how Adam, on the day when he was expelled from Eden, brought an offering to God which included three of spices associated with Lady Wisdom in Sirach 24:

> And on that day on which Adam went forth from the Garden, he offered as a sweet savour an offering, *frankincense, galbanum, and stacte*, and spices in the morning with the rising of the sun from the day when he covered his shame.[20]

A similar tradition is found in the Apocalypse of Moses, where Adam is granted permission to take spices with him from Eden so that he may offer sacrifices to God at a future time:

> And [Adam] said to [the angels]: "Behold, you cast me out. I pray you, allow me to take away fragrant herbs from paradise, so that I may offer an offering to God after I have gone out of paradise that he hear me . . . " And God commanded it to be so for Adam that he might take sweet spices and seeds for his food. And as the angels let him go, he took four kinds: *crocus and nard and calamus and cinnamon* and the other seeds for his food: and, after taking these, he went out of paradise.[21]

Cinnamon is another of Wisdom's aromas mentioned in Sirach 24, and all four spices mentioned here appear in Cant 4:14. With this Edenic background in mind, Sirach is undoubtedly recalling the tradition of Proverbs where Wisdom is called "a Tree of Life to those who take hold of her" (Prov 3:18).[22] Sirach possibly intends to contrast Wisdom's life-giving "glorious and abundant fruit" (24:17) with the fruit of the tree of the knowledge of good and evil, which was "pleasant to the eyes and a

---

20. Jubilees 3:27. See also 1 Enoch 24–32 for another witness to the presence of spices and fragrances in Eden.

21. *Apoc. Mos.* 29:3–6; cf. *Vita Adae Evae* 43:3.

22. Fournier-Bidoz believes that the entire description of verses 13–17 describes the growth of the tree of Eden. Fournier-Bidoz, "L'arbre et la demeure," 8.

tree desirable to make one wise" (Gen 3:6). Whereas the attractive fruit
of Eden deceptively promised wisdom but only brought bitter alienation
and death, Wisdom "satisfies men with her fruits; she fills their whole
house with desirable goods, and their storehouses with her produce" (Sir
1:14–15).

### Trees and Spices in the Tabernacle

Sirach 24's trees and spices also evoke the Tabernacle—and thus Mount
Sinai, where it was originally built. Cedar wood was used for some of
the sacrificial rituals (Num 19:6) and branches of palm trees were an
essential element for the celebration of Sukkot (Lev 23:40). Olive oil
was burned in the menorah (Exod 27:20; Lev 24:2); it was also one of
the ingredients of the anointing oil (Exod 30:24–25) and was offered
with sacrifices (Exod 29:2,40; Lev 2:1–7, 15–16). The menorah was also
beautifully ornamented with flowers (Exod 25:31–34; 37:19). As for the
aroma of spices given forth by Wisdom in Sirach 24:15, all of them served
a liturgical purpose in the Tabernacle. Myrrh, cinnamon, cassia, and olive
oil were the ingredients of the holy oil used to anoint the Tabernacle
(Exod 30:23–30). The other four spices—stacte, onycha, galbanum and
frankincense—were used to make the incense offered in the sanctuary
(Exod 30:34–36). Both the holy anointing oil and incense were strictly
reserved for liturgical purposes; using them for any profane purpose was
severely prohibited (Exod 30:31–33). The spice imagery thus confirms
not only that Wisdom is present in the tabernacle; she also performs a
sacred liturgical service in its inner sanctuary.

### Trees and Spices in the Jerusalem Temple

The trees and spices of Sirach 24 also evoke the Jerusalem Temple. Four
of the trees described in Sir 24:13–17—cedar, cypress, olive, and palm
trees—played an important role in the Temple, either as raw material for
its construction, in its liturgical service, or in the sanctuary's artwork.
Cedar and cypress were the chief woods imported by Hyram of Tyre
from Lebanon (1 Kgs 5:6, 8, 10) for the Temple's construction: It was
lined with beams and boards of cedar (1 Kgs 6:9, 15, 18, 36), and its floor
and doors were covered with cypress (1 Kgs 6:14, 34). Both the cherubim
(1 Kgs 6:23) and doors of the sanctuary (1 Kgs 6:31–33) were made

of olive wood. Olive oil was used as in the Tabernacle—as fuel for the menorah, as ingredient for the anointing oil, and offered with sacrifices. Palm trees were artistically carved over the walls and doors of the sanctuary along with flowers and cherubim (1 Kgs 6:29, 32, 35; Ezek 41:20, 25). The Temple area was profusely decorated with flowers, including the menorah (1 Kgs 7:49), the capitals on top of the pillars (1 Kgs 7:19, 22), and the brim of the molten sea of bronze (1 Kgs 7:26, 2 Chr 4:5).

## Eschatological Fruitfulness

Sirach's trees and plants also recall the eschatological vision depicted by the prophets, who use similar vegetation to describe the messianic age. Isaiah, speaking of deliverance from Babylon, announces that the cypress trees and cedars of Lebanon will rejoice over Israel (Isa 14:8), and "Lebanon shall be turned into a fruitful field" (Isa 29:17) when Israel returns to God. In the future glory of Zion "the glory of Lebanon shall be given to it" (Isa 35:1–2) and "instead of the thorn shall come up the cypress tree" (Isa 55:13). In one rich verse that bears many affinities with Sirach 24, God proclaims: "I will put in the wilderness the cedar, the acacia, the myrtle, and the olive; I will set in the desert the cypress, the plane and the pine together" (Isa 41:19). Elsewhere, Isaiah adds an explicit mention of the sanctuary: "The glory of Lebanon shall come to you, the cypress, the plane, and the pine, to beautify the place of my sanctuary" (Isa 60:13).

One prophetic eschatological passage, Hosea 14:5–9, displays so many common features with Sirach 24 that it seems nearly certain that Ben Sira had it in mind as he wrote his text. These include the lily, Lebanon, spreading branches, the beautiful olive tree, the growing vine, the cypress tree, abundant fruit, and wisdom:

> I will be as the dew to Israel; he shall blossom as the lily (Sir 24:17; Cant 2:1–2,16), he shall strike root like Lebanon (Sir 24:13; Cant 3:9); his shoots shall spread out (Sir 24:16); his beauty shall be like the olive (Sir 24:14), and his fragrance like Lebanon (Cant 4:11). They shall return and dwell beneath my shadow, they shall flourish as a garden; they shall blossom as the vine (Sir 24:17; Cant 2:13), their fragrance shall be like the wine (Cant 1:2, 4) of Lebanon . . . I am like an evergreen cypress (Sir 24:13; Cant 1:17), from me comes your fruit (Sir 24:17; Cant 2:3). Whoever is wise (Sir 24:1), let him understand these things; whoever is discerning, let him know them. (Hos 14:5–9)

Palm trees are also an important feature of Ezekiel's eschatological Temple.[23] Flowers are expected to spring forth in Isaiah's future age, when a "branch" shall grow out of the roots of Jesse (11:1) and "the desert shall rejoice and blossom as the rose" (35:1–2). "As the earth brings forth its bud, as the garden causes the things that are sown in it to spring forth, so the Lord GOD will cause righteousness and praise to spring forth before all the nations" (61:11). The prophets announce that the messianic age will be like the former Garden of Eden: Isaiah prophesies that the Lord will make Zion's wilderness "like Eden, and her desert like the garden of the Lord" (Isa 51:3), and the righteous will be like "a watered garden, and like a spring of water, whose waters do not fail" (Isa 58:11, cf. Jer 31:12, Ezek 36:35).

In summary, Sirach 24's imaginative description of Lady Wisdom—rich in allusions to the Song of Songs—affirms Wisdom's role as the bride of wisdom seekers. The same imagery also evokes the Garden of Eden, the Tabernacle and Temple, and the messianic age announced by the prophets. In other words, pursuing Lady Wisdom is not only a romantic endeavor; it is also a return to Eden by means of Temple worship, which anticipates God's future restoration of creation at the end of days.

## Lady Wisdom's Banquet (24:19–22)

In Sirach 24:19–22, Wisdom invites "those who desire her" to come to a sumptuous banquet to eat their fill of her produce. This recalls the feast of Proverbs 9:1–6, where Wisdom "slaughtered her meat," "mixed her wine," "furnished her table," and invited the simple to come eat her bread and drink of her wine (cf. Sir 1:16–17; 6:19; 15:2–3). Eating and feasting are frequently associated with romantic love; as the universal sign of covenantal bond, fellowship and communion, eating and feasting also took place in Eden, on Mount Sinai, in the Temple, and are expected to continue at the end of days.

### Love Feast

Just as Lady Wisdom gives food and drink to her followers, so the bride of the Canticle also feeds her beloved and gives him to drink (Cant 5:1; 7:13; 8:2). In Sirach, Wisdom adds: "For the remembrance of me is

23. Ezek 40:16, 22, 26, 31, 34, 37; 41:18–20, 25–26.

sweeter than honey, and my inheritance sweeter than the honeycomb"
(Sir 24:20). The sweet taste of Lady Wisdom not only echoes Ps 19:10,
where the judgments of the Lord are deemed "sweeter than the honey
and the honeycomb,"[24] but again the Song of Songs: The lips of the Canticle's spouse have the same taste as Wisdom, dripping of honeycomb,
with honey and milk under her tongue (4:11). At the climax of the Song,
the Shulamite invites her lover to "come to his garden, and eat its choicest
fruits" (4:16); when he does so, he exclaims: "I have eaten my honeycomb
with my honey" (5:1).[25]

## Feasting in Eden

Lady Wisdom's invitation to her banquet evokes a return to the lost paradise of Eden. Although the brief description of Eden in Genesis does not
mention any eating, the presence of "every tree that is pleasing to the sight
and good for food" (Gen 2:9) and the invitation to "freely eat of every
tree of the garden"—including the Tree of Life (Gen 2:16)—assumes that
Adam and Eve were in a place of many delights to the palate. Apocryphal
texts confirm the tradition of feasting in Eden. 1 Enoch recalls that the
Tree of Life had "a fragrant smell more than all fragrant spices" and its
fruit was "like bunches of a date palm tree" (1 Enoch 24:4). In 2 Enoch,
the paradise of Eden is a place of abundant and exquisite foods, including sweet-smelling fruit from sweet-flowering trees and "foods borne
bubbling with fragrant exhalation" (2 Enoch 8:2), with "produce from all
fruits" growing from the Tree of Life (8:4), and springs of honey, milk, oil
and wine (8:5). In the Apocalypse of Moses (6:1–2), Seth recalls the fruits
of paradise that his father Adam used to eat, and he proposes to return
there to bring some back. Eve later recalls to her son how Adam gathered
fragrant herbs and "seeds for his food" just before his expulsion from
paradise to ensure his future survival (*Apoc. Mos.* 29:6).

In light of these texts, Lady Wisdom's offer to "eat your fill of my
produce" sounds like an invitation to partake of the lost fruit of the Tree
of Life and thus to taste of Wisdom's immortality. This stands in contrast
to the serpent's invitation to eat the fruit of the tree of knowledge of good
and evil that brought suffering and death to mankind. Wisdom says that

---

24. Cf. also Ps 119:103; Prov 24:13–14.

25. Other associations of honey with nuptial love are found in Ezek 16:13, 19 and
Prov 5:3.

he who obeys her "will not be put to shame" (Sir 24:22). Before their fall, Adam and Eve were naked and not ashamed (Gen 2:25). Eve mistakenly thought that eating of the forbidden fruit would make them wise, but as a result they hid from God in shame (Gen 3:7–11). Now Lady Wisdom reverses this picture, restoring true wisdom and taking away the shame of the fall.[26]

### Covenantal Feast at Sinai

Given Sirach's identification of Lady Wisdom with the Torah (Sir 24:23), her banquet could also allude to the covenantal feast celebrated between God and Israel at Sinai, when Moses mediated to the people the ordinances of the Torah, the people solemnly vowed their obedience by offering burnt-offerings and peace-offerings, and Moses, Aaron, Nadab, Abihu and the seventy elders went up on the mountain where they "beheld God, and they ate and drank" (Exod 24:3–9). The covenantal ceremony was immediately followed by the coming of the glory of the Lord in the form of the cloud (24:15–18). The close intimacy between God and Israel at Sinai (later understood as their betrothal) was enacted by the sacrifice of whole-burnt offerings (signifying complete dedication between the two parties) and the offering and eating of peace offerings (signifying intimate communion between them), creating an experience where "man, literally, and God, figuratively, partake of the same feast."[27]

### Partaking of the Sacrifices in the Temple

The sacrifices instituted at Sinai were perpetuated in the liturgy of the Tabernacle and Temple, which included among its offerings the presentation of loaves and wine (Exod 29:23; 40–41; Lev 23:13). Just as the covenantal eating and drinking on Sinai celebrated the people's bond with God, so the eating of the sacrifices offered in the Temple was a covenantal meal that solemnly ritualized the alliance between them. In other words, communion with God is attained by "eating with him." In light of Lady Wisdom's liturgical service in the sanctuary (Sir 24:10), her invitation to "eat and drink" her likely alludes to the same worship, its communal

---

26. Wisdom's promise that "those who work in me will not sin" is also a possible allusion to a reversal of the curse on work brought by sin in the Garden (Gen 3:17–19). Fletcher-Louis, "The Cosmology of P," 91.

27. Berman, *The Temple*, 130.

sacrifices and drink libations, and perhaps also the bread of the presence in the sanctuary.[28]

## Eschatological Banquet

Abundant covenantal eating and feasting are also expected in the messianic age. Isaiah announces that the Lord will offer to all people "a feast of fat things, a feast of choice wines—of fat things full of marrow, of choice wines well refined." (Isa 25:6). God will establish his everlasting covenant with Israel within the context of a sumptuous banquet: "Come, buy and eat! Come, buy wine and milk without money and without price . . . eat what is good, and delight yourselves in rich food . . . and I will make with you an everlasting covenant . . . " (Isa 55:1–3).[29] Jeremiah also envisions the final redemption as a time of abundant feasting, when Israel "shall come and sing aloud on the height of Zion, and they shall be radiant over the goodness of the Lord, over the grain, the wine, and the oil, and over the young of the flock and the herd; their life shall be like a watered garden, and they shall languish no more" (Jer 31:12).

In short, Lady Wisdom's banquet appears to be another aspect of her mediating role in the love relationship between God and Israel. This is seen in the banquet's affinities with the delights of Eden and with the covenantal feasting at Sinai and in the Temple, to be fulfilled in the great eschatological banquet.

## Lady Wisdom as Torah Personified (24:23–34)

Following Lady Wisdom's invitation to her covenantal meal, Sirach reveals another facet of her identity in what is perhaps the book's most stunning declaration. Lady Wisdom is the "the book of the covenant of the Most High God, the law which Moses commanded us as an inheritance for the congregations of Jacob" (24:23). This reference to the book of the covenant refers to the Sinai covenant code (Exod 24:7), using an exact quote from Deuteronomy (Deut 33:4; cf. 2 Kgs 23:2; 2 Chr 34:31).

28. Fletcher-Louis argues that the "remembrance" of Wisdom (Sir 24:20) points to the Temple's cultic setting: "the memorial of Wisdom is the Israelite cult, since Wisdom's actions in creation (and history) are recorded, rehearsed and engrained upon the people's corporate memory through the structure and drama of the cult." Fletcher-Louis, "The Cosmology of P," 93.

29. Cf. also Isa 49:9–10; 62:9; 65:13, 21; Amos 9:14; Joel 2:24, 26; Zech 8:12, 9:17.

Sirach thus identifies Lady Wisdom with the Torah—the ultimate source of wisdom.[30] Conversely, wisdom is a necessary virtue to keep the law. As Gilbert has noted, Wisdom expresses in her song of praise the essential contents of the Torah, that is, how God created the world and man, how he chose Israel and gave her the Promised Land with the Jerusalem Temple at its center, where the liturgy to God was celebrated, and whence sprung the word of the Lord (Isa 2:4; Mic 4:2).[31] In Sirach, Wisdom is the "fulfillment of the law" (Sir 19:20), and in our present passage she is nothing less than a personal hypostasis of the Torah (cf. Bar 3:37–4:1). This means that for our author, Wisdom came down and was "given" to Israel at Mount Sinai. At the same time, Wisdom's identification with the Torah considered in light of her presence at the origins of the world implies a close relationship between the Torah and creation. Although Torah/Wisdom was given to Israel through Moses at Mount Sinai, its revelation to the world was already implicit at creation (cf. Sir 16:24–17:20). Thus, the Torah is the supreme actualization of the natural law, the particular revelation to one people at one moment in time of what had been universally given to all humanity at the dawn of history.[32]

### Five Rivers and Two Men (24:25–29)

> [25] It fills men with wisdom, like the Pishon,
> and like the Tigris at the time of the first fruits.
> [26] It makes them full of understanding, like the Euphrates,
> and like the Jordan at harvest time.
> [27] It makes instruction shine forth like light,
> like the Gihon at the time of vintage. (Sir 24:25–27)

Ben Sira now elaborates on how the Torah brims with wisdom by means of an analogy of five rivers. The book of the covenant fills men with wisdom and understanding, making instruction shine forth like the Pishon, the Tigris, the Euphrates, the Jordan, and the Gihon. Wisdom is frequently compared to a fountain or stream in wisdom literature: In Proverbs she is

---

30. Cf. Ps 90:12; Sir 6:32–37; 15:1; 1 Chr 22:12.

31. Gilbert, "L'éloge de la Sagesse," 337–38.

32. Philo (*On the Creation of the World*, 3) expresses the unity between natural and revealed law some two centuries later, saying "that the law corresponds to the world and the world to the law, and that a man who is obedient to the law, being, by so doing, a citizen of the world, arranges his actions with reference to the intention of nature, in harmony with which the whole universal world is regulated."

called a "fountain of life" (Prov 16:22) and a "gushing stream" (Prov 18:4). Sirach writes elsewhere that Solomon, in his great wisdom, "overflowed like a river with understanding" (Sir 47:14). Baruch adds that to turn away from the Torah is to "forsake the fountain of Wisdom" (Bar 3:12). Four of the five rivers mentioned here are the four riverheads that branched out of the river coming out of Eden (Gen 2:10–14). This comparison with the paradisal waters is yet another link connecting Wisdom with the original home of Adam and Eve.[33] The same Edenic context is maintained in the next verse with the mention of the "first man" and a return to the primordial elements of creation—the sea and the great abyss: "Just as the first man did not know her perfectly, the last one has not fathomed her; for her thought is more abundant than the sea, and her counsel deeper than the great abyss" (Sir 24:28–29). These two verses mentioning the first and last man return to the theme of Wisdom's eternity: she is present both at the beginning and at the end of time. The first man, Adam, did not know Wisdom perfectly because the Torah had not yet been revealed. Yet even the last man on earth will never be able to fathom her depths.

## Wisdom's Eschatological Streams (24:30–34)

[30] I went forth like a canal from a river
and like a water channel into a garden.
[31] I said, "I will water my orchard
and drench my garden plot";
and behold, my canal became a river,
and my river became a sea. (Sir 24:30–31)

If the rivers of 24:25–27 evoke the rivers of Eden, the ever-widening stream of 24:30–31 alludes to the river flowing out of Ezekiel's eschatological Temple (Ezek 47:1–12). According to Ezekiel's description, these waters pass south of the altar, trickle out of the eastern gate with an ever increasing and deepening flow down into the Aravah valley and into the Dead Sea, causing the waters of the sea to be "healed" and miraculously revived with an abundance of fish returning to the formerly salty waters. Along the banks of this supernatural river grow lush trees whose "fruit will be for food and their leaves for medicine."[34] With this sixth river,

33. On the waters of Eden as a life-giving symbol in early Jewish traditions, cf. 2 Enoch 8; Apoc. Abr. 21; 1QH 16:4–26. These texts are discussed in Um, *The Theme of Temple Christology in John's Gospel*, 20–55.

34. Cf. also Joel 4:17–18; Zech 14:8–9.

Ben Sira has masterfully drawn a bird's eye view of Wisdom's ongoing presence in human history from Eden to the eschaton. He has also tied the end back to the beginning because the miraculous trees whose "fruit will not fail" growing alongside Ezekiel's river are no doubt another allusion to the Tree of Life. Flowing water, springs and streams are also an important theme of Isaiah's eschatological visions, which speak of drawing water with joy from the wells of salvation (Isa 12:3), and of God being a "place of broad rivers and streams" (Isa 33:21). Other passages are even more richly evocative, describing miraculous waters turning the desert into a blooming garden:

> The wilderness and the dry land shall be glad, the desert shall rejoice and blossom; like the lily it shall blossom abundantly, and rejoice with joy and singing . . . For waters shall break forth in the wilderness, and streams in the desert. (Isa 35:1, 6)

> I will open rivers on the bare heights, and fountains in the midst of the valleys; I will make the wilderness a pool of water, and the dry land springs of water. I will put in the wilderness the cedar, the acacia, the myrtle, and the olive; I will set in the desert the cypress, the plane and the pine together. (Isa 41:18–19)

The wondrous outpouring of water reviving nature and restoring the weary soul is also associated with the outpouring of God's Spirit on those who come to the waters, for they will themselves become a watered garden and permanent spring of refreshing water: "And the Lord will guide you continually, and satisfy your desire with good things, and make your bones strong; and you shall be like a watered garden, like a spring of water, whose waters do not fail" (Isa 58:11).

The motif of springs and fountains is also characteristic of love imagery. The Canticle's mention of gardens, orchards, living waters, and spices (Cant 4:12–15) reveals more connections to Wisdom, Eden, and the eschatological streams of water. Sirach's rivers thus evoke biblical imagery typical of erotic love, as well as recall the streams of Eden and the miraculous streams flowing out of the eschatological Temple that water nature and soul at the end of days.

### Lady Wisdom on Four Holy Mountains

Lady Wisdom concludes her song of praise with an eschatological turn towards the future. She promises: "I will again make instruction shine

forth like the dawn, and I will make it shine afar; I will again pour
out teaching like prophecy, and leave it to all future generations" (Sir
24:32–33). Wisdom's promise to make instruction "shine forth" and to
pour out teaching like prophecy to "all future generations" implies that
Sirach compares her instruction to prophetic speech. We hear echoes
of Isaiah's promise that the radiant light of the Lord will one day shine
not only upon Israel but also on all the nations of the earth (Isa 60:1–3).
Sirach 24:32–33 also recalls Isaiah 2:2–3, which announces that in the
latter days the law of the Lord will go forth from the "mountain of the
Lord's house" in Zion, and all nations will flow to it to learn his ways.
We have mentioned the "mountain of the Lord" as the "high places" of
Wisdom's dwelling (Sir 24:2). By returning here to the cosmic mountain
of the Lord we have come full circle. The entire scene of Sirach 24 takes
place on the Lord's holy mountain, in the Temple on Mount Zion (Sir
24:10). For Sirach, the "holy hill of Zion" is the "mountain of the Lord"
from which flows the river of living waters (Ezek 47:1–12; Joel 4:17–18;
Zech 14:8–9). These eschatological waters of healing are associated with
the rivers of Eden (Isa 51:3; Ezek 47:12; Ps 36:7–10), itself identified with
the "holy mountain of God" (Ezek 28:13–14). The Temple on Mount
Zion was God's dwelling, as he dwelt with Adam and Eve in the Garden.[35]

Let us summarize this dazzling interconnection of themes. For
Sirach, the "holy mountain of God" from which flow streams of living
water is simultaneously:

1. The Garden of Eden (cf. Ezek 28:13–14)

2. Mount Sinai (cf. Exod 3:1; 19:3)

3. Mount Zion, seat of the Temple (cf. Ps 2:6; Ps 46:4; 48:1–2; Wis 9:8)

4. The Eschatological Temple (cf. Isa 2:3; Ezek 47:1–12; Joel 4:17–18;
   Zech 14:8–9)

The close identification of Eden, Sinai, and Zion, and the eschatological Temple is confirmed not only by Sirach 24 and its intricate web

---

35. The cherubim, palm trees, and flowers on the doors of the Temple, as well as
the two cherubim over the Ark of the Covenant made it clear that the Temple was
meant to replicate paradise. Moreover, the setting in Sirach 24 corresponds to all five
attributes of the cosmic mountain of Zion in biblical tradition: (1) the cosmic mountain is situated at the center of the world; (2) it is the point of junction between heaven
and earth; (3) it is a place where time stands still and where a primordial mythical and
sacred time is made present; (4) it is associated with the primal paradise of the Garden
of Eden; (5) it is intimately associated with creation. Levenson, *Sinai and Zion*, 115–37.

of metaphors, but also by the Book of Jubilees (4:25–26; 8:19), as seen above. Eden is thus seen as a temple and sanctuary, identified with *both* Mount Sinai and Mount Zion, for it is "holier than all the earth besides, and every tree that is planted in it is holy" (Jub 3:12). Biblical literature often recalls it in conjunction with the loss of former glory,[36] and with the hope of a future restoration.[37]

## Creation, Tabernacle, and Wisdom's "Incarnation"

We have highlighted Lady Wisdom's nuptial role at four key moments of salvation history through rich intertextuality between Sirach 24, the Song of Songs, and the narrative traditions of creation/Eden, Sinai/the Torah, the Tabernacle/Temple, and the prophetic eschatological visions. It remains to consider how Sirach portrays Wisdom as "incarnated" in the person of the high priest via intertextual connections between Genesis 1–2, Exodus 25–31, Sirach 24, and Sirach 50.

### Creation, Tabernacle, and Wisdom

Some time ago, Kearney argued that the seven days of creation in Genesis 1 roughly correspond to seven speeches spoken by God in Exod 25–31, giving instructions to Moses for building the Tabernacle.[38] This correspondence reveals a view of the cosmos as macro-temple and the sanctuary as microcosm. Its construction, therefore, is a reenactment of the

36. Cf. Gen 13:10; Ezek 28:11–19; 31:16–18; Joel 2:3.

37. Cf. Isa 51:3; Ezek 36:35. Eden is also associated with the future Temple in extra-biblical literature: cf. 1 Enoch 24–32; Test. Levi 18:6; Test. Dan 5:12; Apoc. Mos 29:1–6. 1 Enoch 24–32 remarkably confirms what we have learned from Sirach 24, namely that Eden is situated on (seven) mountains, full of fragrant trees, spices, and beautiful fruit, watered by flowing streams. The summit of the highest mount is "like the throne of God" (25:3), and the Tree of Life will be "transplanted to the holy place, to the temple of the Lord" (25:5).

38. For example, on the first day God created the light separating the day and night (Gen 1:3–5); in the first speech, Aaron is made responsible for tending the lampstand providing light in the sanctuary between day and night (Exod 27:20–21; 30:7–8). On the third day, God created the sea (Gen 1:9–10); in the third speech, Moses is told to make the bronze laver, later called the "sea" (1 Kgs 7:23). On the seventh day, God "rested" from all His work (Gen 2:2–3); the seventh speech stresses the importance of the Sabbath rest (Exod 31:12–17). Kearney, "Creation and Liturgy: The P Redaction of Ex 25–40"; Villeneuve, *Nuptial Symbolism*, 83–84.

creation of the world, and Aaron's liturgical ministry is an act of *imitatio Dei*.[39] Building upon Kearney's work, Fletcher-Louis discerned in Sirach 24 a literary structure that follows the pattern of the days of creation and building of the Tabernacle.[40] He noted that while the second section of Sir 24 (vv. 25–33) borrows from the imagery of Genesis 2, the first section (vv. 3–23) is especially indebted to Genesis 1. Fletcher-Louis saw in Sir 24:1–22 a "carefully crafted sapiential meditation on the Priestly account of creation," indebted not only to Gen 1:1–2:4, but also to the priestly narrative of the building of the Tabernacle.[41] These correspondences carry over into another key text: the hymn of the High Priest in Sirach 50.

## *The High Priest as "Incarnation" of Wisdom (Sir 50)*

Sirach 50 ties the creation account, the building of the Tabernacle, and Lady Wisdom's hymn, so that many of the metaphors applied to Wisdom in Sir 24 are also applied to Simon the High Priest. The unit begins with a reference to Simon immediately following a mention of Adam (49:16–50:1). The juxtaposition of the two figures possibly testifies to the ancient tradition of Adam as first high priest of humanity.[42] Ben Sira could be portraying Simon the high priest and representative of Israel as a type of second Adam.[43] This association of Simon with Adam sets the stage for a description of the High Priest that shows many common features with the days of creation and the building of the sanctuary.[44]

1. Although the beginning of Sir 50 shows no obvious parallel with the first day of creation, given the cosmic symbolism of the high

---

39. Fletcher-Louis, "The Cosmology of P," 77, 79.

40. Fletcher-Louis, "The Cosmology of P," 79–94.

41. Fletcher-Louis, "The Cosmology of P," 93; Villeneuve, *Nuptial Symbolism*, 84–87.

42. Rabbinic writings attest to the tradition that Adam's garments were the high priestly robes, handed down through successive generations until they reached Aaron. Cf. *GenR* 20:12; 97:6; *Numbers Rabbah* 4:8. Hayward, *The Jewish Temple*, 45. Adam's role as high priest is known from the account of his offering a sacrifice of frankincense, galbanum, stacte and spices (Jubilees 3:27).

43. As Hayward writes (*The Jewish Temple*, 45), Ben Sira seems to imply that "the privileges granted to the first man, and thus to all humankind, are also peculiarly summed up in Israel whose representative is Simon in his function as sacrificing high priest."

44. Cf. Fletcher-Louis, "The Cosmology of P," 94–111.

priest and Temple developed in the following verses, it is possible that the action of Simon, who "repaired the house" and "fortified the Temple" (50:1), is intended to reflect the creation of the universe.

2. Sirach reports that Simon "laid the foundations of the high double walls, the high retaining walls of the temple enclosure" (Sir 50:2). The Temple, situated on God's cosmic mountain, was thought to cover the expanse between the upper and lower realms (cf. Ps 78:69), analogous to the firmament's separation of the upper and lower waters on the second day of creation. It could be that Simon's foundations and high walls hint at these lower and upper limits of the cosmos.

3. In Simon's days, "a cistern for water was quarried out, a reservoir like the sea in circumference" (Sir 50:3). This corresponds well to the creation of the sea on the third day (Gen 1:9–10), to the instructions for the building of the laver in God's third speech to Moses (Exod 30:17–21), and to the sea over which Wisdom rules (Sir 24:6a). Moreover, the high priest's identification with many of the same trees, plants and flowers as Lady Wisdom in chapter 24 could well reflect God's creation of the vegetation on the third day.[45]

4. The high priest comes out of the sanctuary glorious "like the morning star among the clouds, like the moon when it is full; like the sun shining upon the temple of the Most High, and like the rainbow gleaming in glorious clouds" (Sir 50:5–7). This clearly echoes the creation of the sun, moon and stars on the fourth day.

5. The high priest is then compared to "fire and incense in the censer . . . and like a cypress towering in the clouds" (Sir 50:9–10). The rising smoke matches God's fifth speech to Moses on making the sacred incense (Exod 30:34–38); the clouds perhaps allude to the creation of birds on the fifth day.

6. Sir 50:11–13 describes Simon clothed in splendor, serving at the altar and offering sacrifices while surrounded by his fellow priests. This matches the sixth day, when Adam was created. Fletcher-Louis argues that Sirach is drawing a picture of the high priest as new

45. The High Priest is "like roses in the days of the first fruits, like lilies by a spring of water, like a green shoot on Lebanon on a summer day . . . like an olive tree putting forth its fruit, and like a cypress towering in the clouds" (50:8, 10). As he stood by the hearth of the altar he was "like a young cedar on Lebanon; and [the priests] surrounded him like the trunks of palm trees" (50:12).

Adam, clothed with his "garments of glory" and restoring the "true image of God ruling over every living creature which he was given on the sixth day of creation."[46] As he receives portions of the sacrificial offerings from the other priests, one hears echoes of Adam's dominion over every living thing, of the Tabernacle sacrificial worship, and of Lady Wisdom's feast (Sir 24:20–22).

7. Finally, Sir 50:14–21 describes how the high priest "finished ministering at the altar and arranged the offering to the Most High." The end of the liturgical ministry mirrors the accounts of creation and of the building of the Tabernacle, with a common language of completion and blessing. Just as God "finished" and "blessed" the work of creation (Gen 2:1–3) and Moses "finished" the construction of the Tabernacle and "blessed" the people, so Simon "finished" ministering at the altar and "blessed" the whole congregation (Sir 50:14, 19–20).[47]

Sirach evidently wishes to connect not only Lady Wisdom and Simon, but also his predecessor Aaron, the first high priest ordained by Moses at Sinai. This is seen by comparing our text with Sir 45:6–16: Sirach describes how God made an "everlasting covenant" with Aaron, entrusting him the priesthood, clothing him with a "glorious robe" and "superb perfection," and calling him to continually burn the offerings with "incense and a pleasing odor as a memorial portion" (Sir 45:7–8, 15–16). Simon now fulfills the same role in the Temple, clothed with a similar "glorious robe" and "superb perfection," bringing offerings to the altar with a wine libation pleasing to the Most High, concluding his liturgical ministry with a trumpet blast for *remembrance* before him (Sir 50:11, 15, 16). Recall that the same terms are used of Lady Wisdom, who gives forth an "aroma of spices" and "pleasant odor" (24:15), is compared to a vine (24:17) and is "drunk" (24:21), and whose banquet is called a "*memorial*" meal, serving as a *remembrance* of her presence and actions in creation and salvation history (24:20). Liturgical worship, sacrifices, the pleasant odor of frankincense and pouring of wine all serve to illustrate the communion between God and his people rendered possible

---

46. Fletcher-Louis, "The Cosmology of P," 105.

47. The linguistic parallels between the completion accounts of creation and the Tabernacle were noted by Cassuto, *Commentary on the Book of Exodus*, chap. 39–40; Berman, *The Temple*, 13–14; Levenson, "The Temple and the World," 287–88; *Sinai and Zion*, 143; *Creation and the Persistence of Evil*, 85–86.

through the mediation of Lady Wisdom and the high priest—originally Aaron at Sinai and now Simon in the Temple. Accordingly, just as Lady Wisdom's sacred meal is "sweeter than honey," so the liturgical singers praise the high priest in a "sweet melody" (50:18).

In summary, Sirach 24 and 50 appear to be "two carefully crafted halves of a literary dyptich modeled on the canonical dialectic between creation and Tabernacle," [48] according to which the creation of the world is in a close symmetrical relationship to Israel's construction of the Tabernacle. The Tabernacle is a "mini-cosmos," and its liturgical service is correlated to the right ordering of the universe. Israel's worship brings creation towards its completion. The metaphysical link between creation and Tabernacle is the presence of omnipresent Wisdom, who rules over the universe on the one hand, and serves in the sanctuary as the high priest on the other. Ben Sira thus sees the high priest as the impersonation and "incarnation" of Wisdom, possessing the same attributes and officiating in the Temple (as she does), filling the sanctuary with the Lord's glory as Lady Wisdom fills the earth with the same glory. Just as Simon in his liturgical service fills the court of the sanctuary with glory, so Wisdom, planted in the land and people of Israel, prospers and attests to their holiness. As God sent Wisdom to dwell among men, the Temple cult counts among God's greatest gifts to his people.[49] The "incarnation" of Wisdom in the High Priest constitutes a striking precursor to the Incarnation of the Logos.

## Lady Wisdom at Four Moments of Salvation History

For Sirach and the wisdom authors, Wisdom is the sustaining principle of all creation. Yet she is more than an impersonal force over creation. Her female identity, her seductive invitation to men to join her at her feast, and her self-description in the language of the Song of Songs indicate that she communicates herself to her people in a nuptial way. Moreover, she is concretely at work in the history of Israel. Sirach 44–50 presents a hall of fame of great biblical figures who distinguished themselves by their wisdom. From Enoch to Simon the high priest, these men were "leaders of the people in their deliberations and in understanding of learning for the people, wise in their words of instruction" (Sir 44:4). The

---

48. Cf. Fletcher-Louis, "The Cosmology of P," 112.

49. Fournier-Bidoz, "L'arbre et la demeure : Siracide XXIV 10–17," 9.

Wisdom of Solomon (chapters 10–19) also reviews the history of Israel by highlighting Wisdom's activities in history from Adam to the conquest of Canaan, thus attributing an active, saving role to Wisdom in Israel's history. Indeed, we have found Lady Wisdom to be particularly active at four milestones of the nation's history:

1. She is present at creation or identified with the Tree of Life in the Garden of Eden.

2. She is the Torah given at Mount Sinai.

3. She is the cloud of the divine presence dwelling in the Tabernacle and in the Temple.

4. She is expected to be present in the messianic age at the end of days.

These four milestones underline the interplay between Wisdom's particularism and universalism. Eden represents the common origin of all mankind. Sinai is the moment of the birth of Israel as nation and their adoption (or betrothal) as a "kingdom of priests and holy nation" (Exod 19:6). The Tabernacle and Temple are the liturgical extension into time of the Sinai theophany and the meeting point (or nuptial chamber) between God and Israel. The messianic age is the final destination of the course of history and the return to its universal dimension for the entire human family.

## Lady Wisdom at Creation and as the Tree of Life in Eden

The wisdom authors believed that Lady Wisdom was present at the creation of the world.[50] Eden is her primordial sanctuary and dwelling, for in her universality she belongs to and is even "married" to all mankind. At the same time, Wisdom's gift of self to God's people is seen as a renewed access to Eden's lost Tree of Life (Prov 3:18). Accordingly, the fruit of the righteous man who pursues her is also a Tree of Life (Prov 11:30). The motif of Wisdom as source of life returns frequently, echoing the choice in Eden between the Tree of Life and the Tree of Knowledge whose fruit brought death: He who finds wisdom "finds life," but he who hates her "loves death" (Prov 8:35–36). Lady Wisdom promises to the wise man: "By me your days will be multiplied, and years of life will be added to you" (Prov 9:11). Moreover, the fear of the Lord, known to be the beginning

50. Prov 8:22–30; Sir 1:4; 24:9; Wis 6:22; 9:9; 10:1.

of wisdom, is "health to your flesh" and "strength to your bones" (Prov 3:8); it "prolongs days" (Prov 10:27) and is a "fountain of life" (Prov 14:27; 19:23). The allusion to the Garden and to life continues in Sirach, where Wisdom's blossoms produce "glorious and abundant fruit" (Sir 24:17) and she is compared to the four rivers of Eden (Sir 24:25–27). Hence Sirach considers the fear of the Lord to be "the crown of wisdom, making peace and perfect health to flourish" (Sir 1:16). Baruch concurs: in wisdom there is "length of days and life" (Bar 3:14; cf. 4:1).

## Lady Wisdom as the Torah

Wisdom is also identified with the Torah and commandments given at Mount Sinai. Sinai is the place where she "contracted herself" and gave herself to the people of Israel as the Torah in a type of "betrothal" event. Accordingly, the commandments, like wisdom, are the source of life. Proverbs declares that remembering the Torah and keeping the commandments will grant "length of days and long life" to the wise man (Prov 3:2). In Sirach, not only is the Law the source of wisdom (Sir 6:32–37; 15:1) and wisdom the fulfillment of the Law (Sir 19:20). Wisdom is, in fact, the Torah itself, "the book of the covenant of the Most High God, the law which Moses commanded us as an inheritance for the congregations of Jacob" (Sir 24:23; cf. Bar 3:36–4:1). Moreover, Ben Sira views the creation of the world and the giving of the Torah as two sides of the same coin: Within the same passage, he describes the establishment of the cosmic order (16:26–28), the creation of man (16:29–17:4) and capacity of human understanding (17:6–10), then goes on to describe the divine granting of a "law of life" and establishment of an "eternal covenant" to those who saw "his glorious majesty, and their ears heard the glory of his voice" (Sir 17:11–14). The Wisdom of Solomon makes a comparable association between pre-existent Wisdom, Torah and (eternal) life: One passage describes in logical sequence how an initial desire for instruction as an expression of love for wisdom is translated into a practical keeping of her laws, which leads in turn to immortality in the presence of God and his kingdom:

> The beginning of wisdom is the most sincere desire for instruction, and concern for instruction is love of her, and love of her is the keeping of her laws, and giving heed to her laws is assurance of immortality, and immortality brings one near to God; so the desire for wisdom leads to a kingdom. (Wis 6:17–20)

## Lady Wisdom in the Sanctuary

The wisdom writers viewed the Tabernacle and Temple as the privileged places of God's encounter with Israel throughout the nation's history—an encounter initiated at Sinai and expressed liturgically through sacrificial worship. The betrothal at Sinai is thus extended into time in the sanctuary established on God's holy mountain (recalling Eden and Sinai) as the "nuptial chamber" of Wisdom and Israel. In Sirach, Lady Wisdom "ministered" before God in the holy tabernacle and found a "resting place" in the Temple on Mount Zion (Sir 24:10–11). Since the sanctuary was Wisdom's resting place, Ben Sira sought her before the Temple (Sir 51:14). In the Wisdom of Solomon, Wisdom sits by God's throne (Wis 9:4), and Solomon asks God to send her down to earth so she can assist him in the work of building the Temple (Wis 9:8–10). The fact that she is found primarily in the Temple, combined with the insistent invitation to men that they embrace and love her[51] implies that this union is to take place in the sanctuary, where the people are represented by the High Priest (Sir 50). This means that the wisdom writers see the Temple as a nuptial chamber and the impartation of divine wisdom to man as a spousal union.

## Lady Wisdom in the Last Days

Finally, Wisdom is oriented towards the future. Since she is eternal, "established from everlasting" (Prov 8:23) and sitting by God's throne (Wis 9:4), she is expected to be present at the end of human history. Baruch identifies her with "the law that endures forever" (Bar 4:1). Sirach affirms that she established an eternal foundation among men (Sir 1:13), and she announces: "for eternity I shall not cease to exist" (Sir 24:9). The imagery used to describe her in Sirach 24 reveals many parallels between her presence and the messianic age of the prophets. The Temple serves as a permanent reminder and hope of the paradisal world to come at the end of time when Torah, the source of all Wisdom, will stream from the top of God's mountain to all nations as the sign and pledge of the consummated marriage between Lady Wisdom and redeemed humanity. In Fournier-Bidoz's words, Wisdom evokes the earth and the sanctuary as a coherent whole, both being places of rest and of festive rejoicing that recall paradisal images, either at the origins of creation or in the eschatological future.[52]

---

51. Prov 4:6; 9:1–6; Sir 4:11–12; 15:2–3; 24:19–21; Wis 7:10; 8:2–3.

52. Fournier-Bidoz, "L'arbre et la demeure," 4.

# III

## Christ and the Church:
## Divine Marriage in the New Testament

*7*

# The Bridegroom and the Kingdom

## *The Gospel of Matthew*

THE MARRIAGE BETWEEN GOD AND ISRAEL UNDERGOES a significant development in the New Testament as it metamorphoses into the espousals of Christ and the Church. This transformation represents more of an organic growth than a break with the Jewish tradition out of which Christian nuptial symbolism was born. In the New Testament's nuptial passages, the Church is not portrayed as a rival to Israel but rather as her historical continuation. In addition to this ecclesial nuptial symbolism, the New Testament authors apply many ideas from Wisdom literature to the mystical marriage between Christ and the soul of the believer. It is also in the New Testament that we find some of the earliest known allegorical interpretation of the Song of Songs. In all four Gospels, Jesus matter-of-factly refers to himself as "the bridegroom" whose friends and followers rejoice in his presence.

The Gospel of Matthew introduces the nuptial motif within the context of the question on fasting. Matthew adds two nuptial parables: In the parable of the wedding feast (Matt 22:1–14), the kingdom of heaven is compared to a sumptuous wedding feast prepared by a king for his son, to which all people of good will are invited. In the parable of the ten virgins (Matt 25:1–13), Jesus exhorts the Church to be watchful in preparation for the eschatological *parousia* of the bridegroom-Messiah.

## Behold the Bridegroom: The Question on Fasting
### (Matt 9:14–15)

When the disciples of John ask Jesus why his disciples do not fast like they do, he replies with a rhetorical question: "Can the sons of the bridechamber mourn as long as the bridegroom is with them? The days will come, when the bridegroom is taken away from them, and then they will fast" (Matt 9:14–15). [1] Some exegetes see in this saying a simple parable comparing the coming of the messianic kingdom with the joy of a marriage feast. [2] The time of the eschatological wedding between God and Israel has come, and by its very nature it excludes fasting and mourning. For others, the passage is eminently Christological. Jesus is comparing himself to a bridegroom, and his very presence turns the scene into a joyful wedding feast. Thus, the era of the Messiah is the era of the divine-human espousals, which presupposes that the Messiah is the bridegroom. [3] The wedding feast is a common metaphor used by the prophets to describe the age of salvation, a time of great rejoicing when the ascetic practices of fasting and mourning are inappropriate and even unthinkable. Whereas John's disciples and the Pharisees fast as a sign of repentance in preparation for the coming of the messianic kingdom (and perhaps to hasten the Messiah's coming), the presence of Jesus is the joyous sign that both have already arrived, and the "new wine" (Matt 9:17) an indication that the festivities are already under way. As Pitre observes, "Jesus is identifying his public ministry with the Jewish wedding week, in which the bridegroom and his wedding party would celebrate together." [4] Jesus' disciples take on the role of the "sons of the bridal-chamber" (sometimes translated "wedding guests" or "friends of the bridegroom") who, according to most rabbis, were exempt from performing ordinary religious duties during the week-long Jewish wedding celebration. [5]

The context of the question on fasting is significant. The passage follows the calling of Matthew and the banquet at his house where Jesus eats with tax collectors and sinners, drawing the ire of the Pharisees. [6] In response to their grumbling, Jesus quotes Hosea 6:6: "I desire mercy

1. Cf. Mark 2:18–20; Luke 5:33–35.
2. Jeremias, *The Parables of Jesus*, 52.
3. Infante, *Lo sposo e la sposa*, 85.
4. Pitre, *Jesus the Bridegroom*, 87.
5. *B. Sukkah* 25b–26a. Cf. Pitre, 88–89.
6. Matt 9:9–13; cf. Mark 2:13–17; Luke 5:27–32.

and not sacrifice" (Matt 9:13). This leads to the question on fasting, followed by Jesus' statement contrasting an old garment and wineskins to new wine and wineskins (Matt 9:16–17). Some see the Hosea quotation within the context of the conflict between the disciples of Jesus and the Pharisees, where the term "sacrifice" alludes to "the Pharisaic program of extending the rules of ritual purity for priests in the Jerusalem Temple to all Israel."[7] The feasting at Matthew's table and reference to the Temple sacrifices juxtaposed to the question on fasting, the announcement of the bridegroom's presence, and the contrast between old and new wineskins may imply a cultic significance to Jesus' self-identification as bridegroom. Thus, the "old wine" relates to pre-70 Judaism, its Temple service and Messianic expectation, and the "new wine" means the arrival of the bridegroom-Messiah and the new law and new cult centered around him. The wine's common association in the Old Testament and early Judaism with covenantal feasting, Torah, temple sacrifices, nuptial love and celebration of the eschatological age reinforces the historical dimension of the bridegroom's presence as the culmination of salvation history, following the expectation of the "old order" centered around the temple.

The bridegroom is thus already with his people—but only for a short time, for the next verse marks a shift from his current presence to the expectation of a future absence: "The days will come, when the bridegroom is taken away from them, and then they will fast" (Matt 9:15). This allusion to Jesus' disappearance is a prophecy pointing to his passion and death—the "night of consummation" when the bridegroom is "taken away" from his friends and enters the bridal chamber (*chuppah*) to be joined to his bride.[8] The cultic and nuptial dimensions of Christ's passion are confirmed by the fact that, for the sages, the *chuppah* was a type of mini-tabernacle (and the Tabernacle a *chuppah* where God was joined with Israel).[9] Thus, whereas Jesus initially speaks about a new age embodied in the bridegroom's presence, he follows it with a passion prediction of the bridegroom's loss. If the present time is one of rejoicing in the bridegroom's presence, the text announces a moment when he will be removed, and then will come the time for fasting and mourning.

Is Matthew attributing to Jesus the role of the divine bridegroom of the Old Testament? There are good reasons to believe that this is the

---

7. Harrington, *The Gospel of Matthew*, 129.

8. Pitre, *Jesus the Bridegroom*, 89–91.

9. *M. Baba Bathra* 6:4; *Numbers Rabbah* 13:2; cf. Pitre, 92–94.

case. The idea of the bridegroom-Messiah would be a new development of an old idea because it is foreign to the Old Testament and literature of Second Temple Judaism.[10] Noteworthy, however, is the absence of the bride. Although the text does not explicitly depict a marriage between Christ and his followers, Jesus' identification with the divine bridegroom does provide a foundation for the idea of the Church as bride.

## What God Has Joined: Jesus' Teachings on Marriage (Matt 19:3–12)

Jesus' teachings on marriage and divorce are informative because they shed light on the nuptial symbolism employed elsewhere by the New Testament authors.[11] In Matt 19:3–12,[12] Jesus castigates the laxity of the Pharisees' interpretation of the Torah in matters of divorce (cf. Deut 24:1), grounding his argument on the original unity of Adam and Eve described in Gen 1:27 and 2:24. The implication is three-fold: first, marriage is rooted in creation and in the very origin of mankind; second, the one-flesh union between man and woman creates a substantial unity and interpersonal communion between them at the deepest level of their being; third, in the sexual union, God permanently joins the two parties in such a way that they must no longer be separated: "Therefore what God has joined together, let not man separate" (Matt 19:6). In reminding his listeners that "from the beginning it was not so" (Matt 19:8), Jesus contrasts the Law of Moses permitting divorce with a more primitive and pristine "Law of Eden" where divorce was unheard of, and he calls for a return to this original and superior understanding of marriage. When one adds to these two dispensations the restored economy of marriage that Jesus institutes and the final eschatological state when marriage as we know it will cease, we distinguish four historical periods in the institution of marriage:

---

10. The identity of the Messiah as bridegroom is found in later texts such as the Targum on the Song of Songs 8:1 and Targum on Ps 45. Jeremias, *The Parables of Jesus,* 52.

11. Paul, especially, seems to take these teachings for granted. Cf. 1 Cor 6:15–20.

12. And parallels Matt 5:31–32; Mark 10:2–12; Luke 16:18; cf. also 1 Cor 7:10–11.

1. The original state in paradise as God intended it, when Adam and Eve became "one flesh." The divinely ordained original unity provides the ground for the indissolubility of marriage: "what God has joined together, let not man separate."

2. A "period of compromise" under the Mosaic Law, when divorce was allowed because of man's "hardness of heart."

3. A new period introduced by Jesus that returns to the original order of creation and to the unity and inviolability of marriage.

4. The time of the resurrection where "they neither marry nor are given in marriage, but are like angels of God in heaven" (Matt 22:30).

Human marriage is therefore an institution of the present age that originates in creation, was wounded by sin and became subject to provisionary regulations under the Torah, was restored by the Messiah, but will pass away in the world to come. This model is closely related to our "four nuptial moments" of early Jewish thought. As we shall see, Jesus' four-fold scheme of human marriage also forms the underlying foundation for the marriage between Christ and the Church as developed in the Johannine and Pauline writings.

## Come to the Feast: The Parable of the Wedding Banquet (Matt 22:1–14)

In Matt 22:1–14, the kingdom of heaven is compared to a sumptuous wedding feast prepared by a king for his son, to which all are invited.[13] No expenses are spared, and the oxen and fatted calf are killed in honor of the guests—an action that underlines the abundance of the feast and generosity of the king. But the generous invitation transmitted twice by the king's servants is met first with apathy and then with hostility on the part of the invitees, who go on with their business or mistreat and kill the monarch's envoys. The outraged king sends armies to destroy the offenders and burn their city in retaliation, after which he sends more servants to invite "all whom they found, both bad and good" to the wedding feast. But when a guest is found without wedding garment he is rejected and cast out into the "outer darkness."

---

13. The parable is similar to the parable of the great supper in Luke 14:15–24, though Luke leaves out the marriage motif.

Matthew's comparison of the kingdom of God with a banquet is explicit here. Some have suggested as background to the parable Lady Wisdom's invitation to her sacred banquet in Proverbs, where she slaughters her meat, mixes her wine, furnishes her table, sends out her maidens and invites all to her feast (Prov 9:1).[14] But if in Proverbs Wisdom sends out the invitations to her feast, in Matthew it is the king who invites the guests on behalf of his son. Feuillet tied the parable to the messianic feast of the prophets (c.f. Isa 25:6–8; 55:1–5) where the Lord offers an abundance of delightful foods to all people on Mount Zion.[15] He also saw connections with the feast of the lovers in Cant 8:1–2, which the Targum interprets as the "Feast of Leviathan" that Israel will share with the King-Messiah in his eschatological Temple.[16]

The main point of the parable is the choice between rejecting or accepting the king's invitation to the wedding feast. Matthew allegorically alludes to the rejection of the prophets and persecution of the apostles by the Jews or Jewish leaders, who treat with contempt the invitation to salvation extended to them. As a result, they must suffer the dire consequence of seeing Jerusalem burned. The new guests gathered from the streets may refer to the marginal people within Israel (the "tax collectors and sinners") or perhaps the gentiles who have received the gospel. The wedding feast is the eschatological day of salvation; the king's inspection of the guests is the last judgment; the "wedding garment" may refer to the righteous deeds of the saints;[17] and the "outer darkness" to hell. Matthew has thus "transformed our parable into an outline of the plan of redemption from the appearance of the prophets, embracing the fall of Jerusalem, up to the Last Judgment."[18] Both the bridegroom and bride, however, remain in the shadows. All that is said about the wedding party is that the bridegroom is the king's son—a clear reference to Jesus given his identity as bridegroom in 9:15 and 25:1, and as the son in the preceding parable of the vineyard and wicked tenants.[19]

The parable of the wedding feast is a miniature depiction of salvation history, with the wedding banquet as its eschatological consummation.

14. Harrington, *The Gospel of Matthew*, 307.

15. Feuillet, "Les épousailles messianiques," 205–7.

16. Feuillet, "Les épousailles messianiques," 207–9.

17. Infante (*Lo sposo e la sposa*, 87–88) has noted that the wedding garment recalls Rev 19:7b–8 and *b. Shabb.* 153a.

18. Jeremias, *The Parables of Jesus*, 69.

19. Cf. Matt 3:17; 8:29; 14:33; 16:16; 21:33–46.

The historical dimension is visible in the role of the rejected servants as the prophets of the past and apostles of the present, and the destruction of the city emphasizes the break between the original invitees (the Jews or their leaders) and the guests found on the highways (those who have accepted the Gospel). Since the community of disciples is portrayed as the wedding guests and not as bride, however, we cannot properly speak of nuptial union between Christ and his followers here.

## The Parable of the Ten Virgins (Matt 25:1–13)

The parable of the ten virgins (Matt 25:1–13) is the last occurrence of the nuptial motif in the Gospel of Matthew, this time presented as an eschatological exhortation to watchfulness for the Church in preparation for the *parousia* of Christ. The parable is placed in the midst of a long section on eschatological events: it is preceded by Jesus' discourse on the destruction of the Temple, the end times and coming of the Son of Man, and the parable of the good and wicked servants (Matt 24:1–51), and followed by the parable of the talents and the last judgment scene (Matt 25:14–46). The central message of these two chapters is watchfulness in preparation for the coming of the Son of Man.

In our parable, ten virgins await the bridegroom's arrival with their lamps, presumably outside in the dark. According to the customs of Jewish weddings at the time, the scene takes place at the groom's house. The bridegroom has gone to the house of the bride's father to get her and bring her to his house, where the bridal table and chamber are ready.[20] Five of the virgins are wise and take sufficient oil with them to last through the night, but the other five virgins are foolish and neglect to take enough oil. Caught by surprise by the bridegroom's sudden arrival, they must rush away to buy oil, but then are caught in front of closed doors after the wise virgins have gone in to the wedding feast with the bridegroom.

Here the context makes it clear that the bridegroom is Christ, the Son of Man whose glorious coming was just described in the previous chapter. The other elements of the allegory are easy to identify: the ten maidens are the community of believers waiting for Christ; the bridegroom' delay is the postponement of the *Parousia*; his sudden coming

---

20. Harrington, *The Gospel of Matthew*, 36–37, 349; Jeremias, "νύμφη, νυμφίος," *TDNT* 4, 1100. On ancient Jewish marriage customs, cf. De Vaux, *Ancient Israel: Its Life and Institutions*, 1:24–38.

is the unexpected coming of the Son of Man; the foolish maidens left behind the closed door symbolize the last judgment; and perhaps the foolish virgins represent Israel and the wise ones the Gentiles.[21]

This parable is the nuptial passage in the synoptics that comes closest to alluding to the God-Israel marriage. The torch-light entrance of the bridegroom was known in early Judaism as a metaphor for God coming to meet his bride Israel.[22] Moreover, there are several affinities between the parable and Cant 5:2–8: the Canticle's bride sleeps, as do the virgins in Matthew; yet the bride's heart is awake, and the virgins keep their light lit; in both cases the bridegroom appears in the middle of the night; in both cases his arrival is announced with a voice or a cry; the Canticle's bride is not ready and slow to open the door, and the foolish virgins are caught unprepared; when the bride finally opens the door, and when the virgins return, it is too late: the bridegroom has gone away.[23] These parallels seem close enough to warrant some inter-textual relationship between Matthew and the Song of Songs.

This parable, as the previous one, is peculiar insofar as the bride is absent from the story.[24] Jesus' followers are represented not by the bride but rather by the ten virgins, perhaps as a sign of their call to purity, holiness, and consecration—though evidently this calling does not guarantee their automatic entrance into the wedding feast. There may be a correlation here with Paul's depiction of the Corinthian church as a "pure virgin" who is in danger of being distracted and led astray from her devotion to Christ her bridegroom (2 Cor 11:2–3). Several ancient and modern authors, in fact, have suggested that the bride in Matthew's parable should be identified with the ten virgins.[25]

It is also significant that the parable of the ten virgins depicting the coming of the bridegroom immediately follows Jesus' eschatological discourse, in which he dramatically describes the destruction of the Temple

21. Harrington, *The Gospel of Matthew*, 349.

22. *Mekh* on Exod 19:17 interprets Deut 33:2 (The Lord came from Sinai . . . at His right hand was a fiery law unto them) as: "like a bridegroom who goes to meet the bride." Cf. Jeremias, *The Parables of Jesus*, 172.

23. Feuillet, "La synthèse eschatologique de Saint Matthieu," 74–77. See also Winandy, "Le Cantique des Cantiques et le Nouveau Testament," 166; Infante, *Lo sposo e la sposa*, 89–90.

24. A few manuscripts add "and the bride" at the end of Matt 25:1 ("[The ten virgins] went out to meet the bridegroom *and the bride*.").

25. Cf. Infante, *Lo sposo e la sposa*, 90.

that will precede the coming of the Son of Man (24:1–31). The depiction of the "abomination of desolation"—standing in the holy place immediately before its destruction, accompanied by the coming of many false Messiahs and symbolizing the ultimate desecration of the holy dwelling of God—stands in stark contrast to the coming of the bridegroom and joyous wedding feast of chapter 25. This creates a dramatic juxtaposition of the chaotic and destructive end of the old cultic order with the expectation and preparation required for the arriving of the new.

## Jesus as Temple and Shekhinah (Matt 18:20)

It is worth mentioning another motif in Matthew that is closely related to our study. This is the identification of Jesus with the Temple and divine presence (the *Shekhinah*). Jesus claimed to be "greater than the Temple," and he announced that he would "rebuild it in three days."[26] The ripping of the Temple veil from top to bottom at the time of his death is commonly interpreted as signifying the opening of the way to God's formerly inaccessible presence in the Holy of Holies.[27] In addition, Jesus' saying that "where two or three are gathered together in my name, I am there in the midst of them" is a probable allusion to the *Shekhinah*, given similar statements found in the Mishnah. According to Rabbi Hananiah ben Teradion, "if two sit together and words of Torah [are spoken] between them, the *Shekhinah* rests between them." Rabbi Halafta ben Dosa replies: "if ten men sit together and occupy themselves with Torah, the *Shekhinah* rests among them." He then proceeds to argue that not ten people are necessary to usher in the *Shekhinah*'s presence, but five, three, two or even just one devout person, for "in every place where I cause My name to be remembered I will come to you and bless you" (Exod 20:24).[28] The striking similarity of language between those statements certainly points to a relationship between them. If these rabbinic sayings were known oral traditions circulating in the first century, it is probable that Jesus purposefully employed this language to identify himself with both the Torah and the *Shekhinah*.

26. Matt 12:6; 26:61; 27:40; cf. Mark 14:58; 15:29; John 2:19–22.

27. Matt 27:51; Mark 15:38; Luke 23:45; cf. also Heb 6:19, 9:3, 10:19–20.

28. *M. Avot* 3:2, 6.

## Summary: Nuptial Imagery in the Gospel of Matthew

Matthew clearly portrays Jesus as bridegroom. Yet it is not entirely obvious that he is attributing to him the role of divine bridegroom. The parables certainly reflect the Old Testament theme of the marriage between God and Israel, and Jesus could be thought of as the "messianic bridegroom of Israel." Yet the conspicuous absence of the bride and the fact that the community of believers is usually given another role in the nuptial parables and sayings (friends of the bridegroom, guests, virgins) indicate that Matthew does not depict a fully thought-out marriage between Christ and his disciples. His nuptial symbolism focuses on realized eschatology (the presence of the bridegroom during Jesus' ministry), the prediction of his future absence, watching and waiting, and the eschatological wedding feast and coming of the bridegroom. One notes a certain tension between Matt 9:15, where the day of the wedding banquet is already taking place during the life of Jesus, and Matt 25:1–13 where the festivity awaits his return. In short, Matthew's nuptial symbolism is discrete. Much different is the nuptial symbolism of the Fourth Gospel, to which we now turn.

# 8

# The One Whom My Soul Loves

## *The Gospel of John*

THE GOSPEL OF JOHN IS FULL OF subtle yet profound nuptial symbolism. The ministry of John the Baptist prepares the way for the wedding at Cana, where Jesus manifests his glory (John 2:1–12) in an echo of both the Genesis creation account and the Sinai theophany. With the cleansing of the Temple, Jesus identifies his body as a new Temple (John 2:19–21), hinting at a correlation between nuptial and temple themes. John the Baptist declares that Jesus is the bridegroom, his disciples are the bride, and the Baptist is the friend of the bridegroom responsible for arranging the wedding (3:29). Jesus' encounter with the Samaritan woman alludes to Old Testament betrothal-type scenes where a man meets a woman at a well and the encounter leads to a marriage (4:5–42). Finally, the anointing at Bethany (12:1–3) and the resurrection appearance to Mary Magdalene (20: 1–18) both allude to the Song of Songs, framing the narrative of Christ's passion and resurrection as his "messianic wedding."

## Prologue: The Glory of the Word Made Flesh
## (John 1:1–18)

A central theme in the Gospel of John is the manifestation of Jesus' "glory" (Gk. *doxa*). The theme is introduced in the prologue with John's proclamation of the Incarnation: "and the Word became flesh and dwelt among us, and we beheld his glory, the glory as of the father's only son, full of grace and truth" (John 1:14). The Greek word for "dwelt" (*skeno*) evokes the Tabernacle (Heb. *mishkan*, Gk. *skene*) and home of God's presence—the *Shekhinah*—at the time of Israel's wilderness wanderings.[1] Israel hoped that the divine presence would one day transcend the boundaries of a tent or temple structure: Joel announced that at the great day of judgment God would "dwell in Zion" (Joel 3:17); Zechariah had God promise to the daughter of Zion, "I will dwell in the midst of you" (Zech 2:10).[2] In this light, John's use of *skeno* suggests that Christ's flesh was a tabernacle in which abode the *Logos*, his human body becoming the new localization of God's presence on earth and replacement of the ancient Tabernacle.[3] It also reflects the idea that Jesus is the divine *Shekhinah* and Wisdom of God, the dwelling place of the Father among his people. Given the memory of the divine glory that formerly dwelt in the sanctuary and the identification of Jesus with the Tabernacle, we gain a better appreciation of John's words "and we beheld his glory." The glory of the *Shekhinah* formerly revealed at Mount Sinai and in the Tabernacle is now seen in Jesus,[4] and the relationship between God and the *Logos* is now expressed as an intimate father-son relationship (1:18).[5]

The last words of John 1:14, "full of grace and truth" are another allusion to the Sinai theophany, for this was the moment when God revealed himself to Moses as "abounding in grace and truth" (Exod 34:6). The expression is a witness to God's covenant love underlying the Old Testament manifestations of his glory. Just as the great revelation of this love first took place at Sinai, where the Tabernacle became the dwelling

---

1. In the Septuagint, the Greek verb *skeno* denotes the indwelling of the divine presence (Num 35:34; Ezek 43:7; Joel 4:21; Ps 14:1). In the New Testament, *skeno* only appears in John 1:14; Rev 7:15, 12:12, 13:6, 21:3, describing either God's dwelling among his people or his people dwelling in heaven. For a summary of the rabbinic sayings on the *Shekhinah* and early Christian and rabbinic literature on the doctrine of the divine immanence, see Gillet, *Communion in the Messiah*, 81–87; Patai, *The Hebrew Goddess*, 96–111; Coloe, *God Dwells with Us*, 31–63.

2. The indwelling of the *Logos* among us also recalls passages in wisdom literature where Wisdom dwells among men. Cf. Sir 24:4, 8; 1 Enoch 42:1–2.

3. For treatments of Jesus as new tabernacle and echoes of Exodus in John 1:14–18, cf. Boismard, *St. John's Prologue*, 135–45; Brown, *The Gospel According to John I–XII*, 32–35; Beasley-Murray, *John*, 14–15; Kerr, *The Temple of Jesus' Body*, 117–26; Coloe, *God Dwells with Us*, 23–27.

4. Beasley-Murray, *John*, 14. Ps Sol 17:32 announces that the future royal Son of David will reveal the glory of the Lord to all nations; Cf. Ps 17:32; Ps 97:6; Isa 60:1–2; 1 Enoch 49:2.

5. It is possible that Jesus' glory "as of the only begotten from the Father, full of grace and truth" (John 1:14) is an allusion to the Synoptic tradition of Jesus' Transfiguration. Cf. Villeneuve, *Nuptial Symbolism*, 122–3.

for God's glory, now the supreme revelation of God's covenantal love becomes manifest in the incarnate *Logos*, the Word made flesh and new Tabernacle of divine glory. The link between the Sinai covenant mediated by Moses and the New Covenant instituted by Jesus is recapitulated in John 1:17: "For the law was given through Moses; grace and truth came through Jesus Christ." The relation between Moses and Christ, old and new, law and grace, continues to be developed in preparation for the Sinai-Cana connection that unfolds in chapter two.

The Fourth Gospel has much more to say concerning the divine *doxa*: it repeats that the true glory of God is found in Jesus (5:41–44). It is manifest at the resurrection of Lazarus (11:4, 40) and at Jesus' death (his "hour"), for his glory is intrinsically related to God's love and eternal life (12:23; 13:31–32; 17:1–5, 22–24). At the same time, Jesus already possessed the glory of God the Father "before the foundation of the world," and at the hour when his glory is manifest he declares that he will pass it on to his disciples (17:4, 22–24). We will return to the theme of the divine glory in our treatment of the Pauline epistles, examining how Paul interprets its action in the life of the believer. For now, Brown's words fittingly conclude our preliminary discussion on the divine glory manifest in the *Logos*:

> The great exhibition of the enduring covenant love of God in the OT took place at Sinai, the same setting where the Tabernacle became the dwelling for God's glory. So now the supreme exhibition of God's love is the incarnate Word, Jesus Christ, the new Tabernacle of divine glory.[6]

## Preparing the Way: John the Baptist and the Sandals of the Bridegroom-Messiah

Following the prologue, the gospel narrative begins with the proclamation of John the Baptist announcing the coming of the Messiah—the Lamb of God who takes away the sin of the world (John 1:29–37). John describes Jesus as one "whose sandal strap I am not worthy to untie" (John 1:27).[7] It is worth reflecting on this declaration, keeping in mind the nuptial context of chapter 2 and the fact that the same John calls Jesus "the bridegroom" in John 3:29.

6. Brown, *The Gospel According to John I–XII*, 35.
7. Cf. Mark 1:7–8; Matt 3:11; Luke 3:16; Acts 13:25.

Exegetes commonly interpret John's saying on the sandal as an expression of his humility before one who is greater than he. Yet another interpretation, well known in the ancient world, tends to be overlooked by modern commentators. The Baptist's reference to the sandal may well be a reference to the law of the levirate and rite of the *halizah* formulated in Deut 25:5–10 and applied in Ruth 4:6–8.[8] The law stipulates that the brother of a man who dies childless must marry his brother's widow and raise offspring who will carry the name of the deceased brother. If the brother does not marry the widow, the ceremony of *halizah* takes place, whereby the woman is released from the levirate obligation and free to marry someone else:[9]

> If the man does not wish to take his brother's wife . . . then his brother's wife shall go up to him in the presence of the elders and pull his sandal off his foot and spit in his face. And she shall answer and say, 'So shall it be done to the man who does not build up his brother's house.' (Deut 25:7, 9)

When the Jewish authorities ask John whether he is the Messiah, he vigorously rejects these claims. In light of John 3:29, to arrogate such a title would mean to supplant the one who has the rights of the bridegroom. Thus, loosening Jesus' sandal would be tantamount to submitting him to the rite of the *halizah* (including spitting in his face!), causing Jesus to forsake marriage with his legitimate bride. Other clues add weight to this nuptial interpretation. John's self-identification with the "voice crying in the wilderness" of Isa 40:3 (John 1:23) may allude to the desert that was the place of betrothal between God and Israel for the prophets. John thus calls the people into the wilderness to prepare them for the coming of the Messiah, just as the prophets led the bride into the wilderness to call her to conversion (Hos 2:16–17; Jer 2:2–3). The desert is the place where the covenant of love between God and his people will be renewed. In this way, the nuptial theme is subtly introduced in the first chapter of the gospel, with the Baptist announcing in veiled terms what he makes explicit in chapter 3—that Jesus is the bridegroom-Messiah.

8. Cf. Alonso Schökel, *I nomi dell'amore*, 111–33; Infante, *Lo sposo e la sposa*, 119–22.

9. Cf. "Levirate Marriage and Halizah" in *Encyclopedia Judaica* 11, 122–130.

# The Glory of the Bridegroom: The Wedding at Cana
## (John 2:1–11)

### The Cana Narrative

The story of the Wedding at Cana is well known: Jesus, his mother and his disciples are invited to a wedding in Cana of Galilee, which takes place "on the third day" (2:1). At some point, the wine runs out, which prompts Mary to inform Jesus: "They have no wine." His response is perplexing: "Woman, what have you to do with me? My hour has not yet come" (2:4). Mary then instructs the servants: "Do whatever he tells you" (2:5). At Jesus' command, the servants fill with water six large stone jars "for the Jewish rites of purification." After the water miraculously turns into wine, Jesus tells them to take some to the master of the feast. After tasting the miraculous wine, the master of the feast calls the bridegroom and congratulates him for having kept the best wine until that moment (2:9–10). The miracle is identified as the "beginning of signs" that Jesus did which "manifested his glory; and his disciples believed in him" (2:11).

On a first reading, the nuptial theme seems almost peripheral to the narrative. Jesus is not the bridegroom but only a guest, and the bride is wholly absent from the story. Still, the fact that Jesus is identified as bridegroom in the following chapter (3:29) indicates that his role at Cana may be more than that of a simple guest. Indeed, the fact that he takes on the responsibility for supplying the wine puts him in the position of the bridegroom, the person traditionally charged with providing the wine at weddings.[10]

### The "Third Day" and Jesus' "Hour"

Jesus "manifested his glory" at the wedding at Cana which occurred on "the third day" (John 2:1, 11). This third day alludes to the manifestation of Christ's glory when he is raised on the third day.[11] The allusion

---

10. This is a classic example of Johannine irony: while the characters in the story see Jesus as a simple guest, the reader is given a deeper insight into his role in the story. "John hints that the Messiah who provides an abundance of good wine is a bridegroom." McWhirter, *The Bridegroom Messiah and the People of God*, 49. Cf. Feuillet, "Les épousailles du Messie," 373; Fehribach, *The Women in the Life of the Bridegroom*, 29; Pitre, *Jesus the Bridegroom*, 35–45.

11. Dodd, *The Interpretation of the Fourth Gospel*, 300; Schnackenburg, *The Gospel According to John*, 325; Brown, *The Gospel According to John I–XII*, 97; Beasley-Murray,

is strengthened by the relation between Cana's "third day" and Jesus' "hour," which had "not yet come" (2:4). Jesus' hour refers to the hour of his death (7:30, 8:30) when he is glorified (12:23, 27; 13:1; 17:1; 19:27). How is it, then, that he already reveals his glory at Cana? It seems that Jesus manifests his glory in two "installments"—first at Cana and then at the "hour" of his death and resurrection. The two events are distinct but related moments when Jesus manifests his glory, so that Cana is a partial anticipation of the glory later revealed at the resurrection.[12] In this sense, perhaps Jesus' statement that "my hour has not yet come" at Cana means that the hour of *his own wedding* had not yet come—namely the "hour" of his crucifixion.[13]

Significantly, Jesus later speaks of an "hour" that will inaugurate a new worship of God "in spirit and in truth" (John 4:21–24), and of the "hour" of the final resurrection of the dead (5:25–29). The Fourth Gospel thus refers to four moments related to Jesus' hour: (a) Cana, when his hour has "not yet come" but which partially anticipates the revelation of Jesus' glory; (b) Jesus' death and resurrection—his "hour" properly speaking; (c) the "hour" when God will be worshiped "in spirit and in truth;" and (d) the final "hour" of the resurrection of the dead. Jesus' hour thus carries a strong sense of realized eschatology—of "already but not yet": First, the miracle at Cana reveals Jesus as "the giver of God's eschatological gifts, here and now" for those who are at the wedding with him.[14] Second, Cana points to Christ's passion, death, and resurrection, his "hour" when he fully manifests his glory. Third, the paschal mystery inaugurates the "hour" of the new worship "in spirit and in truth," characterized by the "living water" of the Holy Spirit that will become "springs of water welling up to eternal life" in Jesus' disciples (4:14; 7:38). Finally, this new worship will anticipate the final "hour" of the resurrection of the dead (5:25–29), when all who are thirsty will be invited come and drink the water of life (cf. Rev 22:17).

---

*John*, 34; Carson, *The Gospel According to John*, 167.

12. On the moment of the revelation of Christ's glory, Brown (*The Gospel According to John I–XII*, 100–101) writes: "For John the true glory of Jesus is revealed only in 'the hour.' Since 7:39 states clearly that during the ministry Jesus had not yet been glorified, we are to think of 2:11 either as referring to a partial manifestation of glory, or as being part of the capsulizing of the training of the disciples where their whole career, including their sight of the glory of the resurrected Jesus, is foreshadowed."

13. Fehribach, *The Women in the Life of the Bridegroom*, 30–31.

14. Schnackenburg, *The Gospel According to St. John*, 331.

## Seventh Day of a New Creation

It has often been noted that Cana's "third day" concludes a sequence of days introduced in the first chapter of the Gospel describing the beginning of Jesus' public activity. Three times, a new day is introduced with the expression "the next day." After four successive days, the wedding at Cana occurs on "the third day," resulting in the following sequence:

First day (John 1:19) + 1 (1:29) + 1 (1:35) + 1 (1:43)
+ "the third day" (2:1) = Seven days

According to this scheme, the Wedding at Cana takes place at the climax of the first week of Jesus' activity. Commentators have suggested that the succession of seven days in John 1–2 is an allusion to the seven days of creation of Genesis 1.[15] Indeed, there are several parallels between the two narratives:

- Both Genesis and John's Gospel open with the words "in the beginning."

- The creation of light on the first day of creation (Gen 1:3) foreshadows Jesus' identity as "the true light which gives light to every man coming into the world" (John 1:9).

- On the second day, God created the firmament and divided the waters under and below it (Gen 1:6–8). On the second day, John the Baptist baptizes with water and sees "the Spirit descending from heaven like a dove" (1:32), recalling the Spirit of God that hovered over the face of the waters at creation (Gen 1:2).

- God completed his work of creation on the seventh day, which he blessed and hallowed (Gen 2:1–3). The wedding at Cana occurs on the seventh day when the bridegroom blesses and hallows his bride.

These allusions to creation imply that the evangelist is portraying Jesus as a new Adam. In addition, ancient interpreters saw Jesus calling his mother "woman" (John 2:4, cf. 19:26) as a veiled reference to Eve, called "woman" and "mother" in Gen 2:23; 3:15, 20.[16] This Mary-Eve

---

15. Boismard, *St. John's Prologue*, 106–7; Boismard, *Du Baptème à Cana*, 15; Barrosse, "The Seven Days of the New Creation in St. John's Gospel," 507–16; Brown, *The Gospel According to John I–XII*, 105–6; Carmichael, *The Story of Creation*; Kerr, *The Temple of Jesus' Body*, 70–71; Coloe, *God Dwells with Us*, 21–23.

16. Justin Martyr, *Dialogue with Trypho* 100; Irenaeus, *Against Heresies* 3.22.3;

association is confirmed in Rev 12: In a dramatic scene of cosmic warfare, the "woman clothed with the sun" and mother of the Messiah battles "that ancient serpent, called the Devil and Satan" (Rev 12:1–9). The scene clearly evokes the enmity between the serpent and the woman announced in Gen 3:15. That the mother of the Messiah—Mary, the mother of Jesus—battles against the ancient serpent implies that she is the woman of Gen 3:15 who undoes Eve's sin. In this light, John not only portrays the wedding at Cana as the pinnacle of the new creation; he also hints that Mary is the new Eve.[17] In this way, the evangelist adroitly connects the nuptial theme of Cana with creation and the origins of humanity. After Cana, Mary disappears from the narrative until the crucifixion scene—Jesus' "hour" which also becomes her own hour. As we shall see, the evangelist portrays the crucifixion as a messianic wedding which brings forth the fruit of a new birth, where Mary as new Eve takes on the role of a spiritual mother.

## Cana as Echo of Sinai

In addition to alluding to the days of creation, there are good reasons to believe that the sequence of seven days in John 1–2 also refers to God's covenant with Israel at Sinai (which, as we recall, the rabbis considered to be the betrothal between God and Israel).[18] In the following sections, we will highlight the literary and theological relationship between the Cana and Sinai narratives. First, we will compare the sequence of seven days in John 1–2 and Exod 19. Second, we will examine the role of Jesus' statement about Jacob's ladder (John 1:51) and its relation to Sinai. Third, we will consider Mary's role at Cana as mediating voice between Jesus and the servants, paralleling the mediating role of Moses between God and Israel at Sinai. Fourth, we will consider how the wine at Cana alludes to the Torah, cultic worship, wisdom, love, Eden, and the messianic age.

---

5.19.1; *Proof of the Apostolic Teaching* 33. Cf. Hahn, *Hail, Holy Queen*, 31–45; Brown, *The Gospel According to John I–XII*, 107–9.

17. For a thorough exposition of this view, cf. Feuillet, "Les épousailles du Messie," 548–50.

18. The correlation between Cana and Sinai has been studied in depth by Aristide Serra in his *Contributi dell'antica letteratura giudaica per l'esegesi di Giovanni 2, 1–12 e 19, 25–27.*

## Theophany and Covenant on the Seventh Day

We have mentioned the sequence of days in John 1–2 (First day + 1 + 1 + 1 + third day = seven days). In the book of Exodus, we read that the Israelites arrived at the wilderness of Sinai in the third month after coming out of Egypt, on an unspecified day ("on that day") (Exod 19:1). The Lord tells Moses to consecrate the people "today and tomorrow" and warns them to be ready by *the third day*, *"for on the third day* the LORD will come down upon Mount Sinai in the sight of all the people" (Exod 19:10). The Sinai theophany and revelation of the glory of God is thus announced for the *third day*—as is the wedding at Cana when Jesus reveals his glory.

Although the mention of the third day in Exod 19 and John 2 hardly constitutes strong evidence for an intertextual relationship between the two passages, the testimony of rabbinic literature considerably strengthens the correlation, noting that a *week* of preparation preceded the Sinai theophany so that God appeared to Israel on the *seventh day* from their arrival at the mountain. Targum Pseudo-Jonathan narrates the Sinai theophany as occurring over one week, using the same structure of days as found in John 1:19–2:11: four days are listed in succession, followed by "the third day" (1 + 1 + 1 + 1 + 3 = 7). A comparison of the Targum and the Gospel reveals several parallels between the events leading to Sinai and Cana.[19]

---

19. Serra (*Contribuiti*, 64–73) has analyzed in detail the correlation between the Targum of Exodus and the Johannine narrative. See Villeneuve, *Nuptial Symbolism*, 430-433 for the parallel texts of Targum Pseudo-Jonathan Exod 19:1-20 and John 1:19-2:11.

| Day | Targum Pseudo-Jonathan | John 1–2 |
|---|---|---|
| 1 | On the third month of the Exodus . . . *on that day, the first of the month*, they came to the desert . . . (Ex 19:1–2) | And this is the testimony of John . . . "I am the voice of one crying in the wilderness." (Jn 1:19–28) |
| 2 | And Moses on the *second day* went up to the summit of the mount . . . (Ex 19:3–8) | *The next day* he saw Jesus coming toward him, and said, "Behold, the Lamb of God . . . " (Jn 1:29–34) |
| 3 | And the Lord said to Moses on the *third day*: I will reveal Myself to thee in the depth of the cloud of glory. (Ex 19:9) | *The next day* again John was standing with two of his disciples. (Jn 1:35–42) |
| 4 | And the Lord said to Moses on the *fourth day*, Go to the people, and prepare them today and tomorrow . . . (Ex 19:10–15) | *The next day* Jesus decided to go to Galilee; and he found Philip . . . (Jn 1:43–51) |
| 7 | And it was *on the third day* . . . that on the mountain there were voices of thunders, and lightnings, and mighty clouds of smoke. (Ex 19:16–20) | *On the third day* there was a wedding at Cana in Galilee. (Jn 2:2–11) |

### First day: Setting the stage and anticipation

On the first day, the Israelites come to the wilderness of Sinai; John the Baptist is introduced as a voice crying in the wilderness. Both the Targum and the Gospel describe the physical setting of their respective scenes: the wilderness. It is a time of preparation and anticipation of the imminent revelation.

### Second day: Divine gift and consecration

On the second day, both texts describe a person standing as mediator between the divinity and the people: Moses mediates between God and Israel; John the Baptist between Christ and the disciples. God tells Moses that Israel will receive the Torah and be consecrated as "kingdom of priests and holy people." John sees Jesus receiving the Holy Spirit as sign that he is the Son of God. Torah and Holy Spirit are divine gifts that communicate divine revelation, enable communion with God, act as signs of the covenant, and serve as guarantors of divine adoption.

**Third day: Announcing the imminent revelation to awaken faith**

On the third day, God announces that he will reveal himself to Moses in the cloud of glory, so that the people may *hear* God's voice and *believe* in Moses. On the Gospel's third day, the disciples *hear* John speak and they are thereby convinced to *follow* Jesus—which is the practical application of believing in him. To their question "where are you staying?" he replies, "come and see."

**Fourth day: Warning to stay at a distance and personal invitation**

On the fourth day, a marked contrast between the two stories is apparent: whereas the revelation at Sinai is awesome and frightening, and the people are warned not to approach the mountain and to purify themselves in preparation for the theophany, Jesus extends a personal invitation to his disciples to follow him. Whereas the Sinai narrative prohibits marital relations in preparation for the heavenly vision, Jesus alludes to Jacob's ladder and declares that his disciples will "see heaven opened, and the angels of God ascending and descending on the Son of Man."

**Seventh day: Revelation of divine glory**

Both narratives end with the revelation of divine glory—of God at Sinai and Jesus at Cana—"on the third day" which completes the sequence of seven days. Moses is mediator at Sinai; Mary is mediatrix at Cana. But while Sinai emphasizes distance between a Holy God and an unworthy people (through thunder, lightning, smoke, flames, and trumpets), Cana underlines the closeness of intimate communion and joy flowing from the abundance of wine at the wedding.

The similarities between the Cana narrative and the Targum's account of the Sinai revelation are too close to be mere coincidence. This indicates that the Targum's traditions were probably known at the time of the Gospel's redaction, and that John relied on them to craft his Cana narrative as echo of the Sinai revelation and as the moment of the nuptials between Christ and his people.

## Jacob's Ladder: Stairway to Heaven

> And [Jesus] said to [Nathanael], "Amen, amen, I say to you, you
> will see heaven opened, and the angels of God ascending and
> descending on the Son of Man." (John 1:51)

Jesus' saying in John 1:51, when viewed in light of rabbinic literature,
is another link connecting the wedding at Cana not only with the Sinai
covenant but also with the Jerusalem Temple.[20] Jesus refers to the dream
of the patriarch Jacob on his journey from Beer Sheva to Haran. In this
vision, "a ladder was set up on the earth, and its top reached to heaven;
and there the angels of God were ascending and descending on it"
(Gen 28:12). Although the most ancient interpretations take "it" to mean
the ladder, most rabbis in later rabbinic literature interpret "it" as "him"—
meaning that the angels ascended and descended not on the ladder but
on *Jacob*.[21] By referring to Jacob's ladder, Jesus is identifying himself (the
Son of Man) with either Jacob's ladder or perhaps the patriarch himself
upon which the angels ascended and descended.

Why would Jesus make such a declaration? The answer may lie in
the fact that the rabbis considered Jacob's ladder to be a prophetic figure
of the Sinai revelation. If this tradition was known in the first century
and the evangelist is alluding to it, Jesus would be introducing the wedding at Cana (where Christ's glory is revealed ) as a fulfillment of the
Sinai covenant (where God's glory was revealed). In this light, note how
*Genesis Rabbah* interprets Genesis 28:12–13 by linking every element of
Jacob's vision of the ladder with an aspect of the Sinai theophany:

> *Then he dreamed, and behold, a ladder*: this represents Sinai.
> . . . *that was set up on the earth*: "and they stood at the foot of
> the mountain" (Exod 19:17). . . . *and its top reached to heaven*:
> "and the mountain burned with fire to the midst of heaven"
> (Deut 4:11). *And behold the angels of God*: "The chariots of
> God are twenty thousand, even thousands of thousands; [the
> Lord is among them as in Sinai, in the Holy Place]" (Psa 68:17).
> . . . *and behold the angels of God*: These are Moses and Aaron.

---

20. For discussions of John 1:51, cf. Kerr, *The Temple of Jesus' Body*, 136–66; Serra,
*Contribuiti*, 260–301.

21. The two views are presented in *GenR* 68:12. Commenting on the view that the
angels were ascending and descending on Jacob, the Midrash states that while Jacob's
body lies on the earth, his true features are in heaven. Applying this to Jesus would
mean that he is the connection between heaven and earth.

*. . . were ascending*: "and Moses went up to God" (Exod 19:3).
*. . . and descending*: "So Moses went down from the mountain"
(Exod 19:14). *And behold, the LORD stood above it*: "Then the
LORD came down upon Mount Sinai, on the top of the mountain" (Exod 19:20).[22]

According to the Midrash, Jacob's ladder represents Mount Sinai.
The earth upon which the ladder stood and its top reaching to heaven are
respectively the foot and top of the mountain. The angels of God ascending the ladder are either the chariots of God at Sinai or Moses and Aaron
climbing the mountain. Just as God stood above the ladder, so he stood
upon Mount Sinai. Jesus' statement on Jacob's ladder thus functions as a
transition between John's prologue and the Cana narrative: the prologue
announced that we beheld Christ's glory, that is, the glory of God revealed
at Sinai that dwelt in the ancient Tabernacle. Now, by identifying himself
with Jacob's ladder upon which the angels ascended and descended, Jesus
associates himself with Mount Sinai, the place where the glory of God
was manifest to Israel and dwelt among them.[23] His saying anticipates the
revelation of his own glory at Cana.

The same Midrash also understands Jacob's dream to symbolically
refer to the Temple:[24]

> No dream is without its interpretation. *And behold a ladder*
> symbolizes the stairway; *set up on the earth* – the altar, as it
> says, *an altar of earth thou shalt make unto me* (Exod 20:24);
> *and the top of it reached to heaven* – the sacrifices, the odour of
> which ascended to heaven; *and behold the angels of God* – the
> High Priests; *ascending and descending on it* – ascending and
> descending the stairway. *And behold, the Lord stood beside him*
> (28:13) – *I saw the Lord standing beside the altar* (Amos 9:1).[25]

The Biblical text already indicates that the place of Jacob's vision is
the "house of God" and the "gate of heaven" (Gen 28:17). The Midrash
elaborates: The ladder symbolizes the ramp that led to the altar of the
Temple. The earth on which it stood refers to the altar. The heaven
towards which its top reached represents the sacrifices, whose odor

22. *GenR* 68:12.

23. The Targums on Genesis (Onkelos and Jerusalem) also support this view, placing God's *Shekhinah* on Jacob's ladder.

24. Kerr, *The Temple of Jesus' Body* (136–66), examines at length the relationship
between John 1:51 and the Temple.

25. *GenR* 68:12.

rises towards the heavens. The angels are the high priests who go up and down the ramp of the altar, and the Lord standing above the ladder (or above Jacob) is associated with his presence before the altar. Moreover, the Midrash and Targum add that the site of Jacob's vision was the place where the Temple was later to stand.[26] The identification of Jacob's vision with the Temple is further confirmed by the repeated use of the word *place* (Heb. *makom*, Gk. *topos*, mentioned 6 times in Gen 28:10–19), which commonly refers to the Temple in the Old Testament and Jewish tradition.[27] The association of the ladder with the Temple sheds light on Jesus' saying in John 1:51: By identifying himself with Jacob's ladder, Jesus also identifies with the Temple—in continuity with his revelation of the glory of God's *Shekhinah* (1:14) and of his body as new Temple (2:21).

## Mary's Role: "Do Whatever He Tells You"

Another connection between Cana and Sinai is Mary's instruction to the servants at the wedding: "do whatever he tells you" (John 2:5). This exhortation echoes the words pronounced by the people of Israel on three occasions at Mount Sinai.[28] The first proclamation occurs after God's preliminary meeting with Moses and before the theophany to Israel, when the people tell Moses: "All that the LORD has spoken we will do" (Exod 19:8). The second instance occurs after the theophany, at the time of the sealing of the covenant, when the people proclaim: "All the words which the LORD has said we will do" (Exod 24:3). The third instance comes immediately afterwards, following Moses reading the book of the covenant to them as they respond in unison: "All that the LORD has said we will do, and be obedient" (Exod 24:7).

Apart from the affinity of language with Mary's words, these proclamations follow a common pattern: first comes the discourse of a mediator (Moses), standing between God and the people and recalling the salvific acts of God and the conditions of the covenant. Second, the people unanimously respond by giving their assent to the covenant and

26. Tg. Ps.-Jon. Gen 28:17: "This place is not profane but the holy house of the name of the Lord, the proper spot for prayer, set forth before the gate of heaven, founded beneath the throne of Glory." Cf. also *GenR* 69:7.

27. Cf. Exod 15:17; Deut 12:5, 11–14; 2 Sam 7:10; 2 Chr 17:9; Jer 7:3–4, 7, 12, 14; 2 Mac 1:27–29; 2:17–18; John 4:20; 11:48. Cf. Kerr, *The Temple of Jesus' Body*, 152–56; 303–306.

28. Cf. Serra, *Contributi*, 139–226; *Marie à Cana*, 39–47.

its stipulations. Third, the ceremony displays liturgical features. It is a cultic assembly with a fixed form that can be repeated at regular intervals by a feast in which the people commemorate and renew their alliance with God.[29] In the Gospel, the role of mediator is shared by John the Baptist, who testifies to the salvific role of Jesus, and Mary, who urges the servants to do as Jesus says. As mediatrix, Mary prompts the servants to obey Jesus and their obedience is seen in their actions. The presence of the jars used for ritual purposes adds the liturgical dimension to the Cana narrative.

The nuptial symbolism associated with Sinai sheds new light on Mary's role as mediatrix between Jesus and the servants at Cana, similar to Moses' role as mediator between God and Israel at Sinai (Deut 5:5, 27). The obedience of the servants to Mary's words, modeled on the obedience of Israel at Sinai, thus becomes a model of the docile obedience required of the disciples of Christ so that they may enter into the new nuptial alliance and joy of the wedding by which it is sealed.

## Cana's Wine

Jesus' miraculous transformation of ordinary water into a great abundance of superior wine stands at the heart of the sign of Cana. Wine is a symbol of the goodness of creation in the Old Testament, echoing the psalmist's view that God generously provided the world with "wine to gladden the heart of man" (Psa 104:15).[30] In ancient Judaism, wine was also associated with Torah, cultic worship, wisdom, spousal love, the Garden of Eden, and the eschatological feast of the end of days.

### Wine as Torah

Wine is one of the signs of the covenant. It is a gift of God and a sign of his blessing to Israel as a reward for faithful Torah observance (Deut 7:11–13; 11:14; Prov 3:10). Failure to keep the covenant results in the absence of wine (Deut 28:39). In Jer 23:9, wine is related to the reception of the Word of God, which has an intoxicating effect on the prophet: he is "like a drunken man . . . whom wine has overcome, because of the Lord

29. Other instances of such liturgical covenant-renewal ceremonies are found in Josh 1:1–18; Josh 24:1–28; 2 Kgs 23:1–3; 2 Chr 15:9–15.

30. Cf. Job 1:13; Eccl 9:7; 10:19.

and because of his holy words." In Philo[31] and rabbinic literature, wine is one of the preferred symbols of the Torah, and Mount Sinai is sometimes represented as the "wine cellar" of the Torah.[32] For example, the Targum on the Song interprets the "house of wine" of Cant 2:4 as "the house of study at Sinai" where the assembly of Israel studies Torah and declares its acceptance of God's commandments.

### Wine as Symbol of Cultic Worship

The contrast between the water for the Jewish rites of purification and the wine at Cana has often been interpreted as the sign of the old order of law transformed into the new order of grace.[33] Jesus' bridegroom role as provider of the "new wine" of grace is also highlighted in his identity as "true vine" in John 15:1–10. As we have seen, the bridegroom-wine association is also found in the Synoptics, where the question on fasting is juxtaposed with Jesus' saying on the "new wine," denoting the inappropriateness of fasting at a time when the bridegroom and provider of the best wine is present among his people. Wine was offered as drink offerings with the sacrifices in the Temple (Exod 29:40–41; Lev 23:13, 18; Num 15:5–10). Given Jesus' roles in the Fourth Gospel as new Temple and sacrificial Lamb offered at the "hour" of his crucifixion (anticipated at Cana), and given the association between Jesus' blood and the Eucharistic wine (6:53–56), it is likely that the wine of Cana carries additional cultic or sacrificial allusions.

### Wine as Wisdom

Wine is also associated with wisdom. In Prov 9:1–6, personified Lady Wisdom has "mixed her wine," and she invites those who seek her to come and drink it: Seeking and finding divine Wisdom is tantamount to finding an attractive wife and drinking abundant wine with her at a sumptuous feast. John associates the traits of Lady Wisdom with the Logos: Both were pre-existent, existing in the beginning with God (Prov 8:22–25; John 1:1–2) and active in the work of creation (Prov 8:26–30; John 1:3); both came into the world to dwell among men (Prov 8:31; Sir

31. *On Flight and Finding* 176; *On Dreams* 2:190; *On the Life of Moses* I:187.
32. *Sifre Deut* 48; *PRK* 12:5; *CantR* 1:2; *TgCant* 2:3–4.
33. Cf. Schnackenburg, *The Gospel According to John,* I:339.

24:7–12; John 1:14); both provided wine and bread for them (Prov 9:1–5; John 2:1–11; 6:4–14).[34] Philo sheds further light on Jesus' role as Logos or incarnate Wisdom and his connection with wine. Commenting on King Melchizedek, the "priest of God most high" who brought out bread and wine for Abraham (Gen 14:18), Philo writes that Melchizedek, as "priest-logos," will also perform a miraculous transformation of water into wine.[35] For Philo, wine represents the wisdom that intoxicates men and gives them delight and joy. Moreover, Philo calls the Logos "cupbearer" and "master of the feast."[36] John may have been aware of this Philonic identification of wine with wisdom. He may have intended to associate the wine of Cana with wisdom, or contrast the wine of the new doctrine of the Logos with the old Torah represented by the jars of water.

## Wine as Love

Lady Wisdom's invitation to come "drink her wine" in Prov 9:5 also reveals an association between wine and nuptial love. Wine flows in abundance in the Song of Songs as sign of the inebriation of the lovers for each other. The king's love for his beloved is "better than wine" (Cant 1:2) and so is hers for him (Cant 4:10). At the climax of the Song, when the lover "comes to his garden," he exclaims: "I drank my wine with my milk" (Cant 5:1). His beloved's navel is "a rounded bowl that never lacks mixed wine" (Cant 7:2) and her palate is also "the best wine" (Cant 7:9), while she desires to bring her man into the house of her mother so that she may give him "spiced wine to drink, the juice of my pomegranates" (Cant 8:2).

## Wine in Eden

Although the Bible does not attest to the presence of wine in Eden, the tradition is known from apocryphal sources: According to 2 Enoch 8:5, "two springs come out [of paradise] which send forth honey and milk, and their springs send forth oil and wine." The tradition of wine in the

34. Boismard, *St. John's Prologue*, 74–76; *Du Baptême à Cana*, 137–43. All those characteristics also apply to Lady Wisdom in Sir 24.

35. *Allegorical Interpretation* III:82. Cf. Dodd, *Interpretation* 298. Cf. Heb 5:6, 10; 7:1–17.

36. *On Dreams* II:249; II:183; cf. Dodd, *Interpretation*, 298–99; Schnackenburg, *The Gospel According to John*, I:339.

garden of delights is also preserved in rabbinic literature. In Targum Canticles 7:2, the beloved's "mixed wine" represents the words of Torah that are compared to the water of the great river of Eden. The Targum also renders the wine of Cant 8:2 as "old wine preserved in its grapes since the day the world was created and from pomegranates and fruits prepared for the righteous in the Garden of Eden."

### Wine as Sign of the Messianic Age

Wine is also connected to the messianic age in prophetic and apocalyptic literature. It is the sign of the happiness and deliverance that will characterize the age of salvation. Jesus' miraculous supply of "the good wine" for the wedding feast, sign of abundance and joy, is one of the consistent Old Testament figures for the coming of the kingdom of God, often represented by a great feast with abundantly flowing wine. Jewish tradition associates the coming of the Messiah with an abundant outpouring of wine.[37] Jacob's blessing to Judah claims that the future ruler from Judah will be "binding his donkey to the vine, and his donkey's colt to the choice vine, he washes his garments in wine, and his clothes in the blood of grapes." (Gen 49:11–12). Amos' eschatological vision sees mountains dripping with sweet wine, and he announces that the captives of Israel will return and "plant vineyards and drink wine from them" (Amos 9:13–14). For Hosea, the scent of eschatological Israel will be "like the wine of Lebanon" (Hos 14:7). Isaiah also anticipates an abundance of wine on the mountain of the Lord at the end of days (25:6; 55:1). Wine is sometimes linked with God's promise to restore his nuptial alliance with his people (Hos 2:19–22; Isa 62:4–5, 8). The apocryphal 2 Baruch also speaks of an abundance of wine in the messianic age (2 Bar 29:3, 5).[38] In rabbinic writings, wine represents the Torah taught by the Messiah at the end of days: for example, the Targum on the Song of Songs (8:1–2) turns

---

37. Brown writes: "Thus the headwaiter's statement at the end of the scene, 'You have kept the choice wine until now,' can be understood as the proclamation of the coming of the messianic days" (*The Gospel According to John I–XII*, 105). Schnackenburg, *Gospel*, 338–40; McWhirter, *The Bridegroom Messiah*, 47–49. As seen above, the messianic symbolism of wine appears in the Synoptics within the context of the question on fasting.

38. On the abundance of wine in the eschatological age, see also Joel 3:18; Jer 31:5,12; Zech 9:17; 1 Enoch 10:19. Cf. Schnackenburg, *The Gospel According to John*, 338 and n. 34.

the lovers' joyful drinking of spiced wine into a joyful acceptance of the precepts of the Torah in the last days.

The wine of Cana has been traditionally interpreted to signify things such as the Eucharistic wine, the Holy Spirit, the New Covenant, the teachings of Christ, or the goods of the messianic age. The Sinai-Cana typology reveals that just as God revealed his glory on the third day at Sinai by revealing the old wine of Torah, Jesus reveals his glory on the third day at Cana by taking on the role of the bridegroom, providing better wine as symbol of his new Torah and the great eschatological wedding feast to come.

## Summary: The Wedding at Cana

John carefully crafts the first two chapters of his Gospel with a series of allusions pointing to key moments of salvation history: First, he depicts Cana as the culmination of a new creation, occurring on the seventh day of Jesus' first week of ministry, with Jesus figuring as new Adam and Mary as new Eve. Second, John alludes to the Sinai revelation and the nuptial covenant between God and Israel by means of clever literary hints. These include the sequence of seven days leading to Cana as echo of the seven days leading to Sinai, Jacob's ladder as symbol of Sinai, Mary's mediating role recalling Moses' mediating role, and the association of Cana's wine with the Torah. These parallels indicate that the revelation of Christ's glory at Cana echoes the revelation of God's glory at Horeb, and that Jesus is the bridegroom who renews God's nuptial union with Israel at Sinai. Third, John points to Jesus' role as Tabernacle and Temple, describing him as the Logos dwelling among us, just as the *Shekhinah* dwelt in the former Tabernacle. The evangelist continues to develop this realized eschatology in the next pericope on Jesus' body as the New Temple.

# The New Temple (John 2:13–22)

## The Bridegroom-Messiah as New Temple

Just as Matthew juxtaposes the nuptial coming of the bridegroom (Matt 25:1–13) and the destruction of the Temple at the time of the *parousia* (Matt 24:1–44), John also closely associates the themes of marriage and Temple, placing the episode of the cleansing of the Temple (John 2:13–22) immediately following the marriage of Cana (John 2:1–12). This arrangement is no mere coincidence. Both episodes refer to the fulfillment of timeless Jewish institutions—the water for ritual purification and the Temple—in the new cult centered on the person of Jesus. Both incidents also foreshadow the passion, death and resurrection of Jesus which are at the heart of his role as bridegroom-Temple. Unlike the Synoptics, however, John places the cleansing of the Temple at the beginning of his Gospel.[39] This means that his life and ministry are portrayed in light of his identity as new Temple, as the narrative moves towards the climax of Jesus' "hour."

John reports that Jesus went to Capernaum for a few days after leaving Cana, and then continued up to Jerusalem at the time of the Passover. Upon entering the Temple complex he violently drove out the sellers and their animals with a whip and overturned the tables of the money changers, accusing them of making his "Father's house" a house of trade (John 2:16). Asked for a sign to justify his action, he foretells the Temple's demise and announces the raising of a new Temple: "Destroy this temple, and in three days I will raise it up" (John 2:19). When the Jews respond with outrage at the suggestion that what had taken forty-six years to build could be raised in three days, no reply comes from Jesus' mouth—yet the evangelist adds a clarifying note for his readers:

> But he spoke of the temple of his body. When therefore he was raised from the dead, his disciples remembered that he had said this; and they believed the Scripture and the word which Jesus had spoken (John 2:21–22).

As Schnackenburg has noted, "this explanation makes Jesus the 'place' where God is to be adored, the true 'house of God.'"[40] Numerous studies have been made on Jesus' role as new Temple in the Fourth Gospel.[41] Here I will focus on the nuptial theme. We have mentioned above the link between John the Baptist's saying on Jesus' sandals and the law of the levirate, which hints that Jesus is the bridegroom of Israel. In the formulation and application of the levirate law in Deut 25:9–10 and Ruth 4:11–12, the producing of offspring for the deceased brother

---

39. The Synoptics place the incident near the end of Jesus' ministry: Matt 21:12–13; Mark 11:15–17; Luke 19:45–46.

40. Schnackenburg, *The Gospel According to John*, 1:352.

41. Cf. Coloe, *God Dwells with Us*; Kerr, *The Temple of Jesus' Body*; Um, *The Theme of Temple Christology in John's Gospel*; Hahn, "Temple, Sign, and Sacrament."

is called "building up his house"—a common expression denoting the establishment of a marriage and family and the raising of children. The Temple at the time of Jesus was commonly called "house of the Lord" and the Holy of Holies was thought of as a nuptial chamber where God united himself with Israel. Here Jesus calls the Temple his "Father's house." In other words, he is in the Temple as a Son is in his father's home. When Jesus cleanses the Temple, foretelling its demise and the raising of the "Temple of his body," could he be referring to the "building up of God's house," that is, the renewal and transformation of the marriage covenant with Israel, in continuity with the law of the levirate? Is Jesus' reference to the destruction of the Temple an allusion to the "death" of the older brother (the Jewish Temple service) pointing to his "levirate marriage" with Israel as he takes on the role of the firstborn son marrying the wife (Israel/his disciples) of his deceased brother (Temple Judaism)? Such an interpretation is in line with John's contrasts between old and new, law and grace, water for the purification of the Jews and new wine of the Messiah.

## New Temple, New Sacrifice

When Jesus cleanses the Temple, his disciples remember Ps 69:9: "Zeal for your house has consumed (*katephagen*) me" (John 2:17). This psalm belongs to a group of psalms of the Righteous Sufferer, often associated with the Passion of Christ. Just as the Righteous Sufferer in the psalm was persecuted for remaining loyal to the Temple, so Jesus' action in cleansing the Temple will arouse enmity against him and eventually lead him to his death and "consummation."[42] The new Temple is inextricably linked with the bridegroom's self-sacrifice, suffering and death. Jesus' action in the Temple took place during Passover (2:13) when lambs were slain to commemorate Israel's deliverance from Egypt, and in anticipation of his own paschal sacrifice as "Lamb of God who takes away the sins of the world" (1:29). The sacrificial element of Jesus' death is further displayed in the citation of Ps 69 and its use of the verb *kataphagetai*, which is often used to describe the fire consuming the sacrifices offered to God on the altar.[43] By disrupting the trade taking place in the Temple courts necessary for

42. Dodd, *Interpretation*, 301.

43. E.g. Lev 6:10; 9:24; 1 Kgs 18:38; 2 Chr 7:1. Cf. Kerr, *The Temple of Jesus' Body*, 85.

the animal sacrifices, Jesus is foreshadowing the cessation of sacrificial worship in the Temple and its replacement by his own sacrifice, a prerequisite for the institution of the new Christological Temple worship. Although the Logos already "tabernacled" among men at the moment of the Incarnation, Jesus becomes a Temple properly speaking only after the resurrection, as indicated by his intention to raise up the Temple in "three days."[44] In addition, the use of *kataphagetai* (which can mean eat up, consume or devour) may also be connected to Jesus' exhortation to his followers in the bread of life discourse to eat (*phagein*) his flesh (John 6:51–53).[45] The Eucharistic allusion is plausible when one considers Jesus' role as sacrificial lamb of God and the fact that it was necessary for the Israelites to eat (*phagein*) the flesh of the paschal lamb (Exod 12:8). The connection is strengthened in that our three relevant passages, the cleansing of the Temple, the bread of life discourse, and the crucifixion are all described as occurring at the time of the Passover (John 2:12; 6:4; 19:14).

## Eschatological Revelation of Divine Glory

The idea that Jesus is a Temple that will surpass the Jerusalem sanctuary is the logical development of his identity as the *Shekhinah* who tabernacled among men and revealed the divine glory. The Synoptics also promote the idea that Jesus is one who is "greater than the Temple" and a new, spiritual Temple "made without hands" (Matt 12:6; Mark 14:58). Matthew identifies Jesus with the *Shekhinah* and associates his death with the ripping of the veil in the Temple that allowed access to the innermost sanctuary (Matt 27:51). The promise of a new Temple announces that God's glory will no longer be manifest in a building but rather in the person of Jesus, especially at the hour of his glorification (John 17:1–5). Jesus' prediction that he will raise up a new Temple also ties in with eschatological promises of a renewed Temple worship (Ezek 40–48; Tob 13:10; 14:5), and with prophetic passages declaring that the Temple will be rebuilt by the messianic Davidic "Branch" (2 Sam 7:12–13; Zech 6:12).[46]

---

44. Schnackenburg (*The Gospel According to John*, 1:352): "John sees this spiritual temple as coming about only through the death and resurrection of Jesus, and he sees it portrayed in the body of the risen Lord."

45. Hahn, "Temple, Sign, and Sacrament," 113.

46. The Targums on Zech 6:12 and Isa 53:5, and *Sib. Or.* 5:422 refer to the Messiah as builder of the Temple.

## New Birth, Baptism, Mystical Marriage (John 3)

### Faith and Baptism as Mystical Marriage

So far, nuptial imagery in the Gospel of John is subtle, beginning with the sandals of the bridegroom-Messiah (pointing to the levirate law) and the wedding at Cana (pointing to the Sinai revelation), where Jesus is the implicit bridegroom who provides miraculous wine for the wedding guests. The nuptial imagery becomes more explicit in 3:29 when John the Baptist calls Jesus the bridegroom. Yet this raises a crucial question: If Christ is bridegroom, then what is the nature of the wedding between Christ and his bride? Part of the answer is found in the response expected of those who come into the presence of the bridegroom-Messiah: *faith.* The reason why the Logos became flesh was to grant light and life to men (1:4–9) so that they may become children of God (1:12) by *believing* through him and *believing* in his name (1:7, 12). This faith is not just abstract intellectual assent; it is expressed through close communion with Jesus: The first two disciples "follow him" and "stay with him" (1:37–39, 43)—a response of faith that carries nuptial connotations. Faith is also the response of Nathanael as he encounters Jesus (1:49–50), of the disciples at Cana when Jesus manifests his glory (2:11), and of the same disciples after the resurrection when they remember Jesus' words concerning the temple of his body (2:22).

The theme of faith continues in chapter 3 with Jesus' conversation with Nicodemus: to find salvation and eternal life it is necessary to *believe* in the Son of God (3:14–18, 36). Yet a second action is required of those who wish to attain eternal life and enter the kingdom of God through communion with the bridegroom-Messiah: this is the "new birth" or "birth from above" of "water and the Spirit" (3:3–8). While Nicodemus fails to understand what this means, the context indicates that this new birth is *baptism.* Water baptism was already introduced in the Gospel narrative in the ministry of John the Baptist. Although little is said about the effect of John's baptism in the Fourth Gospel, we know from the synoptic tradition that it was a baptism of repentance and forgiveness of sins.[47] By contrast, Jesus will baptize in the Holy Spirit (1:31–33). Since Jesus also baptizes in water (3:22), it appears that this water-baptism is the baptism in the Holy Spirit announced by John and the new birth "of

---

47. Matt 3:2,6,11; Mark 1:15; Luke 3:3; Acts 19:4. Cf. Koester, *Symbolism in the Fourth Gospel,* 178.

water and the Spirit" required to enter the kingdom of God and receive eternal life. This gift flows out of God's great love for the world declared in John 3:16, a love ultimately revealed through the sacrificial gift of his Son. It is also related to the Exodus: the lifting of the son of Man is compared with Moses lifting up the serpent in the wilderness (3:14–15; cf. Num 21:9). Baptism is also the spiritual enlightenment that enables men to escape the world's darkness and come into the light of the Logos and of the kingdom of God (1:4–9; 3:19–21).[48]

## Bridegroom, Bride, and Friend of the Bridegroom
### (John 3:29)

The third chapter of John contains the only occurrence in the Fourth Gospel where Jesus is explicitly called "the bridegroom." When the Baptist's disciples express concern that Jesus is competing with John's own ministry by baptizing and attracting more followers than him, John responds: "He who has the bride is the bridegroom; the friend of the bridegroom, who stands and hears him, rejoices greatly at the bridegroom's voice. Therefore this joy of mine is now full" (John 3:29). This is also the only nuptial passage of the four gospels where Christ's bride is explicitly mentioned. With these words John the Baptist explains to his followers, in continuation with his discourse in chapter one, that his role was only preparatory; they ought to follow Jesus, the bridegroom-Messiah, and not him. John is but the best man or "friend of the bridegroom," the *shoshbin* responsible for arranging the wedding and for bringing the bride to her bridegroom.[49] The bride does not belong to him but to the bridegroom. Since the dispute which gave rise to John's statement is over the issue of the disciples' allegiance to him or to Jesus, it is clear that the bride here represents the community of believers.[50] As *shoshbin*, John joyfully

---

48. This is further illustrated in John 9:5–7, where the opening of the eyes of the blind man is accomplished through a washing in water from the pool of Siloam. On baptism as enlightenment, cf. Heb 6:4; 10:32.

49. On John the Baptist as *shoshbin* and the *shoshbin*'s role in early Judaism, cf. Brown, *The Gospel According to John I–XII*, 152; Barrett, *The Gospel According to John*, 186; Jeremias, "νύμφη, νυμφίος," 4:1101; Pitre, *Jesus the Bridegroom*, 33–34.

50. Batey agrees: "The identification of the Bride with the messianic community which at present is being received by Jesus is unmistakable." Batey, *New Testament Nuptial Imagery*, 49–50.

presents the bride as a people purified by the waters of baptism to the bridegroom-Messiah.

## The Voice of the Bridegroom: Echoes of Jeremiah and the Canticle

One element particular to John 3:29 is the "voice of the bridegroom." This expression occurs four times in Jeremiah, three times in a context of condemnation and once in a context of consolation (Jer 7:34; 16:9; 25:10; 33:11). Worthy of note is Jeremiah's first mention of the disappearance of the "voice of the bridegroom and voice of the bride" (Jer 7:34) as a result of the imminent doom of the Temple, which has become a "den of thieves" (7:11).[51] Now, seemingly in response to Jeremiah, after Jesus has foretold the rise of the new Temple of his body, John rejoices at hearing again the bridegroom's voice. The passage that reveals the most similarities with John 3:29, however, is Jer 33:10–11. McWhirter cites six correspondences between both passages: (1) both locate the action in Judea (John 3:22); (2) both refer to the "voice of the bridegroom;" (3) both feature the bridegroom in the company of the bride; (4) both celebrate the presence of the matrimonial couple (as opposed to Jer 7:34, 16:9, 25:10 which foretell their absence); (5) both state that someone hears the voice of the bridegroom; and (6) both associate the bridegroom's voice with great joy and gladness.[52] John's allusions to Jer 33:10–11 thus imply that Jesus is the bridegroom whose joyous return was prophesied by Jeremiah. He is also presumably the messianic "righteous branch from David" spoken of by the prophet (Jer 33:15). Significant is also the fact that the voice of the bridegroom was to be heard "as they bring thank offerings to the house of the Lord" (Jer 33:11). This establishes yet another connection between the bridegroom and the Temple.

Scholars have noted that the bride and bridegroom, the friend of the bridegroom and the bridegroom's voice are also found in the Song of Songs.[53] Both Cant 2:8–14 and 5:2–4 describe the woman's joyful response to the voice of the beloved. Stronger parallels are found in Cant 8:13: "You who dwell in the gardens, the companions listen for your voice.

---

51. This is the verse that the Synoptics cite to justify Jesus' action in cleansing the Temple. Cf. Matt 21:12–13; Mark 11:15–17; Luke 19:45–46.

52. McWhirter, *The Bridegroom Messiah and the People of God*, 54–56.

53. Cambe, "L'influence du Cantique des Cantiques sur le Nouveau Testament," 15.

Let me hear it!" Perhaps John the Baptist is appropriating to himself the role of the Song's companions as he hears the bridegroom's voice—the voice of Jesus.

To those who see Jesus as a competing practitioner of the same ritual, John replies that the baptism of Jesus, the bridegroom-Messiah, must now take precedence over his own (3:22–30). Just as the water of the Jewish rites of purification stood in the background of the new Messianic wine (2:6), here too the Jewish purification rites provide the background to the baptism of Jesus (3:25). Perhaps the predominance of ritual water and baptism alongside the nuptial imagery of chapters 1–3 alludes to the idea of a nuptial bath. The nuptial union between Christ and his followers is therefore accomplished through faith in him and baptism in water; communion between them is attained through the divine gift of the Spirit "without measure" (3:34). Moreover, the mystical marriage takes places between heaven and earth, between the one "who comes from above" and those who are "from the earth" (3:31). Dodd's discussion on the Logos is useful:

> The incarnation of the Logos, is . . . the descent of the Son of Man, or heavenly Man, into the lower sphere, the realm of *sarx* (flesh). It is the heavenly man alone . . . who, having descended, ascends to heaven again. His descent and ascent open to men the possibility of receiving eternal life, that is, of ascending to the sphere of *pneuma* (spirit); in other words, the possibility of rebirth. The possibility becomes an actuality for those who have faith in the Son—which is tantamount (in terms of the Prologue) to 'receiving the Logos', with the consequent *exousia* (power) to be children of God.[54]

Dodd's reflection may be taken further when considered in light of John's nuptial aspect. When the Logos became flesh, he 'tabernacled' among men so that they could see the *doxa* (glory) of the Father. The divine *doxa* dwelt in Jesus' *sarx* when the heavenly Logos took on earthly human nature. Recall that the Tabernacle and Holy of Holies were understood to be a nuptial chamber in early Judaism. In their union with the bridegroom-Messiah by faith, through the gift of the Holy Spirit obtained in the nuptial bath of baptism, therefore, those who believe in Jesus are introduced into the nuptial chamber, so to speak, so that they too may contemplate the divine *doxa* and be joined to it. This seems to be John the

---

54. Dodd, *Interpretation*, 305.

evangelist's idea of the mystical marriage between Jesus the bridegroom and his ecclesial bride. From there it is but a small step to arrive at the Pauline doctrine of the body of the believer, which becomes a sanctuary of the Holy Spirit as a result of its union with the bridegroom-Messiah. The mystical consummation of the marriage as a one-flesh union between heavenly bridegroom and earthly bride, however, must still wait until chapter six of the Gospel to be disclosed.

## The Woman at the Well: Living Water and New Worship (John 4:4–42)

Following the Baptist's declaration that Christ is the bridegroom and his followers are his bride, the next chapter brings forth a concrete example of a woman encountering Jesus in a "betrothal-type scene" that turns to a discussion of living water, husbands and marriage, places of worship, the coming of the Messiah, and ends with many people from the woman's community coming to faith in Jesus. The new order of worship announced at the cleansing of the Temple now finds its exposition in nuptial terms through the redemptive presence and action of the bridegroom-Messiah. The close relation between the account of the Samaritan woman at the well and the first three chapters of the gospel was noticed by Dodd, who saw John 2:1–4:42 as bound together by a single theme, best characterized by Paul's expression: "The old things have passed away, see, the new have come!" (2 Cor 5:17). In 2:10 the water of the old purifications is replaced by wine; in 2:14–19 the old Temple makes way for a new one in the risen body of the Messiah; chapter 3 speaks of a new birth; and chapter 4 contrasts Jacob's ancient well with Jesus' 'living water,' and the ancient cults of Jerusalem and Mount Gerizim with the new worship 'in spirit and in truth.'[55]

### Echoes of the Patriarchs

Already in the second century, Origen compared the episode of the Samaritan woman at the well with three well known Old Testament "betrothal-type scenes" where a man on a journey meets a maiden at a well and the story ends with a marriage. In his *Commentary on John*, Origen compared the Samaritan woman with Rebekah in Gen 24:1–67;

55. Cf. Dodd, *Interpretation*, 297; Beasley-Murray, *John*, 31.

in his *Homily on Genesis*, he extended the connection to the stories of Jacob and Rachel in Gen 29:1–20 and Moses and Zipporah in Exod 2:15–22.[56] Origen saw in the Old Testament well-scenes prefigurations of Jesus' encounter with the Samaritan woman, itself a type of the marriage between Christ and the Church: "There, one comes to the wells and the waters that brides may be found; and the Church is united to Christ in the bath of water."[57]

McWhirter has surveyed the recent scholarship on John 4:4–42 and offered new insights into the matter.[58] She noted that all three accounts of Gen 24, Gen 29 and Exod 2 reveal details of plot, characters, setting and diction that appear in John 4. A traveling man stops at a well and is met there by a woman who comes to draw water (John 4:4–7; Gen 24:10–15; 29:1–9; Exod 2:15–16). One of them draws water from a well and gives it to the other (John 4:7–15; Gen 24:16–20; 29:10; Exod 2:17). The woman then rushes home to tell her family about the stranger; the family proceeds to offer him hospitality (John 4:28–29, 40; Gen 24:28–33; 29:12–14; Exod 2:18–19), and the story leads to a betrothal and marriage—literal in the Old Testament stories and inferred in the Gospel. Three other details are absent from the Moses-Zipporah encounter and present only in the Genesis stories: first, the question of the woman's eligibility for marriage in terms of her family/ethnic background and current marital status (positive for Rebekah and Rachel, but negative for the Samaritan woman); second, the initial hidden identity of the traveler which is only revealed later in the story; third, the interest generated by the stranger leading to someone coming to the well to meet him.[59] Yet some unique characteristics of the narrative present only in Gen 29:1–20 and John 4:4–42 indicate that John alludes especially to the encounter between Jacob and Rachel. These include the time of day in "broad daylight" (Gen 29:7) or "about noon" (John 4:6) and especially the central role of Jacob, the main character of the Genesis narrative who is mentioned three times

---

56. Origen, *Commentary on the Gospel of John* 13.175–78; *Homily on Genesis. Gen.* 10.5; cf. McWhirter, *The Bridegroom Messiah*, 1.

57. Origen, *Hom. Gen.* 10.5.

58. McWhirter, *The Bridegroom Messiah*, 6–7, 58–76. Cf. also Fehribach, *The Women in the Life of the Bridegroom*, 45–81; Koester, *Symbolism in the Fourth Gospel,* 47–50; Kerr, *The Temple of Jesus' Body*, 167–204; Carmichael, "Marriage and the Samaritan Woman;" Coloe, *God Dwells with Us*, 85–113; Um, *The Theme of Temple Christology in John's Gospel*, 130–188; Pitre, *Jesus the Bridegroom*, 55–81.

59. McWhirter, *The Bridegroom Messiah*, 60–61.

in John: both scenes occur at the same place, at Jacob's well (John 4:6), near the plot of land that he gave to his son Joseph (John 4:5), and the Samaritan woman is a descendant of Jacob (John 4:12). Moreover, just as Jacob was a man on a journey who became a bridegroom, Jesus is identified as a bridegroom a few verses prior to his encounter with the woman (John 3:29). One difference, however, is significant: While the encounter between Jacob and Rachel ends with a marriage, John's account does not lead to a marriage but rather to many of the Samaritans from the woman's city coming to faith in Christ (4:39–42). This correspondence between marriage and faith in Jesus is consistent with the same correlation seen in John 2–3. Moreover, elements found in Gen 29:1–20 become vehicles for John's central themes, which we will now briefly review.

## Jesus and the Samaritan Woman in Light of Gen 29:1–20

### Water from the Well and Eternal Life

Jesus asks the woman for a drink of water as a rhetorical device to tell her about the "living water" that he has to offer her.[60] Echoing targumic traditions holding that the water from Jacob's well overflowed miraculously for twenty years,[61] the living water that Jesus promises will become "a fountain of water springing up into everlasting life" (John 4:14) in whoever drinks it. This attractive offer illustrates the gift of eternal life introduced in the previous chapters: The prologue stated that the Logos is the source of eternal life (1:4); Jesus revealed to Nicodemus that this eternal life is shared with those who believe in the Son of God (3:15–16, 36) and are joined with him in a nuptial union (3:29) entered through baptism (3:5, 22). This finds a practical application as the narrative moves from the waters of baptism to Jesus' offer of living water, source of eternal life, to the Samaritan woman in the "betrothal-type scene" at the well. The contrast between the water of Jacob's well and Jesus' living water recalls

60. The offer of living waters would be an indication of Jesus' messianic claims according to 1 Enoch 48:1; 49:1, which associates the Messiah with "an inexhaustible spring of righteousness, and many springs of wisdom surrounded it, and all the thirsty drank from them and were filled with wisdom."

61. The Targum claims that the well where Jacob met Rebekah "overflowed, and the water rose to its edge, and continued to overflow all the time he was in Haran" (Targum Pseudo-Jonathan on Gen 28:10; 29:10). Jesus' promise of living waters seems to assume Jacob's miraculous drawing of water. Cf. Neyrey, "Jacob Traditions and the Interpretation of John 4," 423; Coloe, God Dwells with Us, 91.

again the contrast between old and new, law and grace (1:17), ancient Wisdom and newly revealed Logos, water of purification and new wine at Cana, and between the water of John's baptism and the new birth "of water and the Spirit."

### Eligibility for Marriage and Worship in Spirit and in Truth

A second point of contact between Gen 29 and John 4 is the woman's eligibility. Whereas Rachel is a beautiful young virgin from Jacob's family (and therefore a perfect candidate for marriage with him), the Samaritan woman's ethnic/religious background and her irregular marital situation, having had five husbands and currently in an illicit relationship with a sixth man, renders her ineligible for communion with the Jewish Messiah. Commentators have seen in the woman's five husbands a symbol of the five religious cults that were brought into Samaria after the Assyrian conquest (2 Kgs 17:29–31), in the sixth man who is not her husband the syncretistic cult of God that was offered in illicit high places (2 Kgs 17:32–33, 41),[62] and in the Samaritan woman a representative of the Samaritan people. Three other correspondences make the allusion to 2 Kings probable: First, both passages strongly emphasize the differences between Samaritan and Jewish worship of God with the frequent use of the verb *proskuneo* (2 Kgs 17:35–36; John 4:20–24); second, both attribute the differences between Jews and Samaritans to ancestral customs (2 Kgs 17:41; John 4:20); third, both passages state that the Samaritans do not know the God of Israel (2 Kgs 17:26; John 4:22). The evidence, therefore, indicates that "the Samaritan woman with her six men is like the Samaritan people with their six religions."[63] But whereas in the former order of things the Samaritans worshiped "what they do not know," the bridegroom-Messiah now announces to her that the cultic dispute between Gerizim and Jerusalem will soon fade into oblivion because "the hour is coming, and now is, when the true worshipers will worship the Father in spirit and truth" (Joh 4:23). Significant is the reference to the "hour," pointing again to Christ's crucifixion and resurrection as source of the new worship in spirit and in truth, and the ambiguous use of both present and future tenses, indicating that the hour has in a sense arrived,

---

62. McWhirter, *The Bridegroom Messiah*, 69–70; Dodd, *Interpretation*, 313; Fehribach, *Women in the Life of the Bridegroom*, 58–69; Kerr, *The Temple of Jesus' Body*, 179.

63. Cf. McWhirter, *The Bridegroom Messiah*, 71.

but in another sense is not quite here yet. Jesus tells the woman that at that "hour," her Samaritan background will no longer be an obstacle to the true worship of the Father. Unbeknownst to her, John is implying that her negative marital and religious baggage no longer constitute an obstacle to entering into a mystical nuptial relationship with the Messiah. The implication of Jesus' words is twofold: cultic and nuptial. On the one hand, Jesus' announcement of a new worship "in spirit and in truth" alongside his declaration that he is the Messiah (4:25–26) means that the dawn of a new era of Israel's cult has arrived. On the other, John's allusion to the courtship between Jacob and Rachel implies that

> Jesus replaces the former "husbands" of the woman with the true *ba'al*, viz., himself. Since the woman is portrayed as accepting Jesus as Messiah (4:39), he effectively becomes her *ba'al*; and he replaces Samaritan expectations when they too confess him as "Savior of the world" (4:42). The Jacob matrimonial allusions then seem to lie in Jesus' becoming the husband/lord of these new converts, even his replacement of their former allegiances.[64]

### Jacob's Self-Disclosure and Jesus' Messianic Identity

The climax of both stories is the revelation of the traveler's hidden identity: Jacob reveals himself to Rachel after watering Laban's flock (Gen 29:10–12); Jesus discloses his messianic identity to the woman after the discussion on the living water (John 4:25–26). This is another personalized revelation to the woman of what was announced earlier by John the Baptist (John 1:41; cf. 3:28).

### Rachel's Report and the Samaritan Woman's Testimony

After Jacob reveals his identity to Rachel, she runs home to tell her father Laban about the unexpected visitor (Gen 29:12). Likewise, the Samaritan woman goes into the city and calls her fellow citizens to come and see the man who may be the Messiah (John 4:28–29). This is another courtship application of a theme introduced in the prologue, namely that of testimony. Just as John the Baptist came "for testimony, to give witness" to Jesus so that "all might believe through him" (John 1:7–8), the Samaritans

---

64. Neyrey, "Jacob Traditions and the Interpretation of John 4:10–26," 426.

come to believe in Jesus thanks to "the word of the woman who testified" (John 4:39).

### Offer of Hospitality, Betrothal, and Faith

In both Genesis 29:13-14 and John 4:40, the people who were brought to the well by the woman invite the traveler home. Laban brings Jacob into his house, and the Samaritans ask Jesus to stay (*meno*) with them, "and he stayed (*meno*) there two days." This is yet another echo of John 1, where the disciples ask Jesus where he is staying (*meno*) and then at his invitation remain (*meno*) with him that day (John 1:38–39). The idea of "staying" with the bridegroom-Messiah, recurring frequently in John, is a fitting conclusion to the nuptial imagery of the narrative. Betrothal is not the end of a love story but rather its beginning, when husband and wife commit to "stay" together to establish a home and family. Yet whereas the story of Jacob and Rachel ends with a wedding, the story of Jesus and the Samaritan woman ends with many of the Samaritans believing in him (John 4:39, 41–42). This is not only a spiritual wedding but also a new, spiritual "birth" (3:5) coming out of the symbolic union of Jesus and the woman. This is a fitting fulfillment of the ultimate purpose of the Word becoming flesh as set in the prologue: all are invited to believe in the Logos, Son of Man and Son of God (1:7,12,49–50; 2:11,22; 3:14–18) and enter into a nuptial relationship with the bridegroom-Messiah (3:29) for the sake of attaining eternal life through communion with him and the gift of the Spirit, thereby becoming children of God (1:12).

## Living Waters Flowing out of the New Temple

### The Symbolism of Living Water: Word and Spirit

The theme of water moves from the waters of John's baptism in chapter 1, to the water of Jewish purification in chapter 2, to Jesus' new birth "of water and the spirit" in chapter 3, to the discussion of Jesus' living water in chapter 4.[65] We have briefly reviewed the symbolism of water in prophetic and wisdom literature in our discussion of Sirach 24, and it

---

65. On the symbolism of water in the Fourth Gospel cf. Koester, *Symbolism in the Fourth Gospel*, 175–203; Um, *The Theme of Temple Christology in John's Gospel*, 130–66; Ng, *Water Symbolism in John*; Jones, *The Symbol of Water in the Gospel of John*.

behooves us to return to this topic here. Water typically symbolizes either divine revelation or the Holy Spirit in biblical imagery. It is a symbol of God's word or of the knowledge of the Lord in the prophets (Isa 11:9; 55:1, 10–11; Hab 2:14), and it is extended to wisdom in later writings (Prov 13:14; 16:22; 18:4). Water in the Old Testament is also a symbol of the Holy Spirit (Isa 32:15; 44:3; Joel 2:28; Ezek 36:25–27) and some-times of God himself, called a fountain of living waters (Isa 33:21; Jer 2:13; 17:13). Geographically, water is associated with the Garden of Eden (Isa 51:3; Ps 36:7–10; Sir 24:25–27), with the Temple (Ezek 47:1–12; Joel 4:17–18; Zech 14:8), and with the eschatological redemption (Isa 12:3; 35:1, 6–7; 41:17–19).[66] Anthropologically, it is a sign of the restoration of the soul (Isa 44:3–4; 58:11; Ezek 36:25–27) and it is characteristic of love imagery (Cant 4:12–15; Prov 5:15–18).

The first passage that John 4 evokes is Sirach 24, not only because it encapsulates all the above themes, but also because John 4:14 ("whoever drinks of the water that I shall give him will never thirst") seems to echo the words of Lady Wisdom in Sirach 24:21: "those who drink me will thirst for more." The two seemingly contradictory statements really say the same thing, namely, that the person who drinks of the supernatural water will be fully satisfied so that he will want it in ever increasing mea-sure and will never need anything else. Recall that Wisdom is identified with the Torah in Sirach 24, filling men with wisdom like the four rivers of Eden and having the likeness of the ever-widening river flowing out of Ezekiel's Temple (Ezek 47:1–12). Ezekiel's eschatological Temple also likely stands in the background of John 4. Just as the waters that flowed from Ezekiel's sanctuary brought healing, abundance, and life, so now Jesus, the new Temple, provides a "fountain of water springing up into everlasting life."[67] That he has come to provide miraculous healing, abun-dance, and life is attested throughout the Gospel, such as in the healing of the official's son (John 4:46–54), the multiplication of the loaves and fish (6:1–15), and the raising of Lazarus (11:1–44).

66. These associations are consistently sustained in Second Temple literature, where water is a symbol representing life in three temporal settings: as a life-giving symbol in the Garden of Eden (2 Enoch 8; Apoc Abr 21:6; Jos. Asen. 2:17–20; 1QH 14:12–18; 16:4–26), as a life-giving blessing in the present age (1 Enoch 26:1–3; 28:1–3; 30:1–2; 89:28; 4 Ezra 6:42–48; Sib Or 4:15–17; Apoc Abr 7:4), and as a prophetic symbol of the end-time blessing in the new creation (1 Enoch 60:20–22; 76:6–13; 2 Bar 10:11; 29:5–8; 36:3–4; 39:7; 72:1–2; T. Jud. 24:4; T. Job 33:6–7; T. Adam 2:10). Um, *The Theme of Temple Christology in John's Gospel,* 15–67.

67. Cf. Coloe, *God Dwells with Us,* 94–96.

## Jacob, Jesus, and the Temple

Jesus' announcement of a new spiritual worship and his identification with Ezekiel's Temple builds upon the prologue's revelation that the Logos "tabernacled" among us, and the identification of Jesus' body as new Temple. The Temple motif could also lie behind the woman's awareness that Jews refer to Jerusalem as "the place (Gk. *ho topos*) where one ought to worship" (John 4:20) since a strong tradition in Judaism identifies *ho topos* (Heb. *hamakom*) as the Temple. Given the close correlation of John 4 with the story of Jacob, it is worth noting that rabbinic sources associate Jacob with Temple worship, asserting that he was endowed with special knowledge concerning the future sanctuary. Recall the midrashic understanding of Jacob's ladder as sign of the Temple. To cite another example, consider the rabbinic treatment of Isaac's blessing of Jacob (Gen 27:27): the Targum compares the smell of Jacob's garments with the smell of incense offered in the Temple:

> See, the smell of my son is like the smell of the fragrant incense that will be offered on the mountain of the Sanctuary, which has been called 'field which the Lord blessed,' and where it has pleased him to make his Shekhinah dwell.[68]

This rabbinic interpretation of Jacob's smell as figurative of the fragrance of the Temple worship gives an even stronger cultic foundation to Jesus' identification with Jacob. In addition, the Midrash on Gen 29:2 associates the well where Jacob met Rachel with the presence of the *Shekhinah* at Mount Sinai, with the water coming out of the rock at Meribah after Moses struck it (Num 20:8; 21:16–17), and with the "drinking of the Holy Spirit" in the Jerusalem Temple during the water libation ceremony of the Feast of Tabernacles.[69] These allusions are all familiar to John in his portrayal of Jesus as bridegroom and temple.

In short, the fourth chapter of John's Gospel depicts the encounter between Jesus, the Bridegroom-Messiah, and the Samaritan woman, representative of her Samaritan community, as a symbolic betrothal. The Samaritan cult (and, likewise, the Jerusalem cult), symbolized by the woman's five husbands, is to be replaced by the new worship in spirit and in truth centered around the person of Jesus who, as source of the living

---

68. Targum Pseudo-Jonathan on Gen 27:27. The Midrash on the same verse associates Jacob's smell with the Temple itself, its destruction and future reconstruction (*GenR* 65:23). Cf. Neyrey, "Jacob Traditions," 431.

69. *GenR* 70:8 on Gen 29:2.

water of eternal life, is identified with Israel's eschatological Temple. Out of this symbolic union between Jesus and the woman comes out the "new birth" of many Samaritans coming to faith in Christ.

## Bread from Heaven and One-Flesh Union (John 6)

The sixth chapter of John's Gospel is set at the time of a second Passover, when Jesus feeds the five thousand by multiplying loaves and fish (John 6:1–15). The proximity of Passover, the identification of Jesus as the awaited prophet who was to come into the world (6:14; cf. Deut 18:15), and the ensuing discussion on the manna and bread from heaven indicate that the miracle is fulfilling the hope of a second Exodus.[70] The Exodus setting recalls the nuptial passages of the prophets, who hoped that the renewal of the marriage covenant between God and Israel would take place in the wilderness as in days of old (Hos 2:14). The Eucharistic connotations of both the miracle and ensuing discourse on the Bread of Life are well known: the formula recalling that Jesus took the loaves, "gave thanks" (*eucharisto*) (6:11), and distributed them to those who were seated closely resembles the institution narratives in the Synoptics and Paul. Other elements such as the nearness of Passover, the idea of the body of Christ offered sacrificially for others, its identification with bread, the idea of eating his body and drinking his blood, and the reference to Judas' betrayal all point to the Eucharistic tradition of the primitive Church.[71]

As with the other signs in the Fourth Gospel, the goal of the miraculous multiplication is that the people may believe in Jesus (6:29) and thereby receive eternal life (6:39–40). As in the dialogue with Nicodemus, faith is an essential prerequisite to receive the gift of life (6:47), but it is not enough. To live forever, one must also *eat* the bread of heaven, which is Jesus' own flesh (6:51). The sign (bread) points to the sacrament (Jesus' flesh), for it is the sacrament that unites heaven and earth: As living bread that came down from *heaven*, Jesus invites those *on earth* to eat this bread—his flesh and blood—to receive eternal life and the hope of resurrection on the last day (6:50–55). The result is mutual communion

---

70. Cf. Beasley-Murray, *John*, 88.

71. Cf. Matt 26:21–28; Mark 14:18–24; Luke 22:19–23; 1 Cor 11:23–24; Brown, *The Gospel According to John I–XII*, 243, 247–48, 284–87, 291–93; Hahn, "Temple, Sign and Sacrament," 121–22.

between Christ and the believer, again characterized by the verb *meno*: "He who eats my flesh and drinks my blood abides in me, and I in him" (John 6:56). Keeping in mind Jesus' role as bridegroom in the Fourth Gospel, the Eucharistic invitation to "eat his flesh" in order to "abide in him" sounds much like a veiled invitation to a mystical "one-flesh" nuptial union with him.

## Feast of Tabernacles and Eschatological Temple (John 7)

In chapter 7, the narrative moves from Passover to the Feast of Tabernacles (Sukkot), and from the theme of the "Bread of Life" back to that of "living water." Jesus goes up to Jerusalem for Sukkot, and on the last day, the "great day of the feast," he proclaims: "If anyone thirsts, let him come to me and drink. He who believes in me, as the Scripture has said, out of his heart shall flow rivers of living water" (John 7:37–38).[72] The Feast of Tabernacles had an intrinsic connection with water. In the days of the Temple, an integral part of its celebration was the daily libation ceremony when water was drawn from the pool of Siloam and poured on the altar along with wine.[73] The main purpose of this ceremony was to invoke God's blessing for rain, for "at the Feast of Tabernacles judgment is made concerning the waters."[74]

The "great day of the feast" is presumably the *Hoshannah Rabbah* (the Great Supplication), known as the day of the final sealing of judgment which had begun a few weeks earlier at *Rosh HaShanah*. On the last day of the feast, believed to be the day when God judges the world for rainfall after the hot and dry summer months, the people's prayers for rain reached their climax; it was the height of the feast's eschatological expectation, which included prayers expressing hope for the speedy coming of the Messiah. It is within this context that Jesus announces that he is the source of living waters, and whoever "drinks from him" will have living waters flow from his heart. John explains that "he spoke concerning the Spirit, whom those believing in him would receive; for the Holy Spirit was not yet given, because Jesus was not yet glorified" (John

---

72. On the *Sukkot* background to John 7, cf. Beasley-Murray, *John*, 113–14; Coloe, *God Dwells with Us*, 115–143; Kerr, *The Temple of Jesus' Body*, 226–250.

73. *M. Sukkah* 4:9.

74. *M. Rosh Hashana* 1:2.

7:39). The living water about which Jesus told the Samaritan woman thus represents the Holy Spirit, but it was not yet given because the "hour" of Jesus' glorification had not yet come." This adds to the complex interconnection of Johannine themes: The "hour" of Jesus—the time of his death and resurrection—is the moment when he is "glorified" (partially anticipated at Cana). It is also the moment when the Spirit is poured out. Throughout the Gospel, there is an atmosphere of anticipation of Jesus' hour and glorification, a sense of "already but not yet," a tension between realized and future eschatology: the bridegroom-Messiah has arrived and is already in communion with his bride-people, but at the same time the gift of the Spirit must await his death and resurrection.

But what passage of Scripture does Jesus refer to when he says "*as the scripture has said*, 'out of his heart shall flow rivers of living water'" (John 7:38)? These words do not match any passage of the Old Testament, but they do hint at texts that we have examined. When read in continuity with chapter 4, John 7:38 possibly alludes to the living waters flowing out of Ezekiel's eschatological Temple (Ezek 47:1–12). Supporting this is the fact that the rite of water libation at *Sukkot* was linked to the anticipated gift of water expected to flow from Jerusalem at the establishment of the kingdom of God. The *Tosefta* attests to the rite's connection with Ezekiel's living waters, identifying the Water Gate though which the libation ceremony entered with the south gate of Ezekiel's Temple.[75] The *Tosefta* also calls these eschatological waters the "waters of creation," and it associates the libations with the "well that was with Israel in the desert," referring to the water that came from the rock smitten by Moses during the desert wanderings.[76] It also attests to the tradition that the rock *moved* and *travelled* with the Israelites in the desert:

> And so the well which was with the Israelites in the wilderness was a rock, the size of a large round vessel, surging and gurgling upward, as from the mouth of this little flask, rising with them up onto the mountains, and going down with them into the valleys. Wherever the Israelites would encamp, it made camp with them, on a high place, opposite the entry of the Tent of Meeting. (*t. Sukkah* 3:11)

The water libation was also understood as the outpouring of the Holy Spirit from the "wells of salvation" spoken of by Isaiah 12:3:

---

75. *T. Sukkah* 3:3–11. Cf. Coloe, *God Dwells with Us*, 131–32.

76. Exod 17:1–6; Num 20:8–11; 21:16–18.

Says R. Joshua ben Levi, why is its name called the place of drawing water? Because, from thence "they draw the Holy Spirit," as
it is said, "and ye shall draw water with joy out of the wells of
salvation."[77]

The context of the Feast of Tabernacles thus indicates that Jesus is
again identifying himself with Ezekiel's Temple, in continuity with his
identification as new Temple in John 2 and his offer of living waters in
chapter 4. This implies that the river of life will not come out of a physical
structure but rather out of himself. Moreover, he will pass on this gift to
his followers, for those who believe in him will also become a source of
living water. This further confirms that the Incarnation of the Logos who
"tabernacled" among us is likened to God coming to dwell in his Temple.
Jesus' signs and healings become the spiritual embodiment of the healing waters flowing from God's house on his holy mountain that were to
bring life to the arid desert, quench the thirst of weary souls, bestow upon
them God's Spirit (Isa 44:3–4, 58:11; Ezek 36:25–26), and bring them
into communion with divine Wisdom (Sir 24). By extension, Jesus the
bridegroom-Messiah and spiritual temple becomes the new source of the
waters of Eden and the way back to paradise.

## The Anointing at Bethany
## (John 12:1–3)

The next nuptial passage in John, the anointing at Bethany, displays
several possible allusions to the Song of Songs. Following Jesus' *Sukkot*
discourse, the narrative of the Gospel continues with the implementation
of the program outlined in the prologue and initiated in John 1:19–4:42.
As the story unfolds, Jesus faces increasing opposition and hostility, and
with the raising of Lazarus in chapter 11 the narrative begins to turn
towards Jesus' own death. Like the sign of Cana, the raising of Lazarus
is another anticipatory revelation of the *doxa* of God and of Jesus (11:4,
40) that will be fully disclosed at Jesus' "hour." Then, six days before his
final Passover, Jesus is invited to a supper in Bethany with Lazarus and
his sisters Martha and Mary. The presence of Judas (11:4) indicates that
the other disciples are there, possibly with other people (11:9). During
the meal, Lazarus is reclining at the table with Jesus while Martha serves
the guests. But it is Mary who quickly becomes the center of attention:

77. *GenR* 70:8. Cf. Brown, *The Gospel According to John I–XII*, 321–23.

Mary took a pound of costly ointment of pure nard and anointed
the feet of Jesus and wiped his feet with her hair; and the house
was filled with the fragrance of the ointment. (John 12:3)[78]

## The King Anointed with Nard and the Song of Songs

Mary's use of her hair to wipe the feet of Jesus has often been considered
perplexing. Her motivation for the anointing is unclear. Does this passage carry nuptial connotations? Winsor has noted that on five occasions
in the Song of Songs the beauty of the man or woman is described with
a reference to his or her hair.[79] More convincing is the Gospel's possible
allusion to Cant 1:12, noted by several scholars:[80] "While the king was on
his couch, my nard gave forth its fragrance." The verse has four characteristics in common with Mary's anointing at Bethany: a king on a couch,
a loving woman, nard, and its fragrance. First, just as the lover of the
Canticle is a king and bridegroom reclining on a couch, so is Jesus a king
(John 1:49; 6:15; 12:13, 15; 18:33–19:22) and bridegroom (John 3:29) reclining on a couch. Second, both men are the object of a woman's intense
loving attention—the beloved of the Canticle and Mary of Bethany. Third,
the presence of the nard is significant in that in the entire Bible it appears
only in the Canticle (1:12; 4:13, 14) and in Mark's and John's accounts
of the anointing at Bethany. Fourth, John's description of the fragrance
of the perfume filling the house recalls the beloved's nard giving out its
fragrance in Cant 1:12, as well as the prominence of scents and fragrances
in other passages in the Canticle.[81] John's text also seems to echo Cant 1:3
with its description of the beloved's name as poured ointment and the
love of the maidens for him: "your anointing oils are fragrant, your name
is oil poured out; therefore the maidens love you."

---

78. All four Gospels include an account of a woman anointing Jesus (Matt 26:6–13;
Mark 14:3–9; Luke 7:36–50), but notable differences between them have resulted in
an unsolvable puzzle of intertextuality. Cf. Brown, *The Gospel According to John I–XII*,
449–52; Villeneuve, *Nuptial Symbolism*, 166–67.

79. Cant 4:1; 5:11; 6:5; 7:5; cf. Winsor, *A King Is Bound in the Tresses*, 20–22.

80. Winandy, "Le Cantique des Cantiques et le NT," 166; Cambe, "L'influence du
Cantique," 15–17; Fehribach, *Women in the Life*, 93; McWhirter, *The Bridegroom Messiah*, 82–88; Winsor, "A King is Bound," 22–23, 25–27.

81. Cf. Cant 1:3–4; 2:13; 4:10–11; 7:9, 14.

## Midrashic Parallels

Here too the Midrash on the Canticle provides some helpful insights. According to Rabbi Judah, Cant 1:12 refers to the theophany at Mount Sinai when Israel declared their obedience to the Lord:

> What then is meant by *while the king was at his table*? While the supreme King of kings, the Holy One, blessed be He, was at His table in the firmament, Israel sent forth a fragrance before Mount Sinai and said, *All that the Lord has said we will do and obey* (Exod 24:7).[82]

R. Eliezer and R. Akiba concur that the Canticle's king represents God in the firmament: For R. Eliezer, the smell of nard represents the pillars of smoke rising from Sinai when *the mountain was burning with fire* (Deut 4:11); for R. Akiba, the fragrance is the *glory of the Lord [which] abode upon Mount Sinai* (Exod 24:16). Cant 1:12 is also associated with the Sinai theophany in the *Mekhilta*, where God (the Canticle's lover) receives Israel (the Shulamite) "as a bridegroom comes forth to meet the bride."[83] These midrashic traditions associating the nard with the Sinai theophany may well stand in the background of the scene at Bethany. Could it be that the evangelist is not only portraying Mary's anointing of Jesus' feet as the woman of Cant 1:12, but also, as in the Midrash, Jesus the king receiving the woman "as a bridegroom comes forth to meet the bride" because of her loving devotion to him?


## John and the Prophets: Bridegroom, Bride and Temple

We may add two observations about the "fragrance of the ointment" of John 12:3: first, the expression occurs in the Septuagint's rendition of Jer 25:10: "And I will destroy from among them the voice of joy, and the voice of gladness, the voice of the bridegroom, and the voice of the bride, the fragrance of ointment, and the light of a candle." As we have seen, this is one of the prophet's oracles about the voice of the bridegroom and the bride that John 3:29 possibly alludes to. Could the "fragrance of the ointment" of John 12:3 be an allusion to Jeremiah's "fragrance of ointment" accompanying the voices of the bridegroom and bride—implying again that Jesus is the mystical bridegroom and Mary a symbolic bride?

82. *CantR* 1:12 §1.

83. *Mekh Baḥodesh* 3.

Second, the word "fragrance" (*osme*) in the LXX usually refers to the pleasing odor of a sacrifice, and only four times does it refer to the fragrance of perfume (with three of these four references found in Cant 1:3–4 and Jer 25:10).[84] Could the evangelist be hinting at the impending sacrificial death of Jesus by emphasizing the pleasing "fragrance" (*osme*) of the sacrifice filling the house? This seems likely since the narrative tells us that Mary's anointing is oriented towards Jesus' death: The scene takes place six days before the Passover on which he would die (John 12:1), and Jesus himself defends the woman's action by announcing that "she has kept this for the day of my burial" (John 12:7).

When one considers the importance of the Temple in the Fourth Gospel, the recurring theme of a new worship centered on the person of Jesus, the sacrificial allusion in John 12:3, 7, and the narrative moving towards his paschal sacrifice, it is possible that Mary's anointing of Jesus in John 12 is a veiled reference to the Temple. The house in Bethany, filled with the fragrance of perfume, is thus a place of worship equivalent to the smoke-filled Temple and House of the Lord.

The association of Jesus with the king-bridegroom of the Song of Songs and Mary of Bethany as the Song's beloved woman seem to portray Mary as fictitious betrothed or bride of Jesus, perhaps representative of the Jewish people, just as the Samaritan woman was representative of the Samaritan community in chapter 4.[85] Fehribach has pointed out that the intimate act of anointing Jesus with perfume with her hair indicates a close relationship between the two, most unusual for acquaintances of the opposite sex in first-century Judea. Perfume was usually reserved for burial rites, cosmetic purposes, and romantic purposes. Since the anointing of a man's feet with perfume was often associated with a romantic setting, and given the love of Jesus for Mary, Martha and Lazarus, it is conceivable that the anointing could have been understood as a romantic action.[86] Moreover, for Mary to let her hair down publicly in the presence of Jesus could have been considered scandalous.[87] In this case, the fact that her action and physical contact with him are described as praiseworthy calls for a context in which the two would have been related. This leads the reader to see Mary as the betrothed or bride of Jesus, and the meal

84. Cf. Gen 8:21; Exod 29:18; Lev 1:9,13,17; 2:2.

85. Fehribach develops this argument in *The Women in the Life of the Bridegroom*, 86–93.

86. Fehribach, *The Women in the Life of the Bridegroom*, 88–89.

87. Brown, *The Gospel According to John*, 450.

that he shared with her and her family at Bethany as a betrothal meal in preparation for his coming passion and death as his messianic wedding.

## The Last Supper as Wedding Ceremony?
## (John 13–17)

### The King and the Daughter of Zion

The day after the anointing in Bethany, Jesus enters Jerusalem. John associates his entrance into the city with the words of Zechariah: "Fear not, daughter of Zion; behold, your King is coming, sitting on a donkey's colt" (John 12:15; cf. Zech 9:9). The use of the term "daughter of Zion" in the singular indicates that Jesus is making use of the well-known personification of the city of Jerusalem and evoking the rich Old Testament imagery which portrayed her as virgin or mother. Once again, temple symbolism and nuptiality intersect: The verse recalls Zechariah's promise that God would dwell in her midst (Zech 2:10). It also evokes Isaiah's promised salvation to the daughter of Zion, with God rejoicing over her as the bridegroom rejoices over the bride (Isa 62:4–5, 11). Yet more than recalling the former promises to the daughter of Zion, Jesus' entrance in Jerusalem signifies that his "hour" and glorification are now imminent.

### Into the Father's House

Fehribach has argued that John depicts Jesus' death as a blood sacrifice that establishes a patrilineal kinship group between him and his followers. This would make Jesus' death to be a messianic wedding between him and his bride. The crucifixion narrative is prepared by Jesus' "farewell discourse" at the Last Supper (13:1–17:26), which contains several temple and nuptial allusions. Chavasse has proposed that Jesus, in the Last Supper, was "as much enacting a Marriage Feast as keeping the Passover." He claimed this on the basis that the Old Testament marriage between God and his people was made and ratified by the Passover. Moreover, Chavasse argued that the outward ceremonies of the Last Supper suggest the customs of a first century Jewish marriage:

> The house was prepared as for the reception of the bridegroom who had absented himself with his friends; at a given signal, he and his party returned to find the room prepared for the

wedding feast. The feast itself began with the prescribed hand-washing and benediction. Then the great winecup was filled, and the principal personage, taking it, and holding it, recited over it the prayer of bridal blessing. Then the men seated themselves. Only the men sat at the marriage supper. After the supper the bridegroom left the feast with the bride.[88]

It is worth examining a few themes in the farewell discourse that point to marriage, family, and temple symbolism. In anticipation of his death, Jesus says that he is going to "prepare a place" for his disciples in one of the "many dwelling places" that are in his "Father's house" (John 14:2–3). In the first century, the wedding ceremony consisted in the groom bringing the bride into his house. In this light, our text may well allude to the fact that as messianic bridegroom Jesus is taking his bride (the community of believers) into his Father's house.[89]

## The Bridegroom's Love in John 13–17

The overarching theme of Jesus' farewell discourse is his love for his disciples. Of the 37 occurrences of the verb *agapao* in the Fourth Gospel, 25 of them appear in chapters 13–17. Jesus introduces the topic by example, washing the feet of the disciples as the humble sign that "having loved his own who were in the world, he loved them to the end" (John 13:1). He then proceeds to discuss the subject extensively, touching upon several dimensions of divine-human love, including the Father's love for Jesus (15:9; 17:23–24, 26) and for the disciples (14:21, 23; 17:23), Jesus' love for the Father (14:31) and for his disciples (13:1, 34; 14:21; 15:9), the exhortation that they abide (*meno*) in Jesus' love (15:9–10; 17:26), love him back (by keeping his commandments, 14:15, 21, 23, 28; 15:12) and also love one another (13:34; 15:12, 17).

## God Dwelling in Man and Man Dwelling in God

It is within this context of love that Jesus announces to the disciples that he is going to prepare a "place" (*topos*) for them in one of the many rooms

---

88. Chavasse, *The Bride of Christ*, 60–61. Pitre elaborates on the Synoptic account of the Last Supper as "a kind of 'new Sinai,' in which he inaugurates a new union between God and his people." Pitre, *Jesus the Bridegroom*, 48–52.

89. Fehribach, *The Women in the Life of the Bridegroom*, 123.

in the Father's house (14:2).[90] The reference to the *topos* in the Father's house possibly refers again to the Temple.[91] The terminology also recalls Jesus' designation of the Temple as his "Father's house" in John 2:16. Since these are the only two places where the "Father's house" is mentioned in the Fourth Gospel, it is probable that Jesus is now announcing the imminent establishment of the new Temple that he foretold in chapter 2. The new eschatological Temple of Jesus' body, out of which flow the rivers of living water (John 4:14; 7:38–39; 19:34), is therefore also the "Father's house" into which the bridegroom-Messiah will bring his bride.[92] As Kerr points out, the "Father's house" bears a degree of identification with the Messiah, for he promises: "If I go and prepare a place for you, I will come again and *receive you to Myself*; that where I am, there you may be also" (John 14:3). The union of love between Christ and his disciples is underlined by the repeated use of *meno*, expressing the Father dwelling in Jesus and Jesus in the Father (14:10–11, 20), Jesus dwelling with the disciples and the disciples in Jesus (14:20, 25; 15:4–10), [93] and the Spirit dwelling with the disciples (14:17). In one of Jesus' strongest statements, he declares: "If anyone loves me, he will keep my word; and my Father will love him, and we will come to him and make our home with him (John 14:23). The idea of Jesus "staying" or "abiding" (*meno*) with his disciples, introduced in an obscure dialogue at the beginning of Jesus' ministry (John 1:38–39), metaphorically illustrated by Jesus "staying" with the Samaritan community (4:40), sacramentally attained by "eating Jesus' flesh and drinking his blood" (6:56) now finds its culmination in the analogy of the vine and branches (John 15:1–17) and with the idea

90. On the "Father's house" and Temple connections in John 13–14, see Kerr, *The Temple of Jesus' Body*, 268–313; Coloe, *God Dwells with Us*, 157–178.

91. In John 11:48, Caiaphas uses the word *topos* to refer to the Temple. Cf. Hahn, "Temple, Sign, and Sacrament," 128; Coloe, *God Dwells with Us*, 164–67.

92. Kerr argues for the Temple symbolism of the "Father's house" of John 14:2–3 based on parallels between the cleansing of the Temple and the Last Supper. Moreover, Jesus washing the feet of his disciples may allude to the ritual washings required of priests as they approached the sanctuary (Exod 30:17–21; 40:30–32; 1 Kgs 7:38; 2 Chr 4:6). Philo sees foot washing as a cleansing preparation before entering the Temple or offering sacrifice (*Questions on Genesis* 4.5; *Questions on Exodus* 1.2). Kerr suggests that John 13 portrays a similar situation: "By washing the disciples' feet, is Jesus preparing them for entry into the new Temple he is going to establish through his death, resurrection and ascension?" Kerr, *The Temple of Jesus' Body*, 278–92.

93. Perhaps the analogy of the vine and branches to illustrate the union between Christ and the disciples also carries nuptial allusion. Cf. Isa 5:1–7; Jer 2:21; Hos 10:1; Ps 128:3.

of the Father and Son making their home in the believer through the presence of the Holy Spirit who was promised in the earlier discourses on living waters.

As Jesus previously declared to the Samaritan woman, the new place of worship and "Father's house" is not spatial (John 4:23). Referring back to its Davidic context, the term "house" carries a double connotation; it can mean either a Temple or a family: David wanted to build a "house" for God (the Temple), but God instead built a house for him (a dynasty or family, 2 Sam 7:5, 11; 1 Chron 17:1, 4, 10). This provides the background to the idea that the "Father's house" is located not only in Jesus but also in his community of disciples.[94] As Hahn writes, "the sense of the new Temple is being extended from Jesus' physical body to the community of God, that is, to God's 'household' or 'family.'"[95] Out of this comes the paradox that, on the one hand, the disciples can find a *topos* in one of the rooms of the Father's house, yet at the same time Jesus and the Father will make their home within the believer. The many "dwelling places" or "rooms" in the Father's house evoke both the rooms of the Temple and the family home where the community-bride can finally abide and "stay" (*meno*) with her bridegroom-Messiah—in response to the first question of the disciples asking Jesus where he is "staying," and his invitation that they come and see (John 1:38–39).

Yet before the disciples can find their definitive home in the Father's house, they must undergo severe tribulations—and these too are described in nuptial terms. Jesus refers to his impending death as the birth pangs of a woman in labor whose "hour" has come. Just as the woman in travail has sorrow at her "hour," so the disciples will have sorrow now that the Bridegroom-Messiah's hour has come. But as the woman's anguish is transformed into joy when she delivers her new-born child, so will the disciples rejoice when they are reunited with Jesus (John 16:21–22). The imagery recalls the labor pains of Zion that the prophets expected before the age of redemption.[96]

Another possible allusion to the messianic wedding in Jesus' farewell discourse is seen in the prayer he utters shortly before he is arrested,

94. The idea of the community as Temple is known from the Qumran texts (1QS 9:5–7; 1Q Flor 1:6; 1QS 8:9; 9:3; 4QFlor 1:6) and the Pauline corpus (1 Cor 3:16–17; 6:19; 2 Cor 6:16; Eph 2:21). Kerr, *The Temple of Jesus' Body*, 54–57; 296–98.

95. Hahn, "Temple, Sign, and Sacrament." 128; cf. Coloe, *God Dwells with Us*, 160–62.

96. Isa 26:17–18; 66:7–10; Hos 13:13; Mic 4:9–10; 5:2; Rev 12:2–5.

saying to his Father: "I made known to them thy name, and I will make it known" (John 17:26). This could be an allusion to Ps 45:17 ("I will make your name to be remembered in all generations")—an ode for a royal wedding in which the psalmist promises progeny and immortality to the royal bridegroom. A reference to this verse would imply that Jesus, as messianic bridegroom, promises that the name of his heavenly father will be eternally remembered through his own progeny.[97]

## The Hour Has Come (John 19)

Jesus' farewell discourse prepares the way for the "hour" of his crucifixion and death (John 17:1) that he anticipated since the Wedding at Cana. The crucifixion narrative includes several points of interest that are worth examining: the Eden typology of the Garden of Gethsemane, Jesus' Paschal sacrifice as a Messianic wedding, the Adam/Eve and birth allusions at the crucifixion, and the symbolism of the water and blood flowing out of Jesus' side.

### In the Garden: Echoes of Eden?

The mention that Jesus was arrested and buried in a garden (John 18:1,26; 19:41) is unique to John's Gospel. Some Church Fathers and modern scholars have argued that this is an allusion to the Garden of Eden.[98] As Satan in the form of the serpent (cf. Rev 12:9) caused Adam's fall in a garden, Satan in the form of Judas (cf. John 6:70–71; 13:27) causes Jesus' death in a garden. As Adam, the archetypal king, was buried in the garden of Paradise according to some traditions,[99] so Jesus, the King of the Jews, is buried in a garden. But Satan's plan backfires as Jesus' death turns into the source of new life. In this way, the evangelist would be suggesting a reversal of the events that caused the original fall and a renewed access to the Garden of Eden.

97. Fehribach, *The Women in the Life of the Bridegroom*, 122–23.

98. Cyril of Jerusalem, *Catechesis* 13:32 (PG 33, 811A). Lightfoot, *St. John's Gospel: A Commentary*, 321–22; Brown, *The Gospel According to John XIII–XXI*, 806; Moloney, *The Gospel of John*, 484, 513; Fehribach, *The Women in the Life of the Bridegroom*, 124–25.

99. Apoc. Mos. 37:5; 40:2.

## Paschal Sacrifice and Messianic Wedding

We have mentioned Fehribach's suggestion that Jesus' death is portrayed as a blood sacrifice establishing a patrilineal kinship group between him and his followers. The idea is in line with the relationship between blood sacrifices and patrilineal descent that was common in both the ancient Greco-Roman world and in biblical tradition.[100] In light of Johannine nuptial imagery, Jesus' death appears to be the consummation of the messianic wedding between him and his bride whereby she becomes, so to speak, his family.

### Jesus' Death as Paschal Sacrifice

The predominance of Passover symbolism in the Fourth Gospel is well known. For John, Jesus is crucified on Passover Eve, the 14th of Nissan (John 18:28; 19:14).[101] The Fourth Gospel thus presents the death of Jesus as a paschal sacrifice. The motif was already announced in the Gospel's first chapter, where John the Baptist calls Jesus "the Lamb of God who takes away the sin of the world" (1:29, 36), and it is confirmed by some Paschal features at the moment of his death: First, Jesus is condemned to death at noon on the day before Passover (John 19:14), at the same time when the priests began to slay the paschal lambs in the Temple. Second, as hyssop was used to smear the lamb's blood on the doorposts of the Israelites in Egypt (Exod 12:22), a hyssop sponge is used to give Jesus wine while he is on the cross (John 19:29). Third, as no bone of the paschal lamb was broken (Exod 12:46), so none of Jesus' bones is broken (John 19:31).[102]

### The Passion as Messianic Wedding?

Could the passion and death of Jesus be interpreted as a messianic wedding leading to the subsequent birth of the children of God as announced in John 1:12? We have mentioned Jesus' promise to "prepare a place" for

---

100. Fehribach, *The Women in the Life of the Bridegroom*, 116–21.

101. On the difficulties in dating the Last Supper and the conflicting accounts of the Synoptics and John, cf. Brown, *The Gospel According to John XIII–XXI*, 555–56.

102. Brown, *The Gospel According to John I–XIII*, 62. Cf. also Coloe, *God Dwells with Us*, 190–196.

his disciples and the reference to the nuptial Psalm 45:17 in his priestly prayer. In addition, several details of the crucifixion and resurrection narrative hint at the idea of the Passion as Messianic Wedding:

1. During his trial, Jesus wore a crown of thorns and a purple robe (19:2). Could this be an ironic reference to ancient wedding traditions whereby the bridegroom clothed himself with special garments and decked himself with a crown?[103]

2. Jesus was stripped naked before he was crucified (19:23), perhaps pointing to the total vulnerability of the Bridegroom-Messiah at the moment of his self-offering.

3. Jesus' words to his mother, "Woman, behold your son" (19:26) allude to a spiritual birth.

4. Jesus' words, "I thirst" (19:28) echo his previous discussion with the Samaritan woman about thirst, living water and husbands (4:13–15), the Bread of Life discourse (6:35), and his speech in the Temple during the Feast of Tabernacles (7:37). It may also allude to Old Testament betrothal-type scenes at the well, such as the scene where Abraham's servant thirsted and was given to drink by Rebekah (Gen 24). Is the Bridegroom-Messiah now declaring his thirst to his bride?

5. Jesus is given sour wine while on the cross (19:29). The bitter drink stands in contrast with the "best wine" he provided at Cana, indicating that his hour has finally come. While Jesus provided the best wine for others, now he drinks the bitter cup of death for the sake of his bride.

6. Could Jesus' last words before dying, "it is finished" (19:30) be translated as "it is consummated" and understood in a marital sense?

7. The blood and water coming out of Jesus' side (19:34) carries overtones of birth imagery.

8. Nicodemus brings 100 pounds of myrrh and aloes to anoint the body of Jesus. These spices are always mentioned in a nuptial context in the Old Testament (Ps 45:7; Prov 7; Cant 4:14).

---

103. Cf. Isa 61:10; Cant 3:11; 2 Bar 10:13; *m. Sotah* 9:14. Cf. Fehribach, *The Women in the Life of the Bridegroom*, 123; Zimmermann, "Nuptial Imagery in the Revelation of John," 154–56; Pitre, *Jesus the Bridegroom*, 103–4.

9. Jesus is laid to rest in an empty, "virginal" tomb in a garden. The earth as place of generation and birth is likened to a womb in Old Testament thought (cf. Ps 139:15).

10. The resurrection scene in John 20:1–18 reveals a correlation with Cant 3:1–4 (see below).[104]

## New Adam, New Eve, New Birth?

Just before he dies, Jesus sees his mother and "the disciple whom he loved" standing by the cross. He tells her: "woman, behold your son!" and to him "behold your mother!" (John 19:26). The last time when Jesus called his mother "woman" was at Cana, where they were portrayed as new Adam and Eve figures. The same connection now returns at the crucifixion (the only other place where the mother of Jesus appears in the Fourth Gospel). In both scenes Jesus calls her "woman." Cana announced Jesus' "hour" and Calvary fulfills it. Cana was portrayed as the seventh day of a new creation, featuring Jesus and his mother as new Adam and Eve figures. Now, at Jesus' "hour" when he entrusts the beloved disciple to Mary as her "son," the new Adam and new Eve bring forth their first spiritual fruit—the disciple as representative of the new messianic community.[105]

Ironic is Jesus' last plea for a drink when, on the brink of dying, he says "I thirst." As in his dialogue with the Samaritan woman, the one who is the source of the waters of eternal life (4:14; 7:38) is asking again for a drink. One sees here a mirror of the previous dialogue, taken to a higher plane: Jesus asked the woman for a drink while claiming to be the one who could satiate her spiritual thirst by giving her "living water." Here, at the cross, Jesus again declares his thirst just before he "gave up his spirit"—perhaps as the sign that the Spirit promised earlier is to be released now that his "hour" has come. The full impartation of the Spirit, however, only comes after the resurrection (John 20:22).

---

104. These points were noted by John Bergsma at a conference at Franciscan University of Steubenville, July 30, 2009.

105. Brown notes: "the Johannine picture of Jesus' mother becoming the mother of the beloved disciple seems to evoke the Old Testament themes of Lady Zion's giving birth to a new people in the messianic age, and of Eve and her offspring." Brown, *The Gospel According to John XIII–XXI*, 925–26; cf. Fehribach, *The Women in the Life of the Bridegroom*, 127–131.

## Stream from Jesus' Side: Eden, the Rock, and Zion

Related to the idea of the crucifixion as birth is the description—unique to the Fourth Gospel—of the Roman soldier piercing Jesus' side with a spear after his death, "and immediately blood and water came out" (John 19:34). Commentators have seen in this feature a rich symbolism pointing to the streams that flowed in the Garden of Eden, out of the rock in the desert, and out of the Temple on Mount Zion.

Many Church Fathers related the outpouring of water and blood from Jesus' side with the Garden of Eden by means of a reference to Gen 2:21: As Eve was taken out of the side of Adam, so the blood and water, representing the new Eve, the community of believers, flowed out of Christ's side.[106] Some modern exegetes continue to see in the passion narrative the birth of the new family of God, whether this be in the newly formed filial relationship between the mother of Jesus and the beloved disciple (John 19:26–27), or in the emission of blood and water suggestive of both natural birth and the new birth "of water and the Spirit" that Jesus announced to Nicodemus (cf. John 3:5).[107] Eve, called "woman" and "mother of all living" (Gen 2:23; 3:20), is associated with the mother of Jesus, called "woman" and made mother of the beloved disciple. At the same time, Eve is identified with the blood and water coming out of Jesus' side.[108] This again renders Jesus as an Adamic figure, out of whose side his bride comes forth. In this light, the evangelist could well have intended to represent the passion and death of Christ as the culmination and consummation of his messianic marriage, followed by his giving birth to the "children of God" announced in John 1:12.

---

106. Tertullian (*De Anima* 43) wrote: "As Adam was a figure of Christ, Adam's sleep shadowed out the death of Christ, who was to sleep a mortal slumber, that from the wound inflicted in his side might in like manner (as Eve was formed) be typified the Church, the true Mother of the living." Augustine (*Exposition on the Psalms* 127:4) makes the same point. Cf. Chavasse, *The Bride of Christ*, 131; Brown, *The Gospel According to John XIII–XXI*, 935, 949; Fehribach, *The Women in the Life of the Bridegroom*, 127–28; Coloe, *God Dwells with Us*, 207; Pitre, *Jesus the Bridegroom*, 110–11).

107. Fehribach, *The Women in the Life of the Bridegroom*, 127–28, n. 42–43.

108. This double symbolism explains why Mary was known as a symbol of both the Church and the New Eve in early Christianity. Cf. Justin, *Trypho* c. 5; Irenaeus *Adv. Haer.* III 22:4; Brown, *The Gospel According to John I–XII*, 108.

## Water from the Rock

Another possible background to the water and blood flowing out of the side of Jesus is the episode of the water gushing forth from the rock in the desert (Num 20:11). While the biblical account only speaks of water coming out of the rock, the Targum on Numbers adds that not only water but also *blood* flowed out of the rock: "And Moses raised his hand and smote the rock with this staff twice: the first time blood dripped, but the second time much water came forth, and he gave the congregation and their livestock (water) to drink."[109] If this Targumic tradition was already known in the first century, it is possible that the evangelist had it in mind as he wrote the account of the crucifixion, in line with the Exodus motif pervading the Fourth Gospel.

## Streams from the Temple

Commentators agree that the flow from Jesus' side most strongly evokes the Temple and its sacrifices.[110] This is evidenced by the Mishnah, which describes a flow of blood and water streaming from the Temple altar into the Kidron brook: "And at the south-western corner there were two holes like two narrow nostrils by which the blood that was poured over the western base and the southern base used to run down and mingle in the water channel and flow out into the brook Kidron." (*m. Mid.* 3:2)

Other scholars see in the blood and water coming out of Jesus' side a fulfillment of Zech 12:10 and 13:1. According to John 19:37 the crucified Jesus is the pierced one of Zech 12:10. Looking at the wider context of Zechariah, the water and blood flowing from Jesus' side could allude to the prophecy that "a fountain shall be opened for the house of David and for the inhabitants of Jerusalem, for sin and for uncleanness" (Zech 13:1). Brown has noted that the themes of *pouring out*, of *spirit*, and of a *fountain* opened for the *cleansing of sins* together evoke a fulfillment of the living water of the spirit announced in John 4:14 and 7:38–39.[111] The still wider context of Zechariah also features living waters flowing out of Jerusalem (Zech 14:8)—a variation of Ezekiel's waters flowing out of the Temple (Ezek 47:1–12). Keeping in mind that for John, Jesus replaces the

109. Targum Pseudo-Jonathan on Num 20:11. Cf. Coloe, *God Dwells with Us*, 206 n. 80.

110. Coloe, *God Dwells with Us*, 206–208.

111. Brown, *The Gospel According to John XIII–XXI*, 955.

Jerusalem Temple (2:21), and recalling that the rivers flowing out of Eden are associated with Zion and its streams in several texts,[112] Fehribach's conclusion seems quite plausible:

> Thus, the blood and water flowing from the side of the King of the Jews as he dies on the cross can easily be equated with these two streams in Eden/Zion that give life to the world. When one adds to this the notion that Zion is also described as the Bride of YHWH (Isa 50:1; 54:1–8), then the blood and water from the side of Jesus takes on marital/wedding overtones.[113]

### Baptism and Eucharist?

Commentators have also seen the flow from Jesus' side as representative of baptism and the Eucharist, which would naturally derive from the prior connection with the living waters flowing from the Temple and the Holy Spirit.[114] The sacramental meaning is not far-fetched when one considers the intratextual witness: the only other mention of blood in the Gospel is found in John 6:53–56, where Jesus emphasizes the need to "drink his blood," and the water points not only to the previously announced "living waters" but also to the new birth of water and the spirit that was discussed with Nicodemus. This sacramental symbolism would be the culmination of a number of typological layers cleverly thought out by the evangelist: from physical Temple to the body of Jesus to the community of believers in whom dwells the Holy Spirit, received through the sacraments of baptism and the Eucharist.[115]

---

112. Isa 51:3; 58:11–12; Ps 36:9–10; 2 Enoch 8:5–6.

113. Fehribach, *The Women in the Life of the Bridegroom*, 124.

114. Brown (*The Gospel According to John XIII–XXI*, 950) suggests that the verse should be read in light of 1 John 5:6–8, which identifies water, blood and the Spirit as the three witnesses to Christ.

115. Hahn's summary is fitting: "Jesus is the New Temple from which flows the bloody stream of sacrifice, dying as the true Passover lamb to fulfill that great feast, as part of the great 'sign' of his death and resurrection. And now, at what may be considered the heart or climax of Jesus' final 'sign,' there flows forth water and blood, the river of the Spirit, baptism and Eucharist" ("Temple, Sign, and Sacrament," 135–36).

## The Beloved in the Garden (John 20:1–18)

Scholars have identified a final nuptial passage attesting to Jesus' role as Bridegroom-Messiah in his resurrection appearance to Mary Magdalene (John 20:1, 11–18).[116] Curious elements in the text have traditionally puzzled commentators, such as the repetition of Mary's "turning" (John 20:14, 16) and Jesus' command not to hold him (20:17). These odd bits begin to make sense when read in light of Cant 3:1–4.

According to the narrative, Mary Magdalene arrives alone at Jesus' tomb early on the first day of the week, "while it was still dark" to find that the tomb is empty (John 20:1). After an interlude focusing on Peter and John's arrival at the tomb (20:2–10), the narrative returns to Mary (20:11): she is standing outside the tomb weeping, then stoops down to look inside the tomb. Mary sees two angels sitting where the body of Jesus had lain who ask her why she is weeping. She replies: "Because they have taken away my Lord, and I do not know where they have laid him" (20:13). Suddenly, Mary "turned around and saw Jesus standing there" (20:14). At first, she does not recognize him and supposes him to be "the gardener" (20:15). When Jesus identifies himself, calling her by name, "she turned and said to him, 'Rabboni!'" (20:16). Jesus then tells Mary: "do not hold me, for I have not yet ascended to the Father, but go to My brethren and say to them, I am ascending to My Father and your Father, and to My God and your God" (20:17).

There are several parallels between this text and Cant 3:1–4. As Mary arrives at the tomb at night while it is still dark, the Canticle describes the Shulamite rising by night, wandering alone through the city to search for the one she loves. Whereas Mary stands outside the tomb weeping and looking inside the tomb for her beloved, in Cant 3:2 the woman declares: "I will rise now and go about the city . . . I will seek him whom my soul loves." Both narratives have the woman rising or standing to search for her beloved. Mary's encounter with the angels and her reply to them, "I do not know where they have laid him," echoes the Shulamite's complaint: "I sought him, but I did not find him" as she encounters the city's watchmen and asks whether they have seen her beloved (Cant 3:2–3). When Mary sees Jesus and thinks him to be the gardener, we are reminded that the site of the crucifixion and Jesus' tomb is located in a garden (John

116. Cambe, "L'influence du Cantique," 17–19; Winsor, *A King is Bound in the Tresses*, 34–44; Fehribach, *The Women in the Life of the Bridegroom*, 143–67; Mc-Whirter, *The Bridegroom Messiah*, 88–105.

19:41). This alludes to the garden setting of the Song, often used as a euphemism for the Shulamite.[117] When Jesus identifies himself and she exclaims 'Rabboni!', this seems to be a pictorial representation of Cant 3:4: "Scarcely had I passed by them, when I found the one I love." The fact that Mary recognizes Jesus at the sound of his voice when he calls her name may also allude to the voice of the beloved that so enthralls the Shulamite (Cant 2:8; 5:2). In Cant 5:6 his voice causes a deep emotional reaction within her: "My heart leaped up when he spoke." Also, the odd repetition of Mary's "turning" in John 20:14, 16 may echo the verbs used in Cant 2:17; 3:2; 7:1, meaning either "turning around" or "turning back."

Jesus' command to Mary "do not hold me, for I have not yet ascended to the Father" (John 20:17) is another textual anomaly, given that there is no prior indication that she is holding him. The verse is enlightened by Cant 3:4: "I held him, and would not let him go until I had brought him into my mother's house, and into the chamber of her that conceived me." The parallel is interesting not only because of the woman holding her beloved and not letting him go, but also because of the father/mother context. While the Shulamite ardently desires to bring her lover into the "house of her mother," the Gospel reverses these words and has Jesus declare to Mary that he is ascending "to My Father and your (pl.) Father, and to My God and your (pl.) God." With this statement, Jesus' Father and God also becomes the Father and God of Mary and the disciples. It is a familial adoption of Jesus' friends into "God's home." This verse is one of those pointing to the establishment of a patrilineal descent group by means of Jesus' paschal sacrifice. For the first time in the Fourth Gospel, Jesus calls his disciples "brothers," and announces that what God the Father was always to him, he is now to his disciples. This indicates that Jesus' death and resurrection

> enabled the disciples to become 'brothers' of Jesus, just as Jacob's blood sacrifice reclassified Laban as a 'brother' to Jacob. Jesus' words, 'my Father and your Father,' indicate that Jesus' fraternal relationship with his disciples is based on a common heavenly Father, a common patrilineal descent established through his blood sacrifice.[118]

---

117. Cf. Cant 4:12–13,15–16; 5:1; 6:2,11; 8:13.

118. Fehribach, *The Women in the Life of the Bridegroom*, 121.

## Receiving the Holy Spirit: A New Creation

On the evening of the same day (John 20:19), Jesus breathes on his disciples, imparting the Holy Spirit to them (20:22). The Spirit had accompanied Jesus since the beginning of his ministry (John 1:32–33). Identified with Jesus' "living water" (7:39), it was announced as an essential requirement for entering the kingdom of God (3:5–6) and for true worship (4:23–24); Jesus had repeatedly promised its future coming and dwelling in the disciples (John 14:17, 26; 15:26; 16:13). As Jesus died on the cross, he "gave up the spirit." Now, after the resurrection, he imparts the Spirit to the apostles by breathing on them. The verb used here for "breathe" (*emphusao*) is not used elsewhere in the New Testament and is rare in the Old Testament. Significantly, it is used in Gen 2:7 to describe God imparting the breath of life to Adam. The author of the Wisdom of Solomon uses the same verb to describe the creation of man, whom God inspired with an active soul and "breathed into him a living spirit" (Wis 15:11). The word is also used to describe Elijah's "breathing" on the dead son of the widow which brings him back to life (1 Kgs 17:21), and the breath of the spirit bringing the dry bones back to life in Ezek 37:9. John's use of *emphusao* likely continues the theme of the new creation initiated in the Gospel's prologue. Jesus breathing on the apostles and imparting the Spirit to them signifies that he is completing in them the new creation and new birth that he announced earlier (John 3:3–5, 16:21). Yet unlike the first creation, where Adam was a passive instrument in the hands of the Creator, here the new Adam is the creator of the "new Eve" who came out of him—the community of believers.[119] We must keep in mind that this day of the "new creation" is precisely the "third day" on which Jesus raises the new Temple (of his Body) as he had announced in John 2:19–21.

## Summary: Nuptial Imagery in the Gospel of John

For John, Jesus is the Bridegroom-King-Messiah. Although this is announced only once explicitly (3:29), the nuptial theme consistently returns throughout the Gospel by means of hints, allusions, and irony: John the Baptist's statement about Jesus' sandals pointing to the law of the levirate, Jesus' hidden role as bridegroom providing the best wine at

---

119. Feuillet, "Les épousailles du Messie," 386. Cf. Seaich, *A Great Mystery*, 174–75.

Cana, the betrothal-type scene with the Samaritan woman modeled on the conversation between Jacob and Rachel, the anointing of Jesus' feet by Mary of Bethany evoking Cant 1:12, his promise at the Last Supper to prepare a place for his disciples in his Father's house, the comparison of his death to a woman's labor pains, the allusions to birth at the cross as Jesus entrusts the beloved disciple to Mary as her son and water and blood pour out of his side, and the resurrection appearance to Mary Magdalene evoking Cant 3:1–2—all these point to a sustained use of nuptial imagery throughout the Gospel. This nuptial imagery, moreover, relates to our key moments of salvation history.

## New Creation and Eden, New Adam and Eve

John interweaves his nuptial symbolism with several allusions to creation, Eden, Adam and Eve. The language of the prologue and the sequence of seven days leading to Cana indicates that Jesus is inaugurating a new creation and taking on the role of a new Adam. At Cana, Jesus' mother, called "woman," takes on the role of a new Eve. Jesus' arrest and burial in a garden evokes the Garden of Eden, where by his obedient death on a "tree" he reverses the disobedience of the first Adam. The river of living water coming out of Jesus (4:14; 7:38; 19:34), alluding to the water flowing out of Ezekiel's Temple, recalls the rivers of Eden, and his imparting of the Holy Spirit on the apostles by blowing on them alludes to the creation of the first Adam and completes the work of the new creation.

## Sinai and Paschal Mystery

John's nuptial symbolism is also related to Sinai and Exodus typology: Jesus' revelation of the divine glory at Cana and at his "hour" recalls the divine glory revealed at Sinai (1:14; 17:1–5; Exod 24:16–17); his role as sacrificial lamb of God is modeled on the paschal lamb (1:29; Exod 12); the sequence of days leading to Cana, the allusion to Jacob's ladder, Mary's words to the servants, and the symbolism of wine at Cana all point to the Sinai theophany (2:1–11; Exod 19–24). Jesus' lifting up is compared to the lifting up of the brazen serpent in the desert (3:14; Num 21); the reference to the manna in the Bread of Life discourse (6:16–21; Exod 16), the allusions to the water from the rock (4:14; 7:38; cf. Exod 17; Num 20), and Jesus' role as "the prophet" (6:14; 7:40) all point to a close connection between John's narrative and the Exodus.

## New Temple

Jesus' role as new Temple pervades the Fourth Gospel. The prologue announces that he "tabernacled" among us (1:14), and the declaration that his body will be a new Temple (2:21) sets the tone for the entire book. The Temple theme is developed in the dialogue with the Samaritan woman about the coming new form of worship, and in the recurring theme of the living waters recalling the river flowing out of Ezekiel's Temple (Ezek 47:1–12). At the Last Supper, the discussion on preparing a "place" in the "Father's house" not only employs nuptial and familial language but also Temple allusions, implying that the new Temple will be extended from Jesus' own body to the community of believers. This is prefigured by the role of the women in John (Mary the mother of Jesus, the Samaritan woman, Mary of Bethany, and Mary Magdalene) who represent the ecclesial community. The link between Jesus as Temple and the disciples as Temple is the gift of the Spirit, obtained through washing in the "living water" of baptism (3:5), and the Eucharistic "eating his flesh and drinking his blood" (6:53–58, 63).

## Realized Eschatology

Characteristic of the Fourth Gospel is its (partly) realized eschatology: in contrast to the synoptics, which acknowledge the bridegroom's presence during his ministry on earth but also anticipate his relative absence (cf. Matt 9:15) until his eschatological second coming (25:1–13), John has a more pronounced emphasis on the continued presence of the Bridegroom-Messiah, perpetuated *now* in the community of disciples. Cana is already an anticipation of the great eschatological wedding feast, and Jesus told the Samaritan woman that "the hour is coming and *now is* when the true worshipers will worship the Father in spirit and truth" (John 4:23). Though there is an awareness of the eschatological resurrection in John, the emphasis keeps returning to the immediate life-giving presence of the bridegroom (cf. John 11:24–26). Even when Jesus speaks at length about his departure, he promises his disciples that he will not leave them orphans, but will come and make his home in them (14:23) through the presence of the Holy Spirit (14:26), mediated by the water and blood of baptism and the Eucharist (19:34; cf. 1 John 5:6–8).

## In Conclusion

The rich sacramental imagery of the Fourth Gospel paints the following picture: Jewish types (e.g. Sinai, the Temple, betrothal of Jacob & Rachel, the manna) are fulfilled in Jesus the Bridegroom (e.g. Cana as new Sinai, Jesus as new Temple, "betrothal" of Jesus & Samaritan Woman, the Bread of Life). This fulfilment in Christ is actualized and re-lived in the community of believers who are the bride (3:29) and the extension of the new Temple on account of the Father's love (14:23). They take on this role via Jesus' death when he "gives up the spirit" and the flow of blood and water, representing baptism and the Eucharist, comes out of him, and when he imparts the Holy Spirit to them after his resurrection. As Coloe writes:

> The blood and water is the link between the events narrated and the community of believers of later generations . . . When Jesus is no longer a physical presence with them, the community can still be drawn into his filial relationship with God and participate in the sacrificial gift of his life in their sacraments of baptism and Eucharist.[120]

---

120. Coloe, *God Dwells with Us*, 200.

# 9

# Temple of the Holy Spirit

## First Corinthians

### Introduction

JOHN NOT ONLY PORTRAYS JESUS as Bridegroom-Messiah, temple, and dwelling place of the *Shekhinah*; he also connects these roles to the community of believers through his mystical sacramental theology. Nevertheless, John's nuptial and temple typology remains primarily Christological. The matter is treated differently by St. Paul, who extends nuptial and temple typology to the Church—presented as bride, temple, and body of Christ—and to the individual Christian—called a "temple of the Holy Spirit" in whom dwells the divinity. Commenting on John's account of the cleansing of the Temple, Raymond Brown discerned three strains of early Christian thought pertaining to the spiritual temple:

1.  the temple is the *Church* (Eph 2:19–21, 1 Pet 2:5, 4:17)

2.  the temple is the *individual Christian* (1 Cor 3:16, 6:19)

3.  the temple is *in heaven* (Heb 9:11–12, Rev 11:19) [1]

These are precisely the three levels of nuptial symbolism that we will continue to explore in our study. Paul is the champion of the first two, while the third is especially found in the Apocalypse. Three Pauline

---

1. Brown, *The Gospel According to John I–XII*, 124.

epistles are particularly relevant to our study because of their treatment of nuptial imagery and its relation to Adam, Sinai, and temple typology: 1 and 2 Corinthians, and Ephesians. These reveal a clear confluence of the nuptial and temple motifs, with the mystical marriage between Christ and the Church taking place in the Temple of the Holy Spirit (the believer) while recalling the Adam-Eve union and Sinai/Exodus typology. We will consider how Paul applies nuptial symbolism to the Church and the Christian, and how he uses temple symbolism to express the union between Christ and his bride.

In the First Epistle to the Corinthians, Paul makes no direct allusion to an allegorical or mystical marriage, but he has plenty to say about earthly marriage and sexuality, the Church and believer as Temple of the Holy Spirit (1 Cor 3:16–17; 6:19–20), and the Church as Body of Christ (6:15–17; 10:17; 11:29; 12:12–26). First Corinthians has been criticized as being "poor in doctrinal content," yielding "the very least for our understanding of the Pauline faith"[2] because it is "an occasional, *ad hoc*, response to the situation that had developed in the Corinthian church"[3] addressing problems such as disunity and strife, doubts concerning Paul's authority, sexual immorality, marriage and consecrated virginity, food sacrificed to idols, customs and conduct in Christian worship, and spiritual gifts. Paul's primary concern for ethics is apparently interspersed with some doctrinal, philosophical, and theological remarks for the sake of strengthening his moral exhortations, including an excursus on wisdom, agricultural and architectural metaphors for the Church, the necessity and importance of love, and the resurrection of believers.

A close examination of the text, however, reveals that Paul is in fact using sustained temple imagery and typology throughout the epistle. When viewed in light of this temple typology applied to the believer (or *mystagogy*), Paul's practical directives to the Corinthians turn out to be much more than casuistic moral exhortations. They are, rather, a description of the sanctified life of love that ought to flow from the believer's consecrated nature as temple of the Holy Spirit. First Corinthians is rich in a temple mystagogy that describes the intimate indwelling of the deity within the believer and is associated with nuptial or sexual themes: Through baptism, the body is consecrated as temple of the Holy Spirit, and the believer experiences a personal union with God comparable

2. Walter Bauer, *Orthodoxy and Heresy in Earliest Christianity*, 219; quoted in Conzelmann, 1 *Corinthians*, 9.

3. Fee, *The First Epistle to the Corinthians*, 4.

to the union that took place between God and Israel in the Jerusalem Temple. This human temple, however, can become desecrated through sexual immorality; Paul refers to the "one-flesh" union between Adam and Eve to make this point (1 Cor 6:16). He also argues that the man-woman hierarchy derives from the created order (11:3–16), recalling the tradition of the first androgynous man from whose side God created the woman. For Paul, not only the Eucharist (11:23–32) but also the community of disciples is the Body of Christ that is "joined" to him (12:12–31). Moreover, Christ's identity as the New Adam (15:22, 45–49) (and the Church as New Eve) reveals an additional link between temple symbolism and the origins of humankind in Eden.

## Wisdom and Temple Building (1 Cor 1:10–3:23)

Paul begins by expressing his concern about schisms in the Corinthian church that contradict the unity signified by the common baptism of all believers (1:10–17). This concern for unity is interrupted by a long excursus on the wisdom and folly of God and of men (1:18–2:16), until the theme of unity is resumed in 3:1–4. To drive home the importance of unity, Paul uses two metaphors to describe the Corinthian church: it is "God's field," in which different workers plant and water but where God alone gives the increase, and "God's building," in the process of being constructed (3:9).[4] The foundation of this building is Jesus Christ, though Paul "as a wise master builder" has laid its foundation. Given the preceding excursus on wisdom and the temple metaphor that follows (3:16–17), it is possible that the "wise master builder" is an allusion to Solomon, the builder of the Temple so reputed for his wisdom. Paul goes on to describe the building materials of this spiritual structure: gold, silver, precious stones, wood, hay, and straw (3:12). The first three are frequently mentioned in the Old Testament as the building materials of the Temple.[5] Perhaps the context of burning (where each one's work "will be revealed by fire," 3:13) alludes to the latter three materials as those used to feed the fire on the altar of sacrifices. Paul specifies that the building being erected is indeed God's Temple: "Do you not know that you are the temple of God

---

4. Conzelmann (75) has shown that the mixing of these two metaphors is traditional in the Old Testament, in Judaism, in Hellenism and in Gnosticism; E.g. Jer 1:10; Philo, *On the Cherubim* 100–112.

5. Hag 2:8; 1 Chr 22:14, 16; 1 Chr 29:2; 2 Chr 3:6. Cf. Fee, *The First Epistle to the Corinthians*, 140–41.

and that the Spirit of God dwells in you?" (3:16). Paul employs temple mystagogy to describe the intimate indwelling of the deity within the Corinthian church: through baptism (1:14–17; 6:11), they have received the Spirit of divine wisdom to build a holy temple—themselves: "For God's temple is holy, and that temple you are" (3:17). The use of the plural pronoun indicates that the temple of God is the community, and it is through the community that the Spirit is communicated to individuals.[6] It is thus within the Church that the Corinthians can experience a union with God comparable to the union that took place between God and Israel in the Jerusalem Temple. As God is *hagios* (holy), so is his temple—his people— also *hagios*, consecrated and set apart for him. The Corinthians are in a sense already sanctified "in Christ;" yet in another they are still called to become saints (*hagiois*) in practice (1:2). But through their factions they are defiling their own temple, undermining their identity in Christ, and corrupting the very mystery they are celebrating. The dire consequences of such behavior are evident: If one destroys the temple and dwelling of God, God will also destroy him (3:17).

## Porneia as Defilement of the Human Temple (1 Cor 5–9)

In chapter 5, Paul condemns the sexual misconduct that is plaguing the church in Corinth with a brief mystagogical allusion to Passover and the cleansing of leaven, which is equated with sin (5:6–8). After expressing his shock at a case of litigation in the community (6:1–8), he returns to his concern for bodily purity and explains more thoroughly the gravity of sexual immorality (*porneia*) and why it defiles the temple of the Holy Spirit. With the words "but you were washed, but you were sanctified, but you were justified in the name of the Lord Jesus and by the Spirit of our God" (6:11), Paul again reminds the Corinthians that the washing of their common baptism is the foundation of their unity, sanctification, and consecration to God in the Church.[7] When he states that "the body is not

6. Cf. Corriveau, "Temple, Holiness, and the Liturgy of Life in Corinthians," 157–59. Gärtner notes four points of contact between this passage and the temple symbolism of the Qumran community: (a) identification of God's temple with the community; (b) the Spirit of God 'dwells' in the congregation; (c) the Temple of God is holy; (d) it requires the purity of the members. Gärtner, *The Temple and the Community in Qumran and the New Testament*, 56–60.

7. For discussions on the baptismal context of 1 Cor 6:11, see Fee, *The First Epistle*

for *porneia* but for the Lord, and the Lord for the body" (6:13), he subtly alludes to the marriage between Christ and the Church: The body of the baptized believer, consecrated, sanctified, and set apart for God, can no longer be joined in passing and illicit "one-flesh" unions with women, since this body is now consecrated for a holy union with the deity: it is "for the Lord, and the Lord for the body." In the Epistle to the Ephesians, Paul formulates a positive description of the love between Christ and the Church as model and blueprint of the ideal "one-flesh" union between husband and wife. Here he deals with the opposite, negative example, forcefully telling the Corinthians what *not* to do: fornication is not only a sexual sin; it is also a desecration of their own bodily temple and an act liable to destroy their union with Christ, of which they are the members:

> Do you not know that your bodies are members of Christ? Shall I then take the members of Christ and make them members of a prostitute? Never! Or do you not know that he who is joined to a prostitute becomes one body with her? For, as it is written, "The two will become one flesh." But he who is joined to the Lord becomes one spirit with him. Flee from sexual immorality. Every other sin a person commits is outside the body, but he who commits sexual immorality sins against his own body. Or do you not know that your body is a temple of the Holy Spirit who is in you, whom you have from God? You are not your own, for you were bought with a price. So glorify God in your body (1 Cor 6:15–20)

This passage goes beyond 3:16–17 in specifying that not only the community is a temple of the Holy Spirit but also the believer's *body*.[8] Because of the body's sanctity, Paul explains the serious implications of sexual immorality. The problem of *porneia* was a widespread one in Corinth, a city renowned for its sexual vice and for the cultic prostitution that took place in its pagan temples.[9] The passage highlights how the "one flesh" union affects the bodily temple of the Holy Spirit, which is also a member of Christ. Interestingly, Paul quotes the one-flesh

---

to the Corinthians, 246–47; Orr and Walther, *I Corinthians*, 199; Conzelmann, *1 Corinthians*, 107.

8. As Corriveau notes: "What is important here is the application of the identity of the Church as Temple to the body of the individual member of the Church. The message is that we cannot separate the community and its members." ("Temple, Holiness, and the Liturgy of Life," 162)

9. On Corinth's reputation, see Fee, *The First Epistle to the Corinthians*, 2–3; Conzelmann, *1 Corinthians*, 11–12.

union of Gen 2:24 not as a metaphor for Christ and the Church but to describe the contemptible union of a Christian with a prostitute. This sin is graver than all others because it is an offense against one's own body, the temple of the Holy Spirit, and against the members of Christ who are "joined to the Lord" and "one spirit with him" in a covenantal relation of love sealed at baptism. For this reason, Paul is much harsher against those believers who engage in *porneia* than those "of this world" who are not of the household of faith and whose bodies are not temples of the Holy Spirit (5:9–13).

But what precisely is wrong with union with a prostitute? It is obviously not the sexual act in itself that defiles the spiritual temple and harms the union with Christ, since this union is permitted and even encouraged between husband and wife in the very next chapter (and exalted in Ephesians as sign of the union between Christ and the Church). In sexual intercourse, two bodies become one. Being joined to a prostitute, therefore, means to become a "member" of her body (6:15)—the body of a person who is not a member of Christ and therefore not destined for resurrection (6:14). The Christian is holy (Heb. *kadosh*, Gr. *hagios*)—sanctified and set apart for God's service. A harlot, on the other hand—*kedeshah* in Hebrew, from the same root *kadosh*—is not consecrated to God but rather "consecrated" to her sinful trade that openly contradicts the divine purpose of sexuality.

Paul's discussion assumes Jesus' teachings on the permanence of marriage. In Matthew 19:4–6, Jesus refers to Adam and Eve's union as the prototype of the "one flesh" union between man and woman as it was "in the beginning"—alluding to the ancient tradition that God originally made Adam an androgynous being, "male and female" (Gen 1:27; 5:2). By taking Eve out of Adam, God made two complementary persons, leaving in them the insatiable desire to return to their primeval unity and again be joined as "one flesh." This original unity, separation, and longing to return to union forms the ground for Jesus' radically new teaching on marriage: "So then," he declares—since God made them "male and female," since woman was "taken out of man" and is "bone of his bones and flesh of his flesh," and since a man "shall leave his father and mother and be joined to his wife"—when they return together to their primal unity, "they are no longer two but one flesh. Therefore what God has joined together, let not man separate" (Matt 19:6). In this light, the problem with union with a prostitute becomes obvious: the one-flesh union, far from expressing the sacred, permanent bond of body and soul that sexual union is meant to represent, becomes degraded to a contract of convenience where the body is used as an object of consummation, temporarily "purchased" for the man's pleasure, and "disposed of" after use. It is thus the innate contradiction of becoming "one flesh" with a prostitute without becoming "one spirit" with her by an enduring covenantal bond that constitutes the offense against the temple of the Holy Spirit, whereby the very nature of the one-flesh union as witness to God's faithful love is distorted and contradicted.

Returning to 1 Corinthians 6, Paul concludes his argument against *porneia* by going back to the analogy of the body as temple of the Holy Spirit. Illicit sexual union defiles the holy temple consecrated to God, which was "bought at a price" (6:20) by Christ's death and represents the sacred space where God enters into communion with man. Paul is probably evoking the Jewish concept of *tum'at mikdash,* whereby the Temple becomes defiled because of Israel's sins.[10] The Temple, as God's house, is the place where the covenant with his people is enacted, maintained, and perpetuated. Any breach in the covenant, therefore, has negative ramifications for the Temple. "When sin taints the covenant, its symbol in the realm of space, the Temple, becomes tainted as well."[11] Likewise, the sin of Christians violates the covenant with Christ and taints the bodily temple of the Holy Spirit. The passage fittingly concludes with an exhortation that the Corinthians "glorify God" in body and spirit through sanctified behavior that is befitting of their new identity as consecrated sanctuaries of God's presence, since their body and spirit now entirely belong to him (6:20).

The concerns about the effects of *porneia* on the temple of the Holy Spirit are followed by a more systematic and positive exposition of the principles of marriage in chapter 7. Worthy of note are the instructions regarding marriages between a believer and an unbeliever. Paul encourages the Christian spouse to remain with the non-Christian, "for the unbelieving husband is sanctified by the wife, and the unbelieving wife is sanctified by the husband; otherwise your children would be unclean, but now they are holy" (1 Cor 7:14). He is teaching here the remarkable idea

---

10. Israel's sins are often described as defiling God's sanctuary: When they offer their offspring to Molech they "defile my sanctuary and profane my holy name" (Lev 20:3). The sin offering is said to "atone for the holy place because of the uncleanness of the children of Israel, and because of their transgressions" (Lev 15:15–16).

11. Berman, *The Temple,* 142.

that the faith of the believing party confers sanctity upon the other and upon their children through the union of marriage.[12]

Chapter 9 provides another example of temple mystagogy: Paul defends his right to eat, drink, and earn a living from his ministry by comparing himself to the priests and workers in the Temple who offer sacrifices and "partake of the offerings of the altar" as a sign of the Lord's approval that "those who preach the gospel should live from the gospel" (9:13–14). Preaching the gospel is thus equated with the priestly sacrificial ministry in the Temple.

## Of Sinai, Sacrifice, and Sacraments (1 Cor 10)

Chapter 10 is probably the richest chapter of our epistle in its typological references to Sinai and the Exodus—the setting of the betrothal between God and Israel that was later commemorated and perpetuated in the Tabernacle and Temple. It begins as follows:

> [O]ur fathers were all under the cloud, and all passed through the sea, and all were baptized into Moses in the cloud and in the sea, and all ate the same spiritual food, and all drank the same spiritual drink. For they drank from the spiritual Rock that followed them, and the Rock was Christ. (1 Cor 10:1–4)

Paul uses the example of Israel in the desert as a warning to the Corinthians, recalling that the Israelites experienced a situation similar to theirs. The passage mentions well-known events of the Exodus: the cloud (Exod 13:21), the sea (Exod 14:21f), the manna (Exod 16:4, 14–18), and the spring (Exod 17:6; Num 20:7–13). Commentators have seen in the cloud "a veiled reference to the presence of God in Israel's midst, comparable to the Spirit for Christians"—or the indwelling *Shekhinah*.[13] Yet what is remarkable here is how Paul daringly retrojects "proto-sacraments" of baptism and Eucharist back into the history of Israel's wanderings as prefigurations of the sacraments of the New Covenant. The crossing of the sea becomes the Israelites' baptism ("into" Moses), and the manna and water from the rock as "spiritual food" and "spiritual drink" are a sort of proto-Eucharist. Paul goes as far as identifying the rock itself with

---

12. This may reflect the concept of *sancta contagio*, whereby the Temple was believed to act as a source of divine power, transmitting holiness to the beholder of its sacred objects (Seaich, *A Great Mystery*, 65–68, 176–77).

13. Fee, *The First Epistle to the Corinthians*, 445.

Christ, who accompanied the Israelites through the desert.[14] Yet despite the divine presence that dwelt among them and the "sacraments" that accompanied them along the way, "God was not well pleased" with them and most died in the wilderness. These things, Paul writes, became "our examples" (or "types"), and were written "for our instruction" (10:6, 11). The Corinthians, therefore, should beware that the same does not happen to them. Of particular significance is the connection between idolatry and sexual immorality in the recounting of the golden calf episode (10:7; Exod 32) and the similar incident at Baal Peor (10:8; Num 25:1–9). *Porneia* is tantamount to idolatry and betraying Christ; idolatry is spiritual adultery. Both, therefore, must be equally shunned (10:14). The invective against idolatry continues the argument that Paul began in 8:1 concerning the eating of things offered to idols. Why is the issue of food important? Because participation in cultic meals is equivalent to communion (*koinonia*) with the deity that is worshiped—whether in the Jewish Temple (10:18), in the Christian Eucharist (10:16–17), or in pagan cults (10:20). The word *koinonia* is significant because of the close intimacy that it signifies ("fellowship," "participation," or "to share with someone in something").[15] Just as sharing in the sacrifices of the Temple means to be "partaker of the altar" and to share in *koinonia* with God, participating in pagan sacred meals involves *koinonia* with demons—a union incompatible with the *koinonia* with Christ in the Eucharist. Partaking of the Lord's body and blood (10:16) is equivalent to becoming one with him: it is a "one-flesh" union as real as the one described in the Fourth Gospel (John 6:56). Eating food sacrificed to idols, therefore, is a sort of "eucharist" with demons. It is spiritual adultery, a betrayal of Christ tantamount to Israel's worship of the golden calf and her subsequent betrayals of God as lamented by the Old Testament prophets.

## Woman as Temple? (1 Cor 11:3–16)

In chapter 11, Paul addresses the issue of head coverings for women and men. This initially seems like a minor, cultural question following the

---

14. Recall the midrashic traditions that the rock out of which came living waters followed the Israelites through the desert. For Philo, the rock is "the wisdom of God . . . out of which he gave a drink to the souls who love God." (*Allegorical Interpretation* 2:21). Cf. Fee, *The First Epistle to the Corinthians*, 448; Orr and Walther, 1 *Corinthians*, 245.

15. On the meaning of *koinonia*, cf. Fee, *The First Epistle to the Corinthians*, 466.

greater problems of fornication and idolatry. Paul has just discussed how worship in temples—whether Jewish, Christian, or pagan—is equivalent to *koinonia* with the respective deity. Then, suddenly, he turns to the hierarchy of subordination between man and woman (itself subordinated to the hierarchy of God and Christ) and the need for women to cover their heads with a veil. Paul explains that the subordination of woman to man is not an arbitrary, culturally bound custom but stems metaphysically from their origins in creation: "For man is not from woman, but woman from man. Nor was man created for the woman, but woman for the man" (1 Cor 11:8–9). Since woman was taken *from* man and *for* man, man has been given authority over her. This recalls again the tradition of the first androgynous man out of whom God created the woman. Yet the hierarchical relation between them is not one of qualitative superiority or domination. Man is the "image and glory of God; but woman is the glory of man" (11:7). The first part of the verse is an allusion to Gen 1:26, which states that man was created "in the image and likeness" of God. Paul thus equates God's *glory* with God's *likeness*, which man reflects. Yet if what is last in creation was first in intention, then woman is the ultimate achievement of God's creation. If man is the crown of creation, then woman is the crown jewel. In Batey's words: "Man who has been created in the image of God reflects the divine nature of his creator. Woman is a reflection of that reflection, for she has been taken from man."[16] First Corinthians thus reveals a close affinity between the man-woman hierarchy and the order of creation (cf. Eph 5:31's quote of Gen 2:24). But why the diversion to the subject of veils? Perhaps because veils are found both on women and in temples. Thus, a woman's body is a sacred temple, consecrated to her husband and reflecting his glory, just as the temple is a sacred space, consecrated to God and reflecting his glory—an association that follows from the metaphors of the Church as temple, body, and bride.[17]

16. Batey, *New Testament Nuptial Imagery*, 22–23.

17. Batey (*New Testament Nuptial Imagery*, 23 n. 4) notes: "In the first century the veil was not primarily a symbol of modesty or dignity. The direct symbolism is that of being taken possession of, and as a result taken out of circulation as a free woman. The woman wearing the veil was to be unapproachable in a similar sense as a holy object, because she had been set apart for her husband—sanctified for him exclusively. For a wife to refuse to wear the veil was not just a breach of modesty but the rejection of God's created order of authority."

## Unity of the Body (1 Cor 11:17–12:31)

Saint Paul returns to the topic of the Lord's Supper (11:17–33), whose sanctity derives from the fact that it is both a memorial of Jesus' death and the anticipation of his future *parousia* (11:23–26). In this setting, too, there are divisions and factions; some approach the Supper out of carnal desires to satisfy their hunger; others are drunk. Paul warns those who approach the Lord's Table in an "unworthy manner" that they become "guilty of the body and blood of the Lord" (11:27). Such behavior contradicts the essence of the Lord's Supper, for the partaking of the Eucharist is the source and sign of the Church's unity, and all members of Christ are "one bread and one body" when partaking of the one eucharistic bread (10:17). Factions at the Lord's Supper (11:17–22), therefore, negate the very mystery that is being celebrated: to be "guilty of the body and blood of the Lord" and to "not discern his body" is to break *koinonia* with the Lord and his body. It is another form of desecration of the sacred.

In chapter 12, Paul continues to discuss the unity of the body, now addressing the diversity of gifts within it. The body "is one and has many members, but all the members of that one body, being many, are one body, so also is Christ" (12:12). Paul again reminds the Corinthians that they have become members of this spiritual body at baptism when they were "made to drink into the one Spirit" (12:13).[18] The unity of the body is not one of bland uniformity but rather displays a rich diversity in its members, comparable to the members of the human body where each plays a different yet indispensable role (12:15–31). What, then, builds up God's building, God's temple and Christ's body? Not worldly wisdom nor knowledge, but *agape*: "Knowledge puffs up, but love edifies" (8:1). According to Paul's famous hymn of love in chapter 13, it is the patient, generous and joyful gift of self, in imitation of Christ (11:1), along with a deep love of truth that "bears all things, believes all things, hopes all things, endures all things" (13:7), which constitutes "the more excellent way" by which Christians are to build up the Body of Christ and Temple of the Holy Spirit.

---

18. The Pauline connection between baptism and "drinking" the Spirit seems related to the water symbolism of baptism and drinking of living water in John 3–4.

## New Adam (and New Eve?) (1 Cor 15)

In chapter 15, Paul deals with eschatology and the resurrection of the dead. He portrays Jesus as the last Adam who reverses the curse of death incurred by the first Adam: "For as in Adam all die, even so in Christ all shall be made alive" (15:22).[19] If the natural, earthly body of the first Adam was sown in corruption, dishonor, and weakness, the spiritual, heavenly body of the last Adam is raised in incorruption, glory and power (15:42–44). While the first Adam, from the earth, passively received life as a "living being," the last Adam, from heaven, gives life as a "life-giving spirit" (15:45–47). Believers, already bearing the image of the man of dust in their mortality, are also called to bear the image of the man of heaven by putting on immortality (15:48–56). The hope for the final day of the resurrection of the dead, "at the last trumpet," means that the human temple of the Holy Spirit will reach the fullness of its stature.

From Paul's multiple metaphors we can infer the following: Since Christ is the last Adam raised in *doxa* (15:43), by considering that "woman came from man" (11:8), that man is the *doxa* of God and woman the *doxa* of man (11:7), and that the Church is Christ's body (10:17; 12:27) who is sustained by the eucharistic communion of his body and blood (10:16) and will inherit his life and *doxa* (15:49), one comes very close to the concept of the Church as "new Eve," the bride who was "taken out" of the new Adam and endowed with his glory.

## Summary: First Corinthians

Although the First Epistle to the Corinthians does not explicitly refer to the marriage between Christ and the Church (with the possible exception of a veiled reference in 6:12–20), its Adam, Exodus, and Temple mystagogy is rich with many nuptial allusions: Christ is the new Adam (15:45) and his body is the Church (12:27); believers have been baptized into this (collective) body by the Holy Spirit (12:13). The Christian life is understood as temple worship and sacred service; the (individual) body of the believer is a temple consecrated to Christ and inhabited by the indwelling presence of the Holy Spirit (6:19). As living temple, the believer shares in intimate *koinonia* with Christ, especially through sharing at his table and

---

19. On the relation between Adam, bringer of death, and Christ, restorer of life, cf. Rom 5:12–21.

partaking of his body and blood—in itself a kind of "one flesh" union. Yet this intimate *koinonia* can be destroyed through illicit sexual union, which is tantamount to idolatry (6:18; 10:7–8). Baptism and the Eucharist, the sacramental means of entering into communion with Christ, are depicted as fulfillments of the Sinai theophany and Exodus (10:1–4). The concrete expression of this communion is the call to the members of the community to love each other with a generous and selfless *agape* love (8:1; 13:1–13). All of it is directed towards a definitive eschatological fulfillment on the day of the final resurrection of the dead (15:51–54).

*10*

# Living Between the Times

## *Second Corinthians*

### Introduction

PAUL'S SECOND EPISTLE TO THE CORINTHIANS betrays a much tenser relationship between the apostle and the Corinthians. The epistle, which has been called "uneven and digressive,"[1] is a combative *apologia* for Paul's person and apostolic ministry, in which he must defend himself against a plethora of accusations raised against him. Paul's most personal letter reveals him as suffering greatly, having recently narrowly escaped death, yet finding all his consolation and placing all his trust in "God who raises the dead" (1:9). Precisely because of his intense sufferings, the epistle is permeated by the contrast between Paul's own weakness and the strength of Christ working in him, between his old, passing "outer man" and the new "inner man" that is gradually being transformed "from glory to glory." To his detractors, Paul answers that just as it was precisely in the paradox of Christ's sufferings that his glory was revealed, so it is in the sufferings of the apostle: "Christ himself must be the Christian paradigm of one who lives in God's presence," and his ministry on the cross as a sacrifice must function "as the visual image of the appearance of those who have entered God's presence through the new covenant."[2]

---

1. Barnett, *The Second Epistle to the Corinthians*, 15.
2. Renwick, *Paul, the Temple, and the Presence of God*, 52.

The epistle's development of some earlier Pauline themes, its description of the glory of the New Covenant in contrast to that of the Sinai covenant, and its identification of the Church as Christ's bride make 2 Corinthians an important document for our study. Jesus manifests the divine glory formerly revealed on Mount Sinai and in the Tabernacle and Temple (2 Cor 3:7–18) but now hidden in weak human bodies—called "tabernacles." The disciple of Christ lives "between the times," having received by faith the guarantee of the glorious promise but not having attained the fullness of union with the beloved. A strong mystical longing for divine union is felt throughout the epistle—and this longing is nuptial: Paul is a father-betrother who has betrothed the Corinthians to one husband so that he may present them "as a pure virgin betrothed to Christ" on their eschatological wedding day (11:2). The ecclesial bride—betrothed but not yet married and still prone to infidelity—is compared to Eve who was deceived by the serpent, thus revealing another instance of Adam and Eve as types of Christ and the Church.

## Letter and Spirit, Old and New, from Glory to Glory (2 Cor 3)

Paul tells the Corinthians that even in the midst of suffering, by finding their entire sufficiency in God through the Spirit Christians become an "epistle of Christ" written "by the Spirit of the living God, not on tablets of stone but on tablets of flesh, that is, of the heart" (3:1–6). Paul contrasts "the letter that kills" of the Old Covenant—the commandments that had been written on tablets of stone—with "the Spirit that gives life" now outpoured in the New Covenant. This is an allusion to the prophecy of Ezekiel 36:26–27 and its promise of giving a new heart (of flesh instead of stone) and new spirit to Israel. The contrast between letter and spirit, stone and flesh, death and life, leads to a further contrast between the glory of the two ministries and two covenants.

This comparison between the glory of the Old and New is developed in a "Christian midrash" based on Exod 34:29–35—the narrative of Moses coming down from Mount Sinai with the tablets of the testimony, with the skin of his face "shining with beams" of the Lord's glory. If the passing ministry of "death" and "condemnation" of the Old Covenant was already glorious, how much more the permanent "ministry of the Spirit" and "of righteousness" that is revealed in Christ. The "glory" (*doxa*) of God, or

"Christ in you, the hope of glory" (Col 1:27) is the divine promise and hidden inner reality that empowers the apostle to continue his work in the midst of trials. We have discussed how the divine glory that filled the Tabernacle and Temple was appropriated to the person of Jesus in John's Prologue. The divine *kavod* or *doxa* is also one of the central themes of 2 Corinthians, appearing ten times as noun and verb in the present section (3:7–11). The superiority of the glory of the New Covenant over the Old also evokes Haggai's prophecy that the Lord would one day fill the new temple with glory, and that "the glory of this latter Temple shall be greater than the former" (Hag 2:8–9). This glory and radiance of God that Christ now imparts to the believer is the ultimate goal of the Christian life (3:18); it is permanent (3:11), eternal, and "heavy" (4:17).[3]

The second part of the metaphor (3:12–18) focuses on the veil that covered Moses' face and hid the shining glory radiating from him when he spoke to the children of Israel after his encounter with God. As "their minds were hardened" then, so "to this day, whenever Moses is read a veil lies over their heart" and they are unable to perceive the all-surpassing glory of the gospel. This veil is taken away "in Christ," "when one turns to the Lord" (3:14–16), and the glory is experienced by receiving the "deposit" of the Spirit, as anticipation and guarantee of the fullness that will be received at the end of the earthly journey (1:22; 5:5). Believing in the gospel illuminates the understanding so that "we all, with unveiled face, beholding the glory of the Lord, are being transformed into the same image from glory to glory" (3:18). Why is the glory seen "as in a mirror"? Because the glory of the Lord is reflected through Christ "who is the image of God" (4:4). In other words, "the light of the knowledge of the glory of God" is seen "in the face of Jesus Christ" (4:6). It is precisely into this glorious image that Christians must be transformed, from the *image* of the man of dust (Adam) into the *image* of the man from heaven (Christ).[4]

## Treasures in Jars of Clay: the Symbolism of Sacrifice (2 Cor 4)

Barnett suggests that Paul's description of the *doxa* is autobiographical: he is describing the glory that he saw and experienced on the Damascus road when he encountered the glorified Christ shining in a dazzling light

---

3. See Barnett, *The Second Epistle to the Corinthians*, 45–46, 178–209.

4. Cf. 1 Cor 15:49; Rom 8:29.

from heaven. Indeed, in the book of Acts, Paul recalls his conversion as an experience of heavenly glory: "I could not see for the glory (*doxa*) of that light."[5] But for now, this unsurpassable glory is temporarily hidden within weak bodies, and Christians struggling in the midst of trials guard a treasure hidden in "earthen vessels," living by God's surpassing power rather than their own (4:7). Just as Haggai encouraged his audience not to focus on the visible *doxa* of the Second Temple (disappointingly inferior to the glory of the former Temple of Solomon), Paul says that the superior *doxa* of Christ is not yet visibly manifest.[6] The life and resurrection of Jesus is manifest in "mortal flesh"—through the "outward man" that is perishing—while "the inward man is being renewed day by day" (4:16). It is precisely the temporary "light affliction" that works "a far more exceeding and eternal weight of glory": the sufferings of this present age are preparing believers for the glory of the coming age.[7]

Paul's expression "earthen vessels" or "jars of clay" describes the vessels used to bear the sin offering after its sacrificial death in the priestly legislation (cf. Lev 6:28). If such an association is intended, it would mean that Paul is portraying his own life as one in which the "sin offering" of Christ's death has been placed.[8] Given that he is "always carrying in the body the death of Jesus" (4:10), this implies that the "earthen vessel" (the believer's body) is the container for the sin-offering, and the "treasure" (Christ's sacrifice) is the sin-offering. This cultic allusion is consistent with the language describing the "fragrance" and "aroma" of Christ propagated by his disciples in 2:14–16. Paul uses similar terms elsewhere, either referring to material gifts received as a "sacrifice acceptable and pleasing to God" (Phil 4:18), or to Christ's own sacrifice (Eph 5:2). This terminology is common in the Septuagint as describing the pleasing odor

---

5. Acts 22:11; cf. 9:3–4; 26:13. Cf. Barnett, *The Second Epistle to the Corinthians*, 184, 206. The glory that Paul saw at the moment of his conversion is perhaps related to the glory that Peter, John and James witnessed at the transfiguration (Luke 9:35), possibly evoking the "glory of the Lord" at Sinai, in the Tabernacle and in the Temple.

6. Cf. Renwick's discussion on the relationship between Hag 2 and 2 Cor 3:1–11 (*Paul, the Temple, and the Presence of God*, 113–121).

7. 2 Cor 4:16–18. The future glory of God often appears in the NT as the fruit of present weakness, sufferings and afflictions. Cf. Rom 8:18–21; 2 Cor 11:30; 12:5–10; Eph 3:13; 2 Thess 1:4; Heb 2:9–10; 1 Pet 1:7–8; 4:13; 5:1, 10.

8. Christ is called *"hamartia"* in 2 Cor 5:21. This is often translated as Christ becoming "sin," but it could also mean "sin-offering" because the LXX translates "sin-offering" as *"hamartia"* (Lev 4:24, 29, 34; 5:6). Renwick, *Paul, the Temple, and the Presence of God*, 83.

of a sacrifice offered to God on the altar.[9] The same terms also appear in Sir 24:15, describing the fragrance of Lady Wisdom as being "like the fragrance of frankincense in the tabernacle" that manifests the presence of God. This cultic interpretation would mean that Paul views the life of the believer as "the smoke that arises from the sacrifice of Christ to God, diffusing as it ascends the knowledge of God communicated in the cross."[10]

## From Earthly Tent to Heavenly Dwelling (2 Cor 5)

In chapter 5, the text becomes directly relevant to our study. Here the anthropological dualism between the "outer person" of this present age and the "inner person" of the coming age adopts tabernacle language that is reminiscent of John 1:14 and the human temple of 1 Corinthians:

> For we know that if the tent that is our earthly home is destroyed, we have a building from God, a house not made with hands, eternal in the heavens. For in this tent we groan, longing to put on our heavenly dwelling, if indeed by putting it on we may not be found naked. For while we are still in this tent, we groan, being burdened—not that we would be unclothed, but that we would be further clothed, so that what is mortal may be swallowed up by life. (2 Cor 5:1–4)

Paul contrasts the frail human body—"the tent that is our earthly home"—with our permanent home, the eternal "building from God," a "house not made with hands" and "heavenly dwelling." If the earthly tent-house is the mortal human body,[11] the eternal, heavenly building from God is undoubtedly the resurrected body, given the resurrection mentioned in the immediate context (4:14) and the language of being "clothed" and of death being "swallowed up by life." The believer groans as long as he is subject to his earthly body, not only because of its weakness and proneness to suffering and death, but especially because being "at home in the body" means to be "away from the Lord" (5:6). One feels here Paul's eschatological longing for union with Christ. He views it as infinitely better to depart from the fragile bodily tent (*skenos*) to be "at

9. Cf. Gen 8:21; Exod 29:18; Lev 1:9; Num 15:3; Ezek 6:13.

10. Barnett, *The Second Epistle to the Corinthians*, 99.

11. Cf. also Wis 9:15; 2 Pet 1:13–15 for the use of tent (*skenos*) as a metaphor for the human body.

home with the Lord" (5:8) than to continue living the earthly life away from him.[12] Paul feels "compelled" by the love of Christ, who "died for all, that those who live should no longer live for themselves but for him who died for them and was raised again" (5:14–15). The fullest expression of love was manifest in the Messiah's willingness to suffer and die for his people. Recognizing this love calls for self-surrender and following in his footsteps by "carrying about in the body the dying of the Lord Jesus, that the life of Jesus also may be manifested in our body" (4:10).

The obvious difference between this depiction of the body as *skenos* and the metaphor of the body as temple of the Holy Spirit employed elsewhere is the contrast between presence and absence. When Paul calls the body a "temple of God" or "temple of the Holy Spirit," he is emphasizing the indwelling *presence* of God in the believer, whereas here the frail *skenos*, though evoking the Tabernacle, is characterized by the relative *absence* of the Lord and longing for future union with him. The difference is probably more didactic than of substance. If Paul must remind the Corinthians that they are a temple of God, this is precisely because they have become forgetful of the "treasure in earthen vessels" that they are carrying, and are desecrating their own temple by their fornication.[13] Since the indwelling *Shekhinah* must be apprehended by faith, without this faith (or as a consequence of *porneia*) the real *presence* can easily be cast out and turn into a real *absence*. Thus, the reminder that the divine presence indwells the bodily temple aims at spurring on Christians to lead a sanctified life worthy of the Holy Spirit given to them as guarantor of the eschatological glory to come. On the other hand, the *skenos* metaphor emphasizes the relative *absence* of Christ as an encouragement not to despair of temporary afflictions and to look forward to the eschatological fulfillment of the resurrected body. Thus the Christian lives "between the times," between presence and absence, having received by faith the guarantee of the glorious promise but still waiting for the fullness of union with the beloved. He is betrothed but not yet married, spurred on by confidence in the love of Christ yet struggling to steadfastly live out this commitment to his Lord. By contrasting the fragile, earthly *skenos* with the eternal, heavenly "building from God," Paul is also alluding to the contrast between the temporary, portable, and fragile Tabernacle (*skenos*) that accompanied the Israelites in the wilderness, and the permanent,

---

12. This yearning is similar to the one that Paul expresses in Phil 1:21–23.
13. Cf. 1 Cor 3:16–17; 6:15–20.

imposing, and splendid Temple that replaced it in Jerusalem and was the renown of all nations.

## Temple of God Revisited (2 Cor 6:14–18)

The next passage has much in common with those seen in 1 Corinthians:

> Do not be unequally yoked together with unbelievers. For what partnership has righteousness with lawlessness? And what fellowship has light with darkness? What accord has Christ with Belial? Or what portion does a believer share with an unbeliever? What agreement has the temple of God with idols? For we are the temple of the living God; as God said: "I will make my dwelling among them and walk among them, and I will be their God, and they shall be My people." (2 Cor 6:14–16)

Paul returns to the theme of the spiritual temple of God, again within the context of separation: certain ways of life are incompatible with the believer's sanctified state. Paul exhorts the Corinthians to "not be unequally yoked together with unbelievers."[14] Given the five rhetorical questions that follow, in which Paul pits the sanctified state of the disciple of Christ against the evil ways of the world, it seems that the "unbelievers" are the unconverted pagans and idol-worshippers of Corinth, and the state of being "unequally yoked" with them is likely intermarriage or participation in their cultic life.[15] Paul probably had both meanings in mind since the most common cause of idolatry in Israel had always been intermarriage with pagans.[16]

Paul's plea for keeping the temple of God free from inappropriate unions with unbelievers and idols is supported by a concoction of Old Testament citations recalling God's covenantal promises to his people.

14. This metaphor is based on two OT texts, LXX Lev 19:19 which forbids the crossbreeding of animals, and Deut 22:10 which prohibits the yoking together of an ox and a donkey for plowing.

15. As Barnett notes (*The Second Epistle to the Corinthians*, 345), Paul did not ban all social interaction with "unbelievers" (1 Cor 5:9–10; 10:27; 14:22–24). He did allow believers to remain married with unbelievers (1 Cor 7:12–15), but by this he probably meant situations where one of the spouses, already married, came to faith. It is unlikely that he would have approved the marriage of Christians to unbaptized pagans in normal circumstances.

16. Cf. Num 25:1–9; 1 Kgs 11:1–8; 22:25–26. We also recall the recurring connection between fornication and idolatry in the New Testament (1 Cor 10:7–8, 14; 6:15, 18; Col 3:5).

The first and most important is based on Jer 32:38, Ezek 37:27, and especially Lev 26:11–12: "I will make my dwelling among you, and my soul shall not abhor you. I will walk among you and will be your God, and you shall be My people." These citations help us to better grasp the meaning of our Pauline passage. Both Lev 26 and Ezek 37 refer to God's promise of establishing his sanctuary among his people; all three passages talk about his faithful covenant love and solemn pledge to "be their God." Paul then loosely quotes another group of Old Testament verses to further exhort the Corinthians to separate from the Gentiles and unclean things (2 Cor 6:17–18). This is a reference to Isa 52:11, which urges Israel to separate herself from Babylon and the surrounding pagan nations. By citing Isaiah, Paul is comparing the Corinthians with those who "bear the vessels of the LORD"—a holy people set apart for divine service, fitting to their identity as "temple of the living God." Paul then switches from temple to familial imagery in a loose paraphrase of God's filial covenant with David: "And I will be a Father to you, and you shall be my sons and daughters, says the Lord Almighty" (2 Cor 6:18; cf. 2 Sam 7:14). Separation from the unclean is not only for the sake of the cultic purity of the ecclesial temple of God, but even more so because of the divine filiation that it implies. The status of the Corinthian church as adopted sons and daughters of the Most High already implies their betrothal with the Son of God, which brought them into the divine family.

## A Pure Virgin Betrothed to Christ (2 Cor 11:2–3)

Our last passage from 2 Corinthians reveals evident bridal imagery:

> For I am jealous for you with godly jealousy. For I have betrothed you to one husband, that I may present you as a pure virgin to Christ. But I fear, lest somehow, as the serpent deceived Eve by his cunning, so your minds may be corrupted from a sincere and pure devotion to Christ. (2 Cor 11:2–3)

Paul is playing the role of the father-betrother who zealously guards the betrothed until she is ready to be presented to her husband on the long-awaited wedding day. Alternatively, he takes on the role of the *shoshbin*, elsewhere claimed by John the Baptist.[17] Despite the checkered

---

17. This role of father-betrother is in conformity with ancient marriage customs in Israel when the father was responsible for the daughter's virginity and faithfulness to her betrothed until the marriage (Gen 29:23; Deut 22:13–21). Cf. Barnett, *The Second*

moral record of the Corinthians, Paul continues to describe them using metaphors of perfect sanctity and purity. The holy "temple of the living God" is now a "pure virgin." Both metaphors imply a state of *kedushah*: the community is consecrated and set apart by a solemn oath and binding covenant to her beloved—Christ, the Bridegroom—requiring the zealous exclusion of anything that could defile the sanctified temple and bride.

The betrothal metaphor also shares with temple imagery the state of being "between the times." We have mentioned the tension between the inner *presence* of Christ in the bodily temple, received in baptism and guaranteed by the deposit of the Holy Spirit, and the relative *absence* of the Lord which continues to distress the believer in his temporary *skenos*, requiring commitment, endurance, and faithfulness in the hope of reaching eschatological glory in his heavenly dwelling. Likewise, although the bride is betrothed to her divine bridegroom and belongs to him, this does not make her immune from infidelity while he is still away. The marriage still lies in the future,[18] and she remains for now in danger of being seduced by "another Jesus," "a different spirit," or "a different gospel"—a cause of many worries to her father-betrother! Immediately after announcing the betrothal of the Corinthian community to Christ, Paul expresses his concern that "as the serpent deceived Eve by his cunning, so your minds may be corrupted from a sincere and pure devotion to Christ" (11:3; cf. Gen 3:13). This is another instance where New Testament nuptial imagery evokes Adam and Eve.[19] Paul's association of the Church with Eve is more direct here than in 1 Corinthians 11. In Genesis, the serpent's deception of Eve led to her disobeying God's command, followed by Adam's own disobedience and their expulsion from Eden. Paul may also be drawing from extra-biblical tradition and Jewish legends claiming that the snake seduced Eve in the garden.[20] According to those legends, Eve's sin was not

---

*Epistle to the Corinthians*, 498–99; Furnish, *II Corinthians*, 499; Bruce, *1 and 2 Corinthians*, 234.

18. Marriage in ancient Israel was divided into two separate ceremonies: the betrothal, and the nuptial ceremony that followed a year later and consummated the marriage. Between the two ceremonies the girl was legally the man's wife, but they did not have marital relations and she thus remained a virgin until the wedding. For a good summary of betrothal and marriage customs in ancient Israel, see Batey, "Paul's Bride Image: A Symbol of Realistic Eschatology."

19. Cf. 1 Cor 11:8–9; 15:22, 45–49; Eph 5:31.

20. Cf. *b. Yebamot* 103b; *b. Avoda Zara* 22b; *b. Sabb.* 146a, with variants found in earlier Jewish apocalypses (1 Enoch 69:6; 2 Enoch 31:6; Apoc. Abrah 23). Cf. Martin, *2 Corinthians*, 333; Furnish, *II Corinthians*, 487, 499–500.

only disobedience against God but also infidelity towards her husband. This provides a fitting background for Paul's idea that Christ is the New Adam and the Church is the New Eve, in danger of being tempted and seduced away from her bridegroom.[21]

## Summary: Second Corinthians

Paul emphasizes in 2 Corinthians the situation of the Church living "between the times," suffering in the midst of temporary distress but confident in God's power. The community's relationship with God is expressed nuptially and spans all of salvation history. The Corinthian community is betrothed to Christ as Eve was betrothed to Adam in the Garden, but she is not yet united with him in marriage (11:2–3). She has received a sure deposit of his *doxa*—a glory far superior to the *kavod* of the Sinai covenant (3:7–9)—but this glory is still veiled (4:3–4). For now, it is lived out in mystical union with the bridegroom's self-sacrifice in "earthen vessels" (4:7), rising up to God as a pleasing odor like the Temple's offerings (2:14–16). The *doxa* will only be revealed when the frail *skenos* of the mortal body gives way to the "building from God" and "house not made with hands, eternal in the heavens" (5:1). In the meantime, it must be carefully guarded lest it be lost: The bodily temple must be kept pure through sanctified behavior. Taking on an "unequal yoke" with unbelievers through sexual immorality or intermarriage is tantamount to idolatry: it desecrates the temple, casts away God's presence, and violates the filial covenant by which believers become the Father's sons and daughters (6:14–18). Likewise, receiving "another spirit" or "another gospel" is nothing less than the "pure virgin" betraying her bridegroom. She must therefore be a faithful guardian of the divine *presence* that dwells in her "earthen vessel," while persevering in the relative *absence* of the Lord until the divine espousals that await her at the end of her earthly journey.

21. Cf. Chavasse, *The Bride of Christ*, 70; Batey, *New Testament Nuptial Imagery*, 12.

## 11

# One Flesh

## *Ephesians*

### Introduction

THE EPISTLE TO THE EPHESIANS makes extensive use of temple and bridal imagery in its rich depiction of the Church as Christ's building, temple, body, and bride. It is characterized by a high Christology and rich ecclesiology: Paul accordingly lauds God the Father for having blessed the Church "with every spiritual blessing in the heavenly places in Christ" (1:3). The Messiah has come to disclose the deepest mystery and wisdom of God, formerly hidden but now revealed in the richness of his grace, power, blessing, and love towards those who have been made alive "in Christ." This is for the ultimate purpose of gathering all creation in him, to the praise of God's glory. The epistle's key nuptial passage (Eph 5:22–33) depicts the union of Christ and the Church as the one-flesh union of man and woman in which the bridegroom is to offer himself up sacrificially for his beloved. This marriage between Christ and the Church is described in strong cultic and sacrificial language reminiscent of the temple service. Christ loved the Church in a total self-sacrifice of love that provides atonement, forgiveness, and purification by making reparation for sin, calling to conversion, and restoring communion with God. Christ sanctifies and cleanses the Church "with the washing of water by the word"—an allusion to baptism and possibly to a pre-nuptial bath. He also nourishes and cherishes the Church, called "his own flesh" and "his body" in an echo of the Eden narrative. For Paul, as Eve was originally one with Adam before she was taken out of his side, so the pre-existent Church was originally one with Christ, "of his flesh and of his bones," before she was "taken out of his side."

## Central Themes in Ephesians

Paul delineates a sharp contrast between the former way of life of Christians, which continues to prevail among unbelievers, and the riches and blessings of the glorious Church redeemed by Christ. This results in a striking dualism between sin and sanctity, alienation and reconciliation, darkness and light, where Christ is consistently named as the source and active agent of every promise, blessing, gift, and virtue bestowed upon the Church.[1] If Christ is the agent and cause of the radical transformation of the former children of wrath into God's holy Temple and pure bride, the instrument through which he effects this metamorphosis is *the Church*, described in a rich blend of images and metaphors. The Church is:

- a predestined, eternal, and heavenly community (1:3–6, 2:6)
- the revelation of the mystery and wisdom of God (1:9, 3:9–10)
- the community of the redeemed by Christ's grace (1:7, 2:8)
- holy (*hagios*) (1:1, 4, 15, 18; 2:19; 3:18; 4:12; 5:3)
- God's adopted family and household, reconciled and united in love (1:5, 2:13–19, 3:15)
- created "for the praise of his glory" (1:6, 12, 14)
- the Body of Christ (1:23, 2:16, 3:6, 4:4, 4:12, 4:16, 4:25, 5:23, 5:30)
- recipient of God's rich inheritance and power, and partaker of his promises (1:11–14, 18, 2:7, 3:6)
- a "building" growing into a "holy temple in the Lord" and "dwelling place of God in the Spirit" (2:20–22)
- Christ's fullness (1:23; 4:13)
- the new, holy, "perfect man" (4:13, 24)
- Christ's bride (5:22–33)
- God's army (6:10–20)

1. For an overview of the contrasting traits of the world and the Church, cf. Villeneuve, *Nuptial Symbolism*, 216.

## *Kedushah* and Love

The common thread connecting those metaphors is *kedushah*—holiness. The Greek word *hagios* (holy) and its corresponding verb *hagiazo* (sanctify) appear no less than 16 times in our short epistle. The term describes God's transcendent essence and the state of being set apart or consecrated for a special purpose. Applying it to the Church means that she is the community of the elect, set apart for consecrated service to God "for the praise of his glory." The Church's *kedushah* is not of her own doing but gratuitously inherited, a pure gift of grace from her Maker and Redeemer (2:5–9), just as the *kedushah* of the Temple derived from God's presence within it (Exod 25:8; 29:43–45). Israel's *kedushah* was rooted in God's covenantal bond of love, initiated with the redemption from Egypt, sealed at Sinai through his gratuitous adoption, and guaranteed through promises of rich blessings (Exod 19:6; Deut 7:6–9). Similarly, the Church's *kedushah* is dependent upon Christ's covenantal bond (Eph 1:4–5, 2:6–7), rooted in his all-surpassing love (1:4, 3:17–19, 5:1–2, 25), accomplished in the redemption through his blood (1:7), sealed through the adoption of her members into God's family (1:5, 2:13–19, 3:15), promising them incomparable heavenly blessings (1:3, 11). The moral virtue of the Church and her members, though important, is not a prerequisite for election but rather its fruit. The moral imperative of *kedushah* is "to walk worthy of the calling with which you were called" (Eph 4:1). The Church thus participates in God's *kedushah* only "in Christ," by partaking in his own life and being joined to him as the members of a body are joined to the head. The holiness of each member draws its health from the whole body, just as the cells in a human body must remain attached to the body to stay alive. Thus, if in Christ "dwells all the fullness of the Godhead bodily" (cf. Col 2:9), the Church, in turn, is "Christ's fullness" (Eph 1:23) as long as she remains in communion with him. Just as the Temple "contained" the *Shekhinah*, the living presence of God, so the Church, as God's Temple and Body of Christ, is the mediator of the divine presence and love in the world.

## Ecclesial Body and Temple

The themes of *kedushah* and love in Ephesians imply a third central theme: *unity*. God's plan for the cosmos is to unite all things in Christ (1:10) through the Church, fittingly described as the body of Christ united to Christ the head (4:4–6, 11–16; cf. 1 Cor 12:12–30). The Church is also the locus of unity between Jews and Gentiles: by breaking down "the middle wall of partition" Jesus has put to death the enmity between them and granted to both "access by one Spirit to the Father" (2:14–18). Commentators have often proposed that the reference to the "middle wall of partition" is probably an allusion to the wall that separated the court of Israel from the court of the Gentiles in the Temple, preventing the latter's access to full communion with God.[2] This discussion on the unity of Jews and Gentiles reconciled to God "in one body through the cross" (2:16) in the Church leads Paul to declare that Gentile Christians are

> no longer strangers and sojourners, but . . . fellow citizens with the saints and members of the household of God, built upon the foundation of the apostles and prophets, Christ Jesus himself being the cornerstone, in whom the whole structure is joined together and grows into a holy temple in the Lord; in whom you also are built into it for a dwelling place of God in the Spirit. (Eph 2:19–22)

Paul is describing a building that is curiously *growing* into a holy temple. Now buildings and temples are normally built; plants, living bodies, and people grow; but buildings and temples do not usually grow. The use of this verb reveals that while Paul describes the Church as Temple, he is keeping in mind the metaphor of the Church as Body, combining both metaphors as he does in 1 Corinthians. Yet whereas in 1 Corinthians the Temple of the Holy Spirit is the individual believer and the local community, in Ephesians, it is the *universal Church* that is the "holy temple in the Lord." Unity is thus expressed using the language of both temple and body. Yet it finds its fullest expression in the language of love, of which it is the natural fruit, especially in the "one flesh" union of marriage: The Church is consecrated for the sake of her sanctification, rooted in a covenantal bond of love and expressed in humble self-sacrifice for the beloved.

---

2. Cf. Barth, *Ephesians* 1-3, 283–87; Lincoln, *Ephesians*, 141; Best, *Ephesians*, 253–57.

## As Christ Loved the Church: Ephesians 5:21-33

The richest nuptial passage of the New Testament is Eph 5:21–33, which presents the love of Christ for the Church as the paradigm for human marriage.[3] This is not a simple moral exhortation, as if Paul were taking Christ's love for the Church as an ideal example that husbands should imitate as they struggle with the challenges of married life. No, Paul presents the union between Christ, the heavenly bridegroom, and the Church, his bride, as the *standard*, *prototype*, and *archetype* for the 'one flesh' union between husband and wife.[4] In other words, the relationship between earthly and heavenly love is not metaphorical: it is *metaphysical*. Paul is arguing "from the Heavenly Marriage to human marriages, not vice versa; he is seeing the human in the light of the heavenly, and therefore will have the human model itself on the heavenly."[5]

The passage opens with a description of the hierarchy of subordination by which the husband is head of the wife as Christ is head of the Church—and "savior of the body." This hierarchy is not one of domination but of sacrificial love: the headship of the man is to be modeled on Christ who "loved the Church and gave himself for her." The ultimate purpose of this self-gift is the sanctification and purification of his ecclesial bride. Cultic language is employed in the description of the glorious Church "not having spot or wrinkle" and called to be "holy and without blemish." This spotless condition, unrealistic to expect of any community made of fallible humans, points to eschatological hope for the perfection of the bride. A wife's full identification with her husband is evident in that she is his own body and flesh, to be nourished and cherished as Christ nourishes and cherishes the Church. This leads up to the climax in a citation of Gen 2:24, expressing the "great mystery" of the one-flesh union between man and woman that speaks of Christ and the Church. Since they are truly one, the final exhortation that the husband "love his own wife as himself" is almost self-evident.

3. For studies on Eph 5:22–33, cf. Muirhead, "The Bride of Christ"; Sampley, *And the Two Shall Become One Flesh*; Miletic, *One Flesh*.

4. Lincoln, *Ephesians*, 352, 362.

5. Chavasse, *The Bride of Christ*, 77. Cf. also Barth, *Ephesians 4–6*, 622.

## Echoes of Ezekiel and the Song of Songs

The mystical marriage of Ephesians shows an affinity with the marriage symbolism of the Old Testament prophets. Yet there are also some differences, three of which are worth mentioning:[6]

1. The covenant in the Old Testament is an exclusive, "national" one between God and Israel; the covenant in Ephesians is "international," between the Messiah and the Church, composed of Jews and Gentiles.

2. While human grooms in the Old Testament typically pays a price for acquiring a woman,[7] the divine Bridegroom does not pay any price to acquire his bride Israel. The situation is different in Ephesians: The Messiah loves his bride so much that he is willing to lay down his life for her.[8] He purchased the Church with his own blood.[9]

3. In the Old Testament prophets, the marital metaphor occasionally depicts God as a bigamous husband, married to the two sisters Israel and Judah.[10] He is at times so disgusted by their sins and idolatry that he threatens them with divorce.[11] In Ephesians, however, Christ's marriage to his glorious bride is monogamous and indissoluble. The Church's temporary imperfections are overlooked and transformed by the Bridegroom's perfect sanctity.

Certain features of the mystical marriage of Eph 5:21–33 can be traced directly to two of the main witnesses to God's marriage to Israel in the Old Testament—Ezekiel 16 and the Song of Songs.[12] In Ezek 16:8, the Lord passes by Jerusalem and looks tenderly upon her. Finding her at "the time of love," he declares: "I swore an oath to you and entered into a covenant with you, and you became mine." If this covenantal language depicts a betrothal, then the washing of water that follows (Ezek 16:9) is a pre-nuptial bridal bath, whereby the divine husband purifies his bride whom he has just acquired. This reveals a close affinity

---

6. Cf. Barth, *Ephesians* 4–6, 670–72.

7. Cf. Gen 34:12; 1 Sam 18:20–27; Ruth 4:1–7; Hos 3:2, Isa 43:3–4.

8. Eph 2:13–18; 5:2; 5:25; cf. John 15:13; 10:11–16.

9. Eph 1:7; 2:13; cf. 1 Cor 7:23, 1 Pet 1:18–19.

10. Cf. Jer 3:6–14; Ezek 23.

11. Jer 3:8; cf. Isa 50:1; Ezek 23:18.

12. Cf. Sampley, *And the Two Shall Become One Flesh*, 38–49.

with Eph 5:26, where Christ the bridegroom sanctifies and cleanses his bride in a washing of (baptismal?) water. Moreover, in Ezek 16:14, the Lord lovingly bestows glorious beauty upon his bride Jerusalem, who becomes renowned among the nations: "And your renown went forth among the nations because of your beauty, for it was perfect through the splendor which I had bestowed upon you." Likewise, in Ephesians 5, the Church is depicted as perfect and "glorious" or "in splendor." These parallels lead Sampley to conclude:

> Thus Eph. 5:25–7 has close affinity to Ezek. 16:8ff. in that both reflect a hieros gamos (YHWH-Jerusalem, Christ-church) in which the groom cleanses his bride by a washing with water and in which the result is a strong emphasis on the beauty and purity of the bride. Here is the first clear evidence that behind the Ephesian verses is the pattern of YHWH's marriage to Israel-Jerusalem as the basis for the understanding of the relation of Christ and the church.[13]

Eph 5:21–33 also echoes the language of the Song of Songs. The Song, of course, abounds in references to the rhapsodic love between bridegroom and bride, and to the beauty and splendor of the latter who is repeatedly called 'beautiful,' 'fairest among women,' and 'my perfect one.'[14] Compare Cant 4:7 ("You are all fair, my love; there is no flaw in you") with Eph 5:27 ("that he might present the Church to himself in splendor, without spot or wrinkle . . . that she might be holy and without blemish"). In both texts, a positive statement of the bride's beauty and splendor is followed by a privative one noting the absence of flaws in her perfection. As Sampley notes, these parallels indicate that

> a definite relationship of dependence existed between Ephesians and the YHWH-Israel hieros gamos of Ezekiel and the Song of Songs. Ezekiel and Song of Songs show greatest affinity to Ephesians in their emphasis on the bride's beauty and the groom's love for the bride, the betrothal of the bride and related washing in water.[15]

---

13. Sampley, *And the Two Shall Become One Flesh*, 43.
14. Cant 1:8; 1:15; 2:10–13; 4:1, 7; 5:2, 9; 6:1; 7:7.
15. Sampley, *And the Two Shall Become One Flesh*, 49.

## Authority and Submission, Love and Sacrifice
## (Eph 5:21–25)

> [21] Be subject to one another out of reverence for Christ. [22] Wives, be subject to your husbands, as to the Lord. [23] For the husband is the head of the wife as Christ is the head of the Church, his body, and is himself its Savior. [24] As the Church is subject to Christ, so let wives also be subject in everything to their husbands.

Let us now examine Eph 5:21–33 in greater detail. Following an exhortation to mutual submission, the passage begins by inviting wives to be subject to theirs husbands as a reflection of the Church's subordination to Christ. As mentioned, the image of Christ as head and Church as body is a recurring theme in Ephesians: in 1:22–23 Christ is described as the "head over all things to the Church, which is his body, the fullness of him who fills all in all." In 4:12–16, we read how his body is edified through the synergy of its members' loving service to one another. By "speaking the truth in love," believers "may grow up in all things into him who is the head—Christ." In this way they effect the unity of the body and cause it to grow "for the edifying of itself in love." By joining the Church, Christians become a part of the same living organism, akin to the cells in a body.[16] We have encountered the theme of wife-husband subordination in 1 Corinthians 11 and noted how it derived from the original order of creation of man and woman (Gen 2). The subordination of wives to their husbands in both Pauline texts may be an implicit echo of the subordination of Eve after the fall: "Your desire shall be for your husband, and he shall rule over you" (Gen 3:16). This hierarchical relationship, however, is not one of oppression or domination, but an imperative to sacrificial love. Recalling that in 1 Cor 11:7, woman is "the glory of man" who is himself "the image and glory of God," in Ephesians it is the man who bears the greater responsibility in his vocation to love his wife selflessly as Christ "loved the Church and gave himself up for her."

> [25] Husbands, love your wives, as Christ loved the Church and gave himself up for her,

---

16. Cf. 1 Cor 12:12–27; Rom 12:4–5.

The exhortation to self-sacrifice for the sake of the beloved, in imitation of Christ, is at the heart of the Gospel's message.[17] In Ephesians alone, the word *agape* and its derivatives occur no less than 19 times, either describing Christ's unsurpassable love for the Church or the love by which Christians are called to love him and each other in return.[18] Eph 5:25 returns to the line of thought initiated in 5:1–2, where the Ephesians are called to be "imitators of God as dear children" and to "walk in love, as Christ loved us and given himself up for us, an offering and a sacrifice to God for a sweet-smelling aroma." Christ's self-gift for the sake of the Church takes here the distinct look and smell of Temple sacrifices with the expressions "offering and sacrifice"[19] and "sweet-smelling aroma."[20] Similar sacrificial language is used to describe the gifts that the Philippians sent to Paul (Phil 4:18), and the same expression is alluded to in 2 Cor 2:14–16 to denote all Christians: "we are to God the fragrance of Christ." Elsewhere, Paul describes his sacrificial labor of love as the outpouring of a drink offering by using unmistakably liturgical language: "I am being poured out as a drink offering on the sacrifice and service of your faith" (Phil 2:17). The same expression is used in 2 Tim 4:6 in the context of the author's impending death, figuratively described as a libation upon the altar: "For I am already being poured out as a drink offering, and the time of my departure is at hand." We thus see the language of Temple offering and sacrifice used in several epistles to describe *agape* in action: Christ provides the model (Eph 5:2) to be imitated by his followers, whose gifts (Phil 4:18), works and sufferings (Phil 2:17), lives (2 Cor 2:14) and deaths (2 Tim 4:6) are offerings presented to God and pleasing to him. This is the extent of the call to husbands to love their wives "as Christ loved the Church."

---

17. Cf. Matt 22:37–39; John 3:16, 10:17, 13:34–35, 14:15, 21; 15:10–13, 17:26, 21:15–19; Rom 5:8, 8:35–39, 12:10; 1 Cor 13; 2 Cor 2:4, 9:7; Gal 5:13–14; Phil 2:2; 1 Pet 1:22; 1 John 3:1; 4:7–10, 16–19.

18. Cf. Eph 1:4, 6, 15; 2:4; 3:17, 19; 4:2, 15–16, 5:1–2, 25, 28, 33; 6:23–24.

19. LXX Ps 39:6.

20. LXX Exod 29:18; Ezek 20:41.

## Sacrifice as Means to Communion

### The Symbolism of Sacrifice

It is worth considering the meaning of temple sacrifices to better understand Paul's liturgical and sacrificial language as applied to the love between Christ and the Church. Rabbi Joshua Berman provides valuable insights on the connections between covenant, love, and sacrifice in the context of the Temple service. He explains how sacrifice was viewed in the ancient world as a "bilateral process," whereby the owner of the animal to be sacrificed had to "*renounce* his ownership of the animal so that the gods could *receive* the animal in his place."[21] These two aspects were taken up in the biblical notion of sacrifice in the sanctuary, along with the idea that a sacrifice is *kadosh*—sanctified and set apart for God. An animal dedicated for the purpose of being offered as a sacrifice is designated as *hekdesh*—made holy.[22] Sacrifice thus meant abnegation, renunciation, and forfeiture for the owner. When an animal was brought into the Temple for sacrifice, the owner renounced his claim over it and could no longer use it for his personal benefit. At the same time, the smoke and smell of the animal burnt on the altar, rising to heaven, was received by God as pleasing to him, a "sweet savor to the Lord." Yet the main connotation of sacrifice (*korban*) in the Bible goes beyond the ideas of renunciation, gift, and acceptance. The root of the word *korban* is *k.r.b.* which means "close." A *korban* is therefore "that which has been brought close," something that has come into God's presence in the Sanctuary, and offering a sacrifice ("*lehakriv korban*") means literally "to bring the sacrifice close." The ultimate purpose of the *korbanot*, therefore, is to draw God's people close and bring them into communion with him.

Sacrifices are also symbols of repentance, whereby the gap between God and man caused by sin is bridged by the atoning death of the animal and shedding of its blood. Sin is incompatible with God's presence,[23] and its consequence is death.[24] By offering sacrifices, a man overcomes the alienation and attendant death sentence that sin has brought upon him. This is done by transferring not only his sins onto the animal to be sacrificed, but also his own identity through the act of *semikhah*—laying

21. Berman, *The Temple*, 115. Emphasis in original.
22. Berman, *The Temple*, 116.
23. Deut 31:17–18; Ps 32:1–5; Isa 59:1–2; Ezek 23 :18.
24. Gen 2:7; 3:19; 6:5–7; Exod 31:14–15; 32:33–34; Lev 20.

hands on the animal's head and "leaning" on it. It is a symbolic act of investiture: The animal becomes representative of its owner, and the offering of the sacrifice is "an execution in effigy" with a rehabilitative purpose: "As he stands before God in the Temple and witnesses his own execution by proxy for sins he committed, the owner of the offering is meant to reach a new awareness of his obligations to God so that his breach will not be repeated."[25] The rites of the *korbanot* are thus *punitive measures* that the owner should view as carried out on his own body. By burning and obliterating the animal, he "eradicates the element of his sinful persona that exhibited animalism rather than humanity."[26] The slaughter of the animal, the shedding and sprinkling of its blood, and the annihilation of its body in the flames was no doubt a stark pedagogical experience that was also *purgative* and *cathartic*, deepening the owner's conversion and strengthening his resolve not to sin again.

The different kinds of sacrifices carry various meanings. Three of them are symbols of penitence: The *sin-offering* (*chattat*) represents a purifying or cleansing of the spiritual defilement that has been engendered by sin.[27] The *guilt-offering* (*asham*) carries the connotation of indemnity, reparation payment, repairing damage, and making restitution. The *whole burnt offering* (*olah*), in turn, signifies a complete dedication

25. Berman, *The Temple*, 118–19. Medieval Jewish commentator Nachmanides, in his commentary on Lev 1:9, sheds light on the identification of the sinner with the sacrificed animal: "[The owner] should burn the innards and the kidneys [of the offering] in fire because they are the instruments of thought and desire in the human being. He should burn the legs since they correspond to the hands and feet of a person, which do all his work. He should sprinkle the blood upon the altar, which is analogous to the blood in his body. All these acts are performed in order that when they are done, a person should realize that he has sinned against God with his body and his soul, and that "his" blood should really be spilled and "his" body burned, were it not for the loving-kindness of the Creator, Who took from him a substitute and a ransom, namely this offering, so that its blood should be in place of his blood, its life in place of his life, and that the chief limbs of the offering should be in place of the chief parts of his body."

26. Berman, *The Temple*, 120.

27. The same word also means "to purify" in the Torah (Lev 8:15; 14:49; Num 19:9). Nachmanides (on Lev 4:2) is instructive regarding the purifying role of the *chattat*: "The reason for the offerings for the erring soul is that all sins [even if committed unwittingly] produce a particular 'stain' upon the soul and constitute a blemish thereon, and the soul is only worthy to be received by the countenance of its Creator when it is pure of all sin. It is for this reason that the erring soul brings an offering, through which it becomes worthy of approaching 'unto God who gave it.'" (Berman, *The Temple*, 121–22). See Berman's discussion on the three sacrifices of penitence, 120–24.

to God.[28] The role of the blood sprinkled on and around the altar is also significant. Since the blood symbolizes the soul (Lev 17:11), the animal's blood not only represents the blood of the owner but also his soul. Thus, the sprinkling of the blood upon the altar symbolizes "not the forfeiture of the owner's life, but the rededication of his soul in concert with the rest of his being" to God.[29]

Sacrifices were also covenantal gestures that renewed the covenant between God and his people. The covenant at Sinai was sealed by the shedding and sprinkling of blood (Exod 24:3–8), which signified the depth of mutual commitment between the two parties, and the covenant of circumcision is also characterized by the shedding of blood. The associations of this symbolism with the New Covenant established through Christ's blood are well known.

This discussion helps us understand how "Christ loved the Church and gave himself up for her" within the context of the Temple. When Paul depicts Christ as sacrifice of the New Covenant, he recapitulates in him the different roles of the Temple sacrifices: Christ purchased his Bride with his own blood (Eph 1:7; 2:13)[30] for the purpose of atoning for her sins, making reparation and restitution for them, purifying and sanctifying her, and proving his dedication and love to her. Yet his sacrifice was also necessary to render possible the union and communion with his bride. This is best understood in light of the sacrifice that restores and symbolizes communion with God: the *zevach*, a covenantal feast centered around the consumption of meat (cf. 1 Sam 28:24; 1 Kgs 1:9; 19:21). In its sacrificial context, it is a shared meal that ritualizes the formation of a bond between two parties[31] or celebrates its ongoing renewal, accompanied by the presentation of loaves of bread and wine.[32]

---

28. Abraham was commanded to offer Isaac as *olah* as the ultimate sign of his devotion to the service of God, whom he trusted and loved to the point of being willing to offer up "his son, his only son Isaac whom he loved" (Gen 22:2). Abraham proved his love by the greatness and totality of his sacrifice.

29. Berman, *The Temple*, 125.

30. Cf. also 1 Cor 7:23; 1 Pet 1:18–19.

31. Some examples are found in Gen 26:28–30; 31:44–46, 54.

32. Here too Berman (*The Temple*, 130) is enlightening: "The Temple . . . is the focal point for the commemoration of the *brit*—the covenant between God and the Jewish people. Moreover . . . the covenant is dynamic and is renewed and rejuvenated on an ongoing basis. As the Jewish people continually rededicate themselves as covenantal partners, the notion of *korban* as *zevach* comes into play. The *korbanot* are an expression of a universal convention between partners to a *brit*. As the Jewish people

The *zevach* recalled the original bond made between God and Israel at Sinai, where Moses mediated to the people the ordinances of the Torah, the people solemnly vowed their obedience, burnt-offerings and peace-offerings were offered, the covenant was sealed by the sprinkling of blood on the altar and on the people, and Moses, Aaron, Nadab, Abihu and the seventy elders went up on the mountain where they "beheld God, and they ate and drank" (Exod 24:3–9). This covenant ceremony was immediately followed by the coming of the glory of the Lord in the form of the cloud (Exod 24:15–18). The close intimacy between God and Israel at Sinai was thus enacted by the sacrifice of *olot* (signifying complete dedication between the two parties) and the offering and eating of *zevachim* (signifying intimate communion between them). The *zevach* is thus an experience where "man, literally, and God, figuratively, partake of the same feast."[33]

It is also significant that the offering of every *korban* included the presentation of loaves and wine. The bread of the presence in the sanctuary attests to the idea that communion with God is attained by "eating with him," and that eating is the most hallowed form of worship.[34] We see how this concept would have developed into the sharing of the Eucharistic bread and wine as highest and most intimate form of communion with the incarnate Christ. This is likely one of the allusions in Eph 5:29, which states that the Lord "nourishes and cherishes" the Church, his bride and his own flesh.

In short, the *korbanot* are sanctified and dedicated gifts to God, expiatory symbols (especially the sin and guilt offerings) symbolizing punishment, providing atonement and forgiveness, purifying sin and making reparation for it, and calling to conversion. They are also symbols of covenantal feasting (the whole-burnt and peace offerings) whose ultimate purpose is to draw man close to God, bringing the human into the presence of the divine and into intimate communion with him. Keeping this symbolism in mind helps us to better grasp the great implications of the husband's calling to love his wife "as Christ loved the Church" by giving himself for her as "an offering and a sacrifice to God for a sweet-smelling aroma."

---

continually rededicate themselves to their Covenantal Partner, they bring *zevachim* to the covenantal center to symbolize through celebratory feasts the rejuvenation of the bond between them. Classically, a true feast included wine. With this in mind, the analogy of *korban* as feast is further buttressed by the requirement that the offering of every *korban* include the presentation of loaves and wine (Numbers 15:1–14)."

33. Berman, *The Temple*, 130.
34. Berman, *The Temple*, 136–38.

## On Love and Death

Given our nuptial context, it is worth adding a few words on the relationship between sacrifice and love, and how the element of self-renunciation and death symbolizes the owner's total self-gift to his Maker. The Mishnah comments on the injunction of the *Shema* to love God with one's entire being (Deut 6:5):

> A person must praise [God] for bad things just as for good things, as it is said "And you must love God with all your heart, soul and might." 'With all your heart'—with your two inclinations, the good inclination and the evil inclination; 'soul'—even when God takes your soul from you; 'might'—your property. (*m. Berakhot* 9:5)

Fishbane notes how the Mishnah's exhortation to love God with both one's good and evil inclinations implies the sublimation of both base instincts to divine ends, whereby the inner division of the two impulses is brought in line in a wholehearted and total devotion to God. The duty of loving God with all of one's soul, in turn, means "even if he takes your soul." Love of God is thus a total commitment, even unto death.[35] Rabbinic commentaries on the *Shema* supplement the Mishnah with a verse often used in martyrological contexts: "for Your sake we are killed all day long; we are accounted as sheep for the slaughter" (Ps 44:22).[36] The Sages have raised the question as to how one can be killed "all day long." One answer is that "the Holy One, blessed be He, regards the righteous as if they are killed every day."[37] This may be seen as a kind of martyrdom "in installments" whereby the righteous "kills" his evil inclination and evil heart in a constant act of self-mortification and sacrifice of his base desires for God's sake.[38]

For mystics like Paul, to be "at home in the body" means to be "absent from the Lord" (2 Cor 5:6), and this is the motivation for martyrdom: A willing death for God is not only the ultimate sacrifice of love to him but also the quickest way to consummate the mystical union with

35. As Fishbane states: "Heavenly love is activated by human death. Self-sacrifice thus stands at the heart of Being—a sacrament of love for the salvation of God." Fishbane, *The Kiss of God*, 126.

36. *T. Zera'im* 6:7; *Sifre Deut* 32; *Mekh Shirata* 3. Cf. Fishbane, *The Kiss of God*, 6.

37. Rabbi Simeon ben Menasia, quoted in Fishbane, *The Kiss of God*, 6.

38. Fishbane, *The Kiss of God*, 8.

him.[39] But if martyrdom is the highest expression of love for God, it remains an occasion that occurs only in exceptional circumstances, and few are those who *joyfully* choose that path. In normal circumstances, when the supreme act of martyrdom is not an option, various forms of ritual simulation and substitution symbolize the person's death for God in a more digestible way for the common folk who are not yet ready to die (literally) for God. The biblical sacrifices are the most evident form of ritual substitution whereby a person could "practice death."[40] Reconciliation and union with God are accomplished through sacrifice because of its cost to the owner. His renunciation of something of great value to him is symbolic of his own self-renunciation, self-denial, and death. The essence of sin is disordered self-love whereby a person places his own desires first, even to the point of disobeying God and forsaking his commandments. Sacrifice reverses this process and counters human egoism by forsaking costly goods and offering them as dedicated gifts to God in humble obedience. The animal is thus a symbolic substitute of the owner's self-offering to God. The shedding of the animal's blood and consumption of its body in the flames are a substitute for the death that he should have incurred by his transgression of God's commandments. Free-will offerings and sacrifices of communion are of even higher value precisely because they are optional gifts, gratuitously offered to God out of selfless generosity.

Death can seem like "the limit of love on earth"[41] and the ultimate enemy of love. The earthly love between two spouses can be suddenly terminated by the death of one of them. Yet love can also die while both spouses are still alive. One's own ambitions and desires can easily conflict with the care and devotion for the beloved that love requires. A person willing to bear hardships and forsake his own desires for the beloved has demonstrated love in a tangible way. When human love is not sustained by self-sacrifice and self-gift, however, it runs the risk of weakening, waning, and dying. If this occurs while the spouses are still alive, death has won over love. The former lovers continue to live, but their love has died. A love that has fizzled out is more dead than one interrupted by natural

39. Cf. Phil 1:21–23. A Jewish prayer for the Day of Atonement expresses the same idea: "O Lord! . . . when I am far from You—my life is death; and were I cleave to You—my death would be life." Fishbane, *The Kiss of God*, 11.

40. On the forms of ritual simulation and substitution of death and their development in Judaism, see Fishbane, *The Kiss of God*, 87–124.

41. See Barth's discussion on love and death in *Ephesians* 4–6, 684–87.

death in which the memory of happy love lives on. On the other hand, love that prevails "till death do us part" in fact manifests the victory of love over death. When lovers withstand all trials until the end of earthly life, when death is the only thing able to separate them, then death is defeated by its own apparent victory; love has prevailed—indeed, love "strong as death" (Cant 8:6). This is the love of Christ for the Church: "Greater love has no one than this, than to lay down one's life for his friends" (John 15:13). Jesus demonstrated his love for his bride by his death, bearing all suffering, humiliation, and abandonment until the bitter end. Precisely for this reason, nothing—not even death—can separate the Church from her divine Bridegroom.[42]

## In Imitatio Christi

This is the type of sacrificial love that husbands must imitate for the sake of their brides. This would presumably involve a long and arduous process of "practicing death" in self-denial, self-mortification, and *kenosis* (self-emptying) in imitation of Christ.[43] The language of Eph 5:25 where husbands are called to love their wives "as Christ loved the Church and gave himself for her" is reminiscent of Gal 2:20: "I have been crucified with Christ; it is no longer I who live, but Christ who lives in me; and the life I now live in the flesh I live by faith in the Son of God, who loved me and gave himself for me." Paul extols Christ's love for him and gratefully offers his own life in return so that it no longer belongs to him but to his master who "lives in him." Though no nuptial metaphor is employed, all of its elements are present: the covenantal bond of love, the sacrificial gift of self by the "greater" party and willing self-surrender of the "lesser" party, and the union of flesh and spirit between them resulting in an exchange of persons whereby each offers his life to the other.

The imitation of Christ and identification with him in sacrificial love for the Church is also expressed in Col 1:24: "Now I rejoice in my sufferings for your sake, and in my flesh I complete what is lacking in Christ's afflictions for the sake of his body, that is, the Church." Here Paul sees himself as a kind of *alter Christus*: by taking part in the Messiah's

---

42. Cf. Rom 8:37–39. Fishbane (*The Kiss of God*, 104) provides the same insight from a Jewish perspective: "Self-sacrifice thus stands in the center of world-restorative actions, actually replacing the ancient Temple as the site of ritual at-one-ment."

43. Cf. Phil 2:3, 6–8; Col 3:5.

afflictions he shares in his redemptive role for the sake of his ecclesial body. If these passages place the bar very high as to the sacrificial quality required of the husband's love for his wife—or of the Christian's self-gift to Christ for the sake of the Church—all emphatically affirm that such selfless gift is only possible "with Christ," "in Christ," and inasmuch as "Christ lives in me" (Gal 2:20). Christ's love for the Church is not only the example but also the sacrament that empowers husbands to love their wives and the saints to love one another as Christ loved them.

One last Pauline passage compares the Christians life with the Temple offerings: "I urge you, brothers, in view of God's mercy, to offer your bodies as living sacrifices, holy and pleasing to God—this is your spiritual act of worship (*latreia*)" (Rom 12:1). The word *latreia*, used here to denote the offering of one's body as living sacrifice, can mean "the state of a hired laborer, service" or "the service and worship of God according to the requirements of the Levitical law."[44] In the Old Testament the word is used to describe the commemoration of the Passover (LXX Exod 12:25–26; 13:5), the offering of sacrifices (LXX Josh 22:27), and the work of the priests and Levites in the Temple (1 Chr 28:13; cf. Heb 9:1, 6). All believers are thus to offer up their lives as living and spiritual sacrifices for their Lord in a way reminiscent of the Temple sacrifices and in imitation of Christ's own sacrifice.

## Eros and Agape

A peculiarity concerns the use of the verb *agapao* to denote the love between husband and wife in Eph 5:25. This is practically the only occurrence in the New Testament where *agapao* also includes the sexual union by which a man and a woman become 'one flesh.'[45] While the New Testament writers frequently make use of the words *agapao* and *agape*, they completely avoid *eraomai* and *eros* (referring to sexual love)— presumably to emphasize an attitude of selfless giving in contrast to lustfully using a person for the sake of self-gratification. The high view of the "one-flesh" union in Ephesians, however, categorically rules out any Platonic or Gnostic denigration of the body and the sexual union in marriage.

---

44. Liddell-Scott, *Greek Lexicon*; Thayer, *Greek-English Lexicon of the NT.*

45. On *agape, eros,* and sex in Ephesians, see Barth, *Ephesians* 4–6, 621 n. 48; 715–20.

Pope Benedict XVI, in his Encyclical Letter *Deus Caritas Est*, provides helpful insight into the biblical relationship between *eros* and *agape*, opposing an alleged antithesis between a descending, oblative love (*agape*) that would be typically Christian and an ascending, covetous love (*eros*) that would be typical of Greek culture:

> *Eros* and *agape*—ascending love and descending love—can never be completely separated. The more the two, in their different aspects, find a proper unity in the one reality of love, the more the true nature of love in general is realized. Even if *eros* is at first mainly covetous and ascending, a fascination for the great promise of happiness, in drawing near to the other, it is less and less concerned with itself, increasingly seeks the happiness of the other, is concerned more and more with the beloved, bestows itself and wants to "be there for" the other. The element of *agape* thus enters into this love, for otherwise *eros* is impoverished and even loses its own nature. On the other hand, man cannot live by oblative, descending love alone. He cannot always give, he must also receive. Anyone who wishes to give love must also receive love as a gift. Certainly, as the Lord tells us, one can become a source from which rivers of living water flow (cf. John 7:37–38). Yet to become such a source, one must constantly drink anew from the original source, which is Jesus Christ, from whose pierced heart flows the love of God (cf. John 19:34).[46]

Thus, both *eros* and *agape* are essential dimensions of Christian marital love lived out in imitation of Christ. In sum, Christ first loved the Church with a total love encompassing both the passionate *eros* of longing for union with his bride, and the unselfish *agape* of total self-offering for her good. This sacrifice of love takes up the entire symbolism of the Temple sacrifices, providing atonement, forgiveness, purification, making reparation, calling to conversion, and restoring communion with God. At the same time, this love is the model, inspiration and source for the love that is asked of Christians in return, and most especially of husbands for their wives.

---

46. Benedict XVI, *Deus Caritas Est*, 7.

## Holy and without Blemish (Eph 5:26–27)

> [26] that he might sanctify her, having cleansed her by the washing of water with the word,

Returning to our exegesis of Eph 5, verse 26 tells us that the ultimate purpose of sacrificial love is the sanctification of the beloved bride—the Church. We recall the meaning of *kedushah*: it is significant that in rabbinic literature the Hebrew term for "sanctify" (*lekadesh*) expresses the action of betrothal and means "to espouse a wife."[47] Christ's action of sanctifying the Church, therefore, implies not only to 'set her apart' but also to 'set her apart as wife.' Moreover, he sanctifies her "by the washing of water with the word." We have mentioned how this washing of water recalls Ezekiel's metaphor of God forming his marriage covenant with Jerusalem, where he bathes her with water, washes off the blood from her and anoints her with oil. In this light, the "washing of water" of Ephesians may well allude to a pre-nuptial bridal bath in preparation for the bride's union with the bridegroom. The idea of sanctification through the washing of water as a metaphor of salvation also occurs in 1 Cor 6:11.[48] Most ancient, medieval, and modern commentators agree that these passages are direct references to water baptism—the "bridal bath" that precedes the bride's entrance into the bridal chamber to meet with the bridegroom. [49]

When did Christ sanctify and cleanse the Church? This could have occurred either when he "gave himself up for her" or at the moment of the "washing of water"—that is, either at Christ's death or at the believer's baptism. It is probable that Paul refers to both events—the Messiah's universal redemptive death and its individual application to the baptized believer—since the two events are often related in Pauline theology (with baptism explicitly connected to Christ's death).[50] Baptism is thus the sacrament by which the sanctification and cleansing attained by Christ's death are received by individual Christians.[51]

---

47. Sampley, *And the Two Shall Become One Flesh*, 42–43, 129. Cf. *b. Kiddushin* 2a, 41a.

48. Cf. also Acts 22:16; Heb 10:22.

49. Cf. Lincoln, *Ephesians*, 375.

50. Cf. Rom 6:3ff; 1 Cor 1:13; Col 2:12; Heb 10:22; 1 John 1:7, 9; cf. Best, *Ephesians*, 542.

51. "If Christ's death is the point in history at which his love was demonstrated, baptism is the point at which the Church experiences Christ's continuing purifying love for her as his bride." Lincoln, *Ephesians*, 375.

[27] that he might present the Church to himself in splendor, without spot or wrinkle or any such thing, that she might be holy and without blemish.

We have discussed above the parallels between the splendor and beauty of the Church in Ephesians and the bride in Ezekiel and the Song of Songs.[52] Christ will present the Church to himself "in splendor" (*endoxos*), that is, "resplendent" or "glorious." The word *endoxos*, which derives from *doxa*, points again to the theme of God's glory: first revealed at Sinai in the form of a majestic cloud and consuming fire, radiating on Moses' face, filling the Tabernacle and Temple, leaving Jerusalem and appearing to Ezekiel in exile, the *kavod/doxa* of the *Shekhinah* is reinterpreted in the Johannine tradition as the Logos who came to dwell in the new tabernacle of Jesus' body, incarnated in his flesh, temporarily veiled by his humanity but revealed in his glorified body after the resurrection. For Paul, too, the *doxa* is the crowning promise and gift of the New Covenant, as seen in 2 Corinthians: Christians are transformed "from glory to glory" into the likeness of the Lord, even if they must temporarily carry this treasure in the "earthen vessels" of their frail humanity, prone to suffering and death in imitation of their master. In light of the history of the *doxa* among God's people, we can imagine what Paul has in mind by the Church "glorious." This is the final transformation into divine glory, the unsurpassable *doxa* that will radiate from God, through Christ, in the Holy Spirit into his splendid bride, the Church.

Paul also expects Christ to present the Church to himself "without spot or wrinkle . . . that she might be holy and without blemish." We have discussed how this description is similar to the expression "there is no spot in you" of Cant 4:7, pointing to a probable textual relationship between both passages. Purity was prescribed and demanded of brides in the Torah (Deut 24:1). In Old Testament nuptial imagery, God himself provides the purity that he demands of his bride Jerusalem/Israel (cf. Ezek 16:9–14). This purity, both required of and bestowed on the bride by her divine Bridegroom, is inherited by the Church in Ephesians.[53]

In addition, the expression "holy and without blemish" points to the cultic and ritual purity that was required of priests and sacrifices in the Old Testament. Leviticus 21:17–23 specifies that any priest who has a

---

52. Eph 5:27 echoes other Pauline verses that reflect his ongoing concern for the purity of the Church, further revealing the interrelationship between the nuptial and Temple motifs (2 Cor 11:2–3; Col 1:22).

53. Sampley, *And the Two Shall Become One Flesh*, 70.

blemish of any kind is unfit for divine service. Likewise, any animal with a blemish is not acceptable for sacrifice.[54] The word for "blemish" in the Old Testament (*mum*) normally means a physical blemish, as in the case of priests and sacrifices, but it can also mean a moral fault.[55] The Greek word for "without blemish" (*amomos*) is often a translation of the Hebrew *tamim* (wholesome, undefiled, innocent, upright, perfect), a word used to describe both the physical perfection of animals to be sacrificed as well as the moral perfection of the righteous. The New Testament witnesses to the use of both meanings: "without blemish" evokes the context of ritual purity and (especially) that of moral perfection (i.e. "blameless").[56] Eph 5:27 therefore applies the Old Testament concern for holiness and temple cultic purity to the Messiah's bride, the Church. The Mishnah notes a clear confluence of priestly traditions and marital traditions concerning purity: "All defects which disqualify priests, disqualify women also [for marriage]."[57] This priestly and sacrificial language describing the required purity of the Church indicates that the sacrificial character of Eph 5:1–2 remains present in Paul's mind throughout our passage, and that the mystical bride of Christ is held to the same standard of purity as brides, priests, and sacrificial animals. The holiness and purity of the Messiah's bride, of course, also implies sexual purity (cf. 5:3–6, 12), which recalls Paul's similar concerns about sexual immorality in 1 and 2 Corinthians and the destructive effect that such behavior has on the Body of Christ and Temple of the Holy Spirit.

The expression "holy and without blemish / blameless" (*hagios kai amomos*) also appears in Eph 1:4, where individual members of the Church are "chosen in him" and called to be "holy and blameless before him in love." By contrast, in 5:27 the expression refers to the collective, mystical bride. The holiness and purity of the Church can only be attained through the holiness and purity of her individual members. Conversely, the holiness of the members subsists only in union with the Body of Christ, whose holiness derives from its head. Eph 5:27 illustrates with nuptial language the doctrine of "salvation by grace"—explicitly stated earlier in the epistle (2:5, 8–10)—whereby good works are not the

54. Lev 22:17–25; Num 19:2; Deut 15:21; 17:1. The Mishnah specifies that "these same blemishes [of animal sacrifices], whether lasting or passing, likewise render [priests] unqualified [to serve in the temple]." (*m. Bekhoroth* 7:1)

55. See Deut 32:5; 2 Sam 14:25; Job 11:15; 31:7; Prov 9:7; Cant 4:7; Dan 1:4.

56. Eph 1:4; 5:27; Phil 2:15; Col 1:22; Heb 9:14; 1 Pet 1:19; Jude 1:24; Rev 14:5.

57. *m. Ketuboth* 7:7. Cf. Sampley, *And the Two Shall Become One Flesh*, 71.

prerequisite for salvation but rather its fruit. Commenting on this verse, Barth points out a similar case of "justification by grace" in the Jewish interpretation of the Song of Songs. A midrash on Cant 1:5, where the bride says of herself "I am black, but I am beautiful," states: "Israel is black every day of the week, but beautiful on the Sabbath; black she is in this world, but beautiful in the world to come."[58] The natural imperfections and "darkness" of the bride in this life are expected to be transformed into beauty and splendor at the end of the earthly journey—and this perfect beauty is already anticipated on the Sabbath, the sacred time of God's union with his people.

The perfect holiness of the Church in Ephesians 5 has prompted commentators to ask *when* precisely she becomes Christ's bride. Since any Christian community, let alone the Church at large, falls short of the degree of purity described in Ephesians 5, some have assumed that it is only in the end, at Christ's *parousia*, that the Church becomes the Bride. In this case, her perfection described in Eph 5 would not be a present status or possession but rather her promised eschatological future.[59] The problem with this view is that in 5:32 the "one flesh" union is applied to the present relationship between Christ and the Church. If 2 Cor 11:2 clearly depicts a betrothal where the "pure virgin" is still awaiting union with her beloved, here the Church is apparently already married to him. Yet the eschatological expectation is not wholly absent from Eph 5: Christ is still sanctifying and cleansing her "*that he might present* her to himself a glorious church"—implying that this presentation has not yet taken place. The tension between the two passages is another example of the Church living "between the times," having received the deposit of the Spirit and the divine Presence as betrothed bride, yet still longing in expectation of the full consummation of the marital union.

---

58. *CantR* 1:5. Barth, *Ephesians 4–6*, 676.

59. Muirhead (*The Bride of Christ*, 184) writes: "It is only in the End that the Church becomes the Bride." Cf. Barth, *Ephesians 4–6*, 628, 669, 678. Lincoln (*Ephesians*, 377) disagrees and sees the Ephesian church already married to Christ.

## Christ and the Church: One Body, One Flesh
### (Eph 5:28–30)

> [28] Even so husbands should love their wives as their own bod-
> ies. He who loves his wife loves himself. [29] For no man ever
> hates his own flesh, but nourishes and cherishes it, as Christ
> does the church, [30] because we are members of his body, [of
> his flesh and of his bones].

The wife is now identified with the husband's own body or, synonymously,
with his own flesh—in other words, with himself. The exhortation to the
husband that he should love his wife "as himself" alludes to Lev 19:18:
"you shall love your neighbor as yourself." Paul may have known a rabbinic tradition that applies Lev 19 to marriage, praising the man "who
loves his wife as himself and honors her more than himself."[60] With the
mention of the body, Paul's metaphor takes on another dimension. Until
now the husband was exhorted to love his wife with the selfless *agape* love
by which Christ loves the Church. Here the dimension of *eros* comes into
play. The man is to love his wife because she is really a part of him. As the
quotation from Genesis says, it is in the intimacy of the sexual union that
the wife becomes the husband's "own body" and "own flesh." The images of
the Church as bride and Church as body are combined, together with the
sacrificial allusions discussed above. Christ loves his bride, the Church,
because she is his own body.[61] Recalling the identification of the body with
the Temple of the Holy Spirit, and the Eucharistic Body of Christ whose
partaking signifies intimate *koinonia* with him, our passage reveals a rich
array of interrelated metaphors. The Eucharistic allusion continues in
verses 29–30, which describe Christ's constant provision for and building
up of his body whereby he "nourishes and cherishes" his ecclesial bride.
Though the "nourishing" and "cherishing" can be interpreted in various
ways,[62] the most plausible meaning is the Eucharistic one. Paul argued
in 1 Corinthians 10:14–17 that partaking of the consecrated bread and
sharing in the cup of blessing is the communion (*koinonia*) of the body
and blood of Christ, and thus a form of one-flesh union (cf. John 6:56)
that is also the source of the Church's unity. The Church, Christ's bride,

---

60. *b. Yebamoth* 62b. Cf. Barth, *Ephesians* 1–3, 633.

61. As stated in the immediate context (5:23, 5:30), in other passages in Ephesians (1:23, 2:16, 3:6, 4:4, 4:12, 4:16, 4:25), and in the rest of the Pauline corpus (Rom
12:4–5; 1 Cor 6:15; 10:17; 12:12–27; Col 1:18, 24; 2:19).

62. Cf. Barth, *Ephesians* 4–6, 635.

is also his body that was taken out of him. The Messiah nourishes and cherishes his bride by giving her his Eucharistic Body, the *koinonia* of his flesh and blood which commemorates his paschal self-offering for her, bestows upon her his life, and is the means by which he abides in her and her in him.

Verse 30 adds that Christ nourishes the Church because "we are members of his body, [of his flesh and of his bones]."[63] The second part of the verse recalls Adam's exclamation of marvel when he saw Eve for the first time after she was taken out of him (Gen 2:23). The Church is Christ's "flesh and bones" just as Eve was "bone of [Adam's] bones and flesh of [his] flesh." This points again to the Church's role as "new Eve." If the Eve-Church allusions are less obvious and frequent than the Adam-Christ typology,[64] the three passages that we have seen[65] provide sufficient evidence to attest that the idea already existed in Paul's days.[66] The Eve-Church metaphor attests to the apostle's belief in the pre-existence of the Church, "in Christ" "before the foundation of the world" (Eph 1:4): As Eve was originally one with Adam before she was taken out of his side, so the Church was originally one with Christ, "of his flesh and of his bones," before she was "taken out of his side."[67] The creation of Eve is therefore "the prototype or antitype of the universal church's origin." As Barth says, "Eph 5 then proclaims not only the joining of Christ to his Bride, the church, but also the creation of the church out of Christ's side, viz. of his 'flesh and bones.'"[68] The Church, the New Eve, has not only been redeemed by the New Adam. She has been *created* out of him—as Eve was formed from Adam's side.

---

63. The second part of the verse appears in a majority of manuscripts but is missing in several important ones. Although the longer variant is generally considered to be a later addition to the original text, the fact that it is quoted as early as Irenaeus and is the majority text indicates that it stems from an early tradition and is worthy of consideration.

64. The Adam-Christ typology is developed in several NT passages: Rom 5:12–19; 1 Cor 15:22, 45–49; Eph 4:22–24; 5:31–32.

65. 1 Cor 11:8–12; 2 Cor 11:2–3; Eph 5:30.

66. The idea of the Church as New Eve was later developed by Irenaeus' recapitulation theory (*adv. Haer.* III 22:2f) and elaborated by Augustine (*Tract. In Ioann.* cxx 2). Cf. Barth, *Ephesians 4–6*, 722f.

67. Compare our discussion of John 19:34 above, where the water and blood flowing out of Jesus' side are understood as a symbol of the water of baptism and the blood of the Eucharist and thus the "birth of the Church."

68. Barth, *Ephesians 4–6*, 722–23.

## A Great Mystery (Eph 5:31–33)

> [31] "For this reason a man shall leave his father and mother and be joined to his wife, and the two shall become one flesh." [32] This is a great mystery, but I speak concerning Christ and the church;

In quoting Genesis 2:24, Paul has retained the expression "for this reason" from the original verse. For *which* reason, then, would Christ "leave his father and mother" and be joined to his wife, the Church, to become one flesh with her? The antecedent of "for this reason" is most likely that of the original context in Genesis: because woman was taken out of man and is "bone of his bones and flesh of his flesh"—"for *this reason* a man shall leave his father and mother and be joined to his wife, and the two shall become one flesh." The ground for the one-flesh union is the original unity between the bridegroom and bride.[69] Eve was part of Adam's body: they were one before she was taken out of him. Their one-flesh union is therefore not a new event but a *re*-union. The application of this metaphor to Christ and the Church means that they too were originally one; this original unity, followed by the separation by which the Church was "taken out" of Christ, is the root of their mutual desire for union. Thus, Adam's joyous recognition of Eve as a part of himself, as "bone of my bones and flesh of my flesh" is implicitly echoed in Christ beholding his ecclesial bride who was part of him from the very beginning. Theologians and commentators have at times seen in the Church's origin "of his flesh and of his bones" the ground for the idea that the Church is an "extended incarnation of Christ." Chavasse wrote that as "Eve was the continuation and projection of Adam's body . . . so the church, her antitype, is the continuation of Christ's incarnation."[70] The Church, intimately united with her divine Bridegroom, continues to mediate his presence and salvation in the world.

The use of the word *mysterion* in Eph 5:32 within the context of the Genesis quotation has been hotly debated in the history of the verse's interpretation. Translated as *sacramentum* in the Vulgate, it has been traditionally understood by Catholic theologians as the classic proof

---

69. Barth, *Ephesians 4–6*, 637–38; 722.

70. Chavasse, *The Bride of Christ*, 70; cited in Barth, *Ephesians 4–6*, 723. And Batey: "Christians are imitators of Christ (Eph v. 1–2), but they are more than this. They are the historic continuation of his personality." Batey, "The μία σάρξ Union of Christ and the Church," 270–81.

text establishing marriage as one of the seven sacraments instituted by Christ, conveying the grace earned by his suffering and death. According to this interpretation, marriage between man and woman would be the permanent reenactment of the communion of love between God and man in Christ, and the sacralization of what had been until then a mere societal institution, not only symbolizing but even recreating the union of Christ and the Church.[71] Although this interpretation of *mysterion* is rejected by most scholars today,[72] we must grant that it does not merely stem from a proof-text reading of the word *sacramentum* but could be reasonably inferred from the nuptial and sacrificial context of Ephesians 5. Another interpretation would have *mysterion* be the equivalent of the English "mystery," denoting the miraculous or mystical essence of either the man-woman one-flesh union, or the union of Christ with the Church, or the relationship between both pairs.[73] Other occurrences of *mysterion* in Ephesians (1:9, 3:3–4, 9, 6:19) indeed refer to the once hidden purpose of God now revealed in Christ and seem to confirm this interpretation. A third possibility would have *mysterion* indicate that the quotation from Genesis in Eph 5:31 is to be understood in a typological and mystical way, resting on a correspondence between creation (Gen 2:24) and redemption (Christ and the Church).[74]

> [**33**] however, let each one of you love his wife as himself, and let the wife see that she respects her husband.

Following his mystical Christological flight, the apostle returns to the literal meaning of Gen 2:24. Having brought to light the deep meaning of Christ's love for the Church and how their mystical union forms the prototype for human nuptial love, he returns to a final exhortation to conjugal love with a final allusion to Lev 19:18.

---

71. Barth, *Ephesians 4–6*, 746.

72. Cf. Barth, *Ephesians 4–6*, 744–49.

73. Cf. Barth, *Ephesians 4–6*, 642.

74. Cf. Lincoln, *Ephesians 4–6*, 382.

## Summary: The Epistle to the Ephesians

The Epistle to the Ephesians paints a rich picture of the Church as Body of Christ, as "holy Temple in the Lord" and as the Messiah's mystical bride. Their marriage evokes all of salvation history: Since Christ chose the elect "in him before the foundation of the world" (1:4), the Church is pre-existent, even mystically preceding Adam and Eve. The eternal, cosmic union of Christ and the Church was the "cosmic blueprint" for Adam's "one-flesh" union with Eve. At the same time, it is the perfect model that every Christian marriage should imitate (5:31–32). Paul alludes to the Sinai covenant in his mention of the "covenants of promise" given to the "commonwealth of Israel" by means of the "law of commandments and ordinances" that was abolished by Christ (2:11–15), bringing down the "wall of partition" between Jews and Gentiles. The marriage between Christ and the Church is rooted in his self-sacrifice at the cross and shedding of his blood (1:7; 2:16; 5:25) which demonstrated "the width and length and depth and height" of his love for his bride (3:18). The marriage is also portrayed as temple service (5:2) that sanctifies her through the "bridal bath" of baptism (5:26–27) and "nourishes and cherishes" her as his own flesh (5:29)— the Eucharist. Christ's followers are called to imitate this sacrificial love, and husbands especially in loving their wives (5:28). Although in Ephesians the exalted Christ is a heavenly being, the union between him and the Church is viewed as a present relationship. Yet the eschatological dimension of the marriage also remains present as the Church awaits the completion of the Bridegroom's work of sanctification, "that he might present her to himself a glorious Church, not having spot or wrinkle or any such thing, but that she should be holy and without blemish."

# 12

# The Wedding Feast of the Lamb

## The Apocalypse

## Introduction

THE BOOK OF REVELATION GRANTS us a vision of the consummation of the eschatological marriage between Christ, "the Lamb," and his bride, the "New Jerusalem coming down out of heaven from God, prepared as a bride adorned for her husband" (Rev 21:2). Given that John's visions take place before the throne of God in the heavenly Temple, the Apocalypse is also a book replete with temple imagery. Yet at its conclusion even the heavenly Temple disappears, rendered obsolete by the unmediated presence of God and the Lamb (Rev 21: 22). The identification of the wedding feast of the Lamb with the definitive dwelling of God among men (21:3) at the climax of the book reveals a significant connection between nuptial and temple symbolism in the Apocalypse.

Zimmermann has argued that nuptial imagery in Revelation runs through the entire book.[1] The pieces of evidence he proposes for this are the "crown of life" as bridal wreath (2:10; 3:11), the 144,000 as virginal bride (14:4–5), the absence of the voice of the bridegroom and bride in the fallen Babylon (18:23), the wedding of the Lamb (19:6–9), Jerusalem as celestial bride (21:2, 9), and the summons of the bride (22:17). Some scholars have also suggested a possible influence of the Song of Songs in

1. Cf. Zimmermann, "Nuptial Imagery in the Revelation of John."

the Apocalypse, seen in Jesus knocking at the door (Rev 3:20; cf. Cant 5:2) and the woman "clothed with the sun" (Rev 12:1; cf. Cant 6:10). The book also displays connections with Eden, Sinai, and the Temple, such as the woman's war against the dragon (Rev 12:1–17; cf. Gen 3:15), the appearance of the Ark of the Covenant in the heavenly Temple in a Sinai-like theophany (Rev 11:19), and the Tabernacle of God dwelling with men (Rev 21:3).

The first chapter sets the stage with John's initial vision of Jesus in the midst of seven lampstands. Jesus is identified as the one "who loved us and washed us from our sins in his own blood" (Rev 1:5), pointing to the love of the Lamb for his redeemed ecclesial bride and his sacrificial, atoning death for the sake of her sanctification. The vision of the seven lampstands (1:12), representing the seven churches of Asia, is the first of many temple symbols that sketch a picture of heaven as temple. In doing this, the author likely had in mind the tradition that the earthly tabernacle was modeled on the heavenly one (Exod 25:8–9); hence he uses the earthly sanctuary as main point of reference for his depiction of heaven.

## Letters to the Seven Churches (Rev 2–3)

### To Ephesus: First Love and Tree of Life (2:4, 7)

Chapters 2 and 3 consist of seven letters addressed to the seven churches of Asia. In the letter to the church in Ephesus, Jesus reproaches her by saying "you have left your first love" (2:4). For the author of Revelation, this loss of love is a serious failure and a call to repentance, for unless she repents, the community is in danger of losing her lampstand (2:4–5) and, implicitly, of not being admitted to the wedding feast (cf. Matt 22:1–13). This implies that love for the bridegroom is not an option but rather a precondition to be admitted to the coming wedding banquet. To him who overcomes, Jesus promises to give to "eat from the tree of life, which is in the midst of the Paradise of God" (Rev 2:7). The exhortation to the Ephesians to love the bridegroom thus anticipates a return to Eden's Tree of Life, symbolizing an idyllic communion with God that is more fully described at the end of the book.

## To Smyrna: The "Crown of Life" as Bridal Wreath (2:10; 3:11)

To the Church in Smyrna, Jesus promises: "Be faithful until death, and I will give you the crown of life" (Rev 2:10). Although this metaphor is often explained as pertaining to the wreath of victory in games (cf. 1 Cor 9:25),[2] Zimmermann argues that it more likely alludes to the bridal wreath of Jewish and Hellenistic wedding rituals.[3] While the crown or wreath is rarely used as a metaphor for competition in early Jewish tradition, several passages in biblical and post-biblical literature attest to the use of crowns as bridal wreaths: In Isa 62:3, Zion is called a "crown of beauty" and "royal diadem" as she is promised a future marriage with God. In Ezek 16:12 the maiden who represents Jerusalem, adopted and betrothed by God, is adorned as a bride with costly ornaments and a beautiful crown. In Lam 2:15 (LXX), the virgin daughter of Zion is called the "crown of glory, joy of all the earth." In Bar 5:1–2, Jerusalem is told to take off the garment of her affliction and to put on her head "the diadem of the glory of the Everlasting." In Cant 3:11, we read of "the crown with which [Solomon's] mother crowned him on the day of his wedding." These passages indicate that Zimmermann is probably right in seeing the crown of Rev 2:10 (and 3:11) as a bridal wreath, and the exhortation to the church of Smyrna to remain faithful to obtain the "crown of life" as an implicit invitation to the wedding feast of the Lamb.

## To Laodicea: Knocking on Heaven's Door? (Rev 3:20)

In the letter to the last of the seven churches, Laodicea, Jesus extends an invitation to his followers to join him in fellowship at his table: "Behold, I stand at the door and knock. If anyone hears my voice and opens the door, I will come in to him and dine with him, and he with me" (Rev 3:20). The two principal interpretations of this verse are the tropological one, calling the individual to a present, mystical fellowship with Christ (related to the call to repent in v. 19), and the eschatological one, speaking of the imminent return of Christ and messianic feast (related to the promise to sit on his throne in v. 21). Tropologically, the intimacy implied by the expression "I will come in to him" recalls Jesus' promise in the Fourth Gospel that he and the Father will "make their home" within the disciple

---

2. Charles, *The Revelation of St. John*, 1:58; Mounce, *The Book of Revelation*, 94.

3. Zimmermann, "Nuptial Imagery in the Revelation of John," 153–56.

who loves him (John 14:23). Eschatologically, it evokes the promise to his disciples in the Synoptics that they will eat and drink at his table in the kingdom (Matt 26:29). Since both promises were given at the Last Supper—and considering the liturgical setting of Revelation—this makes a Eucharistic interpretation of Rev 3:20 conceivable. Thus the Eucharistic meal of communion with Christ operates as the mystical and liturgical "bridge" between the Last Supper and the eschatological feast which it anticipates.[4]

Commentators who favor the tropological or mystical interpretation have also suggested a parallel between Rev 3:20 and Cant 5:2, where the lover knocks on the door of his beloved's room and invites her to open and let him in.[5] Both verses describe a lover knocking on the door of his beloved, the sound of his voice, and a call to open. This parallel would mean that the author of Revelation is reinterpreting the lover's knocking on the door and the beloved's sleepy, half-hearted response in the Canticle as Jesus "knocking" on the "door" of the lukewarm Laodicean community, calling them to arise from their spiritual sleep and return to the bridegroom's love in preparation for the coming wedding feast.

## Temple Liturgy—Earthly and Heavenly

In chapter 4, it becomes evident that John's vision is a vision of the heavenly temple and liturgy, revealing many familiar symbols from the earthly temple: At the heart of the earthly temple was the Ark of the Covenant; in the center of the heavenly temple is the throne of glory (Rev 4:2–3) and the Ark of the Covenant (11:19). In the earthly sanctuary there was a lampstand and a golden altar of incense; in John's vision of heaven there are seven golden lampstands (1:12) and a golden altar from which incense rises up to God (8:3–5). Four carved cherubim adorned the walls of the earthly Temple; in John's vision four living creatures minister before the throne (4:6–9). Twenty-four priestly divisions served in the earthly Temple; twenty-four elders serve in the heavenly Temple (4:4). Outside the earthly sanctuary there was a laver filled with water and an altar of

4. Cf. Feuillet, "Le Cantique des Cantiques et l'Apocalypse," 336; Harrington, *Revelation*, 75.

5. Charles, *The Revelation of St. John*, 1:101; Feuillet, "Le Cantique des Cantiques et l'Apocalypse," 334–41; Cambe, "L'influence du Cantique des Cantiques sur le Nouveau Testament," 5–9; Massyngberde Ford, *Revelation*, 422; Beale, *The Book of Revelation*, 308.

sacrifices; before the heavenly throne there is a "sea of glass like crystal" (4:6) and an altar under which rest the souls of the martyrs (6:9).[6]

The temple in Revelation is most often called *naos*, but sometimes also *skene* (13:6; 15:5; 21:3). It has different forms: In his letter to the church in Philadelphia, Jesus promises to the one who conquers that he will "make him a pillar in the temple of my God" (3:12). The temple is thus a spiritual structure, made from the communion of saints. These living pillars which constitute the assembly of saints are "before the throne of God and serve him day and night in his temple" (7:15). From the temple also come the orders to carry out God's judgment on earth (16:1) and the angels who execute it (14:15, 17; 15:5–6). In parallel with the liturgy of the heavenly temple, drama unfolds in the earthly temple, which is still the arena of the struggle between good and evil: John is commanded to measure it and its altar, but not its outer court, which is to be trodden by the Gentiles (11:1–2).

As the place of God's throne in heaven, the celestial temple of Revelation is the domain of perfect *kedushah*. The word *hagios* appears 27 times in the book to describe the holiness of God, of Christ, of the angels, of the New Jerusalem, and of the prophets, apostles and saints. In addition, the cosmic battle that rages throughout the book is portrayed as the struggle of God's saints against the forces of evil that epitomize uncleanness, desecration, and defilement. In the final vision, when the Lord God and the Lamb become the temple of the saints, the divine sanctuary radiates with *kedushah*, entirely free from any stain of sin and from "anything that defiles" (Rev 21:27).

## Behold the Lamb: Passover and Exodus Typology

The source of the heavenly Temple's *kedushah* is God himself; his holiness is imparted to the saints by the blood of the Lamb who was slain and whose wedding feast is the climax of the entire book. The imagery is eminently sacrificial, paschal, and nuptial. The connection between these levels of symbolism is anticipated in Jesus' role as the one who *loved* the saints and washed them from their sins in his sacrificial *blood* (Rev 1:5); it comes to the fore in chapter 5 with the revelation of his identity as "Lamb

---

6. Cf. also Rev 7:15; 11:1–2, 19; 14:15–17; 15:5–8; 16:1. On Revelation as a Temple vision, see Briggs, *Jewish Temple Imagery in the Book of Revelation*, 45–110; McKelvey, *The New Temple*; Hahn, *The Lamb's Supper*, 68–69.

who was slain" standing in the midst of the throne of heaven. Jesus' sacrificial slaying and shedding of his blood is the ultimate testimony of his love. It is the act by which he redeemed the saints and made them a priestly kingdom (1:6), just as the slaying of the Passover lamb initiated the redemption of Israel from Egypt and led to their adoption as "kingdom of priests and holy nation" at Sinai (Exod 19:6). It is by his blood that Christ washed the saints from their sins (1:5), redeemed them (5:9), washed their robes and made them white (7:14), and gave them power to overcome Satan (12:11). Jesus' victory through suffering and death is then given over to the saints: Their willingness to die a martyr's death and shed their own blood in imitation of their master is the testimony of their victory over the forces of evil (6:10; 12:11; 16:6; 17:6; 18:24; 19:2). The predominant role of the Lamb who was slain and the constant calling of his followers to imitate him thus point to a strong current of Passover symbolism in Revelation.[7]

The Lamb's sacrifice is also the reason why he is given worship, honor, and glory in heaven (5:8–14). The glory of God filling the heavenly Temple and New Jerusalem is another familiar biblical motif recapitulated in the Apocalypse. The hymns of praise of the angels, elders, and saints resound throughout the book in giving glory to God and to the Lamb.[8] While judgment is executed upon the earth, the heavenly temple is "filled with smoke from the glory of God and from his power" so that no one can enter it until the seven plagues of judgment are completed (Rev 15:8). This language recalls not only the plagues in Egypt but also the divine glory overshadowing Mount Sinai and filling the Tabernacle and Temple.[9]

Other Passover/Exodus/Sinai allusions include the Church as kingdom of priests (Rev 1:6; 5:10; cf. Exod 19:6), the reference to Balaam (2:14; cf. Num 31:16) and the hidden manna (Rev 2:17; cf. Exod 16). John's vision of the heavenly Temple in chapter 4 also strongly evokes Mount Sinai: the seer is invited to "come up" at the sound of a trumpet (Rev 4:1; cf. Exod 19:19–20), so that he sees the throne of God's glory accompanied by thunder and lightning (Rev 4:5; 8:5; 11:9; 16:18; cf. Exod

---

7. This thematic material shows great affinities with Ephesians 5, where the Messiah sacrificially offers himself for his bride, the Church, for the purpose of redeeming, sanctifying, cleansing, and washing her, calling her to imitate him in this self-sacrificial love (Eph 5:1–2, 25–27).

8. Rev 1:6; 4:9–11; 5:12–13; 7:12; 11:13; 14:7; 19:1.

9. Exod 40:34–35; 1 Kgs 8:10–11; 2 Chr 5:14.

19:16). The plagues of God's judgment are modeled upon the plagues of Egypt (Rev 8:7–9:21; cf. Exod 7–11), as is the power of the two witnesses to turn water into blood and to strike the earth with plagues (Rev 11:6). The bitter waters (Rev 8:11; cf. Exod 15:23) and the earth "opening its mouth" to "swallow" the forces that oppose God (Rev 12:16; cf. Num 16:32) also evoke the wilderness wanderings. Finally, the victorious saints over the beast, standing by a "sea of glass mingled with fire" and singing the song of Moses and the song of the Lamb (Rev 15:2–3) clearly echo the hymn sung by the Israelites after they crossed the Red Sea (cf. Exod 15:1).[10] This sustained use of Passover, Exodus, and Sinai typology indicates that John sees the journey of the saints in the Apocalypse as a new Exodus in which they flee the forces of evil and struggle against them while en route to their final destination, the perfect Promised Land in the eternal dwelling of God where all evil will be annihilated.

## The Woman's Return (Rev 12)

In Rev 12, "a woman clothed with the sun, with the moon under her feet, and on her head a garland of twelve stars" cries out in labor and gives birth to a male child who is "caught up to God and to his throne" and will "rule all nations with a rod of iron" (Rev 12:2, 5). This is an obvious reference to Christ in his royal-messianic role via an allusion to Ps 2:9. But for now, the woman and her child are persecuted by Satan, the ancient serpent who was cast down to earth after losing a fierce battle in heaven (12:7–9, 13). They must flee into the desert (12:6) and there must fend off the devil's attacks, aided by the supernatural interventions of divine Providence (12:14–16). At the end of the chapter, the woman's offspring are revealed as those "who keep the commandments of God and have the testimony of Jesus Christ" (Rev 12:17). We have mentioned the Marian interpretation of this figure as "new Eve" in our study of the Fourth Gospel. More commonly, the woman is interpreted as representative of the people of God, in the first place Israel (12:1–5), then the Church of the saints who are her "offspring" (12:13–17). Given her identification with the Church (or as "mother" of the Church) the woman is virtually identified with the New Jerusalem and bride of the Lamb who is fully revealed in the final chapters of the book.

---

10. Cf. Nixon, *The Exodus in the New Testament*, 29.

## New Eve

The woman of Rev 12 evokes Eve and the *protoevangelium* that announced a future conflict between the serpent and the "woman" and between his seed and her seed, and the announcement that the woman would bring forth children in pain (Gen 3:15–16).[11] As foretold in Genesis, the woman of Revelation gives birth in pain, and she and the "rest of her offspring" (the followers of Christ, Rev 12:17) are engaged in a life-and-death struggle against the dragon, identified as "that serpent of old, called the Devil and Satan" (Rev 12:9). This combat between the "woman" and her seed, and the devil and his angels indicates that the woman of Revelation is the "woman" who was announced in Gen 3:15—the "new Eve" whose seed was to bruise the head of the ancient serpent.

## Exodus Typology

Mounce has suggested that Exodus typology is woven through the entire chapter.[12] The dragon's pursuit of the woman and her flight into the wilderness (12:6, 13) recalls Pharaoh's pursuit of the Israelites as they left Egypt and fled into the desert. The "two wings of a great eagle" given to her for her escape (12:14) evoke the "eagle's wings" by which God delivered Israel from the Egyptians (Exod 19:4). The flood of water spewed out of the dragon's mouth to drown the woman may allude to the attempt to drown the Israelite children in the Nile (Exod 1:22) or the flooding of the waters of the Red Sea (Exod 14); and the opening of the earth perhaps evokes the swallowing of the men of Korah into the earth (Num 16:31–33).

## The Woman as Ark of the Covenant

Some authors have suggested that the juxtaposition of the Ark of the Covenant's appearance in Rev 11:19 with that of the woman in Rev 12:1 is no mere coincidence but rather a carefully planned literary device that intends to identify the Ark with the woman. In 11:19, in the aftermath of the judgment of the nations and as the twenty-four elders worship God,

---

11. On the association of the woman of Rev 12 and Gen 3:15, cf. Harrington, *Revelation*, 129–130; Beale, *The Book of Revelation*, 630.

12. Mounce, *The Book of Revelation*, 245.

seemingly out of nowhere we read that "the temple of God was opened in heaven, and the Ark of his Covenant was seen in his temple (Rev 11:19)." This appearance is accompanied by Sinai-like phenomena of "lightnings, noises, thunderings, an earthquake, and great hail" (cf. Exod 19:6). One would expect the author to elaborate upon this stupendous vision of the long-lost Ark, reappearing for the first time in centuries since it went missing when the first Temple was destroyed. But the Ark disappears as soon as it came: in the very next verse it is replaced by the woman who also appears in the midst of heaven. Since the woman carries Christ (the ultimate source of *kedushah*) in her womb and is representative of the Church (Rev 12:17)—elsewhere identified as the holy Temple of God, it seems likely that John wishes to identify her with the sacred Ark of the Covenant.

## Daughter of Zion and Canticle's Bride

The woman of Rev 12 also evokes the prophetic images of the *Daughter of Zion* as a pregnant woman in labor pains, and thus she is closely associated with Israel. One thinks of Isa 26:17–18 (where the defeat of the serpent is also mentioned, 27:1) or Isa 66:7–9 (LXX), which depicts Zion "escaping" and giving birth to a male child. The astral motif in the woman's description (sun, moon, twelve stars) recalls Joseph's dream (Gen 37:9), where the sun and moon represent Joseph's father and mother and the twelve stars the twelve sons of Jacob. This image is consistent with the woman's identity as representative of the twelve tribes of Israel. Others see a closer dependence between Rev 12 and two other texts: the first is Isa 60, which portrays Zion as a glorious sunrise enlightened by the light of God (Isa 60:1), taking on the attributes of the sun and moon (60:19–20), and finding her strength and prestige restored (60:12–14). The second text is Cant 6:10, where the Shulamite "looks forth as the dawn, fair as the moon, clear as the sun, awesome as an army with banners." The two texts may well be related since the beauty of both Zion and the Shulamite are compared to the light of dawn and to the sun and moon, with an emphasis on powerful military strength.[13] These associations with Isa 60 and Cant 6 imply that the woman of Rev 12 takes on the dual role of city

---

13. Feuillet ("Le Cantique des Cantiques et l'Apocalypse," 341–348) and Cambe ("L'influence du Cantique des Cantiques sur le Nouveau Testament," 9–12) argue for the influence of both texts on Rev 12 :1.

and bride—an idea that returns in Rev 21 with the identification of the Lamb's bride as the New Jerusalem.

## The 144,000 as Virginal Bride (Rev 14:4-5)

In yet another nuptial image for the Church, Zimmermann has proposed that the 144,000 redeemed who appear with the Lamb on Mount Zion (Rev 14:4-5; 7:4) represent his virginal bride. Their identity as those who "were not defiled with women, for they are virgins" (14:4) alludes to early Jewish traditions of the fallen angels of Gen 6:1-4.[14] In contrast to the "sons of God" who defiled themselves with women and thereby betrayed the covenant, the 144,000 virgins faithfully follow the Lamb wherever he goes and are "without fault (*amomoi*) before the throne of God" (Rev 14:5). Virginity and immaculateness are the most basic elements of a bride in early Judaism.[15] We have noted in our discussion of Eph 5:27 the cultic context of *amomos* (without blemish) as pertaining to sacrifices, priests, and brides. These three applications of *amomos* also apply to the saints in Revelation who have sacrificially shed their blood in martyrdom (Rev 6:10; 12:11; 17:6, 14; 19:2), perform a priestly ministry serving the Lord in his Temple (7:14-15), and collectively form the Bride of the Lamb, the eternal Temple and the New Jerusalem (21:2, 9-10).

Also related to the nuptial imagery of this passage is the motif of redemption. It was the husband's obligation in early Judaism to ransom his wife should she be taken prisoner.[16] In Rev 14:4, the 144,000 who "follow the Lamb wherever he goes" have been "redeemed from among men, [being] firstfruits to God and to the Lamb." The Lamb redeeming or "buying back" his disciples from the forces of evil points to his role as faithful husband. This verse also shows similarities with Jer 2:2-4, where the Lord recalls Israel's "love as a bride" when she "followed me in the wilderness," being "holy to the LORD, the first fruits of his harvest." The common points are virginity, betrothal, redemption, following the bridegroom, and the bride as first fruits. We also recall the linguistic affinity between sanctity (*kedushah*) and betrothal (*kiddushin*), expressing the

---

14. Cf. 1 Enoch 7:1; 9:8; 10:11; 15:2-7.

15. Cf. Deut 22:13-21; Sir 7:24; Tob 3:14; Philo, *On the Special Laws* III:80; Josephus, *Antiquities* 4:244-248; *m. Ketuboth* 7:7-8; *b. Ketuboth* 46a. Cf. Zimmermann, "Nuptial Imagery in the Revelation of John," 158 n. 19.

16. Cf. *m. Ketuboth* 4:4, 8; *m. Hor* 3:7; *b. Ketuboth* 47b; 51b; 52a.b; *t. Ketuboth* 4:5.

act of setting apart the woman for her husband: the 144,000 are entirely set apart for the Lamb, not having been "defiled with women." In short, the virginity and immaculateness of the 144,000, their promise to follow the Lamb and their identity as ransomed first-born are all nuptial motifs indicating that the vision in Rev 14:1–5 may well be an anticipation of the upcoming wedding feast of the lamb.[17]

## The Fall of the Whore of Babylon (Rev 18)

Rev 18 depicts the judgment and fall of Babylon the great, symbol of the evil nations that oppose God's plan. The city is personified as a woman and set in stark contrast to the pure virgin-bride of Christ about to be unveiled, the New Jerusalem.[18] Babylon is "the mother of harlots" (Rev 17:5) who has fornicated with the kings of the earth and "made all nations drink of the wine of the wrath of her fornication" (Rev 14:8; 18:3), being also responsible for the blood of the Christian martyrs (17:6; 18:24). Though she was "arrayed in purple and scarlet, and adorned with gold and precious stones and pearls" (Rev 17:4), glorifying herself and living luxuriously, she will be stricken with dreadful plagues and all of her riches will come to nothing in one hour (18:7–16). In the description of the gloomy silence that will fall upon the desolate city, we are told that "the voice of bridegroom and bride shall not be heard in you anymore" (Rev 18:23). This recalls the passages about the voice of the bridegroom and bride in Jeremiah and especially Jer 25:10, which speaks of "the grinding of the millstones and the light of the lamp" (as in Rev 18:23). Thus, not only the promiscuity and defilement of the whore stand in contrast to the virginity and immaculateness of the Lamb's bride; the future absence of the voice of the bridegroom and bride will characterize the city of the godless in contrast to the joy and celebration of the wedding that will take place in the city of God.

## The Wedding of the Lamb (Rev 19:6–9)

The nuptial imagery moves to the forefront as the narrative comes to a climax in the last chapters of the book. Following the demise of Babylon, a great multitude proclaims:

17. Cf. Zimmermann, "Nuptial Imagery in the Revelation of John," 157–60.
18. Cf. Zimmermann, "Nuptial Imagery," 160–62.

> Alleluia! For the Lord God Omnipotent reigns! Let us be glad
> and rejoice and give him glory, for the marriage of the Lamb has
> come, and his wife (*gyne*) has made herself ready. And to her it
> was granted to be arrayed in fine linen, clean and bright, for the
> fine linen is the righteous acts of the saints. (19:6–7).

To this acclamation, the angel responds: "Blessed are those who are called to the marriage supper of the Lamb!" (19:9). A great feast is implied, seen as the fulfillment of the eschatological marriage that the prophets (cf. Isa 25:6–8) and apostles (cf. Matt 22:1–13) had announced and longed for. The bridegroom is the Messiah (cf. Matt 25:1–13) and the bride is the people of God (cf. 2 Cor 11:2)—though her identity is only revealed later. Zimmermann has identified an intertextual relation between Rev 19:6–9 and the royal wedding Psalm 45. Both depict an omnipotent king who reigns and is praised, the joy of the wedding and glory of the king, an adorned bride wearing bright garments, and the theme of righteousness and justice. Isa 61:10 is another possible backdrop to Rev 19:69.[19] It too calls for rejoicing and presents the people of God as a bride who is "adorned" for her husband. She is divinely granted "garments of salvation" and a "robe of righteousness" as wedding garment, an image that resembles the bride's garment of fine linen which is "the righteous acts of the saints" in Rev 19:8.[20]

The contrast between the earthly city—the adulteress Babylon arrayed in purple and scarlet who is "mother of harlots" (17:2–5; 18:3), and the heavenly city—the Lamb's pure wife dressed in her clean, bright, fine linen representing "the righteous acts of the saints" (19:8) is evident. The identification of the Lamb's wife with the good deeds of the saints establishes her identity as the Church. The bride's purity recalls the need to keep the Temple of the Holy Spirit pure by fleeing sexual immorality (1 Cor 6:15–20), and the exhortation to the Church to guard her sincere and pure devotion (2 Cor 11:2). The radiant wife is also reminiscent of the "glorious church, not having spot or wrinkle," "holy and without blemish" of Ephesians 5.[21] As in Ephesians, this beauty and purity is not her own but "granted" to her by her bridegroom.

---

19. Fekkes, "'His Bride Has Prepared Herself': Revelation 19–21 and Isaian Nuptial Imagery," 270–74.

20. Ezekiel's personified Jerusalem is also clothed with "fine linen, silk, and embroidered cloth" (Ezek 16:13). Zimmermann, "Nuptial Imagery," 165.

21. The saints in Revelation are said to be "blameless" *amomoi* (14:5), just as the Church in Eph 5:27 is called "holy and without blemish" (*amomos*).

Although Rev 19:6–9 tells us little about the identity of the Lamb's wife, her designation as *gyne*-woman (rather than *nymphe*-bride) recalls the splendidly clothed woman of Rev 12 (the only other woman in the Apocalypse apart from the whore of Babylon). This has led some scholars to conclude that these two women are one and the same—metaphorical figures of the redeemed ecclesial community, identified with the saints by way of different images.[22] Whereas the woman of Rev 19 is clothed with the "righteous deeds of the saints," in Rev 12:17 the woman's "offspring" are those "who keep the commandments of God and have the testimony of Jesus Christ." They differ in that the woman of Rev 12 already gives birth—to a messianic figure symbolizing Christ—and has a numerous progeny in the saints, while the woman of Rev 19 is only just getting married (to Christ the Lamb). Perhaps the woman clothed with the sun focuses on the present ecclesial dimension of the Church, while the woman of Rev 19 underlines the eschatological aspect of the marriage to come. At the time of the writing of Revelation, Christians would have seen themselves as still living "between the times," betrothed to Christ but still awaiting their final marriage with him. In Revelation (as in Eph 5), the Church is Christ's wife uniting herself with her beloved. But if in Ephesians the union is mystical and spiritual, in Rev 19–21 it is eschatological. The imagery highlights the transitory time between present betrothal and future eschatological wedding. As ancient Jewish weddings began with a procession to the bride's house followed by a return to the groom's house for the marriage feast, the Church, now espoused to Christ by faith, "awaits the parousia when the heavenly groom will come for his bride and return to heaven for the marriage feast that lasts throughout eternity."[23]

## Here Comes the Bride: The New Jerusalem (Rev 21)

Rev 19:6–9 is but a preliminary announcement of the wedding feast of the Lamb, still to be preceded by the turmoil of a penultimate eschatological

22. Zimmermann, "Nuptial Imagery," 168. There are several resemblances between the woman of Rev 12 and the bride of the Lamb in Rev 21: both appear in heaven and are clothed with splendor; the woman is crowned with 12 stars while the bride (Jerusalem) has 12 gates and 12 foundations; both are also related to Eden: the woman suffering from the pains of childbirth and threatened by the serpent recalls Eve, cast out of paradise, while the bride of chap. 21 finds the long-lost Tree of Life.

23. Mounce, *The Book of Revelation*, 347.

battle, the millennium, the war of Gog and Magog, the definitive destruction of Satan and his evil forces, the final judgment, and the resurrection of the dead (19:11–20:15). Finally, John sees a new heaven and a new earth, and "the holy city, New Jerusalem, descending out of heaven from God, prepared as a bride adorned for her husband" (Rev 21:1–2). For the first time, the bride is revealed as the New Jerusalem. The image of the city-bride draws upon the rich nuptial prophetic tradition. But who exactly is the bride? Is she literally identified with the community of saints? As we have seen, if the personification of Jerusalem/Zion was originally depicted in relation to its people, in wisdom and pseudepigraphical literature it increasingly took on the role of

> a self-reliant unity that excludes a simplified identification with her inhabitants or the people of God. Zion assumes, like lady wisdom, an intermediary role into which she enters as a person in relation to JHWH and to mankind. From within the intimate relationship with God, the city of God provides for the well-being of her inhabitants and can even create salvation for all people.[24]

Thus, on the one hand the bride is the embodiment of the redeemed from all the nations and the "eternal felicity of all who follow the lamb."[25] On the other hand, her exact identity remains ambiguous. As eschatological Church she is not only the sum of her parts but really an entity that transcends her individual members. In Rev 19:7–9 there seems to be a distinction between the bride and the wedding guests "called to the marriage supper of the Lamb." Likewise, a clear differentiation is made between the city-bride and her inhabitants in Rev 21:9–10; 24–26. Zimmermann's observation, therefore, seems correct: The holy bridal city is "not simply a collective term for the sum of her inhabitants but rather has an independent existence that becomes the counterpart of the bridegroom."[26]

The creation of "a new heaven and a new earth," with the appearance of the glorious New Jerusalem descending from heaven is the culmination of God's salvific action in human history. There, finally, redeemed humanity finds rest from its toilsome journey, dwelling in God's presence with no more suffering or death, freely drinking from the "fountain of the

24. Zimmermann, "Nuptial Imagery," 172–73.

25. Mounce, *The Book of Revelation*, 382.

26. Zimmermann, "Nuptial Imagery," 174.

water of life." The ultimate blissful union of the bride with her beloved is described with temple imagery:

> Behold, the Tabernacle (*skene*) of God is with men, and he will dwell with them, and they shall be his people. God himself will be with them and be their God. (Rev 21:3)[27]

The verb "to dwell" (*skeno*), which in John 1:14 denotes the "tabernacling" of the Logos among men, returns here with the same connotation of the divine Presence dwelling among his bride and people. Yet it no longer dwells mystically and secretly in the life of the believer but is now manifest to all, accompanied by a definitive end of all pain, sorrow, and death (Rev 21:4).[28] Another parallel with the Fourth Gospel is the free gift of the "fountain of the water of life" to whoever thirsts (Rev 21:6). This is no longer a mere promise, as given to the Samaritan woman (John 4:14) and to the Jews at the Feast of Tabernacles (John 7:38), but now a present reality indissociable from the great wedding feast.

In another vision, the New Jerusalem, now called both "the bride" and "the Lamb's wife" descends from heaven on a "great and high mountain," having "the glory of God" (21:9–11). The glory of God reflected in his city-bride-temple on his holy mountain evokes the glory revealed at Sinai and in the Temple, and the familiar "mountain of the Lord" traditions. Ezekiel's Temple also has a prominent place since it was to be built in a city on a "very high mountain" (Ezek 40:2). The light of the New Jerusalem is "like a most precious stone, like a jasper stone, clear as crystal" (Rev 21:11). The adornment and glory of the bride recalls again the "glorious" Church of Ephesians 5:27, now manifest in all her splendor. The city is surrounded by a high wall with twelve gates (representing the twelve tribes of Israel, cf. Ezek 48:30–34) and twelve foundations (representing the twelve apostles, Rev 21:12–14). Its wall is made of jasper and the city itself is of "pure gold, like clear glass" (Rev 21:18).[29] The twelve

---

27. Cf. Exod 29:45; Ezek 37:27; Lev 26:11–12; Jer 31:33; Zech 2:10–11; 8:8.

28. The only places where *skeno* appears in the New Testament are John 1:14 and Rev 7:15, 12:12, 13:6, and 21:3, either describing the indwelling of God among his people, or the indwelling of his people in heaven. "When the Seer writes that the tabernacle of God is with us, he is saying that God in his glorious presence has come to dwell with us." (Mounce, *The Book of Revelation*, 383)

29. The depiction of the New Jerusalem as a bride made of pure gold is perhaps related to the rabbinic tradition describing a "Jerusalem of Gold" as a crown worn by a bride (*t. Shabbat* 4:6; *b. Sotah* 49b), such as the one Rabbi Akiva made for his wife (*y. Shabbat* 6:1; *b. Shabbat* 59b; *b. Nedarim* 50a).

foundations of the wall are adorned with all kinds of precious stones, and the twelve gates are twelve pearls (21:19–21).[30] The correlation between precious stones, nuptial symbolism, and eschatological imagery converges here in the adornment of the New Jerusalem and Lamb's bride.

The perfect union between God and his bride as he "tabernacles" with her forever dispenses with the need for a temple structure. Even the heavenly temple—the setting for the greater part of the book—fades into oblivion in its closing chapters. John sees no temple in the New Jerusalem, "for the Lord God Almighty and the Lamb are its temple" (Rev 21:22). The heavenly city radiates with the *doxa* of the eternal and divine sanctuary: "The city had no need of the sun or of the moon to shine in it, for the glory of God illuminated it" (21:23). In contrast to the various levels of sanctity of the former earthly temple, there is no more separation between sacred and profane, between God's people and God himself in the New Jerusalem. The *Shekhinah* which had abandoned the Temple and Holy City in Ezekiel's time permanently returns to become the eternal dwelling place of God's people, as ultimate fulfillment of God's promise to establish his sanctuary in their midst forever (Ezek 37:26–28).

## Return to the Tree of Life (Rev 22)

### Living Waters Revisited

John's final vision in the closing chapter of Revelation evokes many well-known biblical images:

> And he showed me a pure river of water of life, clear as crystal, proceeding from the throne of God and of the Lamb. In the middle of its street, and on either side of the river, was the tree of life, which bore twelve fruits, each tree yielding its fruit every month. The leaves of the tree were for the healing of the nations. And there shall be no more curse, but the throne of God and of the Lamb shall be in it, and his servants shall serve him. (Rev 22:1–3)

In this idyllic picture, John has skillfully woven traditions of the Garden of Eden with those of Ezekiel's Temple, while also integrating ideas borrowed from the prophets and from Johannine Christology.

---

30. Fekkes has underlined the dependence of Rev 21:18–21 upon Isa 54:11–12 and Tob 13:16–17. Fekkes, "His Bride has Prepared Herself," 274–282.

The vision evokes the gushing forth of miraculous waters endowed with healing power from Ezekiel's Temple (Ezek 47:1–12), reworked into the hymn of personified Lady Wisdom (Sir 24:25–33). In Ezekiel these waters flow from a physical temple; in Revelation they flow out of the throne of God, who together with the Lamb is the eternal temple of the New Jerusalem (Rev 21:22). Aware of the Fourth Gospel's promise of living waters representing the Holy Spirit (John 7:37–39), John seems to make Trinitarian allusions in his description of the return to Eden: the crystal river of life (alluding to the Spirit) flows from God and from the Lamb to effect the healing of the nations. As in Ezekiel's vision, abundant trees which bear fruit each month grow on both banks of the river. The identification with the Garden of Eden is explicit in the return to the Tree of Life and the end of the curse of suffering and death (Rev 22:3; cf. 2:1; 21:4). Moreover, whereas the healing power of Ezekiel's stream was confined to nature—the desert and waters of the Dead Sea—John emphasizes the spiritual healing and reviving of souls announced by Isaiah (Isa 35:1–2, 6–7; 41:17–19; 44:3–4; 49:10; 58:11) and Jesus (John 7:38). Finally, whereas Ezekiel's healing stream was confined to Israel's borders, John's vision is universal: the pure river of water of life brings healing to the redeemed of all nations.

## Bridal Invitation

Just as Jesus' invitation to the Samaritan woman to drink his "living water" was given in a nuptial context, so is the invitation to drink the "water of life" flowing from the eternal Temple:

> And the Spirit and the bride say, "Come!" And let him who hears say, "Come!" And let him who thirsts come. Whoever desires, let him take the water of life freely. (Rev 22:17)

The Spirit and the bride's invitation echoes the early liturgical *marana tha* prayer to Christ (1 Cor 16:22). Could this be an allusion to the Shulamite's invitation to her lover in Cant 2:10 or 7:12?[31] Zimmermann has proposed two interpretations of this invitation: it could be the bride's summon to her bridegroom to come to the house of her parents and take her to his own home for the wedding ceremony. Or, it could be the bride inviting her bridegroom to come to her in their bridal chamber to

31. Cambe, "L'influence du Cantique des Cantiques sur le Nouveau Testament," 12–13.

consummate the marriage.[32] The second option is perhaps preferable: the consummation of the marriage would be more fitting to the drinking of the water of life and the final apotheosis of the book towards which the whole story has moved. Thus, the ultimate union of divine bridegroom and ecclesial bride is at the same time the most intimate communion with him and in him who is the eternal temple, and a return to the Garden of Eden from which flow the rivers of the water of life.

## Summary: The Apocalypse

Zimmermann's thesis that the Apocalypse is permeated with nuptial symbolism is well founded. The *telos* of the book, the eschatological wedding feast of the Lamb and the New Jerusalem, is anticipated and prepared by several nuptial allusions. These include the "crown of life" as bridal wreath, Jesus knocking at the door as echo of Cant 5:2, the woman "clothed with the sun" evoking Cant 6:10, the 144,000 as virginal bride, the absence of the voice of the bridegroom and bride in the fallen Babylon, and the contrast between the immoral whore and the pure bride of the Lamb. The marriage between the Lamb and his bride is portrayed as a return to Eden, announced in the promise that the overcomers of the church of Ephesus will eat from the tree of life in the Paradise of God (2:7), and fulfilled at the end of the book with the renewed access to the tree of life and end of the curse on mankind (22:1-3). The connection with Eden is also seen in the battle between the ancient serpent and the woman whose offspring are the disciples of Christ (12:1-17), evoking Gen 3:15 and implying that the Church, as offspring of the woman, is linked to Eve and to the origins of humanity. The Apocalypse is also replete with allusions to the Passover, Exodus, and Sinai narratives, chiefly in Jesus' identity as slain paschal Lamb and in the vision of the heavenly Temple that echoes much Sinai imagery. It is out of the self-sacrificial shedding of his blood that the Lamb wins the right to redeem his people-bride and to receive the power, glory, and honor that is due to God alone (5:6-13). Finally, the marriage of the Lamb is inseparable from the temple symbolism that permeates the book until it is fulfilled in the eternal communion of God, the Lamb, and his bride, the heavenly Jerusalem.

---

32. Zimmermann, "Nuptial Imagery in the Revelation of John," 176.

# Conclusion

## *From Salvation History to Four Senses of Scripture*

### God's Marriage with Israel at
### Four Key Moments of Salvation History

OUR STUDY OF THE MARRIAGE between God and Israel in the Old Testament and in early Jewish thought has revealed that those ancient sources consistently situate it at four moments of salvation history:

1. **Idyllic prototype of the marriage (Creation/Eden):** God established his original marriage with humanity through his covenant with Adam and Eve. But the covenant was broken by their sin. This necessitated a new redemptive act on the part of God to restore the marriage.

2. **Redemptive covenantal event (Sinai):** God restored and renewed his covenant with creation when he formed a marriage covenant with Israel at Mount Sinai. But it was betrayed again when Israel worshiped the golden calf, requiring a new means by which God could dwell with his people.

3. **Liturgical extension/actualization of the covenant (Temple/Zion):** The Tabernacle and Temple atoned for Israel's sins, commemorated the marriage formed at Sinai, actualized it through Israel's history, and anticipated its eschatological fulfillment in the messianic age.

4. **Eschatological consummation (Messianic Age):** The marriage between God and Israel was expected to reach its ultimate fulfillment in the messianic age when God would restore his covenant with creation and dwell with his people forever.

## Christ's Marriage with the Church at
## Four Key Moments of Salvation History

The New Testament authors developed their nuptial theology in continuity with their Jewish predecessors and contemporaries, adopting the same framework of salvation history that they inherited from them. Despite the unique character of each text, we have seen a remarkable coherence in the New Testament's nuptial theology and in its typological reinterpretation of the four great moments of salvation history.

### 1. Mystical Marriage as Return to the Origins
### (Adam and Eve in Eden)

The mystical marriage between Christ and the Church often displays close ties with Adam and Eve and the Garden of Eden. In the Johannine and Pauline writings, nuptial texts allude to Genesis 1–3, portraying Christ as "new Adam" who restores the damage incurred by the first Adam's sin, and the Church—Christ's spouse and the mother of all believers—as new Eve. In the Fourth Gospel, nuptial symbolism is introduced by the sequence of seven days of a new creation culminating in the wedding at Cana, where Jesus as "new Adam" addresses his mother as "woman"—hinting at the woman of Gen 3:15. The imagery is unveiled at Jesus' "hour" when the new Adam manifests his glory by overcoming temptation in a garden (in contrast to Adam who sinned in the garden), and the "woman" turns out to be a new Eve and representative mother of the community of disciples. At the "hour" of his death, the bridegroom-Messiah sacramentally gives birth to the Church in the pouring of water and blood out of his side. For Paul too, Christ is the new Adam and the Church is the new Eve. Their marriage is a "one-flesh" union (fulfilling Gen 2:24), and the perfect model to follow for baptized spouses. The nuptial-Eden connection culminates in the Apocalypse with the return of the "woman" whose struggle with the serpent evokes Gen 3:15, and who prefigures the New Jerusalem's marriage with the Lamb, effecting a definitive return of mankind to the Tree of Life.

## 2. Mystical Marriage as Redemptive Event
## (Passover, Exodus, and Sinai)

New Testament nuptial imagery is also closely related to Passover, Exodus, and Sinai typology. The new wine provided by the bridegroom-Messiah is a sign of the divine covenant and Torah. In John, the seven days leading to Cana—matching the same pattern of days leading to the Sinai theophany—indicates that the Messiah has come to make a new Sinai-like nuptial covenant with his people. The idea is supported by the allusion to Jacob's ladder, Mary's words echoing Israel's declaration at Sinai, and the revelation of Jesus' glory manifesting the divine glory. At the same time, the new nuptial covenant is inseparable from Christ's redemptive sacrifice for his bride. It is sealed by Jesus' death as paschal "Lamb of God," offered when Israel was commemorating the Exodus and the Passover lambs were being slaughtered in the Temple. Pauline nuptial imagery is also rooted in Christ's sacrificial death, which reenacts and fulfills the Passover sacrifice. It is through the paschal mystery that Jesus becomes the bridegroom and grants the "right" to the Church to become his bride. Other Pauline typological reinterpretations of the Sinai and Exodus motifs include the "sacramentality" of the manna and water in the desert as types of baptism and the Eucharist, the identification of the rock as Christ, and the contrast between the glory of the Old and New covenants. We have also noted the extensive Passover and Exodus typology in the Apocalypse.

## 3. Mystical Marriage and Liturgical Worship
## (Tabernacle and Temple)

The marriage between Christ and the Church is extended liturgically and mystically in the life of the Christian. This is depicted through temple and sacrificial typology revealing how the divine glory is communicated to Christ's disciples. Christ's love for his bride is actualized on two levels: ecclesially, in the Church, and mystically in the body and soul of the believer. The nuptial metaphor thus represents on the one hand the union between the divine bridegroom and his people as bridal community, and on the other hand a mystical union between Christ and the baptized believer who is a Temple of the Holy Spirit. The mystical marriage is anchored in history, connecting the past, present, and future: it commemorates the one-time redemptive event (the Paschal sacrifice) by making it present liturgically and sacramentally in the human tabernacle through baptism and the Eucharist. At the same time, the union with Christ anticipates the eschatological fulfillment of the wedding that will occur either at the moment of death or at the end of time.

## 4. Mystical Marriage as Eschatological Consummation (Heavenly Temple)

The mystical marriage is not only past (rooted in Christ's sacrifice) and present (ecclesially or mystically); it also awaits its eschatological fulfillment in the glorious wedding of Christ and his ecclesial bride. For Paul, the virgin-Church betrothed to Christ lives "between the times," in a moment that is "already but not yet," in frail tabernacles that long to find their permanent home in the eternal building of God. In the Apocalypse, the betrothal between Christ and the Church, sealed by the sacrificial death of the Lamb, reaches its eschatological consummation in the heavenly temple. This will be nothing less than a return to the idyllic, primeval state of Eden and a renewed access to the lost Tree of Life.

## From Four Key Moments to Four Senses of Scripture

The New Testament books we have studied—the Gospels, the Pauline Epistles, and Revelation—reinterpret the four nuptial moments of Old Testament salvation history in different ways. The Gospels focus especially on the person of Christ; the Epistles on the Church and the Christian believer; Revelation on the eschatological fulfillment of the divine marriage. We may summarize the New Testament's treatment of the four great nuptial moments as follows:

1. Nuptial symbolism in the Old Testament develops through the following motifs:

    1. Adam and Eve in the Garden of Eden

    2. The covenantal bond between God and Israel established at Mount Sinai

    3. The actualization of the nuptial covenant in the Temple

    4. The eschatological fulfillment of the covenant in the messianic age

2. These motifs are applied to the person of Jesus by means of Christological typology (esp. in the Gospels): Jesus is the new Adam, the Paschal lamb, and the new Temple. His ministry inaugurates a new age when his disciples will worship him in spirit and in truth.

3. The nuptial motifs are applied to the Church and the believer by means of ecclesiological typology or mystagogy (esp. in the Pauline epistles): The Church is a new Eve, the body of Christ on a new Exodus, and the Temple of the Holy Spirit, awaiting her eschatological wedding.

4. The nuptial themes are fulfilled in the eternal heavenly temple by means of eschatological typology (esp. in Revelation): At the final consummation of the marriage, the Church will return to the Tree of Life as she completes her new Exodus and dwells forever with God in his heavenly temple.

| Primary Texts: | I. Old Testament | II. Gospels | III. Pauline Epistles | IV. Revelation |
|---|---|---|---|---|
| Fulfillment: | | Messianic Age | Worship in spirit & truth | Eschatological wedding |
| Primary Figure: | Israel | Jesus | Church | Christ & Church |
| Primary Typology: | Historical | Christological | Ecclesiological | Eschatological |
| Interpretation of OT: | Literal | Allegorical | Tropological | Anagogical |
| Four Nuptial Moments: | | | | |
| 1. Ideal Prototype: | Adam & Eve; Garden of Eden | Jesus = New Adam | Church = New Eve | Return to tree of life |
| 2. Redemptive Event: | Exodus/Sinai | Jesus = Passover Lamb | Christian life as new Exodus | Paschal Lamb & new Exodus |
| 3. Liturgical Extension: | Zion/Temple | Jesus = new temple | Christian = temple of Holy Spirit | Heavenly temple |
| 4. Eschatological Fulfillment: | Messianic age | Institutes worship in spirit & truth | Waiting for eschatological wedding | Marriage Supper of the Lamb |

This schema is striking in its resemblance to the four-fold framework of biblical interpretation that was later developed by the Church Fathers. The typological treatment of marriage imagery by the New Testament authors, allegorically applied to Christ, tropologically applied to the Church and the believer, and eschatologically projected onto the world to come, closely corresponds to the classic "four senses of Scripture" that became the standard model for the medieval exegesis of the Bible.[1]

It is precisely this interpretive framework that guided the interpretation of the Song of Songs from late Antiquity up to the beginning of the Modern Age.[2] The earliest Christian allegorical exposition of the Canticle was written by Hippolytus of Rome (d. 235).[3] A few years later, Origen wrote his influential commentary (and two homilies) on the Song that would become the foundational text for the great patristic and medieval commentators.[4] Origen was the first to systematize the allegorical interpretation of the Bible, a technique that is particularly apparent in his treatment of the Song. Assuming that the visible world reveals the invisible, the corporeal the incorporeal, and the earthly the heavenly, he argued that the same principle applied to Scripture. He attributed the Platonic tripartite anthropology of body, soul, and spirit to the Word of God, which he saw as a kind of incarnation of the Holy Spirit. To him the carnal sense of the Canticle was its literal meaning—a lofty human love song; the spiritual sense revealed the mystical nuptials of Christ and the Church; and the psychic sense referred to the bridal union of the Logos and the human soul.[5]

Following Origen, other early Christian writers hammered out various theories of allegorical interpretation of Scripture,[6] but none of those were widely accepted until the fifth-century emergence of a model that became the standard for medieval exegesis. This model, first expressed by

1. The fullest treatment of the four senses of Scripture remains de Lubac, *Medieval Exegesis*.

2. For studies on the medieval interpretation of the Canticle, cf. Matter, *The Voice of My Beloved: The Song of Songs in Western Medieval Christianity*; Astell, *The Song of Songs in the Middle Ages*.

3. Only fragments of Hippolytus' commentary have survived. Cf. Murphy, *The Song of Songs*, 14–15; Pope, *Song of Songs*, 114.

4. Origen, *The Song of Songs: Commentary and Homilies*.

5. Origen, 9–10. On Origen's commentary and homilies see Pope, *Song of Songs*, 114–17; Murphy, *The Song of Songs*, 16–21; King, *Origen on the Song of Songs as the Spirit of Scripture*.

6. Cf. Matter, *The Voice of My Beloved*, 53.

John Cassian, distinguished four levels of interpretation in the Scriptures (the first three roughly corresponding to Origen's three senses):

1. Literal sense: the historical meaning conveyed by the "letter" of the text (OT types)

2. Allegorical sense: the typological application of OT events to Christ and the Church

3. Tropological sense: the moral application of OT events to the life of the Christian

4. Anagogical sense: the OT events viewed in terms of their eschatological significance

Cassian's exegetical model is well illustrated in his interpretation of "Jerusalem" in Scripture, which he understood in four ways: "according to history the city of the Jews, according to allegory the Church of Christ, according to anagogy that celestial city of God, which is the mother of us all, according to tropology the human soul."[7] The four senses were eventually encapsulated in the following dictum attributed to Nicholas of Lyra: "The letter teaches events, allegory what you should believe, morality teaches what you should do, anagogy what mark you should be aiming for."[8]

Our study has shown that Cassian was hardly an innovator, for his interpretive model is already visible in the New Testament's treatment of the marriage between Christ and the Church, itself inspired by the ancient Jewish exegesis of the Hebrew Scriptures.[9] This sheds light upon our understanding of the early Jewish and Christian interpretation of the Bible: the interrelationship of these motifs in the New Testament could well have constituted an early framework for biblical interpretation that was adopted by the Church Fathers, and a precursor to what later became known as the four senses of Scripture.

---

7. John Cassian, *Collationes* 2.XIV.8, quoted in Matter, *The Voice of My Beloved*, 54.

8. Cf. De Lubac, *Medieval Exegesis*, 1:1. This interpretive model remains the standard in the Catholic Church today. *CCC*, 115–18.

9. De Lubac (*Medieval Exegesis*, 2:4) has shown that when Church Fathers developed the spiritual/allegorical interpretation of Scripture, they saw themselves not as innovators but merely as followers of Paul: "Christian allegory comes from Saint Paul."

# Epilogue

## *From Divine to Human Marriage*

WE CONCLUDE OUR STUDY with a practical question: can our treatment of nuptial symbolism in ancient Judaism and early Christianity shed light on the nature of human marriage in our own day and age? Can any lessons be learned from the divine marriage that originated at the dawn of creation in the Garden of Eden but was wounded by sin, was redeemed by a great salvific event, is perpetuated through cultic worship, and continues until the final redemption at the end of days? Does this vision of marriage still bear any relevance for citizens of the world in the twenty-first century? We will address this question from three perspectives: first, from a traditional Jewish view; second, from a secular feminist approach, and third, from a Catholic "new feminist" perspective.

### Marriage: A Traditional Jewish View

The traditional Jewish view of marriage embraces many of the ideas that we have observed in our study. The institution of matrimony is, of course, fundamental to Judaism. Even though—oddly enough—there is no explicit commandment to marry anywhere in Scripture, the duty to procreate is so primordial for the survival and propagation of the Jewish nation that it is a holy obligation imposed upon every individual and community.[1] Yet procreation is not the only reason for marriage, as Rubenstein explains:

1. Cf. *b. Kiddushin* 29a: "What are the essential duties of father to son? . . . to circumcise, redeem, teach him Torah, take a wife for him, and teach him a craft." Hence the concept of consecrated celibacy as an ideal is largely foreign to Judaism, though there may be some rare exceptions to this rule for those exceptionally dedicated to the

In traditional Judaism marriage has two fundamental purposes, procreation and the satisfaction made possible by the marital relationship. This satisfaction does not derive from the sexual relationship alone; companionship and intimacy, the sharing of life together, are also a profound source of satisfaction even when the difficulties and tragedies of life are shared.[2]

The obligation to marry translates into mutual responsibilities and benefits for both husband and wife. The man who does not have a wife "lives without joy, without blessing, and without goodness" and is even "not a proper man."[3] He should "always observe the honor due to his wife, because blessings rest on a man's home only on account of his wife."[4]

Despite the lack of a commandment to marry, the basis for the two fundamental purposes of marriage, union and procreation, originates in the first two chapters of Genesis.[5] Indeed, according to the traditional Jewish view, marriage is called to emulate the joy that Adam and Eve experienced in the Garden of Eden. The importance of marital pleasure and joy, along with the connection to Eden, is affirmed in the sixth of the *sheva berachot*—the Seven Blessings that are pronounced over the bridegroom and bride at every Jewish wedding: "Grant perfect joy to these loving companions, as you did your creations in the Garden of Eden. Blessed are You, LORD, who grants the joy of groom and bride."[6]

In addition, marriage is not "a contractual, biological, or sexual union alone, nor even the ability to unite in bringing forth children; it is an *ultimate, transcendental unity*. The goal of marriage is to create the Godly unity of man and woman."[7] Stolper underlines the theological

---

study of Torah: "Whosever's soul craves Torah constantly . . . and clings to [Torah] his whole life, thus neglecting to marry, he bears no sin." Maimonides, *Hilkhot Ishut* 15:3 as quoted in Lichtenstein, "Of Marriage," 13.

2. Rubenstein, "Marriage and the Family in Jewish Tradition," 10.

3. *B. Yebamot* 62b–63a.

4. *B. Baba Metsia* 59a.

5. Procreation is mandated by the commandment to "be fruitful and multiply" (Gen 1:27); nuptial union and intimacy are seen in the purpose behind the creation of the woman: "it is not good that the man should be alone; I will make him a helper fit for him . . . Therefore a man leaves his father and his mother and clings to his wife, and they become one flesh" (Gen 2:18, 24). Cf. Greenberg, "Marriage in the Jewish Tradition," 3–4.

6. *B. Ketuboth* 7b–8a; cf. Rubenstein, "Marriage and the Family in Jewish Tradition," 11.

7. Stolper, "The Man-Woman Dynamic of Ha-Adam," 36.

and mystical connection between every Jewish couple, on the one hand, and Adam and Eve on the other: "In essence every man is a potential Adam and every woman is a potential Eve—their story is the story of all of mankind, their origin represents the origin of each married couple."[8]

Traditional Judaism holds that each human must find a mate "in order to recapture some of the essence of paradise." The Jewish wedding, then, "liturgically dramatizes this 'finding of the helpmate' in the 'Garden of Eden,' which is represented by the enclosure of the *chuppah* or canopy."[9] Stolper adds that the meaning of the marriage ceremony—as expressed in its third blessing recalling God's creation of *ha-adam*[10]—refers to the act of (re-)creating man and woman into the original unity of ha-adam "which bears the potential of becoming the *tzelem elokim* [the image of God]."

> Every wedding restores the bride and groom to the unified state of Adam and Eve, enabling two halves to find their missing half and become whole again. Every wedding resummons the theme of the marriage ceremony blessing, 'Gladden the bride and groom as you gladdened your creation in the primeval Garden of Eden.'[11]

But is it enough for a married couple to draw inspiration from the utopic memory of a long-lost paradise in order to overcome the real tensions and challenges of life? Probably not. They must also be committed to fulfill their mutual responsibilities as the tangible expression of the covenantal relationship that they sealed on their wedding day. The Jewish wedding promotes this idea by dramatizing the Sinai revelation and betrothal between God and Israel. As Chabad states in its *Guide to the Jewish Wedding*, "on the cosmic level, our sages teach us that each marriage ceremony is a reenactment of the marriage between G-d and the Jewish people that took place at Mount Sinai." This is seen in the *kiddushin*—the "sanctification"—when the bridegroom places the wedding ring on his bride's finger and declares to her "with this ring, you are consecrated to me according to the Torah of Moses and Israel." By this act, just as Israel became the Lord's "own possession among all peoples" (Exod 19:5), the

8. Stolper, 36.

9. Bronstein, "Theology and Ritual of Jewish Marriage Rites," 38.

10. "Blessed are You, LORD, our God, sovereign of the universe, who creates man (ha-adam)" (*b. Ketuboth* 7b–8a).

11. Stolper, "The Man-Woman Dynamic of Ha-Adam," 39.

wife is "acquired," so to speak, becoming her husband's "possession," henceforth off-limits to all others.[12] The Sinai dramatization continues with the public reading of the *ketubah*—the nuptial contract detailing the husband's obligations to his wife that serves as symbolic "Torah," which he then gives to her.[13] As Bronstein illustrates, symbolically,

> the couple are standing at Sinai itself. They, like Moses, experience God's mystical presence by encountering the godly image in one another. Standing together under the canopy, they are, as it were, at the mountaintop, isolated from the rest of the gathering . . . In the course of the ceremony the partners are charged to translate the mystery of their brief stay at the mountaintop into a practical formula for living together . . . Thus, as the partners conclude their fleeting emotional and spiritual experience of the wedding service, they leave the scene of the wedding with something in hand, something symbolic of the tablets that represent the social contract called 'Torah.'

In light of these Sinai allusions, the festive wedding banquet that concludes the covenantal celebration between bridegroom and bride also evokes the covenantal feast that took place on Mount Sinai after the sealing of the covenant between God and Israel (Exod 24:9–11).

After the wedding celebration is over, the couple sets out on their journey together, sanctifying their common life and home by fulfilling their obligations amidst daily challenges and trials. Like the relationship between God and Israel, the relationship between husband and wife in a traditional Jewish marriage is not established on modern egalitarian principles. Jewish marriage is based, rather, on a principle of complementarity according to which each party plays a vital yet distinct role: while the husband is to support his wife financially, provide her food and

---

12. "Although marriage in Judaism is in no sense a sacrament, it is *kiddushin*, the sacred relationship whereby the wife is consecrated to her husband and absolutely forbidden to all others for the duration of the marriage. Nevertheless, although the husband acquires rights over his wife's *ishut* (wifehood), he acquires none over her person." (Rubenstein, 11; cf. *b. Kiddushin* 2a–b)

13. According to Chabad (*A Guide to the Jewish Wedding*), "the ketubah document is reminiscent of the wedding between G-d and Israel when Moses took the Torah, the 'Book of the Covenant,' and read it to the Jews prior to the 'chupah ceremony' at Mount Sinai. In the Torah, G-d, the groom, undertakes to provide for all the physical and spiritual needs of His beloved bride."

clothing and attend to her conjugal rights, the wife is responsible for running the home and raising the children.[14]

Now that husband and wife have become one, re-creating in their complementarity the *adam* that reflects the divine image, the two become "so appropriately matched that they create a home which evolves into a miniature sanctuary."[15] Ideally, this is to be reflected in all their activities, from the most mundane to the most intimate. Indeed, the one-flesh union bears such sanctity that it is closely associated with the Sabbath: "relations on the holiest day of the week are not only permitted but encouraged, as 'marital relations are part of the Sabbath delight.'"[16]

And yet the ideal inevitably faces the hardships of reality. As much as earthly marriage may catch a glimpse of the lost bliss of Eden and seek to relive the covenantal bond of Sinai in the sanctuary of the family home, the couple also tastes the drama of Adam and Eve's expulsion and Israel's exile through the vicissitudes of marriage in a fallen world. This is symbolically anticipated when the groom smashes a glass with his heel at the wedding ceremony, a custom that is generally associated with the destruction of the Temple and the subsequent "brokenness" of the Jewish people. As Bronstein notes,

> Many Jewish couples are told at this point in the ceremony that happiness for them cannot be complete until national—even universal—redemption is complete. In this way, even the paradise of marriage cannot give the lovers the complete redemption they seek. Yet their personal covenant of devotion will go a long way toward bringing about the larger redemption in which their own marriage will play a prominent role.[17]

Every Jewish wedding, therefore, implicitly looks forward to the final redemption. This eschatological pining is reflected in the fifth and seventh blessings of the *sheva berachot*—which frame the sixth blessing recalling the Garden of Eden. The fifth blessing invokes Isaiah's eschatological vision of the barren woman (Isa 54:1): "May the barren one [Jerusalem] rejoice and be happy at the ingathering of her children to her midst in joy. Blessed are You L-rd, who gladdens Zion with her children."

---

14. Cf. Exod 21:10; *b. Baba Metsia* 59a; *b. Pesaḥim* 72b; *m. Ketubot* 4:4; 5:5. Rubenstein, "Marriage and the Family in Jewish Tradition," 11–12.

15. Stolper, "The Man-Woman Dynamic of Ha-Adam," 40.

16. Rambam, *Hilkhot Shabbat* 30:14; quoted in Lichtenstein, "Of Marriage," 16.

17. Bronstein, "Theology and Ritual of Jewish Marriage Rites," 41.

The seventh blessing anticipates the fulfillment of Jeremiah's prophecy, longing to hear again "the voice of joy and gladness, the voice of the bridegroom and voice of the bride" in the streets of Judah and Jerusalem (Jer 33:11):

> Blessed are You, L-rd our G-d, King of the universe, who created joy and happiness, groom and bride, gladness, jubilation, cheer and delight, love, friendship, harmony and fellowship. L-rd our G-d, let there speedily be heard in the cities of Judah and in the streets of Jerusalem the sound of joy and the sound of happiness, the sound of a groom and the sound of a bride, the sound of exultation of grooms from under their chupah, and youths from their joyous banquets. Blessed are You L-rd, who gladdens the groom with the bride.[18]

Concerning the eschatological trajectory of marriage, Rabbi Avraham Kook writes: "The sexual inclination goes and pours forth toward the future, toward the perfect existence; it will bring a time when the existence of the world to come will be present in this world. For the future existence is filled with splendor and pleasantness."[19]

In summary, it seems that Jewish marriage has very much preserved the theological structure and meaning of our four key moments of salvation history in both its liturgy and praxis. This vision presupposes that the nuptial covenant is not a mere human invention but is based on a universal, transcendent archetype that has been preserved in the sacred texts and the collective religious memory of the Jewish religion. As Lichtenstein aptly states, marriage

> bears the stamp of a covenantal relationship—entered into between the parties, and with reference to the broader covenant between God and man, generally, and between the *Ribbono shel Olam* [Master of the World] and *Keneset Yisrael* [Community of Israel], particularly—within and through which twin goals [i.e. procreation and love/companionship] are interactively achieved.[20]

18. *B. Ketuboth* 7b–8a.

19. R. Avraham Kook, *Orot ha-Kodesh* 3:38; quoted in Lichtenstein, "Of Marriage," 27.

20. Lichtenstein, 10. Similarly, Chabad asserts: "It is in marriage that we most emulate G-d, creating life and eternalizing the temporal (by reproducing, man and woman not only create a child but also that child's potential to have children, and for his children to have children, ad infinitum). When two become one, they transcend the finite and the mortal, unleashing the single human faculty that is infinite and divine." (*A Guide to the Jewish Wedding*)

Though aware of the contemporary challenges to this vision of marriage, Greenberg affirms the enduring value of such a model, based on a timeless, transcendent paradigm:

> Judaism . . . makes a strong case for traditional marriages: a long-term relationship characterized by love and the bonds of nurturing each other and children, and also bounded by traditional parameters of fidelity, mutual respect, and steadfastness . . . I believe a covenantal model works for human relationships . . . What does Judaism teach? That marriage is good, very good; that it is the Jewish way.[21]

## Marriage: A Feminist Critique

The traditional Jewish vision of marriage stands in stark contrast to contemporary views of love and romantic unions. In recent generations marriage has faced an onslaught of reproaches from feminist critics[22] who have accused it of promoting androcentrism, patriarchy, sexism, male supremacy, and even misogyny— resulting in a long history of control and oppression of women.

This reaction is not surprising. As we have seen, the Scriptural portrait of the divine-human marriage is by no means egalitarian: Despite some important exceptions,[23] the divinity usually plays the role of the dominating male figure, while the human protagonist (Israel, the Church, or the believer) plays the more passive, receptive part of the bride. Thus, it is God, the husband, who sets the terms of the covenant and "calls the shots," so to speak, while the (human) bride is invited to an obedient response of faith and love. This vision clearly clashes with the values of egalitarianism and inclusivism that are so highly prized in contemporary Western culture. Feminists have no great love for the Talmudic view that the husband "acquires" his wife in the act of betrothal. And it is no secret that some streams of Judaism and Christianity have at times promoted quasi-gnostic views denigrating sexuality and the body.[24] Even Green-

21. Greenberg, "Marriage in the Jewish Tradition," 20.

22. Although there are many types of feminism, in the present section, I call "feminism" or "secular feminism" the view that generally rejects divine revelation as the foundation for marriage.

23. Wisdom literature and Philo are two major exceptions that attribute a female role to the divine protagonist.

24. To cite one example: Lichtenstein shows that Maimonides "evidently found no

berg, who praises the merits of traditional Jewish marriage, acknowledges that "much of the literature, law, and language surrounding marriage and divorce reflects hierarchy and sexism."[25]

Dissatisfaction with traditional forms of marriage—and their abuse—has led to a radical rethinking of the notions of marriage and romantic love in recent decades. Although we cannot enter here into the philosophical and theological currents of thought that paved the way for these new models, we may mention some of the main presuppositions and features that demarcate them from the traditional Judeo-Christian views of marriage—and from the model we have examined in the present study.[26]

First, proponents of the "new models" are deeply suspicious of any authority—whether human or divine—that would seek to assert its power over others. Consequently, they reject both the notion of a supernatural personal being who intervenes in human history and traditional sources of religious authority (such as creeds and scriptures).[27] Second, the rejection of an absolute divine authority results in the abandonment of universal transcendent archetypes in favor of an inward turn, where spiritual principles are fashioned "utilizing the human psyche's power to create flexible stories, symbols, myths, and images."[28] Thus, the notion of God as objective, metaphysical reality gives way to largely subjective perceptions of the divine. Third, if the notion of a divinity survives at all, then "liberation from patriarchy" is imperative. This is achieved by replacing the traditional concept of God as father or bridegroom by female or gender-neutral deities. Fourth, the individual will is valued instead of suppressed. The notion of discovering and embracing a predetermined, divine purpose for marriage is supplanted by the "celebration of diversity," where one self-determines the concept of love that best fits one's own desires, thus reaching endless possibilities of self-actualization. Fifth, the linear notion of time that is typical of Judaism and Christianity tends to be rejected in favor of a circular, cyclic concept. Hence the very notion of salvation history, "according to which time starts with Eden,

---

place for either love or companionship as the raison d'etre of marital sexuality." *Hilkhot De'ot* 3:2 in Lichtenstein, "Of Marriage," 17.

   25. Greenberg, "Marriage in the Jewish Tradition," 4, 18.

   26. The characteristics noted here, which apply to most secular feminist movements, are based on Grigg, *Gods after God*, 117–19.

   27. Grigg, 127.

   28. Grigg, 117.

degenerates, and then moves under divine providence to some definite end-point of history,"[29] becomes largely irrelevant. Sixth, this means that bodily growth, decay, and death are cyclic, natural, and not the product of some original sin. There is no need, therefore, to escape these realities or try to "fix" them; one should accept and embrace them as a normal part of human existence. Seventh, the very notion of original sin (and often of sin itself) is emphatically denied, and the concept of objective good and evil is blurred or relativized, so that there is no need to be "redeemed" from sin. Eighth, it follows that sexuality should not be "controlled and repressed but, instead, is allowed to follow its own internal regulatory processes."[30] This is the ethical backdrop for the sexual revolution that has dominated Western culture since the late 1960s. Ninth, sexual self-determination seeks to oust the two traditional moral imperatives of marriage, union and procreation, in favor of "reproductive choice," which translates into free access to contraception and abortion. Finally, the combination of the above factors results in downplaying or rejecting notions of complementarity between man and woman, and of a "gender hierarchy" inherent to the cosmic order that could promote androcentric views.

In short, feminist notions of love and sexuality are generally built "not on notions of an external deity handed down by patriarchal ancestors, but upon the practice of following the leads of one's own spiritual dynamics and developing the images and fantasies that are part of one's own creative spiritual work."[31] This view presupposes—and rejects—a patriarchal notion of God as human projection of male, androcentric views and arbitrary power that is largely or entirely divorced from authentic goodness.

With its rejection of transcendence, of a linear notion of time, of original sin, of redemption, and of a divinely willed male-female complementarity, it goes without saying that the secular feminist view allows no room for a notion of marriage based on the perfect designs of a good God who reveals himself in human history, as seen in the present work. The goal is, rather, to free oneself from the alleged shackles of the dominating patriarchal deity, so that one may freely reach self-actualization and find happiness.

29. Grigg, 118.
30. Grigg, 118–19.
31. Grigg, 119.

## "New Feminism" and "Theology of the Body":
## A Catholic View

In recent decades, a "new feminism" has emerged as an alternative to the "secular feminism" outlined above. Largely inspired by the philosophical, theological, and anthropological vision of Pope John Paul II, it is primarily Catholic in origin, though it also includes non-Catholic proponents.[32] In his 1995 encyclical *Evangelium Vitae,* the late pontiff invited women to

> promote a "new feminism" which rejects the temptation of imitating models of "male domination", in order to acknowledge and affirm the true genius of women in every aspect of the life of society, and overcome all discrimination, violence and exploitation.[33]

The new feminism shares with its secular counterpart the desire to promote the equality of women and fight against all forms of injustices against them. The two movements part ways, however, in their metaphysical and anthropological premises: Metaphysically, the new feminism adopts a position of "openness to God and revelation for understanding human beings." Anthropologically, it insists on affirming not just the equal dignity of men and women, made in the image and likeness of God, but also their complementarity and uniqueness. It thus rejects what it calls "ideological feminism" which "denies the fundamental psychic and spiritual distinctiveness of the sexes and which devalues motherhood and the nurturing role of women in the family and in society."[34]

For the new feminists, it is a foundational principle that (1) male and female are unique, but not identical. Other core principles include (2) marriage as communion, i.e. "a sacred union that entails the self-giving of persons in free, total, faithful and fruitful communion;" (3)

32. Contemporary proponents of the new feminism include Pia de Solenni, Mary Ann Glendon, Sister Prudence Allen, R.S.M., Elizabeth Fox-Genovese, Janet E. Smith, Alice von Hildebrand, Mary Beth Bonacci, Mary Ellen Bork and Johnnette Benkovic. Garcia-Cobb, "'New Feminism' Shines Light on True Genius of Women."

33. John Paul II, *Evangelium Vitae,* 99. Other foundational writings by John Paul II include his series of lectures delivered between 1979 and 1984 that later became known as the *Theology of the Body* (John Paul II, *Man and Woman He Created Them: A Theology of the Body*), his 1981 apostolic exhortation *Familiaris Consortio* ("On the Role of the Christian Family in the Modern World"), his 1988 apostolic letter *Mulieris Dignitatem* ("On the Dignity and Vocation of Women"), his 1994 *Letter to Families,* and his 1995 *Letter to Women.*

34. Garcia-Cobb, "'New Feminism' Shines Light on True Genius of Women."

the celebration of the family and the home, which entails the challenge of balancing domestic and professional work for women, especially in the indispensable role of motherhood; (4) focus on love and service, not power and domination—in contrast to other forms of feminism that emphasize the struggle against "patriarchy;" and (5) freedom grounded in truth, for "the true exercise of freedom involves, not a reliance on purely subjective and changeable opinions, or one's selfish interest or whim, but on divinely revealed and unchangeable truths."[35]

On this last point, two different views of freedom correspond to two different conceptions of happiness: The first is *freedom as autonomy* (literally, *auto-nomos*: "a law unto oneself"), which considers happiness to be "the fulfillment of one's desires, especially desires for wealth, comfort, and influence."[36] This freedom often rejects attempts to objectively assess these desires and tolerates no constraints or obstacles to fulfilling them. The second type is *freedom as the power to love*, which views happiness as the fulfillment of one's need to receive and give love by means of a sincere gift of self.[37] According to this view, marriage is not a mere human institution based on an arbitrary, androcentric will to dominate, rooted in patriarchal cultural norms, but rather a deep mystery that is born in the heart of the God who is love.

Although this is not the place for a full treatment of John Paul II's "Theology of the Body," it is worth noting some of its salient points to consider how it is in continuity with the traditional Jewish view of marriage and the biblical view of nuptial symbolism at key moments of salvation history that has been the object of our attention.

For John Paul II and the "new feminists," the essence of marriage and the family is rooted in the Trinitarian God, who is within himself a "mystery of personal loving communion": "God created man in his own image and likeness: calling him to existence through love, he called him at the same time for love."[38] Hence *"the primordial model of the family is to be sought in God himself*, in the Trinitarian mystery of his life."[39] The divine "We" (cf. Gen 1:26) is the "eternal pattern" of the human "we," especially the "we" that is "formed by the man and the woman created in

---

35. Garcia-Cobb.

36. Garcia, "Authentic Freedom and Equality in Difference," 26.

37. Garcia, "Authentic Freedom and Equality in Difference," 27.

38. John Paul II, *Familiaris Consortio*, 11.

39. John Paul II, *Letter to Families*, 6. (emphasis in the original)

the divine image and likeness." Since the human person is created "from the very beginning" as male and female, asserts the pontiff, "the life of all humanity . . . is marked by this primordial duality" from which derives "the 'masculinity' and the 'femininity' of individuals."[40]

From an initial situation of "original solitude," the first "Adam" (who represents both men and women), discovers that he is different from the animals in that he is endowed with the gift of freedom and called to love—God and neighbor. With the creation of Eve, Adam moves from the state of "original solitude" to a state of "original unity" in which man and woman, as "one flesh," become the image of God, "not so much in the moment of solitude as in the moment of communion."[41] This state of being "naked and unashamed" (Gen 2:25) is the key to John Paul's rich teaching on the "nuptial meaning of the body," whereby spousal love—encompassing both body and soul—is understood as the mutual love of "total self-donation" which has the capacity to bring forth new life as it fulfills the commandment to "be fruitful and multiply" (Gen 1:28). The nuptial meaning of the body, therefore, is the body's *power to express love: precisely that love in which the human person becomes a gift* and—through this gift—fulfills the very meaning of his being and existence."[42]

With the sin of Adam and Eve, however, the rupture of communion with the Creator leads to the breakdown of communion between man and woman. Human sexuality becomes tainted by shame and guilt. It is the "entrance of the fig leaves" into human history (Gen 3:7), when "the union of man and woman becomes subject to tensions, their relations henceforth marked by lust and domination."[43] Later, God establishes a covenant with the people of Israel and gives them the Law of Moses, which regulates and limits the effects of sin on conjugal relations, by "protecting the wife from arbitrary domination by the husband."[44] Yet it is only with the Incarnation of Christ, the divine bridegroom, that

40. John Paul II, *Letter to Families*, 6. In the words of the *Catechism of the Catholic Church* (1604): "Since God created him man and woman, their mutual love becomes an image of the absolute and unfailing love with which God loves man. It is good, very good, in the Creator's eyes."

41. John Paul II, *Man and Woman He Created Them: A Theology of the Body*, 9:3, 163.

42. John Paul II, 15:1, 185.

43. *CCC*, 400; cf. also 1606–1608.

44. *CCC*, 1610.

husbands gain the capacity to love their wives "as Christ loved the Church and gave himself up for her" (Eph 5:25), and wives are able to love their husbands in return with selfless devotion. Spouses are "the permanent reminder to the Church of what happened on the Cross,"[45] as they imitate Christ's self-sacrificial, redemptive, life-giving act by faithfully loving one another, and by remaining open to the gift of new life.[46] This constitutes the essence of their vocation to live as "temples of the Holy Spirit," through which marriage is healed and sanctified anew (cf. Eph 5:21–33) and restored to the divine image. In fact, "the entire Christian life bears the mark of the spousal love of Christ and the Church. Already Baptism, the entry into the People of God, is a nuptial mystery; it is so to speak the nuptial bath which precedes the wedding feast, the Eucharist."[47] The sacraments of baptism, marriage, and the Eucharist, in turn, anticipate the eschatological "marriage supper of the lamb" (Rev 19:7; 21:9) that will bring Christian marriage to its ultimate fulfillment. The Catholic "new feminist" view of marriage is thus based on a scriptural view of salvation history that "begins with the creation of man and woman in the image and likeness of God and concludes with a vision of 'the wedding-feast of the Lamb.'"[48] It remains in continuity with our model of divine marriage at key moments of salvation history, from Eden to the end of days.

---

45. John Paul II, *Familiaris Consortio*, 13.

46. "Thus the couple, while giving themselves to one another, give not just themselves but also the reality of children, who are a living reflection of their love, a permanent sign of conjugal unity and a living and inseparable synthesis of their being a father and a mother," John Paul II, *Familiaris Consortio*, 14.

47. *CCC*, 1617.

48. *CCC*, 1602.

# Bibliography

Abma, Richtsje. *Bonds of Love: Methodic Studies of Prophetic Texts with Marriage Imagery (Isaiah 50:1–3 and 54:1–10, Hosea 1–3, Jeremiah 2–3).* Studia Semitica Neerlandica 40. Assen: Van Gorcum, 1999.

Alexander, Philip S. "The Song of Songs as Historical Allegory: Notes on the Development of an Exegetical Tradition." *Journal for the Study of the Old Testament Supplement Series*, 1996, 14–29.

————. *The Targum of Canticles.* The Aramaic Bible. London: T. & T. Clark, 2003.

————. "Tradition and Originality in the Targum of the Song of Songs." In *The Aramaic Bible*, 318–39. Sheffield: JSOT Press, 1994.

Alonso Schökel, Luis. *I nomi dell'amore: Simboli matrimoniali nella Bibbia.* Casale Monferrato: Piemme, 1997.

Anderson, Gary A. "To See Where God Dwells: The Tabernacle, the Temple, and the Origins of the Christian Mystical Tradition." In *Temple and Contemplation: God's Presence in the Cosmos, Church, and Human Heart*, edited by Scott W. Hahn, 107–43. Letter and Spirit 4. Steubenville, OH: St. Paul Center for Biblical Theology, 2008.

Astell, Ann W. *The Song of Songs in the Middle Ages.* London: Cornell University Press, 1990.

Barker, Margaret. *The Gate of Heaven: The History and Symbolism of the Temple in Jerusalem.* London: S.P.C.K., 1991.

Barnett, Paul. *The Second Epistle to the Corinthians.* NICNT. Grand Rapids, MI: Eerdmans, 1997.

Barrett, C. K. *The Gospel According to John.* London: S.P.C.K., 1955.

Barrosse, Thomas. "The Seven Days of the New Creation in St. John's Gospel." *Catholic Biblical Quarterly* 21 (1959) 507–16.

Barth, Markus. *Ephesians 1–3.* The Anchor Bible. Garden City, N.Y.: Doubleday, 1974.

Batey, Richard. *New Testament Nuptial Imagery.* Leiden: Brill, 1971.

————. "Paul's Bride Image: A Symbol of Realistic Eschatology." *Interpretation* 17, no. 2 (1963) 176–82.

————. "The μία σάρξ Union of Christ and the Church." *New Testament Studies* 13, no. 3 (1967) 270–81.

Beale, Gregory K. *The Book of Revelation.* NIGTC. Grand Rapids, MI: Eerdmans, 1999.

Beasley-Murray, George R. *John.* Word Biblical Commentary. Waco, TX: Word, 1987.

Benedict XVI. *Deus Caritas Est.* Vatican City: Libreria Editrice Vaticana, 2005.

Berman, Joshua. *The Temple: Its Symbolism and Meaning Then and Now*. Northvale, N.J.: J. Aronson, 1995.

Best, Ernest. *A Critical and Exegetical Commentary on Ephesians*. International Critical Commentary. Edinburgh: T. & T. Clark, 1998.

Bloch, Renée. "Ezéchiel XVI, exemple parfait du procédé midrashique dans la Bible." *Cahiers Sioniens* 9 (1955) 193–223.

Boismard, Marie-Emile. *Du Baptème à Cana (Jean 1 :19-2 :11)*. Paris: du Cerf, 1956.

———. *St. John's Prologue*. Westminster, MD: Newman, 1957.

Braude, William G., and Israel J. Kapstein, trans. *Pesikta De-Rab Kahana*. 2nd ed. Philadelphia: Jewish Publication Society, 2002.

Briggs, Robert A. *Jewish Temple Imagery in the Book of Revelation*. New York: Peter Lang, 1999.

Bronstein, Lester. "Theology and Ritual of Jewish Marriage Rites." *Liturgical Ministry* 5 (1996) 34–41.

Brown, Raymond E. *The Gospel According to John I–XII*. The Anchor Bible. Garden City, NY: Anchor Bible, 1966.

———. *The Gospel According to John XIII–XXI*. The Anchor Bible. Garden City, NY: Anchor Bible, 1970.

Bruce, F. F. *1 and 2 Corinthians*. Grand Rapids, MI: Eerdmans, 1971.

Cambe, Michel. "L'influence du Cantique des Cantiques sur le Nouveau Testament." *Revue Thomiste* 62 (1962) 5–26.

Carmichael, Calum M. *The Story of Creation: Its Origin and Its Interpretation in Philo and the Fourth Gospel*. Ithaca, NY: Cornell University Press, 1996.

Carson, D. A. *The Gospel According to John*. Grand Rapids, MI: Eerdmans, 1991.

Cassuto, Umberto. *A Commentary on the Book of Exodus*. Translated by Israel Abrahams. Jerusalem: Magnes Press, 1967.

*Catechism of the Catholic Church*. 2nd ed. Washington, DC: United States Catholic Conference, 2000.

Charles, R. H. *The Revelation of St. John*. 2 vols. International Critical Commentary. Edinburgh: T. & T. Clark, 1920.

Chavasse, Claude. *The Bride of Christ: An Enquiry into the Nuptial Element in Early Christianity*. London: Faber and Faber Ltd., 1940.

Cohen, Gerson D. "The Song of Songs and the Jewish Religious Mentality." In *Studies in the Variety of Rabbinic Cultures*, 3–17. Philadelphia: Jewish Publication Society, 1991.

Coloe, Mary L. *God Dwells with Us: Temple Symbolism in the Fourth Gospel*. Collegeville, MN: The Liturgical Press, 2001.

Conzelmann, Hans. *1 Corinthians*. Hermeneia. Philadelphia: Fortress, 1975.

Corriveau, Raymond. "Temple, Holiness, and the Liturgy of Life in Corinthians." *Temple and Contemplation: God's Presence in the Cosmos, Church, and Human Heart*, Letter and Spirit, 4 (2008) 145–66.

Danby, Herbert, trans. *The Mishnah*. Oxford: Oxford University Press, 1933.

De Vaux, Roland. *Ancient Israel: Its Life and Institutions*. Vol. 1. 2 vols. New York: McGraw-Hill, 1965.

Dodd, C. H. *The Interpretation of the Fourth Gospel*. Cambridge: Cambridge University Press, 1954.

Elior, Rachel. "From Earthly Temple to Heavenly Shrines: Prayer and Sacred Song in the Hekhalot Literature and Its Relation to Temple Traditions." *Jewish Studies Quarterly* 4, no. 3 (1997) 217–67.

———. "The Jerusalem Temple: The Representation of the Imperceptible." *Studies in Spirituality* 11 (2001) 126–43.

———. *The Three Temples: On the Emergence of Jewish Mysticism.* Oxford: Littman, 2004.

Fee, Gordon D. *The First Epistle to the Corinthians.* New International Commentary on the New Testament. Grand Rapids, MI: Eerdmans, 1987.

Fehribach, Adeline. *The Women in the Life of the Bridegroom: A Feminist Historical-Literary Analysis of the Female Characters in the Fourth Gospel.* Collegeville, MN: The Liturgical Press, 1998.

Fekkes, Jan. "'His Bride Has Prepared Herself': Revelation 19–21 and Isaian Nuptial Imagery." *Journal of Biblical Literature* 109 (1990) 269–87.

Fensham, F. Charles. "The Marriage Metaphor in Hosea for the Covenant Relationship between the Lord and His People (Hos 1:2–9)." *Journal of Northwest Semitic Languages* 12 (1984) 71–78.

Feuillet, André. "Le Cantique des Cantiques et la tradition biblique." *Nouvelle Revue Théologique* 74 (1952) 706–33.

———. "Le Cantique des Cantiques et l'Apocalypse." In *Études d'Exégèse et de Théologie Biblique - Ancient Testament,* 333–61. Paris: Gabalda, 1975.

———. "Les épousailles du Messie : La mère de Jésus et l'Église dans le 4è Évangile." *Revue Thomiste* 86 (1986) 357–91, 536–55.

———. "Les épousailles messianiques et les références au Cantique des Cantiques dans les Évangiles Synoptiques." *Revue Thomiste* 84 (1984) 161–211, 399–424.

Fishbane, Michael. *The Kiss of God: Spiritual and Mystical Death in Judaism.* Seattle: University of Washington Press, 1994.

Fletcher-Louis, Crispin. "The Cosmology of P and Theological Anthropology in the Wisdom of Jesus Ben Sira." In *Of Scribes and Sages: Studies in Early Jewish Interpretation and Transmission of Scripture,* edited by Craig A. Evans, 69–113. London: T. & T. Clark, 2004.

Fournier-Bidoz, Alain. "L'arbre et la demeure: Siracide XXIV 10–17." *Vetus Testamentum* 34, no. 1 (January 1984) 1–10.

Freedman, Harry, and Maurice Simon, eds. *Midrash Rabbah.* 10 vols. London: Soncino, 1992.

Fretheim, Terence E. "The Plagues as Ecological Signs of Historical Disaster." *Journal of Biblical Literature* 110, no. 3 (1991) 385–96.

———. "The Reclamation of Creation: Redemption and Law in Exodus." *Interpretation* 45, no. 4 (October 1, 1991) 354–65.

Furnish, Victor Paul. *II Corinthians.* Anchor Bible. New York: Doubleday, 1984.

Garcia, Laura L. "Authentic Freedom and Equality in Difference." In *Women, Sex & the Church: A Case for Catholic Teaching,* edited by Erika Bachiochi, 1–33. Boston: Pauline, 2010.

Garcia-Cobb, Jo. "'New Feminism' Shines Light on True Genius of Women." *Our Sunday Visitor,* August 5, 2009.

Gärtner, Bertil. *The Temple and the Community in Qumran and the New Testament: A Comparative Study in the Temple Symbolism of the Qumran Texts and the New*

*Testament*. Society for New Testament Studies Monograph Series 1. Cambridge University Press, 2005.

Gilbert, Maurice. "L'éloge de la Sagesse (Siracide 24)." *Revue Théologique de Louvain* 5 (1974) 326–48.

Gillet, Lev. *Communion in the Messiah*. London: Lutterworth, 1942.

Green, Arthur. *Keter: The Crown of God in Early Jewish Mysticism*. Princeton: Princeton University Press, 1997.

———. "Shekhinah, the Virgin Mary, and the Song of Songs: Reflections on a Kabbalistic Symbol in Its Historical Context." *AJS Review* 26, no. 1 (April 2002) 1–52.

———. "The Children in Egypt and the Theophany at the Sea." *Judaism* 24, no. 4 (September 1975) 446–56.

———. "The Song of Songs in Early Jewish Mysticism." *Orim* 2, no. 2 (1987) 49–63.

Greenberg, Blu. "Marriage in the Jewish Tradition." *Journal of Ecumenical Studies* 22, no. 1 (1985) 3–20.

Grigg, Richard. *Gods after God: An Introduction to Contemporary Radical Theologies*. Albany: State University of New York Press, 2006.

Hahn, Scott. *A Father Who Keeps His Promises: God's Covenant Love in Scripture*. Ann Arbor: Servant, 1998.

———. *Hail, Holy Queen: The Mother of God in the Word of God*. New York: Image, 2001.

———. "Temple, Sign, and Sacrament: Towards a New Perspective on the Gospel of John." *Temple and Contemplation: God's Presence in the Cosmos, Church, and Human Heart*, Letter and Spirit, 4 (2008): 107–43.

———. *The Lamb's Supper: The Mass as Heaven on Earth*. Doubleday, 1999.

———. "The World as Wedding." In *Catholic for a Reason IV: Scripture and the Mystery of Marriage and Family Life*, edited by Scott Hahn and Regis J. Flaherty, 1–14. Steubenville, OH: Emmaus Road, 2007.

Halperin, David. *The Faces of the Chariot: Early Jewish Responses to Ezekiel's Vision*. Tübingen: Mohr Siebeck, 1988.

Hammer, Reuven. *Sifre: A Tannaitic Commentary on the Book of Deuteronomy*. New Haven: Yale University Press, 1986.

Harrington, Daniel J. *The Gospel of Matthew*. Sacra Pagina. Collegeville, MN: The Liturgical Press, 1993.

Harrington, Wilfrid J. *Revelation*. Sacra Pagina. Collegeville, MN: The Liturgical Press, 1993.

Hayward, C. T. R. *The Jewish Temple: A Non-Biblical Sourcebook*. New York: Routledge, 1996.

Heschel, Abraham Joshua. *The Sabbath*. New York: Farrar, Straus and Giroux, 1951.

Horsley, Richard A. "Spiritual Marriage with Sophia." *Vigiliae Christianae* 33, no. 1 (March 1979) 30–54.

Infante, Renzo. *Lo sposo e la sposa: Percorsi di analisi simbolica tra Sacra Scrittura e cristianesimo delle origini*. Milano: San Paolo, 2004.

Jeremias, Joachim. *The Parables of Jesus*. London: SCM Press, 1978.

———. "νύμφη, νυμφίος." In *Theological Dictionary of the New Testament*, 4:1099–1106, 1967.

John Paul II. *Evangelium Vitae*. Vatican City: Libreria Editrice Vaticana, 1995.

————. *Familiaris Consortio: On the Role of the Christian Family in the Modern World*. Vatican City: Libreria Editrice Vaticana, 1981.

————. *Letter to Families*. Boston: Pauline, 1994.

————. *Man and Woman He Created Them: A Theology of the Body*. Translated by Michael Waldstein. Pauline, 2006.

Jones, Larry Paul. *The Symbol of Water in the Gospel of John*. Journal for the Study of the New Testament Supplement 145. Sheffield: Sheffield Academic Press, 1997.

Kearney, Peter J. "Creation and Liturgy: The P Redaction of Ex 25–40." *Zeitschrift für die Alttestamentliche Wissenschaft* 89 (1977) 375–87.

Kerr, Alan R. *The Temple of Jesus' Body: The Temple Theme in the Gospel of John*. JSNT Sup 220. Sheffield: Sheffield Academic Press, 2002.

King, Christopher J. *Origen on the Song of Songs as the Spirit of Scripture*. Oxford: Oxford University Press, 2005.

Koester, Craig R. *Symbolism in the Fourth Gospel*. Minneapolis: Fortress, 2003.

Landy, Francis. *Paradoxes of Paradise: Identity and Difference in the Song of Songs*. Second Edition. Sheffield: Sheffield Phoenix Press, 2011.

————. "The Song of Songs and the Garden of Eden." *Journal of Biblical Literature* 98, no. 4 (1979) 513–28.

Lauterbach, Jacob Z., trans. *Mekhilta De-Rabbi Ishmael*. Philadelphia: Jewish Publication Society, 2004.

Levenson, Jon D. *Creation and the Persistence of Evil: The Jewish Drama of Divine Omnipotence*. San Francisco: HarperCollins, 1988.

————. *Sinai and Zion*. Cambridge: HarperOne, 1987.

————. "The Temple and the World." *The Journal of Religion* 64, no. 3 (July 1984) 275–98.

Lichtenstein, Aharon. "Of Marriage: Relationship and Relations." *Tradition* 39, no. 2 (2005) 7–35.

Lightfoot, R. H. *St. John's Gospel: A Commentary*. Oxford: Oxford University Press, 1956.

Lincoln, Andrew T. *Ephesians*. Word Biblical Commentary. Dallas, TX: Word, 1990.

Loewe, Raphael. "Apologetic Motifs in the Targum to the Song of Songs." In *Biblical Motifs: Origins and Transformations*, edited by Alexander Altmann, 159–96. Cambridge: Harvard University Press, 1966.

Lubac, Henri de. *Medieval Exegesis: The Four Senses of Scripture*. 3 vols. Grand Rapids, MI: Eerdmans, 1998.

Massyngberde Ford, J. *Revelation*. Anchor Bible. New York: Doubleday, 1975.

Matter, E. Ann. *The Voice of My Beloved: The Song of Songs in Western Medieval Christianity*. Philadelphia: University of Pennsylvania Press, 1990.

McKelvey, R. J. *The New Temple: The Church in the New Testament*. Oxford: Oxford University Press, 1969.

McWhirter, Jocelyn. *The Bridegroom Messiah and the People of God: Marriage in the Fourth Gospel*. Society for New Testament Studies Monograph Series 138. Cambridge University Press, 2006.

Menn, Esther M. "Targum of the Song of Songs and the Dynamics of Historical Allegory." In *The Interpretation of Scripture in Early Judaism and Christianity*, edited by Craig A. Evans, 423–45. Sheffield: Sheffield Academic Press, 2000.

Miletic, Stephen F. *"One Flesh": Eph. 5:22–24, 5:31: Marriage and the New Creation*. Analecta Biblia 115. Rome: Pontifical Biblical Institute, 1988.

Moloney, Francis J. *The Gospel of John*. Sacra Pagina. Collegeville, MN: The Liturgical Press, 1998.

Morris, Leon. *The Gospel According to John*. Revised edition. NICNT. Grand Rapids, MI: Eerdmans, 1995.

Moughtin-Mumby, Sharon. *Sexual and Marital Metaphors in Hosea, Jeremiah, Isaiah, and Ezekiel*. Oxford: Oxford University Press, 2008.

Mounce, Robert H. *The Book of Revelation*. NICNT. Grand Rapids, MI: Eerdmans, 1998.

Muirhead, I. A. "The Bride of Christ." *Scottish Journal of Theology* 5 (1952) 175–87.

Munro, Jill M. *Spikenard and Saffron: The Imagery of the Song of Songs*. Vol. 203. Journal for the Study of the Old Testament Supplement. Sheffield: Sheffield Academic Press, 1995.

Murphy, Roland E. *The Song of Songs*. Hermeneia. Minneapolis: Fortress, 1990.

———. *The Tree of Life: An Exploration of Biblical Wisdom Literature*. 3rd ed. Grand Rapids, MI: Eerdmans, 2002.

Neusner, Jacob, trans. *Genesis Rabbah: The Judaic Commentary to the Book of Genesis*. 3 vols. Atlanta: Scholars Press, 1985.

Neyrey, Jerome H. "Jacob Traditions and the Interpretation of John 4:10–26." *Catholic Biblical Quarterly* 41, no. 3 (1979) 419–37.

Ng, Wai-Yee. *Water Symbolism in John: An Eschatological Interpretation*. SBL 15. New York: Peter Lang, 2001.

Nixon, R. E. *The Exodus in the New Testament*. London: The Tyndale Press, 1963.

Och, Bernard. "Creation and Redemption: Towards a Theology of Creation." *Judaism* 44, no. 2 (Spring 1995) 226–43.

Origen. *The Song of Songs: Commentary and Homilies*. Translated by R. P. Lawson. Ancient Christian Writers 26. Westminster, MD: Newman Press, 1957.

Orr, William F., and James Arthur Walther. *I Corinthians*. The Anchor Bible 32. Garden City, N.Y.: Anchor Bible, 1976.

Parente, Paschal P. "The Canticle of Canticles in Mystical Theology." *Catholic Biblical Quarterly* 6, no. 2 (1944) 142–58.

Patai, Raphael. *Man and Temple in Ancient Jewish Myth and Ritual*. London: Thomas Nelson, 1947.

———. *The Hebrew Goddess*. 3rd enlarged ed. Detroit: Wayne State University Press, 1990.

Pitre, Brant. *Jesus the Bridegroom: The Greatest Love Story Ever Told*. New York: Image, 2018.

Pope, Marvin. *Song of Songs*. Anchor Bible. New York: Doubleday, 1977.

Renwick, David A. *Paul, the Temple, and the Presence of God*. Brown Judaic Studies 224. Atlanta: Scholars Press, 1991.

Robert, André. *Le Cantique des Cantiques*. Paris: du Cerf, 1951.

Rubenstein, Richard L. "Marriage and the Family in Jewish Tradition." *Dialogue & Alliance* 9, no. 1 (1995) 5–19.

Sampley, J. P. *And the Two Shall Become One Flesh*. New Testament Studies 16. Cambridge: Cambridge University Press, 1971.

Schnackenburg, Rudolf. *The Gospel According to John*. 3 vols. New York: Herder and Herder, 1968.

Scroggs, Robin. *The Last Adam: A Study in Pauline Anthropology*. Philadelphia: Fortress, 1966.

Seaich, Eugene. *A Great Mystery: The Secret of the Jerusalem Temple: The Embracing Cherubim and At-One-Ment with the Divine*. Deities and Angels of the Ancient World 1. Piscataway, N.J.: Gorgias Press, 2008.

Serra, Aristide. *Contributi dell'antica letteratura giudaica per l'esegesi di Giovanni 2, 1–12 e 19, 25–27*. Edizioni Herder. Roma, 1977.

Sheppard, Gerald T. *Wisdom as a Hermeneutical Construct*. Berlin: De Gruyter, 1980.

Skehan, Patrick W., and Alexander A. Di Lella. *The Wisdom of Ben Sira*. New York: Anchor Bible, 1987.

Stolper, Pinchas. "The Man-Woman Dynamic of Ha-Adam: A Jewish Paradigm of Marriage." *Tradition* 27, no. 1 (September 1992) 34–41.

Strack, H. L., and Günter Stemberger. *Introduction to the Talmud and Midrash*. Translated by Markus Bockmuehl. Minneapolis: Fortress, 1992.

Um, Stephen T. *The Theme of Temple Christology in John's Gospel*. Library of New Testament Studies 312. New York: T&T Clark, 2006.

Villeneuve, André. *Nuptial Symbolism in Second Temple Writings, the New Testament and Rabbinic Literature*. Leiden: Brill, 2016.

Wacholder, Ben Zion. "Creation in Ezekiel's Merkabah: Ezekiel 1 and Genesis 1." In *Of Scribes and Sages: Early Jewish Interpretation and Transmission of Scripture*, edited by Craig A. Evans, 1:14–32. London: T. & T. Clark, 2004.

Walton, John H. *The Lost World of Genesis One*. Downers Grove, IL: InterVarsity, 2009.

Wenham, Gordon J. "Sanctuary Symbolism in the Garden of Eden Story." In *Proceedings of the Ninth Congress of Jewish Studies*, 19–25. Jerusalem: World Union of Jewish Studies, 1986.

Winandy, Jacques. "Le Cantique des Cantiques et le Nouveau Testament." *Revue Biblique* 71 (1964) 161–90.

Winsor, Ann Roberts. *A King Is Bound in the Tresses: Allusions to the Song of Songs in the Fourth Gospel*. Studies in Biblical Literature 6. New York: Peter Lang, 1999.

Zimmermann, Ruben. "Nuptial Imagery in the Revelation of John." *Biblica* 84, no. 2 (January 1, 2003) 153–83.

———. "The Love Triangle of Lady Wisdom: Sacred Marriage in Jewish Wisdom Literature." In *Sacred Marriages: The Divine-Human Sexual Metaphor from Sumer to Early Christianity*, edited by Martti Nissinen and Risto Uro, 243–58. Winona Lake, IN: Eisenbrauns, 2008.

CPSIA information can be obtained
at www.ICGtesting.com
Printed in the USA
LVHW040458151121
703321LV00003B/4